# ELEMENTARY EDUCATIONAL PSYCHOLOGY

*By*

PAUL L. BOYNTON, PRESIDENT OF STEPHEN F. AUSTIN STATE COLLEGE, NACOGDOCHES, TEXAS.

JOHN W. CHARLES, PROFESSOR OF EDUCATION, IOWA STATE TEACHERS COLLEGE, CEDAR FALLS, IOWA.

PHILIP LAWRENCE HARRIMAN, PROFESSOR OF PSYCHOLOGY, BUCKNELL UNIVERSITY.

FRANCIS F. POWERS, DEAN OF THE COLLEGE OF EDUCATION, UNIVERSITY OF WASHINGTON.

W. CARSON RYAN, HEAD OF THE DEPARTMENT OF EDUCATION, UNIVERSITY OF NORTH CAROLINA.

PAUL A. WITTY, PROFESSOR OF EDUCATION AND DIRECTOR OF THE PSYCHO-EDUCATION CLINIC, NORTHWESTERN UNIVERSITY.

J. WAYNE WRIGHTSTONE, ASSISTANT DIRECTOR, BUREAU OF REFERENCE, RESEARCH AND STATISTICS, BOARD OF EDUCATION, CITY OF NEW YORK.

*Editor*

CHARLES E. SKINNER

PROFESSOR OF EDUCATION
NEW YORK UNIVERSITY

*New York* PRENTICE-HALL, INC. *1945*

PRINTED IN THE UNITED STATES OF AMERICA

# Preface

*Elementary Educational Psychology* has been written for those teachers who prefer a simple and brief presentation of the subject. Without sacrificing scientific accuracy, the present book presents the significant facts and data in a clear, direct style.

The project has been a co-operative undertaking. The outline, attuned to modern education, was presented to a small group of authors who had been selected on the basis of their sympathy with modern educational philosophy. As a result, the book is consistent throughout in its functional and dynamic point of view.

All of the contributors are experienced teachers and experts in their respective fields. Most of them possess first-hand knowledge of the problems of the public school. They are therefore in a position to write with authority on the various phases of educational psychology.

Emphasis has been placed on those basic facts and principles that are generally accepted by today's educators and that can be integrated into the student's own experience and made to function in his educational career.

The authors and editor gratefully acknowledge their indebtedness to the many investigators from whose researches they have drawn material. They also express their appreciation and thanks to authors and publishers who have granted permission to use copyrighted materials. The selections from Billett's *Fundamentals of Secondary School Teaching* and Cutts and Moseley's *Practical School Discipline* are used by permission of, and arrangement with, the publishers, Houghton Mifflin Company. The selections from H. E. Garrett and M. R. Schneck's *Psychological Tests, Methods and Results* and E. R. Guthrie's *The Psychology of Learning* are reprinted by permission of Harper and Brothers. The selections from Bernice Baxter's *Teacher Pupil Relationships* and E. L. Thorndike's *Human Nature and the Social Order* are used by permission of The Macmillan Company, publishers. The excerpts from the several *Yearbooks* of the National Society for the Study of Education are quoted by permission of the Society. The content and organization of a standard course in educational psychology is well indicated in *Visual Outline of Educational Psychology,* by

iii

Guy T. Buswell (Longmans, Green and Company, 1939). Grateful acknowledgment is made to both the author and the publisher of this work for many helpful ideas gleaned from it. Special acknowledgment for assistance is made by the editor to Dr. Philip Lawrence Harriman, of Bucknell University, Dr. Ernest R. Wood, of New York University, Dr. William D. Altus, of the State Teachers College at Santa Barbara, California, and Dr. James Francis Garrett, of Hunter College.

CHARLES E. SKINNER

*New York University*

# Contents

## PART I: INTRODUCTION

## PART II: GROWTH AND DEVELOPMENT

## PART III: MENTAL ABILITIES AND INDIVIDUAL DIFFERENCES

## CHAPTER 1

# The Nature of Educational Psychology

Let us visit a modern school and observe what is going on there. In one classroom we find the pupils busily engaged in a discussion of recent events in Europe. From their contributions we see that the teacher has aroused their interest in critical reading of the daily papers and weekly news magazines. In the biology laboratory we see groups at work making dissections and drawings of their discoveries. Passing by the library, we notice that several groups are preparing materials for debates, or are digging out the answers to worthwhile problems. In a well-equipped small infirmary, the school nurse is testing the hearing or the vision of some boys and girls, and the school physician is making an examination of a pupil's chest or heart. From a cursory glance into the various classrooms, we conclude that the teachers do not seem to be domineering or coercing their pupils, but rather, all of the boys and the girls, as well as the teachers, are engaged in some purposeful activity which they are enjoying very much.

A visit to a modern home would be equally instructive. There we hear the parents discussing the kind of adult they would like their son or daughter to be, and planning how they may guide and counsel the child sanely and wisely toward that end. We hear them speak of ways of setting up various situations to call forth the desired types of response from the child and to enable him to achieve some worthy success.

We learn a great deal if we drop in at a Boy Scout meeting and watch the Scoutmaster inspire and direct the activities of twenty or thirty young adolescents. We notice that he makes the right type of conduct pleasing and desirable to the boys, and that they seem to learn through creative activities, not through dry lectures about the desirability of "being good." Likewise, when we observe an expert guidance counselor at work, we see him assay the feelings, purposes, and capabilities of the child and assist him in formulating a more appropriate and happier pattern for living.

All these people—teachers, parents, and guidance workers—are educational philosophers. They have a definite set of aims, values, and goals for helping young people. We may think of the clergyman as the only person primarily concerned with the improvement of human behavior. Actually, he has many co-workers in that enterprise. Educational psychology can contribute to the work of everyone engaged in guiding and directing the learning and personality development of young people. Although educational psychology does not set the goals (the task of philosophy and religion), it has a great deal to do with the means for attaining those goals.

### What is psychology?

Psychology is the science of behavior—of animals as well as of human beings. It also includes "innate" as well as "learned" behavior. The subject matter of psychology is a body of systematized facts, principles, and laws dealing with the analysis, prediction, control, description, and explanation of behavior. In one sense, the psychologist does in an objective, scientific way what people have always done when seeking to account for the behavior of living organisms. Mankind has always been interested in understanding mental activities, but only recently has this field been explored by science. In gathering his information about behavior, the psychologist employs all the available techniques and methods of science.

### What is educational psychology?

Educational psychology is a branch of psychology and employs scientific techniques in discovering more about the learning process. Since the distinguishing characteristic of human beings is their great capacity to learn, educational psychology is the broadest and most worthwhile phase of psychology.

It is essentially a systematized body of knowledge about the way people learn. The one "big topic" in educational psychology is the nature and the course of the learning process. As a science, educational psychology is concerned with understanding, predicting, and controlling human behavior in situations that involve learning, growth, or adjustment. Since human beings are constantly learning, educational psychology covers a far wider field than the type of learning that goes on in the classroom. Many things are learned which do not make people more efficient or better adjusted to their fellow-men. Educational psychology must take cognizance of all types of learning, both those that are desirable and those that are detrimental. Of course, adults as well as children learn, and educational psychology must also include adult learning. However, since the greater portion of an individual's directed learning does take place in the school, educational psychology is especially concerned with the type and quality of learning that takes place in the classroom.

## Educational psychology—a science

A *science* is a body of knowledge arranged in orderly fashion, developed by careful observation, organized by rigorous thinking, and verified so far as possible by scientific methods. Of course, sciences differ greatly with respect to the way in which they meet this definition. Some sciences, like mathematics and astronomy, are more exact and precise than others, such as biology, psychology, and sociology. Because human beings are in constant change, and because environments differ greatly, psychology cannot approximate the experimental situations that are possible in the physics laboratory. The essential unity of science lies in its method, and not in its body of knowledge. The steps in the scientific method are, briefly: collecting the data; classifying (and, if possible, experimenting with) the data; and drawing conclusions that may be tested again and again by other scientists. Psychology employs the same methods used in other sciences, and although educational psychology does not have a body of knowledge that is in any way as objective and factual as that of chemistry, it does make use of the procedures of science and should be regarded as a science.

Educational psychology, in other words, is concerned not merely with building up a body of scientific knowledge, but with many immediate and practical issues as well. In the solution of these issues it makes use of scientific techniques. A few basic rules of scientific procedure are of sufficient importance to demand careful study:

1. Scientific knowledge is valid if it has been repeatedly tested by other investigators and found to be verifiable.

2. Knowledge based upon experimental and clinical evidence is usually of greater value than that obtained by mere speculation and theorizing.

3. Facts which disprove a theory are fully as important as evidence which supports it.

4. Preconceived notions and speculation are of little value unless evidence can be found to support them.

5. Inaccurate techniques may yield erroneous conclusions.

Admittedly, the body of tested knowledge that comprises the field of educational psychology is still relatively meager; but that does not deter the scientific investigator. Even when the practical exigencies of a particular situation demand that something be done immediately, there is no reason why the educational psychologist should not be scientific in arriving at a solution.

## Sources of data

Many diverse fields of knowledge contribute to a scientific understanding of the learning process. Many branches of psychology make a direct and practical contribution, among them such fields as the following: general, social, developmental, experimental, child, applied, animal, and abnormal psychology. Whatever these branches of psychology have to offer is grist for the educational psychologist's mill. As a matter of fact, the science of psychology in all its branches has contributed an inestimable amount of information that is being constantly utilized in the school.

Many other sciences have contributed a great deal to an understanding of the nature of the learning process and to the practical issues involved in the education of boys and girls. For example, biology, physiology, neurology, endocrinology, biochemistry, psychiatry, cultural anthropology, pediatrics, and sociology have added much to the improvement of educational procedures. The list might easily be extended. Statistics has contributed many techniques that are constantly employed in classifying the data obtained by school tests and measures. In short, educational psychology draws upon many branches of knowledge.

Although the educational psychologist readily utilizes other fields of knowledge, he cannot afford to depend upon them entirely. Within his own domain he must constantly devise new approaches, plan new techniques, and explore new fields. In recent years the changing curriculum has opened up vast fields for exploration in which the educational psychologist may undertake pioneer investigations. For instance, the curriculum makers have in some places set up a course in general mathematics. How to organize such a course, when to commence it, in what ways to measure the outcomes—these are only a few of the new problems that are being tackled by educational psychologists. The emphasis upon the larger task of the school in contributing to the development of the wholesome, socially effective personality of the pupil has raised a tremendous number of problems that the educational psychologist must solve. His discoveries have a direct bearing upon the happiness and welfare of boys and girls in school, and probably upon the entire subsequent course of their lives.

## The scope of educational psychology

Educational psychology covers the entire range of development, learning, measurement, adjustment, and guidance that falls within the province of education. The principles of mental growth and development, the general nature of the learning process as well as the problems incident to the learning of particular phases of the curriculum, mental abilities and individual differences, guidance, measurement, personal and social adjustment, and the psychology of teaching—these are a few of the more important topics that lie within the scope of our study. A glance at the Table of Contents of this book will indicate the broad province included under the rubric *educational psychology*.

## Some objectives of educational psychology

In general, educational psychology has two broad purposes: (1) to inform the student about the field of knowledge included within its province; and (2) to give concrete, practical help to the teacher. Thus, the subject has both a cultural and a professional aim. From the cultural standpoint, it is decidedly worthwhile and important to know something about the work of the public school, the present aims of education, and the various aspects of the learning process. From a professional point of view, educational psychology gives practical help to everyone who is concerned with teaching. Parents and employers, as well as teachers, will find some of the contributions of this subject to have an immediate and practical bearing upon their problems.

For the student of education, the subject is of particular importance. Educational psychology provides the basis for a sound guidance program, for adapting the work of the school to the needs of the individual pupil, and for insuring the development of wholesome personalities. In order to guide young people, the teacher must know the goals to which their behavior should be directed; and she must also know the techniques by which pupils may be brought to attain these ends. Her task requires that she understand the nature of the child, the situations that elicit the desired responses, the possibilities for faulty development, and the facts and principles of learning.

A word of caution: If educational psychology is to make a worthwhile contribution to the work of the young teacher, its principles must be applicable to the teacher in training. Many of the principles will teach the student how to learn more efficiently, how to direct his or her personality development, and how to adjust more happily to other people. If the textbook is memorized in rote, parrot-like fashion, with no attempt to apply the principles or to illustrate the points in one's own experiences, little benefit will be derived from the study. Wherever possible, the student should try to apply the principles of educational psychology in daily life. She should carefully note whether or not the study is improving her ability to profit by visiting classrooms and observing teachers at work. The ability to observe profitably is a most important aim of the course. In many experiences the student should find material that will give constant practice in applying the principles of educational psychology. Throughout the study, the aim should be to make educational psychology really function.

### Teaching as a fine art

While the teacher is availing himself of all the contributions of scientific educational psychology, let him not forget that teaching is a fine art. Teaching at its best will be more than an applied science. A scientific attitude is an important part of the equipment of the artist-teacher. But there are other items which are essential in this equipment. In a list of such requisites by Bagley we find: "(1) a thoroughgoing mastery of the materials that one teaches; (2) a keen appreciation of the significance of these materials to human life; (3) an ardent desire to have others know and appreciate these materials; (4) a sympathetic understanding of the difficulties which the learner will encounter in mastering the materials; and (5) a command of the techniques by which these difficulties may best be overcome." [1]

In dealing with boys and girls the teacher has to adapt himself to a ceaseless variety of situations, no two of which are ever quite the same. The curriculum must be adapted to the needs and capacities of many diverse personalities, and no two pupils are exactly alike in the ways in which they respond to classroom situations. Consequently, we dare not attempt to routinize or mechanize the classroom practice of the teacher. If a teacher should try to meet every classroom problem in some predetermined manner, the results would be disastrous. As a matter of fact, the teacher must make a serious effort to individualize the work of the school, and to meet each issue in a manner appropriate to the particular situation.

The artist-teacher makes use of applied science in his work. He

---

[1] Bagley, W. C., "Teaching as a Fine Art," *Educational Method,* Vol. 9 (May, 1930), pp. 456-461.

benefits by knowing the scientific basis for the educational program of the school. Without a sound comprehension of the scientific foundation of modern education, a teacher would blunder along. In a sense, teaching is somewhat like conducting a symphony orchestra. Long technical preparation is necessary for that work, but each conductor gives a different interpretation to the symphony. He directs the orchestra in such a way as to make the symphony an artistic production. The skilled physician has a sound knowledge of scientific medicine, but he also possesses a rich background of experience and a thorough understanding of his patient. Thus, medicine, like teaching, is a great art. The artist-teacher has a mastery of scientific principles, and he also has an insight into human nature which gives him flexibility and dexterity in social and professional relations.

The prospective teacher should not expect the impossible from "methods" and "theory" courses. Although this training is necessary as a preparation for work in the classroom, many students have expressed their disappointment in finding how little their work in theory contributes to their supervised "practice" teaching. The fault lies principally with themselves. They study basic courses in education and educational psychology in a bookish, academic fashion, making no effort to apply the principles to their own lives or to their observations of other people. The student who studies educational psychology properly will have a scientific basis for all classroom work, pupil guidance, and activities leadership. He will not, of course, have a set of rules to meet every situation which may arise in connection with school work.

## Methods of educational psychology

The ideal method of science is, of course, the experiment. In educational psychology, a field in which laboratory experiments and clinical studies present many real difficulties, a number of other methods are also employed. Since educational psychology has a practical bearing upon immediate problems, there is pragmatic justification for using them. Teachers cannot always wait until laboratory experiments or clinical studies have established the truth or falsity of certain principles. Furthermore, the conclusions drawn from a laboratory experiment on learning may appear to be pedantic and artificial when contrasted with the learning activity that takes place in the school. Certain of the more important methods are the following:

1. *Uncontrolled observation*. Here the experienced student or teacher observes individuals and groups in the normal environ-

ment, such as on the playground, in the theater, at church, in the classroom, in the nursery school, or on the street. Usually the observer keeps a full set of notes on everything that takes place. In order to keep the situation normal and natural, he may try to make himself inconspicuous. For instance, if the problem were to find out what people talk about on the street, the observer would unobtrusively "eavesdrop" to overhear the conversations that took place. Or, if the objective were to find out what store-window displays attract the largest number of spectators and what the onlookers say as they look at the exhibits, that would be an opportunity for the method of "natural" observation. Of course, the interpretations given to data collected in this manner would be difficult and susceptible of error. This type of observation is sometimes referred to as *uncontrolled observation.*

2. *Anecdotes, reminiscences, biographies, and autobiographies.* Many children and adults have kept diaries, journals, and notebooks which contain important material bearing upon educational psychology. Books of fiction, such as *Tom Sawyer* and *Huckleberry Finn*, also contribute a great deal to an understanding of the adolescent personality. Likewise, our recollections of childhood and adolescence, of school and play experiences, and of the problems connected with growth supply data which are of interest to the educational psychologist. Biographies and autobiographies of famous people contain many data which give insight into educational problems. All of these sources, however, are likely to be more or less invalid. Many times, the writer is primarily concerned with producing a literary effect; hence, he does not deal with the data scientifically. Reminiscences are notoriously inaccurate. Thus, when grandfather recalls his days as a schoolboy, the account may be interesting but of little scientific value.

Anecdotes often represent a germ of truth in an exaggerated form. They are told to produce an effect or to dramatize a point, not to state a scientific fact. Like reminiscences and life histories, they have a literary interest but no scientific standing. The fidelity of these reports is lessened with the passage of time. Occasionally, to be sure, they supply some material that is of value to the educational psychologist, but more often they are of limited value. Some experienced teachers, however, have found it worthwhile to keep notebooks in which they jot down anecdotes, incidents, and various experiences of their pupils, and then to return to these records years afterward to see whether they contain anything that might have predicted the present status of these pupils.

3. *Questionnaires, check lists, and interviews.* One of the most popular devices for gathering facts and opinions is the *question-*

*naire*. G. Stanley Hall (1846-1924), often referred to as the father of the child study movement in this country, used it extensively. A questionnaire is a series of questions so framed that the answers will bring out the information desired in some inquiry. It may be long or short, difficult or easy to answer. Properly used, it is an invaluable method of obtaining some types of data. Usually the questionnaire is sent to a representative number of persons who are urged to fill out the form carefully. Sometimes the questions are presented orally, as by a "public opinion sampler," and the responses are recorded by the interviewer.

The questionnaire has several possible shortcomings. It is likely to convey the impression that various problems may be solved in a simple, inexpensive manner by issuing a questionnaire. Questionnaires may be answered facetiously or by people who are not qualified to respond to the questions. Perhaps if a few questionnaires were carefully filled out by experts, the results would be infinitely more valuable from a scientific point of view than if thousands were returned. As Thorndike has said, "The ignorance of a thousand is no better than the ignorance of one." The extensive use of questionnaires has led some people to give undue weight to sheer numbers. Still another difficulty with questionnaire research is that the number of persons who fill out and return the questions may not represent the population which is being surveyed. That is, if persons have a particular interest in one side of an issue or the other, they might take the time to return the questions, whereas those who are indifferent might throw them into the wastebasket. The returns, therefore, would not be representative.

The *check list* is closely related to the questionnaire. It usually consists of a long list of items applicable to a given situation. A teacher might, for instance, draw up a list of play activities observed on the playground, and then check the play of pupils according to their chronological ages, grade status, or sex. Sometimes a check list is used in finding out the type of reading that pupils like to do. A list is drawn up for the pupils to check, as adventure, war, sports, and so forth. Check lists may be distributed for individuals to mark according to the directions, or they may be used by the observer to make a quick and convenient record.

Quite similar to check lists are *rating scales*. A list of traits, characteristics, interests, or any other items is drawn up, and the rater jots down some numerical value which will determine an individual's status on each separate item of the scale. Of the many types of rating scales, the one most commonly employed at the present is the graphic rating scale. On a line after each item on this scale, the rater places a mark indicating the individual's relative status on that given item. Rating scales may be used to record judgments about other people and they may be used for the purpose of self-rating. Owing to the subjective nature of human judgments and to many uncontrollable variables involved in rating, this method does not yield results that are of much real scientific value. For practical uses, however, rating scales furnish a procedure for gathering some data that could be obtained by no other method.

Another technique for gathering data is known as the *interview*. In general, it is similar to the questionnaire. Each has for its purpose the discovery of important or relevant data. Each, however, has its advantages and disadvantages. The interview, or "controlled" conversation, can be used alone, but more frequently it is a part of the case study–clinical method. An interview designed to serve some scientific purpose is far more than just a conversation. To learn how to interview is a whole course in itself. Much literature has been written on the subject, but an abundance of practice is needed to develop a high degree of skill in interviewing.

4. *Classroom investigations.* Classroom investigations are planned on the basis of scientific experiments, the principal difference being that it is difficult to secure adequate control over all the variables when human beings are involved. For instance, the problem for investigation might be to find out whether large classes can be taught as effectively as small classes. The first step, after defining terms and delimiting the problem, would be to select an experimental approach. The investigator might arrange with school principals to have a number of large classes and an equal number of small classes undertake the same unit of study. He would then match the pupils on intelligence, social status, school grade, age, and all other variables he could measure. By comparing the scores on initial tests with those on tests at the end of the unit, he could determine which group made the greater relative progress.

Sometimes an educational experiment is planned in such a way that two methods are tried out successively on the same group. Again, the set-up may provide for the possibility of using one method on the first group and another method on the second group, and then rotating the procedures. Ingenious educational psychologists have devised other variants of the experimental attack on various problems. For the research worker in physics or chemistry, some of these experiments may appear to be loosely conducted and hardly to be worthy of the name *experiment*. It should be apparent, however, that boys and girls are infinitely complex phenomena with which to experiment; hence it is not possible to control all the variables and to conduct laboratory experiments in the strictest way. It is possible, nevertheless, to use a modification of the experimental method and to control as many variables as possible.

The principal objection to much of the educational psychologist's experimental work is that it is artificial. Never does the teacher approximate a laboratory situation in the classroom. Shifting interests, varying degrees of fatigue, divergent backgrounds of experience, diverse home conditions—these are but a few of the factors which militate against the scientific ideal of a controlled situation. Laboratory studies of learning are usually done under more ideal conditions of control, but the results, for that very reason, are often inapplicable to the classroom situation. Furthermore, in laboratory experiments on learning, the investigation is not continued for a very long time, a few weeks or a semester being an unusually long period for such an experiment to run. In school, on the other hand, the long-time results are of great importance; consequently, these short-term experiments are not usually of great value in planning a curriculum or in formulating a methodology.

5. *The experimental laboratory method*. Yet the contribution of the psychological laboratory should not be minimized. As a result of scientific experiments, there are now available for the school a number of objective, precise techniques. Hearing and vision, for instance, may now be measured under controlled conditions. A great deal has been discovered about the span of attention, the learning of poetry and of nonsense syllables, the rate of forgetting, transfer of training, and other topics, as a result of experimental investigations in the laboratory. It is no disparagement of these scientific experiments to say, however, that a great many of them have little practical bearing upon the daily work of the classroom teacher or upon the complex situations encountered outside the laboratory. One of the greatest needs in modern education is for more use of the experimental method in actual school and life situations and for more experiments covering several years.

6. *Developmental methods*.[2] Special forms of the *experimental method* are particularly adapted to the study of development in children. These are often referred to as the *developmental methods*. Three of the more important of these special techniques are the *longitudinal* or *genetic* method, the *cross-section* method, and the *training* method.

The procedure used in tracing the stages of physical, mental, social, or emotional growth from month to month, or from year to year, is called the longitudinal or genetic method. Shirley's study of the sequence of motor development in the infant is a classic

---

[2] Also see Chapter 4.

illustration.[3] Dr. Shirley made repeated tests and observations on a number of children during the first fifteen months after birth. She found with few exceptions a certain genetic sequence: the infant learns to hold his chin up before he can lift his chest, and he learns to sit with support before he can sit alone, and so on. The developmental aspect of educational psychology is a most important one, since behavior must be predicted and interpreted in the light of its development in the individual as well as in terms of group norms.

The cross-section method is used in observing and describing growth characteristics of a hypothetical normal or typical child at one, two, three, five, ten, or fifteen years of age. Representative samplings of children at successive age levels are measured or tested and averages or norms for age, grade, and sex groups are obtained with which the measurements of any particular child may be compared.

The cross-section method puts the emphasis on group norms which do not fit any except the nonexistent and hypothetical average child. The longitudinal or genetic method puts the primary emphasis on the individual and hence gives us a better understanding of the whole child and a more usable scientific basis for prediction.

The training method is used primarily in the study of identical twins. Theoretically, all factors except that of training are kept constant. One member of the pair is trained, the other one is not trained. The resultant differences in behavior are attributed to training. In his classic studies of twins, Gesell used this method.

7. *Tests, inventories, and rating scales.* Educational tests and scales have been issued in great numbers since 1915. A recent bibliography lists over three thousand separate titles. Some of them are carefully constructed, standardized, and validated; others show evidences of haste and superficiality. Intelligence tests and achievement tests are the most satisfactory types of educational measurement thus far brought out. Diagnostic tests, aptitude tests, prognostic tests, character and personality tests, and other measures designed for use in guidance are still in need of great improvement. In collecting the data of educational psychology, a great deal of use is made of tests and scales. Their value in revealing individual differences is great, and their importance in intensive studies of individual pupils is increasing as rapidly as the tests themselves are being improved. Ideally, they give a precise, objective, and

---

[3] Other classic studies involving the use of the longitudinal method include the Berkeley Growth Study (see H. E. Jones and N. Bayley, "The Berkeley Growth Study," *Child Development,* Vol. 12, pp. 167-173) and Gesell's studies at the Yale Clinic.

valid score which represents the status of an individual or a group with reference to a sampling of the population. To the extent to which they achieve this ideal, they bring to light a great many facts which are of importance in educational psychology.

8. *The clinical–case history method.*[4] The most comprehensive method for the intensive study of a single individual is the clinical–case history procedure. Whereas certain other methods are useful in studying groups of people or "man in general," the clinical–case study method deals with the life history of the whole individual in his total environment. His family tree, home life, friends and acquaintances, school career, aspirations and purposes, leisure-time activities, aptitudes, intelligence, physical condition, achievement test scores—these and many more details are brought to light through the application of the clinical–case study method. All pertinent information which contributes to a better understanding of the individual is collected and organized into a case history.

Instead of being interested in gross scores on tests, the clinical worker may be concerned with the individual's response to each item on the test. He may also be interested in finding out everything possible about the individual's attitudes toward tests, his school subjects, his life plans, and everything else that might contribute to a better understanding of the individual or his particular problem. Consequently, every technique or method that seems to have promise may be employed in the clinical approach. As a rule, unfortunately, clinical studies are usually undertaken only when an individual is in some difficulty. Then the immediate purpose is to gain a better understanding of the reasons for his maladjustment or misconduct and to plan a better adjustment. There is a great need for more clinical studies of normal individuals, especially of normal boys and girls in school. No other method is more rewarding than the clinical–case history procedure, even though it does require much patience and time to carry out.

## Summary

Educational psychology can be of definite assistance to all persons who are responsible for the guidance and direction of other people. It is of particular importance for teachers. A comprehensive subject, educational psychology takes for its province all information and techniques that are pertinent to a better understanding of the learning process and to the more effective direction of learning. In some respects it is a unique field of knowledge, since practical

---

[4] Often referred to as the "case study."

necessity has forced it to adopt many novel methods. Although educational psychologists have great respect for the method of laboratory experiment, they do not lose sight of the fact that the scientific laboratory is quite different from a real-life situation. Hence they favor methods that can be used in actual life-situations. From the professional standpoint, the aim of educational psychology is to acquaint the student with a field of knowledge that will enable him to teach more efficiently and to be a more efficient student himself.

### QUESTIONS AND EXERCISES' FOR DISCUSSION AND STUDY

1. As soon as possible, commence observing in schoolrooms. It will also be well to observe pupils at play both on the school grounds and in their own neighborhoods. Try to devise an appropriate check list for recording your observations, particularly for the play activities.

2. Collect samples of children's writing, especially of the type of writing which they do outside of school. Is there any difference in the number of errors between school compositions and out-of-school writing? Which is the more spontaneous and expressive writing? Why?

3. Prepare an acceptable questionnaire for investigating the study habits of college students. Try it out on your acquaintances, and then try to classify your findings.

4. Describe in detail the most recent eye examination you have had. Find out the names and the purposes of the different instruments employed by the eye specialist. How does apparatus help to make observations more valid and precise?

5. Report on some pupil who is definitely maladjusted to the school. Define the problem carefully, and tell what you would do in diagnosing the difficulty and in making recommendations. What type of information occurs to you as being important in a study of maladjusted pupils? Why?

6. Explain the differences between an efficient student and one who is inefficient. Precisely what sort of help would benefit a failing student? What help should a student legitimately expect to get from a course in educational psychology?

7. Differentiate between pure and applied science; between science and art. In what sense is education a science? How is it also an art? Is there actually a basic difference between science and art? Between pure and applied science?

8. What is a science? What is the scientific method? Can the scientific method be applied outside the laboratory? Why cannot the teacher wait for the scientific solution of classroom problems?

9. Induce an experienced teacher to tell you about some of the practical problems which occur constantly in her daily work. Plan a scientific attack upon several of those which seem to be of particular importance. Could all these problems be investigated by the scientific method? Explain.

10. Without using names, describe the poorest and the best teachers you have ever had. Make specific comments about the differences between them.

11. What do you expect to learn from a course in educational psychology? How do you propose to integrate this material into your own personal experience?

12. To what problems is the field of educational psychology limited?

13. Why is learning the most important single topic of educational psychology?

14. Why should the student of education and the teacher be informed concerning the psychology of individual differences and mental abilities?

15. Research in mental and physical growth has resulted in data making possible a scientific study of child development. Explain fully.

16. Why is an understanding of motivation and adjustment of such importance for the teacher? In order to understand delinquency, we must understand motives. Explain.

17. Contrast the experimental and the clinical methods of studying educational psychology, citing both likenesses and differences.

18. What is the case study method? Describe a typical case study.

19. What is the biographical method of studying human behavior? When would you use this method?

20. What is the general use of the questionnaire? Give at least ten suggestions for the construction of a satisfactory questionnaire. Prepare a questionnaire that could be used in the study of some aspect of human behavior.

21. Of what value are tests and scales in educational psychology research? Can you think of any problems of research that would involve the use of suitable tests or scales?

22. Introspection, the act of observing one's own mental operations, is an important method in psychology and educational psychology. What uses do teachers make of pupils introspections? Do physicians make any use of patients' introspections (symptoms)? Explain. What are the limitations of the introspective method? Is it the best method for all studies?

## SELECTED REFERENCES FOR FURTHER READING AND STUDY

Averill, L. A., *Adolescence*. Boston: Houghton Mifflin Company, 1936.

Benson, C. E., *et al.*, *Psychology for Teachers*, rev. ed. Boston: Ginn and Company, 1933. Chap. I.

Boynton, P., *Psychology of Child Development*. Philadelphia: Educational Publishers, 1938. Chap. I.

Bruce, W. F., and F. S. Freeman, *Development and Learning*. Boston: Houghton Mifflin Company, 1942.

Buswell, G. T., *Outline of Educational Psychology*. New York: Longmans, Green and Company, 1939.

Cole, L. P., *Psychology of Elementary School Subjects*. New York: Farrar and Rinehart, 1934.

Commins, W. D., *Principles of Educational Psychology*. New York: Ronald Press Company, 1937.

Douglas, O. B., and B. F. Holland, *Fundamentals of Educational Psychology*. New York: The Macmillan Company, 1938. Chap. I.

Frederick, R. W., C. E. Ragsdale, and R. Salisbury, *Directing Learning*. New York: D. Appleton-Century Company, 1938.

Gates, A. I., A. T. Jersild, T. R. McConnell, and R. C. Challman, *Educational Psychology*. New York: The Macmillan Company, 1942.

Gray, J. S., *Psychological Foundations of Education*. New York: American Book Company, 1935.

Griffith, C. R., *Psychology Applied to Teaching and Learning*. New York: Farrar and Rinehart, 1939. Chaps. I and II.

Hartmann, G. W., *Educational Psychology*. New York: American Book Company, 1941.

Jordan, A. M., *Educational Psychology*, rev. ed. New York: Henry Holt and Company, 1942.

Judd, C. H., *Educational Psychology*. Boston: Houghton Mifflin Company, 1939. Pp. 3-11.

————, *Education As the Cultivation of the Higher Mental Processes*. New York: The Macmillan Company, 1936.

La Rue, D. W., *Educational Psychology*. New York: Thomas Nelson and Sons, 1939.

Leary, D. B., *Educational Psychology*. New York: Thomas Nelson and Sons, 1934. Chap. I.

Mursell, J. L., *Educational Psychology*. New York: W. W. Norton and Company, 1939. Chap. I.

Nelson, M. J., *Handbook of Educational Psychology*. New York: Dryden Press, 1941.

Pintner, R., *et al.*, *An Outline of Educational Psychology*. New York: Barnes & Noble, 1935.

Powers, F. F., *et al.*, *Psychology in Everyday Living*. Boston: D. C. Heath and Company, 1938. Chap. I.

Pressey, S. L., and F. P. Robinson, *Psychology and the New Education*. New York: Harper & Brothers, 1944.

Sandiford, P., *Foundations of Educational Psychology*. New York: Longmans, Green and Company, 1938. Pp. 1-35.

Skinner, C. E., ed., *Educational Psychology*. New York: Prentice-Hall, Inc., 1936. Chap. I.

———— and associates, eds., *Readings in Educational Psychology*. New York: Farrar and Rinehart, 1937. Chap. I.

———— and associates, eds., *Readings in Psychology*. New York: Farrar and Rinehart, 1935. Chap. I.

————, I M. Gast, and H. C. Skinner, eds., *Readings in Educational Psychology*. New York: D. Appleton-Century Company, 1926. Chap. I.

Stroud, J. B., *Educational Psychology*. New York: The Macmillan Company, 1935.

Trow, W. C., *Introduction to Educational Psychology*. Boston: Houghton Mifflin Company, 1937. Chap. I.

Vaughan, W. F., *General Psychology*, rev. ed. New York: The Odyssey Press, 1939. Chap. I.

Witty, P A., C. E. Skinner, *et al.*, *Mental Hygiene and Modern Education*. New York: Farrar and Rinehart, 1939.

# CHAPTER 2

# The Teacher and His Task

## The psychological definition of teaching

One of the most practical concepts for the prospective teacher to acquire is a correct notion of the objective realities of learning and teaching. Confusion with regard to basic learning processes and teaching techniques still persists in the minds of many in spite of the considerable amount of psychological experimentation that has been done bearing upon problems of teaching. And while few psychologists today would be willing to define learning in terms of transfer of ideas, yet some pedagogical procedures imply this background. A considerable gap is always found between the findings of the research laboratory and the practice that this research is calculated to modify—in the business and scientific worlds as well as the educational. For example, one of the most perplexing problems of manufacturing army and navy airplanes in time of war is the necessity of stopping assembly lines to incorporate new research discoveries. One of the purposes of specialized courses and texts in teaching technique is to acquaint the prospective teacher with recent research findings.

When we consider how psychology may be valuable in teaching, we can discern three major lines of influence. The first such line of influence may be termed the *directional* phase of teaching. If learning is viewed as the conditioning of the organism to progressive changes in the environment, rather than as the transplantation of mental pictures, the directive function becomes all-important. From this point of view, the learner is going to be active regardless of teaching; learning does not begin when a teacher appears: it merely takes a different direction.

A second line of influence that teaching may take is *motivation*. Long before the time of the experimental psychology of motivation, common observation had taught men that they do well and vigorously that which they like to do. Modern pedagogy is inclined to the belief that pupils should enjoy what they are learning as much as possible. The old doctrine that we get our best training from what we cordially dislike is no longer in repute. However, there are many things which we must learn to like and, further, it is possible for a teacher to assist the pupil in learning to like them.

A third phase of the psychological influence of teaching is the possibility of the building of *attitudes* in pupils. An attitude is an emotionalized judgment, or an opinion which has become emotionally reinforced. The forming of a judgment involves data or knowledge and a technique of interpreting it.

Of the three phases of the psychological definition of teaching stated above, the development of attitudes is especially important. The present is a time of tremendous strain throughout the world. Dictators have regimented not only labor and government, but education as well. The educational systems of the democracies are on trial—on trial to determine whether in a nation of over a hundred million people with dozens of practically autonomous educational systems, it is possible to secure national integrity of thought. The difficulty in securing this national integrity of thought and attitude is not so much philosophical as psychological. In a dictatorship, a small group of truly expert men can absolutely formulate the methods by which the attitudes are to be built and then enforce their formulation. In a democracy, especially one having a decentralized system of education, it is far more up to the individual school system and teacher to devise the techniques. Consequently, even when there is considerable agreement on objectives, there are likely to be startlingly heterogeneous results owing to lack of uniform methods.

One other thing needs to be said about the psychological definition of teaching: psychology has much to offer in the determination of when subjects should be begun and the order in which their content should be presented. Recently there has been a recrudescence of interest in the topic of learning readiness and periods of optimum learning efficiency. Equally significant is the order of presentation of topics in any field. An examination of a half-dozen standard textbooks on the same subject gives clear evidence of disagreement among authorities not only on what should be presented, but also on the order of its presentation. Mursell [1] has given us a concise statement of the exact way in which psychology should serve in this area:

Psychology can give us insight into the problems of the order of learning. It is always possible to learn any subject in a great many different orders. One can start foreign language with the grammar, or with direct conversation, or in other ways as well. One can start geometry with axioms and postulates, or with

---

[1] James L. Mursell, *The Psychology of Secondary-School Teaching*, rev. ed. New York: W. W. Norton and Company, 1939. Pp. 17-18.

experimental work in the use of pencil and paper, ruler, compass, and protractor. One can start science with the logical foundations of a special science, or with the wide range of information characteristic of general science. And if one goes beyond the beginnings of any subject, the number of variations in the possible order of topics is almost endless. Now it is very probable that there is no such thing in any field as a perfect or ideal order of topics and content. So what we may gain from psychology is not so much an endorsement of one particular sequence, as contrasted with all others, as insight into the fact that difficulties are created, and also removed, for the learner by certain orders and sequences of learning.

## The determination of teaching goals

One of the most perplexing and annoying problems of all education is the method to be used in determining curricular material. Unfortunately, the exact influence which clear knowledge of a goal has upon learning is not yet accurately measured. Purposive learning itself has not been defined by any set of generally accepted criteria. In an extensive and excellent discussion of learning as a purposive process, Mursell [2] says:

The modern curriculum expert contends that children should be taught about the operations of municipal government because such insights will serve them as citizens. The psychologist recognizes the same principle from a different standpoint. On the basis of his understanding of the processes involved he insists that *the purposes for which anything is learned must always become apparent in the learning.* It is not enough to learn Latin without any conscious reference to anything else and then hope that it will improve English. It is not enough to study municipal government in a textbook without any conscious relatedness to surrounding conditions. Means must be recognized by the learner as means, or they cease to be means at all; and then we are acting directly contrary to the requirements of learning as a purposive process.

Some educational psychologists would not go so far as Mursell in contending that everything that is learned must be understood from the purposive angle during the learning. There are situations in which it is virtually necessary to ask the learner to take on faith a delayed utilitarian value of the learning itself. However, it must be freely granted that in instances of this sort, unless there is some compensatory motivation, the efficiency of the learning itself is likely to suffer. Often a situation is materially helped by the borrowed motivation of a remote but strongly reinforced goal. The boy who is desirous of becoming an aviator may not from an intellectual and rational viewpoint comprehend the exact purpose of some of the things that he will be required to do in order to become an aviator, but the carrying force of the highly desired final objective offsets the temporary unrelatedness of what he is studying.

[2] James L. Mursell, *Educational Psychology.* New York: W. W. Norton and Company, 1939. Pp. 170-171.

A moment's reflection reveals many situations in everyday life where learning takes place although its exact purpose is not clearly understood. For example, when a novice is learning to drive an automobile, he is told to do certain things which he accepts on faith as correct. It is doubtful whether the majority of drivers thoroughly understand the results of their actions in driving a car beyond the general results of stirring the vehicle into motion and directing its progress. Where this ultimate motivation is lacking, or where the learner lacks faith in the relationship between what he is being asked to learn and some desired goal, learning suffers materially. The psychological implication, therefore, is quite clear. The teacher should do his utmost to make the goal evident when it is possible to do so, or, lacking means for that, to build up in the learner sufficient confidence to guarantee ready acceptance of the prescribed work.

Much intelligent effort has been expended in attempting to determine the general goals of learning in a democratic society. One of the best of these efforts is that described in the publication of the Educational Policies Commission [3] entitled "The Purposes of Education in American Democracy." This committee finds four educational objectives in the democratic society:

1. The Objectives of Self-Realization.
2. The Objectives of Human Relationship.
3. The Objectives of Economic Efficiency.
4. The Objectives of Civic Responsibility.

Of these four paramount objectives listed by the Educational Policies Commission, it is readily discerned that the first two are definitely psychological; the third, economic; and the fourth, political. The Commission has gone further and worked out in detail some of the things necessary to the attainment of these objectives. These detailed statements [4] are worth reproducing in order to complete the picture.

### THE OBJECTIVES OF SELF-REALIZATION

*The Inquiring Mind.* The educated person has an appetite for learning.
*Speech.* The educated person can speak the mother tongue clearly.
*Reading.* The educated person reads the mother tongue efficiently.
*Writing.* The educated person writes the mother tongue effectively.
*Number.* The educated person solves his problems of counting and calculating.
*Sight and Hearing.* The educated person is skilled in listening and observing.

[3] Educational Policies Commission, *The Purposes of Education in American Democracy.* The Commission, 1201 Sixteenth Street, NW, Washington, D. C. P. 47.
[4] *Ibid.,* pp. 50, 72, 90, and 108.

*Health Knowledge.* The educated person understands the basic facts concerning health and disease.

*Health Habits.* The educated person protects his own health and that of his dependents.

*Public Health.* The educated person works to improve the health of the community.

*Recreation.* The educated person is participant and spectator in many sports and other pastimes.

*Intellectual Interests.* The educated person has mental resources for the use of leisure.

*Esthetic Interests.* The educated person appreciates beauty.

*Character.* The educated person gives responsible direction to his own life.

## THE OBJECTIVES OF HUMAN RELATIONSHIP

*Respect for Humanity.* The educated person puts human relationships first.

*Friendships.* The educated person enjoys a rich, sincere, and varied social life.

*Co-operation.* The educated person can work and play with others.

*Courtesy.* The educated person observes the amenities of social behavior.

*Appreciation of the Home.* The educated person appreciates the family as a social institution.

*Conservation of the Home.* The educated person conserves family ideals.

*Homemaking.* The educated person is skilled in homemaking.

*Democracy in the Home.* The educated person maintains democratic family relationships.

## THE OBJECTIVES OF ECONOMIC EFFICIENCY

*Work.* The educated producer knows the satisfaction of good workmanship.

*Occupational Information.* The educated producer understands the requirements and opportunities for various jobs.

*Occupational Choice.* The educated producer has *selected* his occupation.

*Occupational Efficiency.* The educated producer succeeds in his chosen vocation.

*Occupational Appreciation.* The educated producer appreciates the social value of his work.

*Personal Economics.* The educated consumer plans the economics of his own life.

*Consumer Judgment.* The educated consumer develops standards for guiding his expenditures.

*Efficiency in Buying.* The educated consumer is an informed and skillful buyer.

*Consumer Protection.* The educated consumer takes appropriate measures to safeguard his interests.

## THE OBJECTIVES OF CIVIC RESPONSIBILITY

*Social Justice.* The educated citizen is sensitive to the disparities of human circumstance.

*Social Activity.* The educated citizen acts to correct unsatisfactory conditions.

*Social Understanding.* The educated citizen seeks to understand social structures and social processes.

*Critical Judgment.* The educated citizen has defenses against propaganda.

*Tolerance.* The educated citizen respects honest differences of opinion.

*Conservation.* The educated citizen has a regard for the nation's resources.

*Social Applications of Science.* The educated citizen measures scientific advance by its contribution to the general welfare.

*World Citizenship.* The educated citizen is a co-operating member of the world community.

*Law Observance.* The educated citizen respects the law.

*Economic Literacy.* The educated citizen is economically literate.

*Political Citizenship.* The educated citizen accepts his civic duties.

*Devotion to Democracy.* The educated citizen acts upon an unswerving loyalty to democratic ideals.

## The psychological problem of teaching

Hollingworth,[5] in his *Educational Psychology,* has given considerable attention to the problem of teaching. He uses geography to illustrate a general principle in the psychology of all teaching. The following quotation summarizes the problems in the psychology of teaching:

We may finally sum up what we have said about the teaching of geography in the following words. The problem of teaching geography is that of:

1. Finding or providing a context of such a sort that the desired response will be evoked by the total situation.

2. Presenting this situation vividly and repeatedly until the detailed elements of it, or certain specific details, become effective in evoking the same response.

3. Knowing beforehand what details are the ones which in actual life are likely to be present when this response is needed, and seeing that they become the effective cues.

4. Securing adequate motivation for such a learning process, so that cue reduction most effectively occurs.

5. Determining by testing from time to time the point at which this particular detail or these particular details have acquired the desired effectiveness.

## Teaching as an art

It is not at all uncommon to hear the expression, "Teachers are born, and not made." Those who use this misleading maxim would not for an instant dream of applying this partial truism to any other vocation. It is perfectly true that teachers are born, in the sense that some of the qualities characterizing a master teacher are partially hereditary in nature and, as such, depend upon birth. The inference most frequently drawn, however, is that, since teaching is a hereditary gift, no special technical training is needed for success in it, except, perhaps, mastery of the subject taught. Scien-

---

[5] H. L. Hollingworth, *Educational Psychology.* New York: D. Appleton-Century Company, 1933. P. 158.

dectomy. As a matter of cold fact, there are plenty of parents who do not love children and there are plenty of teachers who do.

Second in personality factors may be noted what has been called an "aptitude for vicariousness." This is simply the ability to put oneself in the other fellow's place. Affection does not guarantee it, although it is not very often found without affection. H. L. Mencken once said that it is necessary for one to have a "child-like" nature in order to be a successful teacher. This is about as accurate a statement of it as one could expect to find.

A third trait that goes far to hold interest and evoke curiosity is facility in explanation and illustration. Even college students will often forget a principle and remember some vivid illustration of it. The teacher who can build toward generalizations and abstractions by a carefully graduated inductive process of explanation and illustration can do much to hold interest and to promote vigorous learning.

Fourth among the requisite factors of the master teacher's personality is emotional balance, mental health, or general temperamental stability. Many children are excitable—as, indeed, are all human beings, for that matter. A teacher who is in a condition of emotional imbalance or temperamental instability has a distinct tendency to promote exactly that type of response in her classes. Lack of balance in the teacher makes for a condition of classroom uncertainty and instability that are a deterrent to concentrated effort and learning achievement.

## The psychology of discipline

The ability to handle classroom discipline successfully is a psychological factor basic in all teaching. No study of first-year teaching failures fails to name as a prominent factor in failure the inability to enforce discipline. Although the causes of disciplinary disorder are legion, and although it is impossible to state a single formula that will encompass all problems of discipline, nevertheless, there are certain general factors which have been carefully worked out and which every beginning teacher should know.

In the first place, a decision must be made as to whether punitive measures are ever in order. One school of thought maintains that punitive discipline is never justified. Undoubtedly, not only is brutalizing a child a reprehensible practice, but it seldom leads to constructive results. On the other hand, one is setting himself a difficult task when he undertakes to control every type of child without any punishment whatever. The writer once taught in a school in which an incorrigible boy slapped the principal in the face because he knew that it was absolutely against the rules of the school for the teacher or the principal to touch a child. Happily, in the instance just mentioned, the principal was able to rise above his own rule and deal with the boy in a language that he was able to understand. This discussion assumes that positive discipline is sometimes necessary, and proceeds to consider the principles which underlie sound psychological disciplinary measures.

There are three or four basic rules of punishment which time and experience have shown to be rather sound. The first of these is that punishment should be not too far separated from the offense in point of time. All human beings have a tendency to rationalize their own conduct and to build up defenses for their own actions, even when those actions are definitely open to censure. When punishment occurs during the period immediately subsequent to the offense, while the offender has a definite sense of guilt, it is much more likely to be provocative of effective results than after a lengthy period in which the offender has had a chance to talk himself out of it. Second, punishment, if possible, should be related to the offense. The rationale of this is that when a situation similar to the one which called out the offending behavior recurs, it will serve as a cue not to further delinquent conduct but to the negative orientation produced by the punishment. Third, corrective measures should be in some sort of proportion to the delinquency itself. This is a highly important and often violated principle. Many parents, for example, in what perhaps may seem to them a commendable spirit of tolerance, endure numerous petty infractions of home discipline and admonitions, only to finally descend in wrath upon the child for a comparatively mild offense and punish him out of all proportion to the misbehavior. The child is not prone to appreciate the cumulative effect of his deviations from rectitude, and is likely to feel much abused. Punitive discipline should be reserved for grave offenses and should be in proportion to them. Finally, discipline should be impersonally administered. Nothing produces hatred in a child so quickly as to feel that he is being punished to give an adult some personal satisfaction. The "this hurts me worse than it does you" attitude should be acted out with all the seriousness possible.

Many parents and teachers are successful with some form of personalized control. Personal loyalty is an extremely potent factor in influencing all persons, especially children. It is probably unsound to categorically condemn personalized disciplinary control, but it is equally impossible to rate it as the highest type. For one thing, the mere factor of personalizing through factors of affection means that the child is likely to get the idea that he does not have

tific experimentation is not needed to expose the childish fallacy of this superstition. Even in the field of pure art itself, such as music, hereditary talent requires the most careful tutelage to bring it to full fruition.

Born plumbers, without training, are not the people to repair broken water-pipes; born engineers, without engineering courses, do not make the best bridges; born cooks may eventually learn to bake angel food cake by trial and error, but they produce plenty of failures in the meantime; born teachers, prepared only with a topheavy load of subject matter, are no better than untrained plumbers, unskilled engineers, and "by-guess-and-by-gosh" cooks.

However, the performance of the master teacher is decidedly puzzling to analyze, and at times it appears almost to be the exercise of some mystical power. In fact, the combination of intuition and adroit skill of a really fine teacher is a beautiful thing to behold. But this fine intuition is the result of planned training and intelligent experience as much as of natural aptitude. We see ample evidence of this fact when talented novices are doing practice teaching and, in spite of their natural aptitude, are making egregious errors. It is also interesting to note that those who essay their practice teaching without the proper background of training, both academic and technical, do far less well than those who have had proper training.

## Psychological factors in teaching methods

A later section of this chapter will discuss the more personalized factors that enter into teaching success. Our purpose in this section is to consider certain general psychological phases of all teaching methods.

Psychologists have long been aware that mere knowledge is no guarantee of teaching success. Judd, for example, pointed this out many years ago in his excellent discussion of the psychology of secondary education: [6]

What has been said with regard to these two simple forms of muscular adjustment can be repeated with regard to any one of the intellectual arts. For example, the teacher who knows a foreign language thoroughly is not, by virtue of that fact, the best-qualified teacher. Indeed, it has been found that in many instances a foreign teacher who comes to an American school with full possession of another language does not understand the difficulties which American children encounter in attempting to acquire this language. The foreigner is unaware of the various stages through which the American mind must pass in adopting strange idioms and forms of thought. An American teacher who does not have as

[6] Charles H. Judd, *Psychology of Secondary Education*. Boston: Ginn and Company, 1927. P. 452.

full a mastery of a foreign language as has the foreigner is sometimes a better
teacher by virtue of his experience with the difficulties that an American meets.

Let us now consider the outstanding general psychological factors which go to make up successful teaching methods. The first of
these is *intelligence*. Contrary to the opinion of many, teachers as
a group, although superior to the general population in point of
intelligence, are far from being in the upper flight of intelligence
groups. Studies at both the high school and the college levels show
that in the matter of sheer natural brilliancy, many students are
superior to their teachers. Even at the secondary level, where students are rather mature, a differential in favor of the teacher is not
sufficient to secure academic classroom mastery. When we couple
the only slightly better than average mentality of a large number
of teachers with the fact that some teachers are teaching subjects
for which they have slight preparation, it is easy to understand
some of the common problems of American pedagogy. Of course,
everyone familiar with the psychology of teaching is aware that
more than intelligence enters into the picture. However, the fact
cannot be lightly overlooked that a young teacher, of equal or
slightly less natural brightness than his student, teaching a subject
for which he has had little preparation, is in real danger of serious
trouble. Looking at the matter from the positive side, it is difficult
to state exactly what should be the minimum intelligence of people
who are allowed to become teachers. Schools and colleges of education throughout the country have shown a decided tendency to
elevate the grade-point average necessary for acceptance into candidacy as teachers. This is roughly the equivalent of increasing the
intelligence necessary, although the correlation between grades in
college and intelligence is not particularly high. Probably, we
should do well to accept into candidacy as teachers only those with
an I.Q. of 120 or better. This figure does not rest upon exact experimental evidence, but rather upon a series of studies in various
subject-matter fields on the college level where the incidence of
low grades becomes greater than that of high grades when the I.Q.
of the learner is less than about 120.

*Social competence* is a vital psychological factor in teaching
method. Social competence means far more than the mere ability
to control children in the classroom. It implies an adequate adjustment to one's administrative superiors and to the community as
well. So many of the modern teaching methods depend upon some
form of socialized procedure that this trait in the teacher is not an
optional but an indispensable one. A high level of social competence implies excellent emotional control or balance, a high

degree of empathy, and practiced attention to the multitude of minimal cues upon which sophisticated adjustment to the social behavior of others is based. Some psychologists believe that underlying social competence are several hereditary factors in social intelligence. To the extent that hereditary factors contribute to social competence, we are dealing with native factors. However much people may differ in social intelligence, there is no doubt that social competence depends upon social intelligence plus considerable social experience. This experience is gained in part vicariously through professional courses designed to acquaint the prospective teacher with some of the situations that he will encounter. It is acquired on a more practical basis, also, in the practice teaching well-nigh universally required as a prerequisite to teaching certification.

Another psychological factor basic to sound teaching method is a highly developed *habit of observation*. This factor is excellently illustrated by the various types of study-hall teachers. A teacher who is in charge of a large study hall, usually held in a library or high school auditorium, has passing before his eyes a complicated and ever-changing panorama of action. Some teachers are blandly unaware of the multitude of violations of sound study habits. As long as the room does not break into a riot, the easy-going teacher seems satisfied. Often he, himself, is reading a book or writing letters, content if the room preserves the outward semblance of order. Other study-hall teachers—they are the superior ones—are keenly aware of every change in tempo of the group over which they have charge. They spot potential trouble-makers and keep them under constant surveillance. While it is very difficult to secure a reliable qualitative measure of comparison between the two types of teachers mentioned, no one with practical school experience doubts for a minute that far more studying is done under the latter type.

## The psychological factors in the curriculum

It should be pointed out at the outset in a discussion of psychological factors in the curriculum that every teacher is a curriculum-maker. All of the better school systems have numerous committees of teachers engaged in the continuous process of curriculum revision.

The old psychological view of the curriculum was a "course of study"-centered point of view. It presumed a fixed amount of material, usually determined by experts, which every child was expected to master. Later on, this view was slightly modified to allow for two or three pupil groups of varying ability, each of which also mastered a rather rigid body of content.

The more modern psychological point of view of the curriculum centers on the individual child, holding that the curriculum should involve a varying amount of material for each child. The expert is not entirely out of the picture, but his work is supplemented by committees of teachers, to which reference has just been made, and often by reactions from the children themselves. The combined judgment of the experts and these other groups results in a core curriculum around which, and in addition to which, each teacher must build an individualized curriculum suited to the needs of each child. This work places a far greater responsibility upon the individual teacher than did the older system which merely required the supervision of the child's mastering of a standardized body of subject matter selected by someone else.

Another important psychological factor of the modern curriculum is its provision for vitalizing and reinforcing learning. An example is very evident in the drastic effort currently being made to effect multiple sensory reinforcement of learning, resulting in the rise in audio-visual devices whose purpose is to enrich the educational program.

## The teaching personality

Practically every modern study of teaching success has thrown emphasis upon the somewhat intangible factor of the personality of the teacher. Thanks to the efforts of numerous competent investigators, this factor becomes more tangible daily. With all due respect to the effort to measure personality objectively, the fact remains that some earlier students of teaching personality, like Palmer, came close to solving the entire problem on an observational and intuitional basis. It is not a bizarre expectation to look, in the near future, for prognostic tests of teaching ability that will correlate highly with later teaching success. In this section we shall consider briefly three of the outstanding factors that contribute to a successful teaching personality.

First, and by all odds most important, one must have a genuine affection for children. Young people and adults are quick to sense any fundamental lack of sympathy with their feelings, aspirations, and efforts. Contrary to the biased observations of some parents, it is not necessary to have had a dozen children in order to be a competent child psychologist or to have a genuine affection for young people, any more than it is necessary for the surgeon to have had his appendix out in order to perform a first-rate appen-

government, which his country originated and to which it has remained faithful. He said that this form of government is a curious compromise between the concept of struggle—natural to individuals—and the concept of unity—the neglect of which means the downfall of society.

"A parliamentary democracy," he said, "is a state in which the minority, after an election, agrees, for a fixed period of time, to be governed by the majority, and even during this period to collaborate with the leaders of the majority in all that is essential to the national existence. Naturally this attitude is possible only *when the minority is sure of being protected by certain fundamental principles which the majority also believes in.* In England these principles have grown up through long usage; in America they are codified in the Constitution; in all free nations they guarantee the minority against the abuse of power.

"If the minority should lose confidence in the good faith of the majority, as far as fundamental principles are concerned, the change from one party to another—which is the essence of democracy—would no longer be possible. A minority which has strong reasons to fear the violence of the opposite party would not let, without a struggle, the police, the army, the finances of the nation fall into the hands of the majority. The reason why parliamentary government is almost completely successful in England is because of the general desire 'to make the thing work.' In England all parties, conservatives, liberals, and laborites, entertain and proclaim the same respect for fundamental liberties. Party conflicts are necessary to the existence and healthy condition of a self-governing country, but they must not be carried so far as to endanger the security of the State. . . . *A house divided against itself cannot stand.*"

A type of democracy which allows dissatisfied minorities to run amuck is not democracy at all, but anarchy. Competent observers are agreed that it was this type of democracy that caused the cataclysmic collapse of the French nation in May, 1940. True, the other extreme is scarcely less to be desired, and modern government is always steering between Scylla and Charybdis as it attempts to preserve individual liberty in a sphere which provides services for which a certain amount of regimentation is inevitable.

The schools should do everything within their power to combat the false democracy which has been described. Love of freedom we should inculcate. Respect for human personality we should assiduously cultivate. But along with these other things, we should teach the child the good sportsmanship which makes him a willing collaborator in a program that the majority have chosen.

Indoctrination on controversial issues is psychologically unwise. Particularly is this true in regard to peculiarities of the personal philosophies of an individual teacher. It is perhaps open to no criticism for a teacher to be a man-hater if she was jilted when a girl. But to attempt to make man-haters out of all the girls coming under one's tutelage is a form of indoctrination not to be condoned. Equally true is this principle in the case of extreme points of view on politics, religion, race prejudice, and so forth. This statement is not inconsistent with what has already been said about democracy, because democracy is not a controversial issue in any real sense of the word in the governmental unit comprised in the United States of America.

Billett,[8] in his excellent discussion of the fundamentals of secondary-school teaching, points out the dangers of indoctrination in some of the modern methods of teaching, with the unit method as an illustration. He lays down some general principles for avoiding indoctrination which are well worth the consideration of every teacher. He says:

If the teacher employs the unit method in the light of the following principles which have been stressed throughout this volume, the pupils will have real freedom of thought and action and a genuine opportunity to exercise choice and to participate in the planning of their own activities, and the results will be the antithesis of indoctrination:

1. In stating the unit and delimiting it, the teacher should not anticipate, hope for, nor have any idea of trying to secure or insure uniformity of educative growth on the part of all pupils. He should seek only to identify some major learning product and some of its most important components in the form of capacities and tendencies to behavior which have meant to those who have possessed them greater understanding and appreciation of the physical and social environment and more intelligent better-intentioned participation in that environment. In other words, the teacher should set up only tentative goals in terms of the educative growth of his pupils.

2. In planning the corresponding unit assignment the teacher should avoid recipes and statements of fact to be followed blindly or to be memorized by the pupils. The pupil should be guided with reasonable economy of his time and energy to a well-balanced sampling of all pertinent data and to different interpretations and points of view. He should meet challenging questions and problems. He should be compelled to think for himself—to hold all conclusions tentative.

3. Although each pupil should be provided with a mimeographed study and activity guide, the pupils should not be expected to engage in the same activities in the same way to the same extent.

a. Even in the core activities the pupil should be encouraged to exercise choice as to what he shall do, and how, and when, and where. During and immediately following the introductory phase of the teaching-learning cycle, each pupil should be encouraged to examine carefully the entire study and activity guide and if desirable to confer with the teacher concerning initial activities. Without the study and activity guide it would be physically impossible for the teacher to allow sufficient choice under reasonable guidance and direction.

b. Some pupils may even begin with some optional related activity. In this connection it is particularly important to note that, no matter how extensive the list of optional related activities prepared by the teacher may be, the list should be closed with an invitation to the pupil to suggest other related activities in which he (the pupil) would prefer to engage.

4. The educative growth actually made by any given pupil in the areas represented by the statement of the unit and its delimitation should be expected

---

[8] Roy O. Billett, *Fundamentals of Secondary-School Teaching.* Boston: Houghton Mifflin Company, 1940, pp. 604-605. Used by permission of, and arrangement with, the publishers.

to be unique in some respects. What a pupil actually learns must depend in part on his aptitudes, abilities, interests, aims, and hence needs, and in part on the educative environment provided him or discovered through his own efforts.

If used by a teacher who does not subscribe to the above principles, or who does not take pains to see that these principles are operative in his courses, the unit method might be perverted easily into an instrument par excellence for indoctrination.

## QUESTIONS AND EXERCISES FOR DISCUSSION AND STUDY

1. What are the three phases in the psychological definition of teaching?

2. Summarize Mursell's discussion of the value of psychology in solving learning problems.

3. Who, in your opinion, are the people who should be charged with the responsibility of determining teaching goals? Why?

4. What are the four basic educational objectives in a democratic society, according to the Educational Policies Commission?

5. Is it your opinion that teachers are born, or that they are made?

6. What are some of the reasons why knowledge is not in itself a guarantee of teaching success?

7. Do you think it is desirable or otherwise that a teacher should be very much more brilliant mentally than his students?

8. Discuss the modern point of view of the curriculum from the psychological angle.

9. Name two or three traits, in addition to those given in the text, which go to make up a good teaching personality.

10. Name the three basic rules of punishment. Decide whether you disagree with any of them, and, if so, why.

11. Why are administrative and community relationships discussed in a treatment of the psychology of teaching?

12. Discuss at some length the meaning of democracy in education.

## SELECTED REFERENCES FOR FURTHER READING AND STUDY

Bayles, E. E., "Obligations of Teaching in a Democracy," *Educational Administration and Supervision*, April, 1939.

Billett, Roy O., *Fundamentals of Secondary-School Teaching*. Boston: Houghton Mifflin Company, 1940.

Briggs, T. H., *Pragmatism and Pedagogy*. New York: The Macmillan Company, 1940.

Cole, Luella, *Psychology of the Elementary School Subjects*. New York: Farrar and Rinehart, 1934.

Commins, William D., *Principles of Educational Psychology*. New York: Ronald Press Company, 1937.

Conklin, Edmund S., and Frank S. Freeman, *Introductory Psychology for Students of Education*. New York: Henry Holt and Company, 1939.

Cooper, J. H., "Democracy and the Classroom Teacher," *National Education Association Journal*, March, 1940.

Crabb, A. L., "Teaching Now and Then," *National Parent-Teacher*, August, 1939.

Davis, C. O., "Rewards of Teaching," *School and Society*, November 25, 1939.

Douglas, Oscar B., and B. F. Holland, *Fundamentals of Educational Psychology*. New York: The Macmillan Company, 1938.

Eby, K., "Intellectual Honesty—An Asset to Good Teaching," *Clearing House*, November, 1939.

Educational Policies Commission, *The Purposes of Education in American Democracy*, Washington, D. C.

Eurich, Alvin C., and Herbert A. Carroll, *Educational Psychology*.  Boston: D. C. Heath and Company, 1935.

Garrison, Karl C., *The Psychology of Exceptional Children*.  New York: Ronald Press Company, 1940.

Garrison, N. L., "Laboratory School Observations," *Teachers College Journal*, March, 1939.

Gragg, C. I., "Teachers Also Must Learn," *Harvard Educational Review*, January, 1940.

Graves, E. B., "What Is Direct Teaching?" *Virginia Journal of Education*, April, 1940.

Gray, J. Stanley, *Psychological Foundations of Education*. New York: American Book Company, 1935.

Gray, William H., *Psychology of Elementary School Subjects*. New York: Prentice-Hall, Inc., 1938.

Hollingworth, H. L., *Educational Psychology*. New York: D. Appleton-Century Company, 1933.

Kilpatrick, W. H., *Art and Practice of Teaching*. New York: W. R. Scott, Publisher, 1937.

Lamb, M. M., *Your First Year of Teaching*. Cincinnati, Ohio: South-Western Publishing Company, 1939.

LaRue, Daniel W., *Educational Psychology*. New York: Thomas Nelson and Sons, 1939.

Maaske, R. J., "Superintendent's Responsibility for Good Teaching," *American School Board Journal*, February, 1940.

Maurois, André, "A House Divided Against Itself," *Harper's*, February, 1941.

Mursell, James L., *Educational Psychology*. New York: W. W. Norton and Company, 1939.

————, *The Psychology of Secondary-School Teaching*, rev. ed. New York: W. W. Norton and Company, 1939.

Patey, Henry C., and George S. Stevenson, *The Mental Health Emphasis in Education*. New York: The National Committee for Mental Hygiene, 1935.

*Peabody Journal of Education*. "Century of Progress Towards the Profession of Teaching; radio programme." September, 1939.

Powers, F. F., and W. L. Uhl, *Psychological Principles of Education*. New York: D. Appleton-Century Company, 1933.

Ragsdale, C. E., "Teaching for Self-discovery and Self-direction." (In *National Commercial Teachers Federation Fifth Yearbook*.)

Reed, Homer B., *Psychology and Teaching of Secondary-School Subjects*. New York: Prentice-Hall, Inc., 1939.

Rivlin, Harry N., *Education for Adjustment: The Classroom Applications of Mental Hygiene*. New York: D. Appleton-Century Company, 1936.

Sandiford, Peter, *Foundations of Educational Psychology*. New York: Longmans, Green and Company, 1939.

Schmidt, Charles C., *Teaching and Learning the Common Branches,* rev. ed. New York: D. Appleton-Century Company, 1939.

Skinner, Charles E., and associates, *Educational Psychology.* New York: Prentice-Hall, Inc., 1936.

Smith, Henry B., *Growing Minds: An Introduction to Educational Psychology.* London: University of London Press, 1937.

Sorenson, Herbert, *Psychology in Education,* 1st ed. New York: McGraw-Hill Book Company, 1940.

Symonds, Percival M., *Education and Psychology of Thinking.* New York: McGraw-Hill Book Company, 1936.

Trow, William Clark, *Introduction to Educational Psychology.* Boston: Houghton Mifflin Company, 1937.

# Part II
## GROWTH AND DEVELOPMENT

---

### CHAPTER 3

# Personality and Behavior

Of all the topics with which the psychologist deals, probably none has greater appeal to or interest for laymen than that of personality. The term has been enshrouded in mysticism to a certain extent, since some people discuss it in much the same way that they would discuss so-called psychic phenomena, or spiritualism, or witchcraft. To these individuals, personality is something which more or less descends upon and envelops the individual from without rather than being "part and parcel" of the individual himself. *Personality,* like other terms, such as *soul* and *spirit,* is taken by many as a kind of link between the individual living in a material universe and a great unknown non-materialism. From this point of view we hear such expressions as "a spark of the divine," "God in man," or "man's better self."

### The Nature of Personality

In general, the point of view that will be considered in this chapter is simply that *personality is behavior.* It is the human individual in action. This should not necessarily offer any disturbance to the theologian, who seeks to define personality as "a spark of the divine," or something to that effect, but it necessitates that he clarify his thinking and recognize the fact that, though the individual may conform to his general hypotheses as to the relationship between God and man, *personality* is a term which simply refers to man in action.[1]

Personality probably has more aspects than simply behavior, as used in ordinary parlance. Thus, we have without doubt the fact that, as we use the term ordinarily, *personality* involves not only behavior on the part of the individual, but response to that behavior on the part of another individual. Thus, if I say of you, "You have a pleasing personality," I am referring not only to your behavioral reaction, but also to the fact that I have responded to

---

[1] Also see Dr. Witty's discussion in Chapter 6.

stimuli involved in your behavior. So, from this point of view, we have to recognize the fact that personality is much as Valentine [2] defined it, "Ourselves as others see us." It is ourselves acted on and providing the stimuli which act on other individuals and cause them to respond to our responses.

## The Factors of Personality

When with this concept of personality we try to understand the development of personality in children, we recognize that we really are dealing with the problem of the development of behavioral responses or habitual modes of behavior on the part of children. Thus, we are left with the problem of determining the factors that influence especially the development of the child's behavior. We come at once to the conventional conclusion that these factors are inheritance, or heredity, and environment, or training and experience.

### Biological inheritance [3]

With respect to the problem of heredity, there seems to be a considerable amount of wishful thinking on the part of some people at the present time in an attempt to eliminate completely the hereditary influences. These individuals would have us believe that the child pays no toll to his inheritance in the development of his behavioral tendencies. To be sure, there is no evidence to indicate that a child inherits behavior as such. In other words, there is no evidence to indicate that he inherits specifically such things as criminality, or politeness, or good manners, or petulance, or independence, or sociability, or any one of a large group of other comparable behavioral responses. To say, however, that a child does not inherit criminality, for example, does not necessarily mean that his hereditary background has no influence on the development of criminal tendencies. Certainly some children, as a result of their inheritances, have certain characteristics which make it more difficult for them to adjust to certain environmental influences, or they possess certain inherent capacities which cause them to fall victim to certain environmental forces much more easily than others. Some individuals with greater inherent intelligence can develop an independence of action in a way that most children of lower intelligence frequently are quite incapable of doing. The thing that must be remembered throughout all of these discussions,

[2] P. F. Valentine, *The Psychology of Personality*. New York: D. Appleton-Century Company, 1929.

[3] Also see the discussions in Chapters 4 and 6.

however, is that personality or behavior is not something which is dependent upon some one factor in isolation. In other words, behavior is not dependent upon inheritance by itself, nor is it dependent upon environment by itself, but it is an outgrowth of the various influences acting on the individual's various capacities and structural organizations.

It may be pertinent to ask what evidence there is to indicate that heredity does produce in the individual these structural characteristics that predispose him to behave in a way different from that in which other individuals possessing other structural characteristics might behave. One of the first things that we meet in this field is the factor of intelligence and the inherited differences in intelligence, which most unbiased investigators would be forced to admit. Despite the work of certain contemporary investigators, some of which seems based upon questionable research procedure and hypotheses of doubtful validity, almost any qualified diagnostician will be able to cite large numbers of cases of individuals who, without question, are mentally incompetent because of their inheritance.

We find evidence of the verity of this hypothesis both in vertical inheritance, that is, inheritance from generation to generation, and in horizontal inheritance, or inheritance within one generation. For example, in a case where there is feeble-mindedness in one generation and in the next generation, in the third generation there is certainly more than mathematical probability of expectancy evident. At the same time, where some six or eight children in one family are all feeble-minded, it is quite apparent that this is not normal expectancy; and especially if these conditions are apparent in early infancy, we are forced to the only logical conclusion possible, namely, that the inheritance of the individuals has determined their mental incapacities. When, for example, you take an adolescent girl who is brought into a home for the feeble-minded as an unquestioned ament and is kept there a few years, but because of overcrowding and certain unfortunate legal conditions is released to her community and then is brought back ten years later with six feeble-minded children whom she has had in the meantime, there is little excuse for assuming anything other than that these six feeble-minded children are feeble-minded because they have inherited the condition from their parents, whoever they might be. Of course, it is a recognized fact that not all amentia results from inheritance, there being a sizable percentage of it which is of secondary origin. On the other hand, we do know that there is very good evidence to indicate that a very large per cent of the aments are amented because of the germ-plasmic condition

out of which they evolved. Then, if intelligence is a factor that is
of any consequence in determining the course of human behavior,
and if intelligence in cases of this type is something that depends
at least in large measure upon inheritance, we find ample evidence
of the effects of heredity on the human individual and the behavioral responses that he develops.

## The endocrine glands

In the field of glandular secretions, it may probably be very
safely assumed that certain individuals have glandular "make-
ups," or constitutions, different from those of other individuals.
In other words, through their inheritance they exhibit different
endocrinological characteristics. In these endocrinological characteristics we find the bases of many of the internal stimuli that are
acting on the individuals and causing them to develop behavioral
responses. If, for example, we find an individual with a hyperactive
thymus, we may discover in him a person who continues to exhibit
certain infantile characteristics long after the early stages of
puberty when he is supposed to have lost them. An individual with
a hypothyroidal condition develops characteristics known as
*cretinism,* or he has certain dwarfish physical characteristics. He is
sluggish, has a thick, swarthy skin, and is mentally incompetent.
Naturally, such a person shows certain personality aberrations or
behavioral differences as a result of these structural changes.

It would seem that the role of inheritance as a determinant in
the development of human personality is more indirect than direct.
That is, there is no evidence to indicate that behavior tendencies
as such are inherited. There are many illustrations, however, of an
indisputable nature which point to the fact that many phases or
aspects of constitutional growth are affected directly by inheritance. Since behavior is always a matter of structure in action, it
is quite natural that different types of structure would and do
respond differently. Two individuals with different hereditary backgrounds would not have definite tendencies to differences in behavior as such, but they would possess different structural characteristics which when acted on by certain environmental stimuli
would result in different behavioral responses or different personality characteristics. The fact that hereditary effects are more
indirect than direct does not lessen the importance of inheritance
in an understanding of the development of human personality. It
merely necessitates a proper allocation of hereditary influences in
the total integration of forces, elements, or influences which go to
shape and regulate human behavior.

## The instinct hypothesis

Attention should be called to an older hypothesis in psychology which, though popular 25 to 50 years ago, has not found many American adherents in recent years. This is the idea that human behavior to a large extent is merely an unfolding of instinctive tendencies. According to this idea, the individual from birth to the grave meets many of his life situations with ready-made forms of response. If this hypothesis had found substantiation in research data, it would have indicated that human personality was primarily an unwinding of hereditary urges anchored in the lost generations of each person's remote ancestry. The accumulated evidence, which seems to indicate how truly human conduct is not the mere outgrowth of these blind dynamic drives, however, has led us to a fuller recognition of the fact that human personality, though influenced by germ-plasmic continuity, as revealed in structural proportions and characteristics, certainly is something far different from the stereotypy which we should anticipate if the instinctivists' hypothesis had been verified.[4]

## Personality-types hypothesis

One other item to which attention should be called is the notion advanced periodically by various people to indicate that human personality is tied up irrevocably and causally with certain specific structural proportions. These typologists would classify human beings into such groups as: asthenics, pyknics, athletics, dysplastics, and so forth. According to this notion, if an individual possesses certain characteristics, and we have to assume that these characteristics are possessed as a result of his inheritance, he is almost sure to develop certain behavioral patterns. To begin with, these body types cannot be found in discrete fashion, and the classification of the vast per cent of mankind on any of these bases would be ambiguous, unreliable, and misleading. Not only is this true, but as long as a sizable percentage of human individuals classified under these typological headings do not conform to so-called personality patterns supposedly associated with the structural characteristics, we can hardly think that these body types at best have anything approximating an individually significant relationship to personality development.

---

[4] Cf. C. Burt, "Is the Doctrine of Instincts Dead? A Symposium. VII. Conclusion," *British Journal of Educational Psychology*, 1943, Vol. 13, pp. 1-15. Also see Vol. 16, pp. 1407, 2658, 3996, and 3980.

## The environmental factors

If we leave the hereditary factor in personality and turn to the influences of environment, we find them to be diverse and multifold in nature. Mention has been made already of the fact that physical structure likely produces an effect on personality reactions in that certain structures predispose the individual to respond to certain stimuli in one way while other structures will predispose him to respond in another way. Very frequently in individual cases, one will notice how structural changes in the individual are accompanied by alterations in his personality reactions. This is noticed often in cases of severe trauma. Though we get widely diverse illustrations of traumatic effects on personality, probably one of the most pronounced is in those cases where cerebral injury is followed by epileptic seizures. Then, of course, there is always a fairly definite group of individuals around any mental hospital who can be cited as cases in whom psychoses have developed following traumatic destruction of cerebral tissue. Disease also has to be considered in somewhat this same connection. The influence of disease is probably noticed subjectively by most individuals during their periods of illness. They themselves recognize the fact that they do not react conventionally to many of the problems that arise around them. In the case of a few diseases, the later personality changes tend to be so well patterned that they have definite classifications. Thus, we have the paretic who is a post-syphilitic case. His paresis, with the consequent paranoidal delusions, usually follows his syphilitic infection from six to twenty years. Then we have the post-encephalitic cases with their gradual mental disorientation and their consequent personality abnormalities. In addition, of course, we have such personality changes as psychoses following pellagra and the various alcoholic and drug psychoses. All of these illustrations in the field of psychotic behavior are more spectacular than common, but serve well to emphasize the fact that environmentally induced changes in the organism can and frequently do produce unavoidable effects on human personality.

## Socioeconomic influences

Probably the most common environmental influence on personality of which most people think is a socioeconomic influence. With the Federal Government attending to cases of economic need and publicizing the results of its work in the way that it has, and with socially minded persons all over the country picking up the cudgel in defense of those who are economically embarrassed, it is little wonder that we find commentators, both lay and professional, taking the position that personality traits are dependent primarily on the formal social and economic aspects of a child's environment. There is an influence of socioeconomic factors on individual behavior without question. There may be a question, however, as to what this influence is at all times. Thus, poverty combined with moronity may lead to personality traits of submissiveness, laziness, untidiness, and the like. Poverty combined with intellectual superiority, however, may lead to vigor, industriousness, and an almost abnormal striving to succeed. Francis [5] at the University of Iowa made a study of socioeconomic influences on children's personality development, and concluded that all such factors were of significance primarily in the influence that they had on the attitudes of other members of the family rather than directly on the developing child. In other words, poverty did not seem to influence the child directly in his personality development in any predetermined manner, but poverty in the home at times was accompanied by parental attitudes which seemed to produce a very definite effect on personality traits and characteristics of the child.

Coleman [6] has made one of the most extensive studies of the relationship of socioeconomic status to performance of children when he studied about 2,800 children in the seventh, eighth, and ninth grades. These children composed the highest 5 per cent, middle 5 per cent, and lowest 5 per cent in socioeconomic status of a population of between twelve and thirteen thousand junior-high-school pupils. With respect to scholastic achievement, he found that children from the favored environment were rather definitely superior to those from the average environment, and these, in turn, were somewhat superior to children from the lowest environmental level. He also found, of course, that there were rather large significant differences in measured intelligence of children from these levels. Rather strikingly, though, the children from the favored environment are achieving less in proportion to their tested intelligence than are the children from the lowest environment in proportion to their tested intelligence. Reference is to averages.

When consideration was given to the problem of personality adjustment or maladjustment as measured by a standard test, in this instance the B. P. C. Personality Inventory, in every comparison but one, children from the highest socioeconomic level made

[5] K. V. Francis, "A Study of the Means of Influence of Socioeconomic Factors upon the Personality of Children," *Journal of Juvenile Research,* 1933, Vol. 17, pp. 70-77.

[6] H. A. Coleman, "The Relationship of Socio-Economic Status to the Performance of Junior High School Students," *Peabody College Contributions to Education* (unpublished), 1940, No. 264.

the lowest (best-adjusted) scores, those from the average environment made the average scores, and those from the poorest environment made the highest or worst-adjusted scores. In the only instance where this was not true, that involving a comparison of boys in the 9th grade, the highest and average boys were of about equal adjustment, the scores being, respectively, 32.94 and 32.42 with the probable error of each about 1.30. Even in this grade, however, there was a statistically significant difference in the degree of adjustment between each of these groups and the boys from the poorest socioeconomic level.

When attention was turned to the hobbies of these children, it was found that those from the more-favored environment had more hobbies than those from the less-favored environments. There was a consistent decrease in incidence of the following hobbies as one went from the more-favored to the average to the least-favored groups: reading novels, mysteries, fanciful stories; reading history, science, biography, and the like; active games or sports; playing musical instruments other than the radio or the phonograph; going to shows; participating in dramatics; building things or shop work; traveling; studying; social activities such as dancing and parties; scouting or other forms of serious group activity; collecting. In turn, there was a consistent increase in incidence of the following hobbies: housework, such as cooking, sweeping, straightening, and so forth; working in a store or on the farm; no hobbies. Children whose families were on relief when studied separately tended to have characteristics quite comparable to those placed generally in the lowest socioeconomic group.

Moncreiff [7] studied problem children and gave especial attention to matters relating to their socioeconomic backgrounds as compared with those of a normative population. These problem children were children whom the teachers in the schools had designated as problems, or who had been designated by the B. P. C. Personality Inventory as possessing personality problems, or children who were selected both by their teachers and by the B. P. C. as problems. Rather strikingly, in this study there did not seem to be the outstanding difference that some would have anticipated. Table I does indicate, however, that in most instances the normative populations come from slightly more-favored backgrounds than the problem children population. On the other hand, these differences are not excessively great. Probably more evidence of difference is seen when consideration is given to certain specific

[7] Ruth Moncreiff, "A Study of Factors Relating to Problem Behavior in Elementary School Children," *Peabody College Contributions to Education,* 1939, No. 294.

TABLE I

Median Socioeconomic Scores of Normative and Problem Children, by Grade and Sex (Moncreiff's Data)

| Sex | Group | Grade | | | | |
|---|---|---|---|---|---|---|
| | | 4 | 5 | 6 | 7 | 8 |
| Boys | Norm............. | 6.4 | 6.5 | 6.5 | 6.9 | 6.7 |
| | Problem........... | 5.8 | 5.8 | 6.1 | 6.1 | 6.6 |
| Girls | Norm............. | 6.2 | 6.5 | 6.6 | 6.8 | 6.7 |
| | Problem........... | 5.9 | 5.9 | 5.9 | 5.6 | 6.1 |

factors in the home than when all these factors are merged into one measure. Thus, normative children much more frequently than problem children tend to have radios in the home, tend to have a telephone in the home, and, in the instance of boys especially, tend to have an auto in the home and take a daily paper. Also, the problem children, with considerably more frequency than normal children, tend to come from homes on relief. Problem children tend to come from larger families, and especially is this true in the instance of those children selected both by teachers and by tests as being problem cases. Furthermore, the only child was not significantly more maladjusted than the average child.

Pledger [8] studied 1,992 children in grades one to three who were rated by their teachers as being well-adjusted personally, and compared them with 1,975 comparably selected cases in the same grades who were rated as being maladjusted. She classified the occupational activities of the fathers of the two groups in accordance with the Taussig-Terman scale. This has five major groups, as follows: I, Professional; II a, Semi-professional and higher business; II b, Lower business; III, Skilled labor; IV, Semi-skilled labor; and V, Unskilled labor. In Table II the reader will see the percentage distribution of adjusted and maladjusted cases whose fathers' occupations fell in each of the designated groups. It will be noticed that ratings of definite adjustment were assigned about three times as often as ratings of maladjustment to children whose fathers were in the two highest occupational brackets. Conversely, the child whose father was in the unskilled-labor group had more than twice as many chances to be rated maladjusted as he had to be rated adjusted. Of course, children of both types were found in

---

[8] M. M. Pledger, "A Study of Maladjusted Children in the Early Elementary Grades," *Peabody College Contributions to Education* (unpublished), 1940.

TABLE II

PERCENTAGE DISTRIBUTION OF ADJUSTED AND MALADJUSTED CHILDREN
WHOSE FATHERS' OCCUPATIONS FALL IN CERTAIN DESIGNATED
OCCUPATIONAL LEVELS (Pledger's Data)

| Type of Child | Occupational Level | | | | | |
|---|---|---|---|---|---|---|
| | I | II a | II b | III | IV | V |
| Adjusted............ | 6.9 | 14.3 | 16.9 | 33.6 | 17.8 | 10.7 |
| Maladjusted........ | 1.9 | 4.4 | 7.1 | 39.6 | 22.4 | 24.8 |

all occupational levels, but there seems to be almost indisputable evidence to the effect that, with these children, environment was likely to be associated in a somewhat schematic pattern with the personality development of the individual.

When Pledger took the socioeconomic ratings of the homes from which children came, as given by the teachers of the children, she found that among the adjusted group 14 per cent came from superior homes, 70.2 per cent came from average homes, and 15.7 per cent came from poor homes. Among the maladjusted group, however, only 3.4 per cent came from superior homes, 44.2 per cent came from average homes, and 52.4 per cent came from inferior homes. Still further, she found that 9.2 per cent of the adjusted children came from homes where the family was on relief, whereas 25 per cent of the maladjusted children came from homes of this type. Pledger's data, showing that the average child comes from a larger family than the adjusted child, agree with the findings of Moncreiff.

One of the most interesting and enlightening phases of Pledger's study came in her analysis of adjustment and maladjustment in relationship to the parental attitudes in the homes of the children. The teachers rated the homes of the children as superior, average, or inferior in terms of the attitudes of the parents toward their children and the general problems of life about them. In Table III is an analysis of these ratings with respect to the expressed attitudes of the parents. It is striking to note that a child from a superior type of home, either boy or girl, has about five to seven times as many chances to achieve an adjusted personality rating as he has to be classified as maladjusted. Conversely, the child from the inferior home is seven or eight times as likely to be rated maladjusted as adjusted. So again we see a rather definite relationship between the training and environmental experiences of a child and the personality rating he is likely to achieve in his contacts in school.

TABLE III

PERCENTAGE FREQUENCIES OF ADJUSTED AND MALADJUSTED CHILDREN
IN HOMES WITH DESIGNATED TYPES OF PARENTAL ATTITUDES
(Pledger's Data)

| Type of Child | Type of Home | | |
| --- | --- | --- | --- |
| | Superior | Average | Inferior |
| Adjusted Boys......................... | 36.9 | 58.1 | 5.1 |
| Maladjusted Boys...................... | 5.2 | 53.3 | 41.5 |
| Adjusted Girls........................ | 37.4 | 57.2 | 5.1 |
| Maladjusted Girls..................... | 6.4 | 58.4 | 36.1 |

Holden [9] studied the characteristics of student leaders in the seventh, eighth, and ninth grades, and compared them with a control group from the same classes. For each sex in each grade there was a rather definitely significant difference in the socioeconomic backgrounds of the two groups, the leaders, on the average, tending to be selected from children with more favorable environmental antecedents. Deer [10] found that children from homes with desirable parental attitudes tended to be much better readers than those from homes with inferior attitudes. Wang,[11] studying fourth-, fifth-, and sixth-grade children, found that, from the standpoint of play interests, girls of low socioeconomic status especially favor Drop the Handkerchief, Farmer in the Dell, Hopscotch, Ring Around the Rosy, London Bridge, Dodge Ball, and Jacks, whereas girls from the most-favored fourth of the socioeconomic distribution prefer hunting, swimming, watching football or baseball, badminton, riding horseback, football, tennis, hiking, and going to the movies. Low-status boys, in turn, especially liked skating, Drop the Handkerchief, and flying kites, as opposed to high-status boys who preferred football, watching football or baseball, badminton, tennis, and swimming.

Armstrong,[12] in one of the most extensive studies available,

[9] B. S. Holden, "A Study of Some Characteristics of Students Participating in Student Government," *Peabody College Contributions to Education* (unpublished), 1940, No. 274.

[10] G. H. Deer, "Factors Associated with Extreme Retardation and Acceleration in Reading," *Peabody College Contributions to Education* (unpublished), 1939, No. 291.

[11] J. D. Wang, "A Study of Certain Factors Associated with Children's Play Interests," *Peabody College Contributions to Education* (unpublished), 1941, No. 210.

[12] L. E. Armstrong, "The Relation of Certain Factors to Children's Behavior Characteristics," *Peabody College Contributions to Education* (unpublished), 1940, No. 259.

analyzed about 18,000 cases in grades one to six. Each child's home had been evaluated by his teacher as either superior, average, or inferior, and the attitudes of each child's parents toward the child and his problems were rated on the same three-point basis. In addition, each teacher had selected from a group of 70 traits, or characteristics, those which she considered outstandingly descriptive of each child in her room. In Table IV is a summary of some of these data, as they pertain to those traits that in the opinion of 50 mental hygienists have either positive or negative hygienic significance. If we note the most outstanding differences between children from superior and inferior socioeconomic backgrounds, we find that superior boys more than inferior boys are likely to be dependable, friendly, happy, and honest, have a sense of humor, be original, adventuresome, ambitious, artistic, energetic, generous, investigative, polite, and precocious, and be leaders. Girls from superior environments show the same superiority, with the addition of self-reliance, over girls from inferior socioeconomic backgrounds. Both boys and girls from the inferior environments, however, are more likely to be rated as dull, inattentive, irregular in attendance, lazy, slovenly, and possessed of a lack of interest than are children from the most-favored environments.

## Parents' attitudes as influences

When the children were studied from the standpoint of their parents' attitudes, boys from favorable environments, as compared with those from unfavorable environments, showed the same superior characteristics, except for adventuresomeness, as did boys from economically superior environments, with the addition of being more self-reliant, persistent, and systematic. Girls from homes with highly favorable parental attitudes showed the same points of superiority when compared with girls from inferior homes as did the boys, with the addition of being more self-controlled and adventuresome. When attention is turned to the traits which are more likely to appear among children from inferior homes of this type than among children from superior homes, the picture is startling. Both boys and girls in these homes are rated as being more likely to cheat, daydream, be disobedient, dull, inattentive, irregular in school attendance, lazy, quarrelsome, slovenly, tardy, and dishonest, and lack interest in their work. Further, these boys are said to be more destructive and rude, and the girls are rated as being more nervous, self-conscious, suggestible, cowardly, and given to pouting.

TABLE IV

PERCENTAGE FREQUENCIES OF APPEARANCE OF CERTAIN PERSONALITY
TRAIT RATINGS FOR CHILDREN WITH DESIGNATED TYPES OF
HOME BACKGROUNDS (Armstrong's data)

| Personality Traits (Grouped according to mental hygienists' ratings) | Socioeconomic Status | | | | | | Parental Attitudes | | | | | |
|---|---|---|---|---|---|---|---|---|---|---|---|---|
| | Boys | | | Girls | | | Boys | | | Girls | | |
| | S* | A | I | S | A | I | S | A | I | S | A | I |
| **Decided Hygienic Value:** Dependable | 38 | 31 | 22 | 51 | 40 | 30 | 49 | 30 | 12 | 59 | 39 | 19 |
| Friendly | 41 | 30 | 19 | 48 | 36 | 23 | 45 | 30 | 11 | 51 | 33 | 17 |
| Happy | 44 | 37 | 29 | 46 | 42 | 34 | 47 | 38 | 23 | 51 | 41 | 25 |
| Honest | 37 | 31 | 24 | 38 | 33 | 25 | 45 | 32 | 16 | 41 | 32 | 18 |
| Original | 18 | 10 | 6 | 19 | 10 | 6 | 24 | 9 | 3 | 22 | 18 | 3 |
| Self-controlled | 5 | 5 | 4 | 8 | 7 | 5 | 7 | 5 | 3 | 9 | 7 | 4 |
| Self-reliant | 10 | 8 | 6 | 15 | 10 | 8 | 15 | 7 | 4 | 18 | 9 | 5 |
| Sense of humor | 23 | 17 | 12 | 15 | 11 | 7 | 24 | 17 | 10 | 15 | 10 | 6 |
| **Some Hygienic Value:** Adventuresome | 19 | 13 | 10 | 10 | 6 | 4 | 8 | 13 | 10 | 10 | 5 | 4 |
| Ambitious | 32 | 21 | 14 | 46 | 33 | 23 | 40 | 18 | 7 | 53 | 30 | 15 |
| Artistic | 11 | 8 | 5 | 26 | 16 | 11 | 14 | 6 | 5 | 28 | 15 | 7 |
| Energetic | 31 | 22 | 18 | 24 | 19 | 15 | 31 | 23 | 16 | 24 | 18 | 14 |
| Generous | 19 | 17 | 14 | 24 | 21 | 16 | 22 | 17 | 10 | 26 | 21 | 15 |
| Investigative | 18 | 9 | 8 | 11 | 7 | 5 | 20 | 9 | 5 | 14 | 6 | 4 |
| Leader | 11 | 6 | 3 | 17 | 9 | 5 | 14 | 5 | 2 | 18 | 7 | 3 |
| Persistent | 13 | 13 | 9 | 15 | 15 | 12 | 15 | 11 | 6 | 17 | 14 | 10 |
| Polite | 33 | 30 | 26 | 42 | 39 | 36 | 41 | 31 | 17 | 46 | 40 | 27 |
| Precocious | 7 | 3 | 2 | 9 | 4 | 2 | 10 | 2 | 1 | 11 | 3 | 1 |
| Systematic | 4 | 3 | 2 | 8 | 6 | 4 | 6 | 3 | 1 | 10 | 5 | 3 |
| **Probably Detrimental:** Cheating | 2 | 3 | 6 | 2 | 4 | 5 | 1 | 4 | 7 | 2 | 4 | 10 |
| Cute; "smart-alec" | 8 | 9 | 8 | 3 | 3 | 2 | 6 | 8 | 9 | 2 | 3 | 2 |
| Daydreaming | 15 | 17 | 18 | 9 | 12 | 13 | 12 | 18 | 20 | 6 | 13 | 17 |
| Destructive | 2 | 3 | 6 | — | 1 | 1 | 1 | 2 | 7 | — | 4 | 2 |

*S—superior; A—average; I—inferior

TABLE IV—(*Continued*)

PERCENTAGE FREQUENCIES OF APPEARANCE OF CERTAIN PERSONALITY
TRAIT RATINGS FOR CHILDREN WITH DESIGNATED TYPES OF
HOME BACKGROUNDS (Armstrong's data)

| Personality Traits (Grouped according to mental hygienists' ratings) | Socioeconomic Status | | | | | | Parental Attitudes | | | | | |
|---|---|---|---|---|---|---|---|---|---|---|---|---|
| | Boys | | | Girls | | | Boys | | | Girls | | |
| | S | A | I | S | A | I | S | A | I | S | A | I |
| **Probably Detrimental** (*Cont.*): | | | | | | | | | | | | |
| Disobedient | 3 | 5 | 5 | 1 | 2 | 3 | 2 | 4 | 10 | 1 | 2 | 6 |
| Dull | 8 | 18 | 30 | 5 | 13 | 22 | 5 | 18 | 39 | 4 | 14 | 31 |
| Gambling | — | — | — | — | — | — | — | — | 1 | — | — | — |
| "Goody-goody" | 1 | 1 | 1 | 1 | 1 | 1 | 1 | 1 | 1 | 1 | 1 | — |
| Immature | 7 | 8 | 7 | 6 | 8 | 7 | 6 | 7 | 8 | 4 | 7 | 6 |
| Impatient | 4 | 3 | 3 | 5 | 4 | 3 | 3 | 3 | 3 | 5 | 4 | 4 |
| Impetuous | 6 | 7 | 6 | 5 | 8 | 4 | 6 | 6 | 7 | 3 | 5 | 5 |
| Inattentive | 15 | 21 | 25 | 8 | 16 | 17 | 9 | 19 | 34 | 6 | 13 | 24 |
| Irregular attendance | 2 | 3 | 10 | 1 | 8 | 9 | 2 | 3 | 12 | 1 | 3 | 11 |
| Lack of interest | 9 | 14 | 19 | 4 | 13 | 13 | 6 | 13 | 28 | 3 | 9 | 19 |
| Lazy | 6 | 10 | 14 | 3 | 4 | 7 | 4 | 10 | 18 | 2 | 4 | 11 |
| Lying | 1 | 1 | 3 | — | 1 | 2 | — | 1 | 4 | — | 1 | 4 |
| Nervous | 12 | 10 | 9 | 9 | 10 | 10 | 9 | 10 | 11 | 7 | 11 | 12 |
| Over-critical | 4 | 2 | 2 | 4 | 4 | 5 | 2 | 3 | 3 | 3 | 4 | 4 |
| Physical cowardice | 2 | 1 | 2 | — | 1 | 1 | 1 | 2 | 2 | 1 | 1 | 12 |
| Pouting | 3 | 4 | 5 | 5 | 5 | 5 | 2 | 4 | 6 | 3 | 5 | 9 |
| Profane | 1 | 1 | 2 | — | — | — | — | 1 | 3 | — | — | 1 |
| Quarrelsome | 2 | 3 | 6 | 1 | 3 | 3 | 2 | 3 | 8 | 1 | 2 | 6 |
| Quitter | 4 | 5 | 7 | 3 | 3 | 5 | 3 | 5 | 9 | 2 | 4 | 6 |
| Rude | 1 | 2 | 2 | — | 1 | 1 | — | 1 | 4 | 2 | 1 | 2 |
| Self-conscious | 4 | 4 | 5 | 4 | 6 | 7 | 4 | 5 | 4 | 3 | 6 | 8 |
| Selfish | 4 | 2 | 2 | 4 | 3 | 2 | 3 | 3 | 2 | 3 | 3 | 3 |
| Sickly | 2 | 2 | 3 | 2 | 3 | 4 | 2 | 2 | 4 | 2 | 3 | 5 |

TABLE IV—(*Continued*)

PERCENTAGE FREQUENCIES OF APPEARANCE OF CERTAIN PERSONALITY
TRAIT RATINGS FOR CHILDREN WITH DESIGNATED TYPES OF
HOME BACKGROUNDS (Armstrong's data)

| Personality Traits (Grouped according to mental hygienists' ratings) | Socioeconomic Status | | | | | | Parental Attitudes | | | | | |
|---|---|---|---|---|---|---|---|---|---|---|---|---|
| | Boys | | | Girls | | | Boys | | | Girls | | |
| | S | A | I | S | A | I | S | A | I | S | A | I |
| **Probably Detrimental** (*Cont.*): Sissy | 2 | 1 | 1 | 1 | 1 | 1 | 1 | 1 | 1 | 1 | 1 | 1 |
| Slovenly | 1 | 4 | 13 | — | 2 | 8 | — | 3 | 21 | — | 2 | 14 |
| Stealing | — | — | 1 | — | — | 1 | — | — | 2 | — | — | 2 |
| Stubborn | 2 | 3 | 4 | 1 | 2 | 2 | 2 | 3 | 6 | 1 | 2 | 3 |
| Suggestible | 3 | 4 | 6 | 2 | 3 | 4 | 2 | 5 | 6 | 1 | 4 | 6 |
| Suspicious | — | 1 | 2 | 1 | 1 | 2 | — | 1 | 3 | 1 | 1 | 2 |
| Tardiness | 1 | 2 | 5 | 1 | 2 | 4 | 1 | 2 | 11 | 1 | 2 | 6 |
| Temper tantrums | 1 | 1 | 1 | 1 | 1 | 1 | 1 | 1 | 2 | 1 | 1 | 1 |
| Too easily frightened | 2 | 3 | 4 | 3 | 4 | 5 | 3 | 3 | 3 | 3 | 5 | 4 |
| Truant | — | — | 1 | — | — | — | — | — | 3 | — | — | 1 |
| **Decidedly Harmful:** Cruel | 1 | 2 | 3 | — | — | — | 1 | 2 | 5 | — | 3 | — |
| Dishonest | 3 | 4 | 5 | 1 | 3 | 5 | 1 | 4 | 10 | 1 | 3 | 9 |
| Isolationist | 1 | 1 | 2 | — | 1 | 2 | 1 | 1 | 2 | — | 1 | 4 |
| Oversensitive | 7 | 8 | 10 | 8 | 11 | 13 | 7 | 8 | 10 | 8 | 11 | 12 |
| Unhappy | 1 | 2 | 4 | 1 | 2 | 4 | 1 | 2 | 4 | 1 | 2 | 5 |

Lester and Barnette [13] found among a group of maladjusted
college women, as compared with a comparable group of adjusted
college women, more "lack of affection and encouragement with
simultaneous domination of parents in choice of friends, inadequate
sex instructions and subsequent worry about sex, stern parents,
harsher punishment." Winfrey [14] found extreme strictness or
leniency in religious instruction during childhood to have scant

[13] O. P. Lester and W. L. Barnette, "Some Factors Relative to Adjusted and
Unadjusted Personalities," *Journal of Juvenile Research*, 1932, Vol. 16, pp. 319-325.
[14] M. E. Winfrey, "A Personality Study of College Girls," *Peabody College
Contributions to Education*, 1936, No. 185.

relationship to the religious ideas of college women, but a rather interesting relationship, especially in certain individual cases, to their personality adjustments. Yourman [15] found that children who were problems under one teacher had twice as many chances to become adjusted if teachers were changed as was the case if the same teachers were continued. Boynton, Dugger, and Turner [16] found a significant difference in the emotionality of children under stable teachers and children under unstable teachers. Mecham,[17] taking his incitation from the latter study, found that specific types of hyper-emotionality among teachers tended to result in the same general types of hyper-emotionality among children.

It would appear that sufficient evidence is available to indicate that specific environmental conditions do produce specific effects on the personality development of children. To be sure, there is no evidence to indicate that any one environmental characteristic is the sole determinant of behavior. For example, there is no evidence to indicate that low socioeconomic status is *ipso facto* evidence of maladjustment. As has been presented earlier in this discussion, behavior, or personality, develops out of an interrelationship of inherited capacities for structural response and the various diverse forces which act on the organism from the time of conception to death. To be sure, specific behavior would seem to be correlated more closely to specific environmental stimuli than to general structural organizations. This position, however, does not eliminate the latter condition as a significant factor. So, by way of conclusion, we might say that every child with whom the school or the home works has certain predetermined limits within which he can develop habits of behavioral response, but, within these limits, the habits themselves will depend upon those forces, influences, and training experiences that his environment provides.

### QUESTIONS AND EXERCISES FOR DISCUSSION AND STUDY

1. How do you account for the interest that so many laymen express in personality?

2. How do you think most laymen would define personality? Compare this with two definitions you can find in psychological literature.

3. Find three physical characteristics which qualified geneticists believe to be inherited. Would fluctuations in these characteristics be likely to affect personality reactions?

---

[15] Julius Yourman, "Children Identified by Their Teachers as Problems," *Journal of Educational Sociology,* 1932, Vol. 5, pp. 334-343.

[16] P. L. Boynton, H. Dugger, and M. Turner, "The Emotional Stability of Teachers and Pupils," *Journal of Juvenile Research,* 1934, Vol. 18, pp. 223-232.

[17] G. S. Mecham, "A Study of Emotional Instability of Teachers and Their Pupils," *Peabody College Contributions to Education* (unpublished), 1940.

4. What is meant by the statement that the role of inheritance as a determinant in the development of human personality is more indirect than direct?

5. What is the meaning of the statement that behavior is structure in action?

6. What evidence can you cite from your own experience that would tend to substantiate a conclusion such as that drawn by Francis?

7. What reasons can you assign for conditions such as Coleman found in the relationship between socioeconomic status and pupil achievements, interests, and personality traits?

8. Are Pledger's findings at variance with Moncreiff's? What was Pledger's most significant finding? Why do you think so?

9. Is there any evidence in Armstrong's findings to indicate that, whereas superior economic backgrounds are more likely to produce noticeable effects on personality reactions than are inferior economic backgrounds, inferior or undesirable parental attitudes are more likely to result in personality differences than are desirable parental attitudes?

10. Can you cite any specific individuals of your acquaintance who tend to illustrate the findings of Lester and Barnette, Winfrey, Boynton *et al.*, and Mecham?

### SELECTED REFERENCES FOR FURTHER READING AND STUDY

Bennett, M. E., and H. C. Hand, *Designs for Personality*. New York: McGraw-Hill Book Company, 1938.

Berg, Louis, *The Human Personality*. New York: Prentice-Hall, Inc., 1937.

Boynton, P. L., *Psychology of Child Development*. Minneapolis: Educational Publishers, 1938. Chap. 10.

Chave, E. J., *Personality Development in Children*. Chicago: University of Chicago Press, 1937.

Hartshorne, H., *Character in Human Relations*. New York: Charles Scribner's Sons, 1932.

Healy, W., *Personality in Formation and Action*. New York: W. W. Norton and Company, 1938.

Heaton, K. L., *The Character Emphasis in Education*. Chicago: University of Chicago Press, 1933.

Jones, M. C., and B. S. Burks, *Personality Development in Childhood*, Monograph of the Society for Research in Child Development, Vol. I, No. 4. Washington: National Research Council, 1936.

Judd, C. H., *Educational Psychology*. Boston: Houghton Mifflin Company, 1939. Part III.

Leeper, R., *Psychology of Personality and Social Adjustment*. Mount Vernon, Ia.: Cornell College, 1937.

Myers, G. C., *Developing Personality in the Child at School*. New York: Greenberg, Publisher, 1931.

Shaffer, L. F., *Psychology of Adjustment*. Boston: Houghton Mifflin Company, 1936.

Stagner, R., *Psychology of Personality*. New York: McGraw-Hill Book Company, 1937.

Theobald, J. J., *Personality and Personalysis*. New York: Prentice-Hall, Inc., 1938.

Thorpe, L. P., *Psychological Foundations of Personality*. New York: McGraw-Hill Book Company, 1938.

Thorndike, J. L., Personality and Personbook, New York: Prentice-Hall, Inc., 1938.

Thorpe, L. P., Psychological Foundations of Personality, New York: McGraw-Hill Book Company, 1938.

# CHAPTER 4

# Growth and Development

### A quarrel with biographers

Admittedly, few types of books are more rewarding to the serious reader than the biographies of men and women who have achieved eminence. The reader gains an insight into the life and times of famous people, he enriches his knowledge of history, and he obtains some understanding of the careers of the great. The conventional biography opens with a few pages dealing with the subject's ancestors; continues with a page or two about the infancy and the childhood of the subject; briefly alludes to the university career, if any; and then proceeds with a detailed account of his adult life. From the standpoint of the psychologist, this method is tantalizing and disappointing. Of course, the subject's fame depended upon his adult career; and, naturally, the biographer is particularly concerned with the task of presenting it and giving it the appropriate interpretations. Since anecdotes make interesting reading, besides serving to illuminate points, the biographer often includes them. The psychologist expresses impatience because he would like to have a full record of the infancy, the childhood, and the adolescence of the person. He would like to know more details about the home, the school, and the teachers, the playmates, and all the other subtle influences which may have determined the life of the subject. Hence, though a reading of biographies may be delightful recreation for a psychologist, it does not contribute very much to his wish to learn more about growth and development.

Like the conventional biography, anecdotes about home lives, play activities, and school experiences of children are frequently rather interesting and often highly diverting. Anecdotes, however, furnish a questionable basis for a genuine understanding of growth and development. In the first place, they usually contain too many data that are uncritically reported. The sources are not properly evaluated, and the teller is frequently intent upon producing an effect. In the second place, only a few dramatic highlights are included in anecdotal records, whether they be written by biographers or related by parents. Consequently, anecdotal records lack continuity. In order to understand the principles of growth and development, we must have continuous records of the same children or cross-section accounts of many children at each successive age. In the third place, anecdotes, like biographies, do not include control or comparison studies. In order to be in a position to judge whether a given type of behavior is commonplace, precocious, or indicative of retardation, we must have adequate standards whereby to make a comparison. These are a few of the reasons why the child psychologist distrusts both the biographical and the anecdotal records of growth and development.

## The longitudinal approach [1]

One of the best ways to understand how children grow and develop is to observe a large group from their first days of infancy to the time of their maturity. By taking copious notes, making photographic records, and using various techniques for creating experimental situations, we might be able to obtain invaluable material. Anyone who has observed the growth and development of an infant during the first year of its life will appreciate how difficult a task this would be. One of the most obvious facts is that the infant does not start life at "psychological zero." On the contrary, the newborn infant (neonate) has a relatively large number of unlearned responses, the cataloguing of which is one of the interesting problems engaging the attention of many psychologists. Among these responses which are observable within the first hour after birth are the following: yawning, unco-ordinated eye movements, crying, movements of legs and arms, twisting of the head from side to side, lip movements, and swallowing. Some of the receptors are ready to function at the beginning of postnatal life. For example, a light touch on the nostrils elicits a sneeze, and a heavy pressure induces a stiffening of legs and arms. When the sole of the foot is stimulated by a light touch, the toes spread upward in a fanlike manner (the Babinski reflex). Many other responses (mass activities and reflexes) are ready to function at the time of birth. These examples have been given in order to correct

---

[1] One of the earliest records of growth and development based upon careful observations is that of Tiedemann in 1787. Among the early writings on this topic, Preyer's *The Mind of the Child* (1881) is often cited as the first thorough report on the early years of life. G. Stanley Hall, of Clark University, did much to stimulate interest in genetic studies. The serious student is advised to commence with Arnold Gesell's "Maturation and the Patterning of Behavior," pp. 209-235 in Carl Murchison's *Handbook of Child Psychology* (Worcester, Mass.: Clark University Press, 1933). M. M. Shirley's *The First Two Years* (Minneapolis: University of Minnesota Press, 1933) is an excellent reference.

the mistaken notion that the infant commences postnatal life at "zero."

An increasing number of observational records of growth and development during the early years of life are now available. Although a detailed account of this material would lead us far afield, many of the most important principles of growth and development are derived from these studies. The earliest investigations in this field were made on individual children, some of them being the children of the psychologists who kept the records. In recent years, small groups of infants have been closely observed by child psychologists. Supplementing the records obtained from observations of infants are many reports of animal growth and development. In dealing with animals, psychologists are able to establish more rigorous controls and to perform more thorough experiments than are feasible with human beings. When the child develops an "inner life" and reaches the age of about three years, the longitudinal method has a limited applicability. An increasing number of gaps appear in the record, and these must be filled in by another method.

### The cross-section approach [2]

Since it is utterly impossible to follow the child day and night, controlling every stimulus, photographing every response, taking full notes on everything that is said and thought, the psychologist makes use of the cross-section approach. He takes groups of children at each successive stage in their development, and then observes characteristic behavior and experiments with, tests or measures, and interviews the children. In general, the findings from these cross-section studies both supplement and substantiate the conclusions that have been drawn from the longitudinal studies of infants. No new principles of growth and development have been discovered by one method that have not been brought to light by the other. Since the longitudinal approach is neither practicable nor feasible with human beings who have outgrown their infancy, observations are made at various chronological ages in the lives of children. For best results, psychologists make use of the same children; but when this requirement cannot be met, they try to obtain children whose backgrounds, health, schooling, and other similar factors are identical.

---

[2] The student is advised to become thoroughly familiar with the normative summaries of development in Arnold L. Gesell's *Infancy and Human Growth* (New York: The Macmillan Company, 1939). It would be interesting and informative to compare infants and young children with these "norms of development," and thus to make an original report of some children in the community. Most intelligent mothers will co-operate when the purpose has been explained to them.

### Some basic principles of growth and development [3]

Although there are many principles of great theoretical interest that would be all-important in a study of the psychology of the infant and the preschool child, we must focus our attention upon a few of the basic principles of growth and development as they relate to the school age. In the first place, growth is an orderly process. For convenience, we often speak of stages in this process. The ones that are generally recognized are infancy, childhood, adolescence, maturity, and senescence. Obviously, there is no sharp break between any of these stages and the one below it or above it.

Growth does take place more rapidly at some periods of pre-adult life than at others. Likewise, different parts of the body have their own rates of growth, and some mature more rapidly than others.[4] The principle of the continuity of the growth processes merely emphasizes the fact that there is no sudden transformation of the individual, not even at the time of the onset of puberty. The investigators who have plotted curves showing the development of physical, mental, and social functions have been impressed by the orderly and continuous nature of growth. In fact, from the large number of data which have been gathered, it is possible to predict, within reasonable limits, the future growth of the child from a careful measurement taken at any given time during his early life. The value of mental tests depends in part upon the fact that, since the developmental processes are orderly and continuous, a sampling of the child's mental abilities at, say, age seven will enable the psychologist to predict his relative standing on a test of intelligence given at a later chronological age.

In the second place, these studies indicate that neither heredity nor environment is the sole determining factor in growth and development. All the investigations support the conclusion that heredity and environment work together. For instance, many people

---

[3] H. L. Hollingworth's *Mental Growth and Decline* (New York: D. Appleton-Century Company, 1928), though a bit out of date, contains much worthwhile material on this topic. See S. L. Pressey, J. E. Janney, and R. G. Kuhlen, *Life—a Psychological Study* (New York: Harper and Brothers, 1939). The prospective teacher will be repaid by reading A. L. Gesell, *Biographies of Child Development* (New York: Hoeber, 1939).

[4] Many knotty problems relating to the growth process remain unsolved, though a promising amount of factual knowledge is now being collected. Evidently, the various tissues and organs of the body have different rates of growth. In many instances, the rate is constant or it proceeds in negative acceleration. In other cases, it appears to be saltatory. Experts differ somewhat in details. See C. E. Skinner and P. L. Harriman, *Child Psychology* (New York: The Macmillan Company, 1941), pp. 78-79, for a summary of some experts' data on the development of posture and locomotion. The voice change of the pubescent boy is an example of what seems to be saltatory growth of the organs of speech.

used to believe that the ultimate stature to which a person would grow at maturity was wholly dependent upon inherited factors. It is now an established fact that good medical care and proper food have increased the height of the average young adult about one and one-half inches over that of his grandparents. On the other hand, this finding does not mean that eventually a race of giants may appear. It does mean that the inherited determiners of growth have a better chance to become operative.

Educators have a practical interest in the controversy about the relative importance of nature and nurture. If it can be shown beyond a shadow of a doubt that some children are by reason of defective heredity incapable of profiting from much schooling, then the taxpayers could be saved much money. If, on the other hand, it can be demonstrated that the environment is all-important, there is justification for unlimited expenditures in mass education from kindergarten through university. Scientific studies of growth and development lend support to neither of these extreme positions. Although the final answers have not yet been found, some of the knotty issues in the nature-nurture debate have been cleared away by science. It has been established beyond question that heredity sets certain limits beyond which human growth and development cannot be forced. It has also been proved that environmental factors may arrest or impair the achievement of these potentialities. Similarly, it is now understood that growth is the result of a continuous interaction between the inherited determiners of development and the environment.

In the third place, there is an important type of growth and development, known as *maturation*, which is often neglected in the schools. Maturation is easier to illustrate than to define. For instance, at approximately one month of age the infant can lift its chin off the mattress when placed on its stomach. A month later it can lift the head and chest, at four months of age it can sit up when its back is supported, by seven months it can sit erect without support, by nine months it can stand up by holding on to something, at fourteen months it can stand without any support, and at fifteen months it can walk alone.[5] In other words, under widely differing environmental conditions this typical sequence in the development of motor patterns may be expected. It is a type of growth that gets its impetus from biological factors. Of course, if the infant is sickly, the sequence may be markedly slowed down. In many instances, the infant develops more rapidly. In all cases, however, it is apparent that this kind of growth cannot be hastened

---

[5] M. M. Shirley, *The First Two Years*. Minneapolis: University of Minnesota Press, 1933.

very much by "hothouse methods." [6] Another example may be of help in illustrating maturation. At about twenty-four weeks of age the infant may grasp a small block by making a looping movement of the arm and a primitive squeeze, but at the end of the first year of life the infant reaches for the block without resting the hand on the tray and with the thumb opposed to the first two fingers.[7] The attainment of full stature, change of voice in boys, and the change in the figure of the adolescent girl are also familiar examples of the process of maturation.

The studies on the maturation of structure and function in the young child have a very important bearing upon the educative process. These studies indicate that there is an optimum age for beginning to train the child, and that, if training is commenced before this age, the results are meager or nil. Of course, observant parents must have noted these facts long before educators fully realized their import for the school. Until the young child has developed certain neuromuscular co-ordinations, it is futile to try to teach the use of a spoon in eating. Parents seldom attempt to teach such things as eliminative control, putting on articles of clothing, speech, and reading until their child has reached an appropriate stage in maturation to be responsive to training efforts. At the present time, educators are giving some attention to the problem of the suitable placement of aspects of the school curriculum with reference to the maturational status of the pupil. They are beginning to realize that if some experiences were introduced at a later age, a great waste of energy might be avoided. For example, it is fairly well established that, with the modern procedures in teaching children to read, best success is achieved when the learners are normal children six and a half years of age. If attempts are made to teach the normal child to read at age four or five, the effort is rather futile. There is likewise a conviction that if the optimum age for introducing certain experiences were known, the rate of progress in learning some things might be increased.

Although educated and observant parents may find little that is unfamiliar in recent studies of child development, the importance of the investigations must not be minimized. First of all, the child psychologist must not confine his observations to a single infant, but must observe a great many. Second, the psychologist, being scientifically trained, is primarily interested in establishing suitable controls before making inferences. Thus, the psychologist is ex-

---

[6] A. Gesell and H. Thompson, *Infant Behavior: Its Genesis and Growth*. New York: McGraw-Hill Book Company, 1934.

[7] H. M. Halverson, "An Experimental Study of Prehension in Infants," *Genetic Psychology Monographs*, 1931, Vol. 10, Nos. 2 and 3.

tremely critical of any sweeping conclusions drawn from observations of a single age level or a restricted group, particularly when the group is limited to the favored social classes. The scientific investigations of child growth and development have broad applications to all children, and the generalizations are supported by impartial, objective evidence. Thus, from the standpoint of a psychologist, the achievement of a given child may be merely typical of the behavior of other normal children at that chronological age and be attributable to the process of maturation, whereas to the fond parent it may be taken as a sign of unusual precocity. Without these thorough observational and experimental investigations of child development, educators and psychologists would have no valid standards of comparison whereby to evaluate the individual child's rate of growth.

## The futility of "forcing" development

Since many parents are apparently eager to hasten the development of their children, it is important to consider the facts regarding this procedure. A psychologist tried to teach a three-year-old child the meaning of the word *opposition*, and his efforts resulted in complete failure.[8] The youngster was entirely incapable of benefiting by patient efforts to instruct him in the connotation of this abstract noun. With a child four and a half years of age, the psychologist achieved some success after a long explanation; but when he explained the meaning of *opposition* to a six-year-old, he met with an immediate success. This simple and interesting experiment has an important bearing upon our problem of understanding the significance of maturation. Apparently, the factor of maturation is as significant in "mental" growth as it is in physical development. Until the child has reached the optimal age for undertaking a task, it is futile to try to teach him. To illustrate this matter further, a broader experiment may be cited. Two psychologists matched two groups of kindergarten children in chronological age, intelligence, and sex; then they gave one group some definite training in memorizing digits. The group made some improvement as a result of their training; but the other group which was given no practice in memorizing digits did almost as well as the practiced group. When the children returned to school

---

[8] K. M. Dallenbach, "A Note on the Immediacy of Understanding a Relation," *Psychologische Forschung*, 1926, Vol. 7, pp. 268-269; and K. M. Dallenbach and George Kreezer, "Learning the Relation of Opposition," *American Journal of Psychology*, 1929, Vol. 41, pp. 432-441. Jean Piaget's studies, for example, *The Language and Thought of the Child* (New York: Harcourt, Brace and Company, 1926), present some findings relative to the conceptual immaturity of young children.

after the long summer vacation, both groups were equal in this ability. In other words, the benefits of the coaching were entirely lost.[9]

A pertinent criticism of the numerous experiments dealing with the effects of coaching is to point out that practically all these investigations deal with the short-time effects, and that most of them involve the use of material outside the pupils' normal range of interests. Indeed, this is a valid objection to some of the sweeping conclusions which have been drawn from such studies. The notion that we must "let nature take its course" is a superficial inference. Furthermore, there is too much dogmatizing about the potency of "intrinsic" factors in physical and mental development. On the other hand, these experiments do emphasize the futility of disregarding the maturational level of the child when a curriculum is planned. We know that many children cannot learn to read easily, with our present methods of instruction, below the chronological age of six and a half. Nevertheless, if better methods of teaching the subject were devised, it is conceivable that the "reading readiness age" might be pushed back six months or more. Many of the attempts to "teach" young children skills and understanding before they are ready to benefit by the instruction, however, result in complete failure or a parrot-like mastery, rather than a genuine act of learning.

Teachers of physical education realize the importance of adjusting games and exercises to the maturational level of the pupil. For example, strenuous sports like distance running and football are likely to be harmful to the young boy. The sports writers apply the expressive term "burned-out athlete" to characterize the condition of the boy who was forced to overexert himself in strenuous competitive sports before he was sufficiently mature to endure the strain. Likewise, the teacher of public-school music must carefully select songs well within the vocal range of the pupils. Where the importance of the maturation factor in relation to the educational program is not recognized, children are often compelled to sit quietly for long periods of time and are reprimanded if they squirm about in their chairs, or the teachers tend to exact close attention to abstract material, to demand neatness in handwriting, and, in general, to expect a maturity of schoolroom conduct and work that would be an effort even for an adult.

In the school, it is right and appropriate that a great deal of

---

[9] Many studies have been made on the problem of the supposed advantages of early coaching. See Myrtle B. McGraw, *Growth, a Study of Johnny and Jimmy* (New York: D. Appleton-Century Company, 1935). There does appear to be some lasting benefit from early "coaching" in music, but the experimental findings on this question have not yet been fully reported and verified.

attention be devoted to the task of adapting the educational program to the maturational level of the pupil. Consequently, a sane program of physical training and health education should be emphasized. If any school practice is likely to have an ill effect upon the child's physical growth and development, the educator must not hesitate to modify or to discard that particular phase of the curriculum. On the other hand, the child should not be allowed to grow up free from all restraint. Graded and directed experiences in the school can facilitate physical growth and stimulate mental development.

To what extent a scientifically planned school program may contribute to the maturation process is a question which as yet has not been fully answered. There are many reasons why educators take a hopeful view. One of the most obvious is that children from the more favored socioeconomic classes tend to be somewhat brighter in school work and more vigorous in physical status than children whose parents live on a marginal income. If all children had good medical care from birth, stimulating and happy home environments, and excellent schools, very likely we should have to revise upward all our standards for growth and development. Such an ideal, however, is quite different from "hothouse forcing methods" in child development.

## Mental development

Earlier in the chapter, the word *mental* was printed in quotation marks because in the early years of life it is difficult to draw any line of distinction between mental and physical development. As a rule, the rate of progress in physical development is the index to the rate of growth in intelligence. Mental development means growth in experience, and it requires no new set of principles or concepts to distinguish it from any other type of growth. There is, however, one great difference between physical development and mental growth. Whereas physical development depends upon biological factors more or less directly, the environment plays a major role in mental development. One of the most convenient indices to the rate of mental development is the child's progress in mastering the vernacular. The earliest vocalizations occur when the infant seems to be experiencing physical discomforts, though some cries, yawns, and other sounds may be made while the infant appears to be comfortable. Later on, these vocalizations acquire some differentiations that serve to indicate delight, surprise, pain, desire for attention, or rage. Long before the infant speaks the first recognizable word, he responds differentially to a limited number of words spoken by the parents. Thus, the very young child learns to understand language before he can use the words. By the end of the first year of life, the average child can speak two or three simple words, and from then on the rate of development is almost too rapid to trace. At the time of entrance into school, the normal child has a speaking vocabulary of between twenty-five hundred and three thousand words.

The growth of ability to combine words into sentences is of great interest to the psychologist. Once a few words have been learned, the child begins to use them in expressive ways, and shortly he commences to combine them into simple sentences. As yet, no psychologists have made an adequate study of the possible relationship between the talkativeness of the young child and the rate of language mastery. There is some basis for believing that there is a slight relationship only, since teachers have found that the most loquacious pupils are not necessarily the brightest. When the normal child enters the first grade, he speaks sentences of approximately five words, usually in the order subject-verb-object and without any subordination. By the end of the twelfth grade, he will have acquired some facility in the use of subordinate clauses and logical co-ordination. Of particular interest as an index to mental development is the acquirement of words to denote shades of meaning and to convey ideas effectively. Obviously, the rate of growth in language mastery is directly related to the environment. If the child has a limited opportunity to hear the language properly used, he cannot be expected to progress normally in his acquisition of it. Also, the relationship between the development of language mastery and physical growth is often overlooked. Though this relationship is indirect, it is of great importance.

At about twelve or fourteen months of age, the normal child speaks the first real word or two. This is approximately the age at which the child begins to walk. If the child does not commence to walk until the beginning of the second year, assuming that he is in good health, his speech is also likely to be delayed. Low-grade idiots never emerge from the level of infantile vocalizations, and neither do they commence to walk until relatively late, if, indeed, they ever develop sufficiently to walk at all. Imbeciles are markedly delayed in the rate of physical development, and likewise they are very slow in acquiring a very limited mastery of the language, seldom progressing beyond the "naming" level. On the other hand, the child who is precocious in learning to talk is usually advanced in physical development. Attempts to "force" development of language facility accomplish very little during the early years of life. One psychologist gave intensive training for six weeks to a child seven years of age, but kept its twin in a situation in which there was a minimum of opportunity to improve the vocabulary during this time. The twin who received the training made great progress, but after a short time there was no significant difference between the vocabularies of the two.[10]

By the time of the fourth or fifth grade, however, the dependence of mental development upon maturation becomes less important, though maturation remains a basic factor until about age fifteen or sixteen. From this point, more attention may be paid to the problem of enriching the experience of the pupil by a properly graded curriculum. It has been conjectured that the normal child might be kept out of school until age ten, and then, being sufficiently matured, he could easily and quickly master the content of the curriculum of the first three grades.[11] For some reasons which we shall presently consider, that might be an unwise procedure; but this statement, probably not meant to be taken literally, serves to emphasize the importance of physical growth during the early years covered by the school program. At about age ten, however, the importance of widening the pupil's breadth of understanding assumes great importance; and it remains as the chief responsibility of the school throughout the upper grades. The means whereby this aim is accomplished is, obviously, the curriculum.

## Is heredity all-important?

The possibilities of improving the race through a sane program of community welfare, public education, and broad opportunities for the hitherto underprivileged are just beginning to attract the attention of psychologists and educators. To support the conclusion that much good may be accomplished through this program, many lines of evidence are now available. In some instances, it must be emphasized, the conclusions are uncritically sweeping and the optimism unjustified by the facts. On the other hand, this program commends itself to teachers much more than does the fatalistic and pessimistic assumption that heredity is all-important. Since the heredity of the pupil has been determined long before he enters school, it seems sensible to concentrate upon the environment. If

---

[10] L. C. Strayer, "Language and Growth," *Genetic Psychology Monographs*, 1930, Vol. 8, No. 3.

[11] Unpublished data from a United States penitentiary, as well as reports on experiments in Army schools, justify the conclusion that adults who have been deprived of opportunities for schooling are able to master the curriculum at an amazingly rapid rate. Although differences in motivation and in general background are important factors in determining the more rapid learning of these adults as compared to that of children, maturation is decidedly important.

the school is to function as an effective social institution, it has to accept the pupils as they are, and then to raise them to the highest possible level of attainment in skills, understandings, personal and social adjustments, and worthy interests. The old problem of the relative importance of heredity and environment is of great theoretical interest to the teacher, but the practical task and the social responsibility of the teacher are to achieve the best results with the material at hand. Consequently, since for better or worse the heredity of boys and girls who come to school cannot be altered, the sensible procedure is to provide the maximum opportunity for each pupil.

In many cases formerly it was thought that the intelligence quotient was constant. However, in a large consolidated school where the writer and some students carried on a program of intelligence testing over a period of six years, it was found that children who came from isolated farms, where their parents eked out a submarginal existence, tended almost without exception to do progressively worse on the tests. If they made scores slightly lower than their classmates in the first grade, by the end of the sixth grade their scores were relatively much lower. In other words, their mental development seemed to be retarded by the impoverished environment from which they came. On the other hand, children living in a good residential area near the school made average or better-than-average scores, and from year to year they remained at about the same relative level of mental development. A few "faculty children" who attended this school made the highest scores of all. Of course, the hereditarian might argue that these results support his position and that the brightest people leave worn-out farms. The incontrovertible fact, however, is that these underprivileged children did relatively better in the first grade than they did at the end of the study. With just a small amount of indirect coaching for the tests, a few of them made average or better-than-average scores in the year they entered school. In the sixth grade, however, their handicap was so pronounced that it seemed quite hopeless to coach them.

Contrary to the opinions of adults who lack a social consciousness, rural children are not so well developed physically as children from privileged urban classes. Uncorrected defects in vision and teeth are much more frequently observed among children who live in slum areas or in submarginal farm regions. Physical examinations almost invariably reveal that children whose parents enjoy comfortable living standards make average or superior scores on tests of learning capacity, do satisfactorily in achievement tests, and are likely to be normal or superior in physical development.

Even today this assertion is disturbing to a few members of highly privileged social classes, who prefer to believe that such conditions are attributable to biological heredity. To be sure, there are many outstanding exceptions to this generalization. Some geniuses have come from city slums or submarginal farmlands, and some children whose parents can afford good medical care and a wholesome environment are puny and dull. On the other hand, many lines of evidence substantiate the assertion that these cases are exceptions to the rule.[12]

Without any doubt, heredity does set definite limits beyond which the growth and development of an individual cannot be carried, no matter how much time and energy may be spent in the process of attempting to reach high goals of achievement. A well-qualified teacher would no more think of minimizing the importance of heredity than a biologist would. Nevertheless, the teacher must regard the slow learner as a challenge, and then proceed on the justified assumption that, if appropriate methods and materials are employed, some degree of mental development will be accomplished.[13] Evidence that attained limits are not necessarily the limits set by heredity is abundant. For instance, it has been reported that the present generation of college students are taller and heavier than the students of a few generations ago. Improvement in the care and feeding of infants and children has effected this remarkable change.[14] Travelers report that the natives in the southern part of India tend to be weak and short, whereas members of the same race in the healthful parts of that country are strikingly superior in intelligence and physique. Since it has been rather convincingly demonstrated that favorable environment fosters wholesome physical growth, educators are encouraged to ascertain to what lengths mental development may be pushed. At least, there

---

[12] See G. W. Hartmann, *Educational Psychology* (New York: American Book Company, 1941), Chapter 6, for a provocative account of the dependence of the I. Q. upon the environment. See L. M. Terman, *Genetic Studies of Genius,* Volume I (Palo Alto: Stanford University Press, 1929), for convincing evidence of the disproportionate number of gifted children from well-to-do parents.

[13] Mistakes about the pupil's real level of intelligence are sometimes made by parents and teachers. For an unusual example, read T. E. Shields, *The Making and Unmaking of a Dullard* (Washington: Catholic Educational Press, 1909).

[14] L. B. Chenoweth, "Increase in Height and Weight and Decrease in Age of College Freshmen," *Journal of the American Medical Association,* Vol. 108, pp. 354-356, 1937. For further evidence on the relationship between socioeconomic status and the rate of physical growth, see: the White House Conference on Child Health and Protection, *Growth and Development of the Child* (New York: D. Appleton-Century Company, 1932), Section I; Medical Service; Parts I-IV. For data on the greater physical development of the present generation, see G. T. Bowles, *New Types of Old Americans at Harvard and at Eastern Women's Universities* (Cambridge, Mass.: Harvard University Press, 1932).

is little justification for the old notion that only the select few can benefit by advanced education.

## Some principles applicable to school procedures

Many ramifications of the problems relating to growth and development are not of immediate importance for the teacher. Some of the very best experimental work has been done on lower animals, such as the salamander (*Amblystoma punctatum*), and hence has little direct applicability to educational work.[15] The best work on growth and development in human beings has been done on infants and young children of preschool age; consequently, these excellent studies are of greatest value chiefly to kindergarten and primary teachers.[16] Data on the growth and development which take place during the years covered by the school program are still rather incomplete, although a promising start has been made.[17] As a result, therefore, it is difficult to set forth specific principles of growth and development that have unquestioned applicability to educational procedures. If the following points are broadly interpreted, however, they may be of considerable practical value. All of them are supported by more or less factual evidence.

1. Growth and development are dependent upon both heredity and environment. To what extent one of these factors is more important than the other, the evidence is insufficient to warrant any dogmatic statement.

2. The school has a responsibility for achieving the best results possible with the boys and the girls who are intrusted to its care. Therefore, the problem of heredity *versus* environment is of more concern to the biologist than to the classroom teacher.

3. In the early years of life, there is a close relationship between the rate of physical maturation and the development of learning capacity. Maturation is an important factor in the determination of suitable placement of items in the curriculum. For example, few

---

[15] For example, G. E. Coghill, *Anatomy and the Problem of Behavior*. New York: The Macmillan Company, 1929.

[16] For an example, see M. M. Shirley, *The First Two Years*, Vols. I, II, and III (Minneapolis: University of Minnesota Press, 1931 and 1933). Studies reported from the University of Iowa, Berkeley, California, and Yale University are well known.

[17] An excellent beginning may be found in B. T. Baldwin, *Physical Growth of Children from Birth to Maturity* (Iowa City: University of Iowa Studies, Studies in Child Welfare, Vol. I, No. 1, 1921). Another important reference is A. Harris, C. M. Jackson, D. G. Paterson, and R. E. Scammon, *The Measurement of Man* (Minneapolis: University of Minnesota Press, 1930). Many of the textbooks on older children and adolescents fill in the gaps in factual knowledge by generalizations which have not been fully validated.

pupils have achieved sufficient neuromuscular co-ordination to write with pen and ink before chronological age ten. Attempts to force maturation seem to be futile, if not harmful.

4. With upper-elementary and high-school pupils, the factor of prior experiences becomes increasingly important. Many of the principles that have been drawn from observational studies on physical growth appear to be applicable to a better understanding of the growth in experience. In fact, all types of growth and development—physical, mental, and social—seem to conform to the same basic principles.

5. There is no justification for assuming that any characteristics appear serially rather than concomitantly. In other words, the developmental process is not marked off by well-defined "stages," with each period different from that which preceded it. There is no support for the old view that elementary-school children are incapable of reasoning and that their curriculum should involve memory work alone. There may be spurts in growth and development; but measurement techniques have not revealed very many of them, with the exception of a tendency to gain in height during the period of early adolescence.

6. During the junior-high-school years, girls tend to be from a year to two years more mature than boys. As a concomitant of this biological advantage, girls at this age often appear to be more mature socially and intellectually than their male classmates. Sometimes difficulties arise at this level of education because teachers do not understand the situation or because they ignore it.

7. The difference between the college freshman entering in September and the senior graduating in June is partly due to the factor of biological maturation rather than being entirely attributable to the program of studies and activities of the college. In other words, teachers sometimes take credit for results which are actually due to the biological processes. During the twelve years of schooling, the normal child increases in height about fifty per cent and in weight about one hundred fifty per cent. The implication is that the school must do nothing that will disrupt or impede this physical development.

8. Teachers must not be impatient if their pupils seem to progress slowly in the growth of understanding and experience. Norms on standardized achievement tests for successive grades reveal the fact that educational progress is gradual. The amount of improvement from year to year is relatively small, but under good teachers it is certain. In some areas of experience, the rate of growth in understanding may be saltatory, but in many others it is slow. There-

fore, an infinite amount of patience is an indispensable asset in educational work.

9. In determining the rate of growth in experience, educators must take into account the factor of motivation. There is evidence that superior motivation will increase the rate of mastery to a remarkable degree. Discouragement, continued frustration, lack of interest, and teacher-pupil antagonisms may be untoward factors in slowing or arresting the rate of intellectual development. Conversely, there is evidence that environmental stimulation fosters optimum intellectual growth. The extent to which excellent teachers and generously financed public education can raise the attainments of pupils has not yet been demonstrated. There is reason to be enthusiastic about the possibility.

## QUESTIONS AND EXERCISES FOR DISCUSSION AND STUDY

1. Look up a few eminent persons in standard biographies and find out how complete a record is given of their early childhood and schooling. Estimate the dependability of these references. Exactly what else would you like to know about their early experiences, childhood, and adolescence? Why would this information be of value?

2. What is the difference between a case history and a biography? Which has the greater interest for the general reader? What are some difficulties you would encounter in writing a complete case history of yourself?

3. Observe children of various ages and try to discover significant differences in activities, topics of conversation, size of groups, and interests. Visit a schoolyard during recess and take notes on the play activities of children at various ages; compare your findings with those of H. C. Lehman and P. A. Witty, in *The Psychology of Play Activities* (New York: A. S. Barnes and Company, 1927).

4. Give some examples of embarrassment from abnormalities in growth. How are small children handicapped on account of their size, and what compensation do they find when older children are in the group?

5. Can you recall some items in the curriculum which seemed very difficult to you at the time they were introduced to you in school but which appeared to be absurdly easy a few years later? Should the curriculum-maker have deferred these items until a high grade level? Explain in full.

6. What is the difference between trying to force the development of a child and controlling the environment so that the most nearly ideal conditions would prevail to stimulate development? Are they essentially the same thing, or is there a real difference between them? Explain.

7. Illustrate from your own experience the effects of repeated failure in some subject or activity. Did the failure spur you on to greater efforts? Is there a relation between the age factor and our reaction to failures? Find some examples from your own life history to support your answer.

8. How would you distinguish between intellect and native mental ability? What is native mental ability, and how can it be observed? Can you isolate any

psychological trait and support the argument that it is solely dependent upon heredity or environment? If heredity sets the limits, how do you account for new records in track and field sports?

9. Are there any situations in certain schools which hamper or even arrest the normal growth and development processes of pupils? What are they, if any? Should such conditions exist, which ones might be difficult to change? Are there situations in the community which might interfere with wholesome development? What are they, if any?

10. Why is much emphasis placed upon the necessity for developing a wholesome personality? How would you define the wholesome personality? Which is the more important, this outcome or a sound mastery of the skills and the facts which the school tries to impart? Are these aims incompatible?

11. Why is it better to have pupils participate in desirable social activities than to talk to them earnestly about the need for co-operation? Would you dispense with exhortations? Why?

## SELECTED REFERENCES FOR FURTHER READING AND STUDY

Breckenridge, Marian E., and E. Lee Vincent, *Child Development*. Philadelphia: W. B. Saunders, 1943. Chapters I and II.

Bühler, Karl, *The Mental Development of the Child*. New York: Harcourt, Brace and Company, 1933.

Gates, A. I., and others, *Educational Psychology*. New York: The Macmillan Company, 1942. Chapters II, III, IV, V, and VI.

Hartmann, G. W., *Educational Psychology*. New York: American Book Company, 1941. Chapters II, IV, VI, XII, and XIII.

Hunt, Leila Wall, *The Child in the Home*. New York: Prentice-Hall, Inc., 1940.

Hurlock, Elizabeth B., *Child Development*. New York: McGraw-Hill Book Company, 1942.

Jersild, Arthur T., *Child Psychology*, rev. ed. New York: Prentice-Hall, Inc., 1940.

Jones, H. E., and N. Bayley, "The Berkeley Growth Study," *Child Development*, 1941, Vol. 12, pp. 167-173.

Jordan, A. M., *Educational Psychology*. New York: Henry Holt and Company, 1942. Chapter II.

Skinner, C. E., ed., *Educational Psychology*. New York: Prentice-Hall, Inc., 1938. Chapters II, IX, and X.

————, ed., *Readings in Educational Psychology*. New York: Farrar and Rinehart, 1937. Chapters II, III, IV, XI, and XXII.

Teagarden, Florence M., *Child Psychology for Professional Workers*. New York: Prentice-Hall, Inc., 1940.

Young, Kimball, *Personality and Problems of Adjustment*. New York: F. S. Crofts and Company, 1940. Chapters III, VIII, and IX.

**CHAPTER 5**

# Stages in Human Life: Infancy, Childhood, Adolescence, Maturity, and Senescence

## Introduction

That all human beings, including children, possess marked similarities of conduct and feeling is self-evident. That no two human beings are exactly alike is also apparent. It is the latter principle that complicates the process of behavior direction known as teaching. Mass education on the scale found in the United States would doubtless be impossible were absolute individualization of instruction required. It is the general similarities in growth, interest, and mental development of children that make a system of mass education practical. But while the similarities make mass education practical, they do not completely remove the necessity for reaching each separate child with a special educational challenge.

Early in the days of free public education in the United States, there emerged with unmistakable clarity the necessity of suiting education to the individual. As educational opportunity expanded, the wider became the selection of pupils from various social, racial, and economic classes and the greater became the range of abilities, interest, and differing early conditioning to which education had to be adjusted. Furthermore, increases in school population during the past twenty-five years took place with such rapidity that, in spite of the willingness of the American public to support education generously, the teacher-pupil ratio in hundreds of instances was in a definite imbalance in the direction of too many pupils per teacher. Through the action of various standardizing and accrediting agencies, this condition is now materially improved and will doubtless be further ameliorated in the future.

One of the honest, but in many ways futile, efforts to meet the critical problem of individual differences arising from a rapidly expanding system of general education has been that to discover some panacea or device which will work educational magic on every child. It could be contended with an obvious plausibility that, since all children are different, the way to individualize instruction is to let each child follow his own inclinations, determine his own curriculum, and pursue it under the general supervision of the teacher. We occasionally find schools organized on this theory in which an effort is made to have each child pursue his own unique destiny. Such a solution of the problem is far more logical than psychological or social. We are training children to take places in a society composed of groups, and many kinds of groups, at that. To make this training effective, there must be not only group training in the course of the educational development of the pupil, but also a resemblance between the training and the probable future environment, which will hardly consist of absolute independence of action. This is a principle that must not be neglected.

No reasonable person of liberal outlook would say that the school has no place in the orderly process of social evolution. But even an enormous institution like education, particularly when it exists in the form that it does in the United States, cannot hope to completely alter the *mores* of society overnight. Society has a right to expect that the educational system which it supports should make a reasonable effort to acquaint the young with the nature of its ideals and processes. Probably, a superior method of making education contribute to social evolution would be to give the learner: (*a*) the thinking techniques that are necessary in solving any problem, social or otherwise; (*b*) methods of gathering data with which to do analytical thinking; and (*c*) the habit of tolerance and suspended judgment.

The foregoing general considerations are intimately related to the problems of certain psychological attributes of infancy, childhood, and adolescence. It is the thesis of this chapter that the true individualization of instruction which results in a highly desirable personal and social adjustment of the individual is to be had through a deep understanding by the teacher of the psychological nature of successive phases of child development. This understanding should encompass a knowledge of the interests and behavior common to all children as well as an understanding of the various possibilities of pedagogical differentiation. Just as the physician must have a wide knowledge of many kinds of bodily behavior in the physical and physiological realms in order effectively to diagnose and treat deviations from the normal, so must the teacher be familiar with analogous phenomena of psychological conduct upon which teaching techniques are based. This basic preparation calls for mastery of experimentally established facts and techniques, rather than subscription to some educational shibboleth or fad. The training program here recommended is well illustrated by a quota-tion from a monograph on the physical and mental growth of girls and boys by Frank K. Shuttleworth,[1] whose excellent and pains-taking research in this field illustrates the difficult but correct approach to a psychological understanding of developmental fac-tors that must be considered in formulating a scientific educational program. The following quotation, which comes from a discussion of physical growth, illustrates the complexity of the factors in-volved and their interaction.

The mere descriptive summary of the major findings concerning twenty-two dimensions as presented in Section 2 is not enough. The theoretical implications of the data need to be indicated. In brief, our theory is that the patterns of physical growth shown by different dimensions and different groups from con-ception to maturity are the resultant of a progressive balancing of endocrine factors, of the timing of endocrine stimulation, of factors peculiar to each dimension, of factors determining mature size, and of factors associated with sex. Each of these five factors represents an exceedingly complex set of forces some of which operate persistently throughout the growth span while others operate for only limited intervals and at different ages. None acts independently. All are inextricably entangled by their mutual action and interaction in a single continuous process. An observed growth pattern is the external manifestation of the constantly shifting balance of such underlying forces.[2]

If the thesis presented here is the correct one, there is a pressing obligation upon the school, namely, to determine the psychological picture which each child presents and to adapt the instruction accordingly. Many splendid new services have been developed to aid the teacher in making this all-important diagnosis. Illustrative of these services are regular school medical examinations, special-ized guidance services, consulting psychiatric services, child re-search clinics, and so forth. When all is said and done, however, it is the classroom teacher who must take the data accumulated from these various specialized services and make practical use of them. It is a task fully as complicated as that performed by the physician, lawyer, or engineer, and should·be so regarded by both society and the teacher.

## Nature of life "stages" in man

The purpose of this chapter is to describe the psychological characteristics of childhood and adulthood and to draw therefrom certain inferences which may prove helpful for teaching.

The title of this chapter implies that there are stages in the life

---

[1] Frank K. Shuttleworth, *The Physical and Mental Growth of Girls and Boys Age Six to Nineteen in Relation to Age at Maximum Growth*. Washington, D. C.: National Research Council, 1939. P. 216.

[2] *Ibid.*

of man. The differentiation of the life cycle of any organism into several partially discrete periods and the designation of these periods by descriptive terminology serve the useful purpose of facilitating discussion. They have the disadvantage, however, of misinterpretation by any who may assume the cleavage in the growth of the organism to be as sharp as it appears from the printed descriptive categories themselves. For example, to state that the period of adolescence is normally from about age twelve to sixteen or seventeen, is only to begin to paint even the general picture, which is different for the sexes, to some extent for races, and certainly for individuals.

This misleading effect of categorical definition has led some students of child psychology to avoid almost entirely the use of terms such as "infancy," "adolescence," or the like. The fact remains that there are several reasonably well differentiated life stages, marked by characteristic physical phenomena and typical mental and social performance. Even a child can distinguish differences in the appearance, bearing, and habits of a baby, an adolescent, and an elderly person. A later section in this chapter will enumerate some of the characteristic behavior patterns of the early life periods.

### Fundamental hereditary wants and desires

One of the salient features of human development which deserves consideration is the nature, number, and educability of the several kinds of "unlearned" response. Unfortunately, although authorities are universally agreed upon the value of considering unlearned behavior, they are far from agreed upon either the nature or the number of "instincts." Some writers have held that the number of "original" hereditary responses is extremely small and that the multiplicity of strongly reinforced actions to be observed in the adult is the result of primary, secondary, and higher conditioning, springing from this narrow base in inverted pyramidal fashion. Others have contended that original behavior is wide in its scope, covering practically the entire gamut of mature adult behavior even in social situations, and that maturity accounts for the appearance of some unlearned behavior at a time considerably subsequent to birth. Obviously, the first theory calls for close attention from students of child psychology, since it throws a much sharper emphasis upon environment and teaching.

Thorndike [3] has maintained that the effort to distinguish the

---

[3] Adapted from E. L. Thorndike, *Human Nature and the Social Order*, pp. 115 *et seq*. By permission of The Macmillan Company, publishers.

unlearned components of behavior from those which are acquired is sociologically and educationally profitable for several reasons which are herewith paraphrased:

First: The successful differentiation of the unlearned in behavior provides knowledge of prepotent behavior trends, of which some are comparatively unalterable, some can be shaped or modified, but none completely eradicated.

Second: The differentiation of hereditary behavior components is valuable, because even though some of the tendencies which are suspected of being fundamental unlearned behavior are later found not to be so, it is likely that such tendencies will still constitute fundamental mixed learned and unlearned patterns from which spring numerous "special desires and aversions."

Third: The mere search for fundamental human behavior clarifies our notion of the dispersion of wants racially and phylogenetically.

Fourth: Any reasonably accurate list of unlearned responses furnishes a cue to basic *qualities* of satisfaction—a list which is superior to one merely of those *situations* which produce satisfaction or annoyance. Many of those situations which produce satisfaction may have the *same quality,* but the psychological essence is the quality itself, and not the situation which happens to contain it.

Fifth: Accurate knowledge of unlearned hereditary behavior permits the genetical classification of desires and aversions.

After elaborating at length on the above and developing other criteria of selection, Thorndike states a definite list of desires and aversions which he regards as basic in human behavior. Because of its fundamental importance psychologically and educationally, this list is herewith reproduced.[4]

*Desires.*
1. bright colors and glitter; sunshine; soft, tinkling, and rhythmical sounds; sweet, fruity, and nutty tastes; touching what is soft and smooth and dry.
2. free bodily movement; rapid motion through space.
3. healthy normal action of the digestive, circulatory, excretory, nervous and other physiological systems.
4. having something behind one's back when resting; "being in a sheltered nook, open on only one side," as James says.
5. the presence of friendly, or at least not inimical, human beings.
6. "concerted action as one of an organized crowd."

---

[4] Adapted from E. L. Thorndike, *Human Nature and the Social Order,* pp. 117 and 118. By permission of The Macmillan Company, publishers.

7. to move when refreshed, especially as in running, jumping, climbing, pulling and wrestling.
8. to rest when tired.
9. vocalization; visual exploration; manipulation.
10. mental control; to do something and have something happen as the consequence is, other things being equal, satisfying, whatever be done and whatever be the consequent happening.
11. witnessing the happy behavior of other human beings, especially of children.
12 successful courtship and love between the sexes.
13. voluptuous sensation, however obtained.
14. to manifest affection.
15. to receive affection.
16. intimate approval, as by smiles, pats, admission to companionship and the like from one to whom he has the inner response of submissiveness; humble approval, as by admiring glances, from anybody.
17. domination, being submitted to by others.
18. to surpass others in the work or play to which original nature leads us and them.
19. submission to a person toward whom it is the "natural" response.
20. In general, when any instinctive behavior series is started and operates successfully, its activities are satisfying and the situations which they produce are satisfying, other things being equal.

*Aversions.*

1. the sight of black; sudden loud sounds; bitter tastes; the odors of putrid flesh; excrement and vomit; sensory pains; over-tension of muscles; impeded or insufficient action of the bodily organs.
2. slimy, wriggling and creeping things on one's flesh.
3. large animals or objects like animals approaching one rapidly; angry scowling faces; solitude; darkness; being suddenly clutched.
4. pain.
5. severe shock of any sort.
6. being interfered with in any bodily movements which the individual is impelled by his own constitution to make.
7. the intrusion of strangers into the neighborhood of one's habitation and the abstraction of any object therefrom.
8. the seizure by others of an object which one is using.
9. being shut up completely within a small, and especially a strange, enclosure.
10. being subdued by a person to whom (or a thing to which) one does not naturally have a submissive attitude.
11. inattention or neglect by human beings whose attention one solicits.
12. the withdrawal of approving intercourse by masters.
13. looks of scorn and derision from anyone.
14. seeing others approved.
15. being outdone by others.
16. In general, when any instinctive behavior-series is started, any failure of it to operate successfully is annoying.

In a later chapter on learning, the mechanism whereby any established response pattern becomes merged with, or transmuted into, other response patterns will be described in some detail. It is to be noted here, however, that this phenomenon applies to the above list of desires and aversions. They seldom appear in simple, uncomplicated form; rather, they are likely to occur in varying combinations and to be modified according to the background and experience of the individual.

## Play

Play appears to be a natural tendency and obviously one closely connected with any system of education. Play is difficult to define. Misunderstanding of the true psychological nature of play activities undoubtedly accounts for many unwise parental and pedagogical practices. While there is no doubt that, to be of recreational value to the organism, play should contain a definite element of spontaneity, it would be overly simple to conclude, therefore, that play activities should never be supervised.

Both observational and physiological studies of work activities give definite evidence that the tension factors involved in the concentration necessary to hard mental work are physical in nature. The cumulative effect of these fatigue factors inevitably tends in the long run to reduce efficiency and augment the fatigue itself. In this situation of hypertension, any activity on a spontaneous and relaxational basis is of value to the organism. Play is a beneficial activity, and as such should be planned for in more curricula.

It is literally true that one man's play may be another man's work. This being the case, it appears that the psychological essence of play is to be found more in its volitional and spontaneous nature than in any set of criteria of a play activity. This is a point which sometimes seems to escape those who are endeavoring to organize a recreational curriculum. Play, like appreciation, tends to lose its qualitative essence when the factor of compulsion becomes strongly in.evidence. This being the case, it is as highly unpsychological to force children into play activities toward which they are strongly disinclined as it is to attempt to compel their appreciation of something for which they have no desire.

Studies have shown a wide variety of play interests in children, with considerable tendency toward sex differences. These play interests tend to run a normal self-determined course without much difficulty, and in most cases little external intervention is required. It is not, for example, often necessary to compel girls to quit playing with dolls, since a combination of changing natural interests and social factors produces this result.

There are those who have maintained that it is possible to organize the entire curriculum on a play basis. Commendable as this objective may be, the chances of success, as events have proved in known instances, are slight. To begin with, the play curriculum, which purports to train the individual for serious later-life activities, is a paradox and contradiction in term and fact. Routine, often not spontaneous, is an inescapable component of all vocations, as Judd [5] has definitely shown. Routine and the ability to follow a routine whether or not one is inclined to do so are contrary to the essence of play.

## The importance of the early years

That first impressions are lasting has long been an axiom of the vernacular. That primary conditioning is persistent is an equally sound premise of the scientific study of behavior. The waste and lost motion in the field of education and child training resulting from incorrect habit formation during the early years are enormous. The entire field of remedial education, for instance, is encumbered with cases that are testimonials to unwise fundamental training.

Merely because the price of errors is not so immediately apparent in education as in medicine is no reason why the teacher should not be as well informed on recent developments in his field as is the medical man. Yet studies of the number of teachers taking even the outstanding journal which reports recent research findings in their particular field show an appallingly low incidence of subscriptions by classroom teachers. Education is a social science, and every day discoveries are being made which little by little can help us build correct early habits and so improve the quality of both mental and social development of our pupils.

## Some phases of child development

It is our purpose in this section to cite certain factors in child development of interest to the teacher. Data corroborating and supporting the generalizations herein laid down are too numerous and technical to be included in this section but can be found in any standard text in the psychology of child development. The following phases will be briefly considered: (a) physical development, (b) social development, (c) language development, (d) creative development, (e) emotional development, and (f) mental development.

a. *Physical development.* Innumerable studies of growth, both physical and physiological, have been made for the purpose of determining height, weight, and health norms as well as periods of

---

[5] Charles H. Judd, *Psychology of Secondary Education.* Boston: Ginn and Company, 1927. Pp. 14 *et seq.*

learning readiness. The present tendency is to use such norms primarily as guides rather than as absolute standards to which every child's growth must be forced. Modern authorities on health have a tendency to feel that, if a child's behavior is effective, adequate, and comfortable, probably growth may proceed in something resembling optimum fashion.

b. *Social development.* The young child quickly discovers methods of social control, and adapts his cries of distress and other behavior to effect such control over others, but this conduct is highly egocentric and its purpose selfish. Unless later training forces him to do otherwise, the infant is likely to carry his methods of social control into an age level when they will be not only ineffective, but definitely conflict-producing.

Children begin to pay attention to their companions at a comparatively early age, certainly before they are a year old. This interest is likely to be diffuse in nature, but it rapidly becomes more specific, and typical human preferences and dislikes begin to appear. Naturally, the processes of social education at this early age are made more difficult by the child's failure to control the language mechanism. It is highly probable that some of the difficulties that older children have in making social adjustments are the result of habits formed previous to the acquisition of language.

Jersild [6] has an excellent discussion of negativistic behavior in infants, a puzzling and irritating trait that causes teachers no end of trouble. Jersild feels it impossible to ascribe negativism to any single factor, but that often it may be the result of overstimulation, such as, for example, asking a child to repeat over and over again something that he is just learning to do. Normally, negative tendencies disappear gradually, but there is evidence that in some instances they become progressively reinforced and result in the chronic dissenter with whom we are all unhappily familiar.

It is important to train children in co-operation during the early period of their social development. Co-operation and the recognition of the nature of personal property are basic for social adjustment to a democratic capitalistic society.

c. *Language development.* Comparative psychologists rank man's ability to communicate with his fellows in symbolic fashion as one of the two or three outstanding distinctions between man and lower animals. Man's entire civilization and social structure would collapse in ruins were language to be taken from him. It is highly probable that any sharp decline in the elaboration with which man can use language would be accompanied by a similar

---

[6] Arthur T. Jersild, *Child Psychology*, rev. ed. New York: Prentice-Hall, Inc., 1940. P. 170.

and proportionate decrease in his social machinery. Not only is language of inestimable value for the purely utilitarian purpose of communication, but it is the mechanism with which modern man does his thinking and solves many, if not the majority, of his problems. It is for the latter reason that some students of the modern curriculum are inclined to feel that systematic vocabulary training should be continued far above levels where it is now customarily stopped, and that, if this were done, it would be possible to increase the functional vocabulary of the average high-school graduate to forty or fifty thousand words in place of the present twelve or thirteen thousand. Thinking power might not increase in direct proportion, but there is little doubt that it would increase materially.

One of the key pedagogical factors to be borne in mind in connection with language development in children has to do with *exact* ideas of meaning. Studies among high-school and college students give clear evidence that knowledge of words in many cases is fuzzy and inexact, being based in countless instances upon careless inferences from the context. It is not at all difficult to trace the parallelism between the vagueness of meanings resulting from a slipshod method of learning words and a thinking process that is weak because it is necessarily dependent upon these words.

There is no doubt that meanings enlarge with experience. It is likewise true, particularly in the case of abstractions, that it is impossible for the child to get the richness of connotation that an adult possesses, but still it is not necessary that all concepts that the child has be vague and nebulous. Knowledge that a giraffe is an animal is satisfactory as far as it goes. To know that it is a certain kind of animal with a definite and characteristic physical structure, that it lives in certain parts of the world and not in others, and that it has typical behavior patterns—all these are highly contributory to the basic concept, although in their totality they still do not represent knowledge sufficient for a biologist. It is sometimes a problem to know at what point to cease expanding a concept, and certainly there is such a thing as over-definition of a term, but the difficulty usually lies in the other direction.

One other thing that should be noted in language development is the use of language as an instrument of deception. All adults are familiar with the fact that language is not always used to communicate realistically. The child at a surprisingly early age learns this falsifying function of language. It is customary to attempt to dissuade him from using language in this way by punishment and moralisms. To these deterrents should be added at least some explanation of the fact that systematic use of language as an instrument of deception inevitably results in some vitiation of thinking, probably because truly deceptive language is almost certain to be a complicated admixture of fact and fiction too involved for even a mature mentality to keep the two separate in memory.

d. *Creative development.* The average child, if left to his own devices and surrounded by physical subjects that challenge his curiosity, will indulge in a limited amount of experimentation and creative effort. In the mental field, also, the child will air his own fancies in such directions as the writing of poetry. It is doubtful, however, whether the development of real creative ability consists primarily of the untrammeled development of these natural tendencies. There is little question that completely unsupervised and spontaneous creative effort may produce masterpieces of interest to a surrealist, but there is more than a little doubt that this method will produce anything else.

One fundamental necessity of all creative expression is sound technique based on principles that have stood the test of experience. A period of free, spontaneous initial activity is far more likely to produce a set of incorrect habits than to effect anything else. The reason why there are so many dub golfers is that too many of us indulged in creative activity in the field of golfing before we had a correct stance, swing, and so forth, and usually the behavior pattern that resulted was not so efficient as the formula developed by generations of experienced professionals.

e. *Emotional development.* From a comparatively small number of instinctive emotional reactions, the child quickly acquires a startlingly large repertoire of conditioned fears, angers, and prejudices. This is the key problem, pedagogically, in the case of emotional development. The basic fact to be borne in mind is that emotion can be conditioned and emotional responses attached to an infinite variety of situations. Sometimes the problem resolves itself into one of reconditioning or the effort to eradicate a response, such as a phobia, which has been established early. Of the several methods that can be employed in reconditioning, probably the best is the introduction of a competitive situation of pleasant feeling tone. Jersild,[7] in discussing the particular technique to be used in reconditioning fear responses, expresses doubt of the efficacy of trying to talk a child out of his fear.

Emotional development presents the same kind of learning problem as any ordinary school subject, a problem that is solved in its major aspects by correct habit formation. It is an error to regard the pedagogy of emotion as qualitatively different from the

---

[7] *Ibid.,* p. 275.

pedagogy of school subjects; in both cases, the correct formation of habits is the primary problem.

The element of fixation is perhaps more in evidence in emotional adjustment than in some of the more prosaic portions of the curriculum. The typical response of any person when thwarted is progressive emotional reinforcement of the tendency toward the desired activity. Whenever a strongly diverting circumstance appears, the problem of insurmountable emotional readjustment seldom arises. The writer witnessed an amusing illustration of this fact when two men were arguing about the present world scene. The situation represented complete blocking on both sides and was highly focalized and vocalized. It was being characteristically reinforced and was approaching a possible beginning of other than verbal hostilities. During the altercation, the chimney of the house caught fire, but the volume of smoke produced was sufficient to convince everyone present that the entire house was in flames. Neither of the parties was sufficiently interested in world affairs to continue arguing about them while the house burned down, nor did they leave the house continuing the argument as they went. Unfortunately, so powerful an external circumstance does not obtrude itself in most cases of emotional blocking. It is, however, possible and practical to form the habit of substituting other activity, beginning at the elementary stage with the habit of counting to ten before getting into a fight and continuing with intelligent investigation, self-analysis, and planning when faced with more fundamental blockings.

f. *Mental development.* It is probable that the individual does not materially increase his potential mental capacity during the course of a lifetime, in spite of the hopeful pronouncements of some optimists. Mental development, therefore, does not consist of increments in basic capacity, but rather involves the development of particular aspects of mentality and the elaboration of knowledge.

In promoting mental growth, we should pay far more attention than we do to the fact, admitted by neurologists and psychologists, that the average person has far more mental power than he usually uses. What the average, normal student needs is not more mental capacity, but more challenge to that capacity which he has.

### Behavior problems and delinquency

One of the persistent problems that plague both parents and teachers is to so direct child development that maladjustment and social delinquency will not occur. In considering this problem, three assumptions will be made:

1. That delinquency is primarily a factor of poor adjustment, and not one of heredity.

2. That *delinquency* is a relative term, descriptive of a low degree of adjustment rather than of a lack of conformity to a list of absolute virtues.

3. That no single cause of delinquency underlies all the major categories of maladjustment.

In some ways, it is surprising that the amount of social maladjustment that one encounters is not greater than it is. Undoubtedly, some well-meaning but poorly conceived training in "individuality" is the cause of some social maladjustment and delinquency. Much delinquency is nothing more than nonconformity with established *mores*. It is far too much to expect an unsophisticated child to divine *mores* by intuition and to generate a desire to conform to them *ex vacuo*. Society owes the child, through its educative agencies, a knowledge of the standard of conduct that it expects, plus some training in the desire to conform. Yet only recently has a systematic effort been made in such fields as safety education to instruct the young in legal standards and conformity to them. We should find the equivalent of the schoolboy traffic patrol in many other phases of modern society.

One thing that criminological studies have shown is the disastrous effect of inconsistency upon the young. We all know the detrimental results of disagreement between parents in the disciplining of the child. Such conflict has a thousand counterparts in social life in general. Obviously, it would be impossible to correct all circumstances of inconsistency in society, but it is not too much to expect that at least those who are in charge of educating the younger generation should be consistent in their conduct. Furthermore, many cases that to the child seem inconsistent can readily be explained, once they are located as the source of difficulty. For example, the writer once taught in a private boys' school where the pupils were forbidden to smoke. The well-meaning headmaster believed it would be easier to enforce this rule if the faculty did not smoke. But, although he had a rule to this effect, certain of the faculty resented this circumscription of their conduct and smoked surreptitiously, a fact which the boys quickly discovered. The discovery was followed by a wave of student infringement of the rule against smoking. When the rule against faculty smoking was abrogated and the entire situation explained to the boys, all difficulties disappeared. The point to be noted is that the inconsistency in the professed beliefs and conduct of the faculty was the root of the student delinquency.

### Behavior trends in the preschool child

This section and the two following give a few of the outstanding behavior patterns of children that are of interest to teachers.

First to be noted in the preschool child's behavior is the geometric expansion of sensory experience and the sensory basis of learning. The preschool child is busy laying experiential foundations for his later learning and thinking. This is accomplished partly by casual experience and sometimes by a planned curricular regimen. A considerable portion of the preschool child's time and energy is devoted to play activities and play-work activities. For example, many progressive schools utilize children's desire to cut out pictures for a beginning step in developing scrapbooks which are the prototype for later and more formal notebooks, laboratory records, and so forth.

The preschool child also experiences the beginnings of adjustment to routine. Often a delicately balanced judgment is required to determine how much routine a child should be forced to undergo. Evidence is given by children who have been forced while quite young through circumstances to assume considerable responsibilities in the household that even young children can become adjusted to a considerable amount of routine activity.

### Behavior trends in the preadolescent

The child of elementary-school age continues to expand his sensory experiences, to play, and to become adjusted to further routine activities. A salient activity of these years consists in the rapid acceleration of vocabulary acquisition. The young child's contact with objects is not always verbalized or expressed. A little later, however, the child desires, and adults are usually willing that he should have, words to describe the objects with which he is dealing.

Another thing that the preadolescent experiences is an increase in contact with social customs. Things that would be regarded as cute in a baby are less likely to be appreciated in a ten-year-old. He is expected to acquire some notion of what personal property means, and to have at least a rudimentary concept of the rights of others. The minutiae of social amenity may still be a mystery to him, but he is expected to know the basic rules.

The behavior of the boy or girl also gives evidence of the beginnings of economic consciousness and the development of a standard of values so necessary in a full-rounded comprehension of the system of private property. It is about this time that savings banks appear and that the child begins to realize that money does not grow on trees, a notion that will not have full meaning for him, however, until he has gone out and tried to earn some of it.

## Behavior trends in the adolescent

Superficially, the adolescent often appears to be completely mature. This opinion may be enhanced because he has by this time acquired a certain amount of poise, backed by a considerable amount of experience and education. Actually, of course, the adolescent is still an immature organism and is yet in the process of development. One of the phases of development in which the adolescent is principally engaged is the acquisition of certain abstract ideas, techniques of judgment, and reasoning. The vocabulary of the younger child tends to consist of definite names for concrete objects. The adolescent has made progress in mastering the meaning of terms where that meaning depends upon the fusion of sensory experiences rather than upon the apprehension of one object.

The behavior of the adolescent should also give evidence of some self-discipline, depending upon the amount of freedom allowed in the family and in the school. He has had experiences in situations where he is his own boss and where his every move has not been under the eye of some monitor.

A final and crucial phase of adolescent behavior patterns is the approach toward personal maturity. While it is true that personality can and does change throughout life, the post-adolescent set is likely to be more or less permanent. In fact, the changes in personality that occur after adolescence are likely to be few and far between.

## Maturity

Maturity is that period of life extending from about the twentieth year to the age of sixty or sixty-five. This general statement, however, admits of numerous exceptions and at best describes merely the average limits of adult life. Actually, *maturity* is a relative term, and no hard-and-fast criteria of maturity or its duration can be laid down. It has been pointed out elsewhere that there are both individual and race differences in the onset of puberty, and the same may·be said for maturity. Likewise, the duration of the mature period of life depends upon so many factors, such as original biological virility, disease, and health habits, that it is impossible to predict such duration in the case of a given individual with any accuracy. In this discussion, "maturity" is taken to mean the span of middle-age years during which the individual is at the height of his potential physical and mental performance.

Physically, one should be at his best during the period of maturity. The physical regimen of that period determines both its duration and the happiness of old age. Unfortunately, many of the common expressions and opinions concerning the health potential at maturity are borrowed from, or influenced by, the field of sports, in most of which for performance purposes one is considered not only mature but actually aged by the middle thirties. Men like William T. Tilden II and William Hoppe constitute the exceptions and marvels of the sport world rather than the average. The sport world is not a valid criterion, and it should not be looked to for an index of the physical nature of maturity. To begin with, the majority of sports, particularly the more strenuous ones, require a completely abnormal energy production and output. It is all very well for coaches and professional athletic performers to point with pride to the magnificent physical condition of athletes. No doubt such condition is beneficial and might well be copied in many of its aspects by all of us. The fact remains that, in highly competitive sports such as boxing, where income depends upon the number of performances and their success, the wear and tear on the organism and the accelerated rate of organic degeneration is very great. Even in a game like baseball, where the performer does not take the same kind of physical beating that he does in boxing, it is rare to find a regular member of an outstanding team past the age of thirty-five. It is true that according to many authorities one reaches the potential physiological peak relatively young and remains for a time at a period of comparatively stable high-level performance declining slowly to a lower level. The significant thing to be noted in the curve of energy output during the individual's life is not that it reaches its peak comparatively early, but that the decline is normally slow and vitally affected by a number of factors such as diet, rational health habits, and so forth, which are more or less completely within the control of the individual himself. Medical science has gone a long way in solving the riddle of many degenerative diseases and other factors that bring on an early senescence. It is up to education to produce a health program that will still further level out and lengthen the plateau of high physical performance during the years of maturity.

In the matter of mental functions and thinking capacity, it is probable that one does not reach his true psychological maturity until the middle or late portion of physical maturity. Some past experiments, indicating that in the mental field also the peak is reached early, were so specialized, particularly of the skill variety, that it is extremely unsound to generalize from them. Insufficient experimentation on higher-level processes is at hand to warrant final conclusions. Such experimentation as there is at the present time on higher-level functions tends to show that certain mental performances, such as discriminating judgment, depend heavily upon experience and maturity. There is another factor which should be borne in mind in a consideration of the learning ability of the mature adult both in physical and mental states—the factor of motivation. Thorndike [8] in an excellent series of experiments on the nature of adult learning has shown that, when adults are motivated equally with younger persons, their learning in many functions is comparable in both quantity and quality. Obviously, in order to come to any sound conclusions concerning the comparative mental capacity and learning ability of persons of various ages, it would be necessary to hold constant all the variables except the one under investigation, and this is difficult to do. The performance of persons of comparatively advanced years in universities and colleges also indicates something to the same purport, although this evidence cannot be taken as experimental or scientific, at least until sufficient cases are gathered. For example, in one case, a mother in her sixties entered a university for the sole purpose of testing the validity of certain of her daughter's contentions. Her daughter, who had been doing rather poorly in school work, when upbraided by her mother, gave the excuse that the mother could do no better. The mother took an entire four-year course and graduated at the head of a class in which her daughter was near the foot. It is recognized that numerous variables enter a picture of this sort, such as additional experience and possible higher original intelligence. The point being emphasized is that a well-motivated adult can often compete successfully with younger people in learning situations such as university classes. This fact should have definite pedagogical implications, particularly for the field of adult education, because frequently older persons feel a needless inferiority in this respect.

The years of maturity should witness the practical completion of the process of socialization. One must learn, and in many ways learn by experience, to become well socialized. While the young adolescent quickly picks up feats of physical skill and can take part in performances requiring such skill, he is notoriously unhappy in many social situations, and the process of his socialization is more often than not, as both he and his teachers will bear witness,

[8] Edward Lee Thorndike, *Adult Learning*. New York: The Macmillan Company, 1928.

a painful one. During the period of maturity, the intelligent and well-educated person makes an effort to analyze and locate his poor habits, both personal and social. Once located, such habits can be either eradicated or changed. Unfortunately, the period of early adulthood is sometimes spent in a crystallization and over-rationalization of bad habits and social maladjustment.

## Senescence

No psychological subject that has been a subject of interest through the ages is of greater importance than old age. Today more than ever before, attention is directed to means whereby so-called "senior citizens" may spend the declining years of their lives in happiness. An enormous volume of social legislation bearing on the problem has been enacted. Sharp differences of opinion exist as to method. For example, those who hold that work is the true salvation from a bored and crabbed old age are inclined to oppose measures, legislative or otherwise, that would insure to the elderly a life devoid of the necessity of working.

Because old age is so often a tragic experience and because of the length of this period in frequent instances, a psychological consideration of the nature and problems of senescence is in order. Like the term *maturity, senescence* is relative. Chronologically it may be taken to mean the period from sixty-five years onward. But senescence is far more than a span of years; it is a state of mind—a fact that has been clearly recognized by those philosophers from Cicero down to the present time who have concerned themselves with a study of this interesting phenomenon. There is no use in blinding oneself to what happens all too often in old age. It is frequently characterized by a crabbed, cynical, querulous disposition. Nor is it possible to excuse the faults of the aged on grounds of infirmity or distress at seeing the mistakes of the young. While such excuses may be valid in a minority of cases of unusually fortunate persons, in the majority of cases the defect is one in the character of the individual rather than intrinsic in the nature of senescence. A quotation from Cicero's [9] delightful and whimsical discussion of old age will show that the recognition of this situation is not new.

But, the critics say, old men are morose, troubled, fretful, and hard to please; and, if we inquire, we shall find that some of them are misers, too. However, these are faults of character, not of age. Yet moroseness and the other faults mentioned have some excuse, not a really sufficient one, but such

---

[9] Reprinted from William A. Falconer's translation of CICERO De Senectute, Loeb Classical Library, Harvard University Press, Cambridge, Mass. Pages 77-78.

as it may seem possible to allow, in that old men imagine themselves ignored, despised, and mocked at; and besides, when the body is weak, the lightest blow gives pain. But nevertheless all these faults are much ameliorated by good habits and by education, as may be seen in real life, and particularly on the stage in the case of the two brothers in the play of that name. What a disagreeable nature one of them has, and what an affable disposition has the other! Indeed the case stands thus: as it is not every wine, so it is not every disposition, that grows sour with age. I approve of some austerity in the old, but I want it, as I do everything else, in moderation. Sourness of temper I like not at all. As for avariciousness in the old, what purpose it can serve I do not understand, for can anything be more absurd in the traveller than to increase his luggage as he nears his journey's end?

Obviously, there is a sharp decline in physical and mental output in persons of advanced age. Although, as in the case of mature persons, inferior performance is partly the result of lack of motivation, in the case of the aged the phenomenon is more real than apparent. Here again, the situation is frequently worse than need be, particularly in the fact that mental output could be much better. While it is true that physical and mental activity are so intimately related as to be practically inseparable, and while decline in physical ability is likely to be accompanied by a corresponding decline in mental functioning, such decline is frequently more sharp than necessary. One of the causes of this is an overly narrow definition of what activity means. The writer once knew an extremely active man whose vocation was commercial fishing. This is a strenuous pursuit, and at a relatively early age this fisherman was forced to retire. For several years he did nothing but mope around, reminisce, and live in the fishing past. His intellectual activities had been conditioned to his day-by-day life. He defined physical activity in terms of commercial fishing. Finally, a discerning member of his household for whom he had deep regard induced him to start reading, particularly books on the history of fishing, boat construction, types of fish, and so forth. Today the same individual is a thoroughly happy member of society, well adjusted, and spending a truly active old age. His activity today is reading—a skilled act. From reading he gets the data for his mental functioning in the same way that he used to get such data from experiences on fishing cruises.

To prevent old age being needlessly dull, it must be planned for instead of merely awaited with mixed feelings of apprehension and distaste. G. Stanley Hall,[10] whose delightful volume on senescence should be read by all persons of forty or over, points this out in a way that needs no elaboration:

---

[10] G. Stanley Hall, *Senescence*. New York: D. Appleton-Century Company, 1922. Pp. 29-30.

It is well at any stage of life, and particularly at its noonday, to pause and ask ourselves what kind of old people we would like, and also are likely, to be—two very different questions. In youth we have ideals of and fit for maturity. Why not do the same when we are mature for the next stage? Why should not forty plan for eighty (or at least for sixty) just as intently as twenty does for forty? At forty old age is in its infancy; the fifties are its boyhood, the sixties its youth, and at seventy it attains its majority. Woman passes through the same stages as man, only the first comes earlier and the last later for her. If and so far as Osler is right, it is because man up to the present has been abnormally precocious, a trait that he inherited from his shorter-lived precursors and has not yet outgrown, as is the case with sexual precocity, which brings premature age. Modern man was not meant to do his best work before forty but is by nature, and is becoming more and more so, an afternoon and evening worker. The coming superman will begin, not end, his real activity with the advent of the fourth decade. Not only with many personal questions but with most of the harder and more complex problems that affect humanity we rarely come to anything like a masterly grip till the shadows begin to slant eastward, and for a season, which varies greatly with individuals, our powers increase as the shadows lengthen. Thus as the world grows intricate and the stage of apprenticeship necessarily lengthens it becomes increasingly necessary to conserve all those higher powers of man that culminate late, and it is just these that our civilization, that brings such excessive strains to middle life, now so tends to dwarf, making old age too often *blasé* and *abgelebt*, like the middle age of those roués who in youth have lived too fast.

There is practically no consideration of the problems of old age in the modern school. As a matter of fact, one would more than likely be laughed out of court if he attempted to get any substantial consideration of this problem by the preadolescent and adolescent. While undoubtedly children would not be likely to be highly attentive to lengthy considerations of what they should be doing when they are eighty, the idea of forcing children to give a little thought to their old age has more psychological merit than may appear on the surface. For one thing, the human mind is extremely retentive and sometimes in peculiar ways. For another, periods of stress and necessity frequently call to mind facts and philosophies placed there long ago. A preview of the entire panorama of life in its normal span would make a worthwhile addition to the personal adjustment courses that are becoming increasingly popular in secondary schools.

So far as old age itself is concerned, its tranquillity and happiness probably depend upon some sort of work, play, or hobby which keeps the individual's attention during his entire waking hours away from himself and his own problems. Any person of any age who has nothing to do or is neglecting what he should be doing can magnify and distort out of all proportion problems and ailments from which no human being is completely wanting. The nature of old age and the undue care which is taken by some to insure that old age shall have no duties or work conspire in a peculiar way to accentuate this general human weakness. Common observation is all that is required to prove that it need not be so. A man with the responsibilities of a Charles Evans Hughes can live to an advanced age with scant time to worry about himself. Remember that when Rome, in one of its hours of most dire peril, turned to an old man to save the day, they did not find Cincinnatus at home musing by the fire on his ancient victories but out in the field behind a plow.

## QUESTIONS AND EXERCISES FOR DISCUSSION AND STUDY

1. *Project:* Find a table giving increases in school population in the United States from 1890 to 1945, and make a graph illustrating the increases. This material may be found in numerous texts, such as those in the history of education, in school statistics, and so forth.

2. Write a one-page argument for or against the thesis that a major function of the school is the revolutionizing of society.

3. Paraphrase the quotation from Dr. Shuttleworth on physical and mental growth in your own words.

4. Why, do you think, is it so difficult to divide life stages in man into exact periods?

5. What are the advantages, according to Thorndike, of attempting to differentiate behavior into learned and unlearned?

6. The text does not give a formal definition of play. Make one of your own which you are willing to defend, or consult a standard dictionary or psychology text for such a definition.

7. Do you think that the evolution of society will involve more routine for the individual or less?

8. Expand the discussion of each of the phases of child development with some ideas of your own.

9. What do you think is meant by the statement that thinking is done with words?

10. Do you believe that it is possible to increase an individual's fundamental mental capacity? Defend your answer.

11. What are the assumptions stated in the chapter upon which the discussion of delinquency as a problem of child development is based?

12. Summarize the discussion on behavior trends in the preadolescent and the adolescent.

## SELECTED REFERENCES FOR FURTHER READING AND STUDY

Alschuler, Rose H., and associates, *Two to Six: Suggestions for Parents and Teachers of Young Children.* New York: Wm. Morrow and Company, 1937.

Conklin, E. S., *Principles of Adolescent Psychology.* New York: Henry Holt and Company, 1935.

Curti, Margaret Wooster, *Child Psychology.* New York: Longmans, Green and Company, 1939.

Horn, John Louis, *The Education of Your Child*. Stanford University Press, California, 1939.

Hull, Clark L., *Principles of Behavior*. New York: D. Appleton-Century Company, 1943.

Hunt, Leila Wall, *The Child in the Home*. New York: Prentice-Hall, Inc., 1940.

Jersild, Arthur T., *Child Psychology*, rev. ed. New York: Prentice-Hall, Inc., 1940.

Jones, H. E., and others, *Development in Adolescence*. New York: D. Appleton-Century Company, 1943.

Judd, Charles H., *Psychology of Secondary Education*. Boston: Ginn and Company, 1927.

Lee, J. Murray, and Dorris May Lee, *The Child and His Curriculum*. New York: D. Appleton-Century Company, 1940.

Merry, Frieda K., and Ralph V. Merry, *From Infancy to Adolescence*. New York: Harper and Brothers, 1940.

National Society for the Study of Education, *Thirty-Eighth Yearbook*. Part I, "Child Development and the Curriculum." Bloomington, Illinois: Public School Publishing Company, 1939.

Rand, Winifred, Mary E. Sweeney, and E. Lee Vincent, *Growth and Development of the Young Child*. Philadelphia: W. B. Saunders Company, 1942.

Shuttleworth, Frank K., *The Physical and Mental Growth of Girls and Boys Age Six to Nineteen in Relation to Age at Maximum Growth*. Washington, D. C.: National Research Council, 1939.

Skinner, C. E., and associates, *Readings in Educational Psychology*. New York: Farrar and Rinehart, 1937. Chap. 25.

———, P. L. Harriman, and others. *Child Psychology*. New York: The Macmillan Company, 1941.

Strang, Ruth, *An Introduction to Child Study*. New York: The Macmillan Company, 1930.

"Teachers Study the Growth and Development of Children," *Educational Method*, Vol. XX, No. 2, November, 1940.

Teagarden, Florence M., *Child Psychology for Professional Workers*. New York: Prentice-Hall, Inc., 1940.

Thorndike, E. L., *Human Nature and the Social Order*. New York: The Macmillan Company, 1940.

# Part III

# MENTAL ABILITIES AND INDIVIDUAL DIFFERENCES

## CHAPTER 6

# Intelligence and Aptitude: Their Nature, Development, and Measurement

During the past twenty-five years, education has been deeply influenced and appreciably enriched by the measurement movement. In the early stages of this development, enthusiasts for objective testing were led to make many extreme statements and unwarranted claims. This tendency led at times to an unjustifiable emphasis on, and a preoccupation with, objective procedures. Accordingly, certain values and outcomes of a more comprehensive educative process appeared to suffer. Despite such limitations, the movement stimulated an unparalleled amount of experimentation and brought a widespread realization of the nature and extent of individual differences in children's abilities and aptitudes. Through the dissemination of the results of objective tests, teachers generally were led to recognize their responsibility for providing a diversified educational program of activities and experiences chosen to suit the varied abilities within every class.

The awareness of individual differences led to many other changes in school practice. For example, objective testing focused attention upon *extreme* deviates. Thereafter, the gifted child, the slow-learning or feeble-minded child, and other types came to be understood and treated more adequately. Educators soon recognized that objective measurement occupied an important place in a guidance program. And, as their research data grew more abundant, they discovered the limitations as well as the values of the objective approach. It became clear that the typical intelligence test measured only one aspect of the child's development, and that adequate understanding and effective guidance depended upon the use and interpretation of many other types of data. Therefore, students undertook to develop additional tests and scales that would supplement intelligence tests. Among the most important and directly useful of these closely related instruments was the aptitude test. Through its use, the teacher was aided in studying the special abilities and latent potentialities of boys and girls.

As the testing movement proceeded, hypotheses and claims of various kinds were tested, and important considerations emerged. Scientists came to question the doctrine of inheritance of mental ability, the dogma of race differences, the assumption of a constant I. Q., and dependence on test results, unsupported by other data, in segregating school children. Today, our perspective is really improved. We are now in a position to use tests sanely and advantageously in an educative process that recognizes the many-sided nature of the child and the need for extensive, subtle investigation to understand his nature and his needs.

Because of the significance of the testing movement, and because false claims and procedures still persist, it appears essential that every student of education and every teacher examine these fundamental developments and formulate his own conclusions. We shall attempt in this chapter to present some considerations basic to such an appraisal.

What is intelligence? How does it grow and develop? Is it inherited? To what extent is it modified by unusual opportunities and favorable conditions in good homes? These and a host of similar questions may be answered dogmatically by many persons despite the fact that the scientific basis for their statements often is lacking. It will repay the student to examine the scientific studies carefully and to weigh the evidence impartially.

## History of Intelligence Testing

Standard testing arose from laboratory investigations and observations. In Germany, scientists directed attention to the measurement and study of reaction time, and other relatively simple abilities and functions. The first psychological laboratory was established in the latter part of the nineteenth century—in 1879 by Professor Wundt in Leipzig.

About this time, important related findings were reported in other countries. In England, the work of Sir Francis Galton was perhaps the most significant. Although Galton did not make an intelligence test, he made many suggestions relevant to this problem. He observed that such a test *could* be made, and that its use would doubtless disclose large individual differences. Some persons would exhibit extraordinary brightness; others would show very little ability; and most would tend to cluster rather closely around the average. During this period, tests were being developed by other workers. In America as early as 1890, J. M. Cattell published a volume entitled *Mental Tests and Measurements*. In it he described tests of single abilities such as sensation, reaction time, speed of movement, and so forth. In the pioneer work, there was implied the belief that intelligent behavior was simply the sum of these separate functions or activities.

Alfred Binet was led to reject this hypothesis, for his studies of memory, attention, and adaptation led him to believe that these factors operated in inseparable combinations; he discovered that the unity or character of the whole pattern was frequently destroyed or altered by attempts to measure each component. Hence, he believed that intelligence could be most reliably observed in activities that called for the combined activity of the various factors. He sought to assemble in order of difficulty the typical reactions of children, young people, and adults. Working with the French physician, Simon, he developed a list, from the reports of parents and from observations, of the everyday experience and behavior of boys and girls. Finally, after considerable experimentation, typical activities were arranged in an age scale from 3 to 14 years. Through its use, it was possible to state crudely a child's intelligence level. If a child of twelve (or of any other age) responded to these tests in a manner typical of the seven-year-old child, he was judged to be seven years of age mentally. If a child of seven years passed the tests in a manner typical of the twelve-year-old child, he was said to have a mental age of twelve years.[1]

The Binet tests were received in various ways; some persons objected violently to the concept underlying them, while others endorsed them enthusiastically. In general, psychologists were skeptical; but the method was adopted by many workers. H. H. Goddard brought the tests to America, published a revision as early as 1911, and soon demonstrated their value in school work. Although many workers were important in the development of testing, it was L. M. Terman who demonstrated best the possibilities in the movement.

In 1916 the Stanford Revision of the Binet-Simon Tests appeared;[2] Terman and his colleagues had spent five years in its construction and standardization. Several of its features are distinctive. For each of years three to ten inclusive, there are six tests. Eight tests are provided for year twelve; and six tests for years

---

[1] Goodenough has pointed out that, in 1897, Chaille published standards for each month of the first year of life, and additional standards up to 36 months. Consult the following: F. L. Goodenough, "Measurement of Mental Growth," in *Handbook of Child Psychology* rev. ed. (C. Murchison, editor) (Worcester, Mass.: Clark University Press, 1933), Chapter VII; and S. Chaille, "Infants, Their Chronological Progress," *New Orleans Medical and Surgical Journal*, Vol. XIV (1887), pp. 893-912.

[2] This revision was accompanied by Terman's *Measurement of Intelligence* (Boston: Houghton Mifflin Company, 1916), which gave a complete description of the test as well as directions for administering and scoring it.

fourteen, sixteen, and eighteen. The tests utilize situations and experiences known to typical American children. For example, the child who succeeds in tests at the three-year level will identify certain objects (such as a watch and a pencil); he will give his name; and he will point to parts of his body. Although the three-year-old child usually will *enumerate* objects in a picture, the seven-year-old child will *describe* the picture, and the twelve-year-old will *interpret* it. These illustrations reveal two characteristics of the revision: (1) its reliance in the measurement of intelligence upon the use of general experience and information; and (2) its attempt to designate *levels* of ability through situations demanding different reactions at different age levels. In giving the tests, the examiner locates the year level at which the child passes *all* items; and the testing is continued until the child fails in all tests in a particular age group. In this way, *range* and *level* of intelligence are gauged.

Although Terman employed the technique developed by Binet, he made several important alterations. He refined the method, added several tests, utilized the mental age concept, and applied Stern's proposal in calculating the I. Q.[3]

This revision appeared in 1916. It was widely used in our schools, and was generally accepted as a necessary instrument in child study. L. M. Terman has continued his experimentation with this approach. In 1937, in collaboration with Maud M. Merrill, he published another revision.[4] Among the significant features of this second revision are: extension of the scale to include children as young as two years of age; the construction of more reliable tests for ages 3 to 5; the improvement of the adult tests; and the development of a second form that makes it possible to offset practice effects in retesting children.

## What Is Intelligence?

It may be observed that psychologists have sometimes attempted to measure intelligence without formulating a clear-cut definition. It is true, of course, that Terman and Binet judged intelligence by its *products*. Moreover, Binet stressed the importance of attention, adaptation, and autocriticism in intelligent

---

[3] The I. Q. is calculated by dividing a child's mental age in months by his chronological age. An average child of exactly 6 years of age will be credited with 6 years of mental age. Thus, his I. Q. will be $\frac{72}{72}$ or 1.00. In general practice, decimals are eliminated; the child's I. Q. is said to be 100. See W. Stern, *Psychological Methods of Testing Intelligence*. Baltimore: Warwick and York, 1914.

[4] L. M. Terman and M. M. Merrill, *Measuring Intelligence*. Boston: Houghton Mifflin Company, 1937.

behavior, and Terman emphasized the ability to do abstract thinking and to succeed in school.

Many thories and definitions of intelligence were advanced.
So contradictory were the various claims that a group of
psychologists prepared a symposium in 1921 in which they
attempted to clarify the situation. At that time, E. L. Thorndike stated that intelligence implied the ability to make "good
responses from the standpoint of truth or fact"; others emphasized
the ability to adjust adequately to new situations; and still others
stressed the ability to learn. Terman asserted that an individual
"is intelligent in proportion to his ability to carry on abstract
thinking," and Spearman and others cited a general factor or
capacity. Thorndike believed that it was necessary to differentiate
kinds of intelligence: for example, abstract, mechanical, and social
types. Then, after several decades of experimentation, he was led to
redefine intelligence, and to state that level, range, area, and speed
are essential characteristics. In *Measurement of Intelligence,* he
reports the construction of four tests, commonly known as the
C A V D scales.[5] These include parts requiring: the completion of
sentences (C), arithmetic (A), vocabulary (V), and ability to
follow directions (D).

Among most workers in this field, it is now agreed that intelligence is reflected by the individual's adjustment and adaptability.
This ability is thought of as comprising a large number of factors
and dispositions. Moreover, it is generally conceded that intelligence tests reflect inborn tendencies and acquired experiences.

## The nonverbal test

For some children, the verbal test is unsuitable. Another type
of test—the performance scale—was devised for use with the deaf
and with children deficient in language or speech acquisitions.
Pintner and Paterson [6] in 1917 presented the first really practical
scale, well-standardized and carefully made, which required little
"conventional" language either in presentation or in response.
Illustrative of the items in this scale is the Seguin Form Board,
which is made up of ten blocks in geometric form—star, circle, and
so forth—to be fitted into appropriate spaces cut in a board. Another in the series is a Picture Completion Test, consisting of a
picture of a child's playground from which ten one-inch squares

[5] E. L. Thorndike *et al., Measurement of Intelligence.* New York: Columbia
University, Teachers College, Bureau of Publications, 1926.

[6] R. Pintner and D. Paterson, *A Scale of Performance Tests.* New York: D.
Appleton-Century Company, 1917.

have been cut. The child selects ten of fifty squares and fits them in their proper spaces. In the complete Pintner-Paterson Scale, there are fifteen tasks of these and similar types. Other performance scales have been constructed. In two surveys, the Porteus Maze and the Arthur Performance Scale were found to be widely used in American psychological and educational clinics.[7] The performance scales prove valuable supplements to the Binet; they are unique in their appeal to children, who generally find pleasure in taking them. These tests yield results that are frequently very illuminating when they are employed with children who are limited in language ability or expression. Intelligence tests have been constructed for other special groups; of significance is the work of Kuhlmann,[8] who has developed an individual test for measuring the intelligence of very young children. Kuhlmann extended the Binet test downward and devised tests and standards for children as young as three months of age. Recently, several students have attempted to devise more comprehensive standards for young children. Arnold Gesell [9] has created developmental schedules for children of ages *below* three. These comprehensive standards have led to penetrating descriptions of the abilities and behavior of very young children. They are useful in child guidance, since they extend the information obtained from an intelligence test and provide a clear indication of different children's needs.

Most of these tests are individual in nature; special training and understanding are required to give them, and considerable time is spent in testing each child. Group tests, therefore, have been developed for children with whom time, money, and lack of trained examiners preclude individual testing. These tests can be administered to varying numbers of persons, for example, a dozen five-year-old children or one hundred or more young people. The examiner needs little training, since precise directions for giving and scoring the tests are available. Characteristic items in these tests include: completion of sentences, completion of number series, general information, arithmetic problems, and vocabulary.

At the end of this chapter is a table listing and describing some widely used individual and group tests. It will be noted that the

---

[7] P. A. Witty and V. Theman, "Psycho-Educational Clinic," *Journal of Applied Psychology,* Vol. XVIII, No. 3 (1934), pp. 369-392; and C. Town *et al.,* "Report of Committee of Clinical Section of the American Psychological Association," *Psychological Clinic,* Vol. XXIII, Nos. 1-2 (1935), pp. 1-140.

[8] F. Kuhlmann, "Revision of the Binet-Simon System for Measuring the Intelligence of Children," *Journal of Psycho-Asthenics, Monograph Supplement,* No. 1. Faribault, Minnesota: 1912.

[9] Arnold Gesell, *Mental Growth of the Pre-School Child.* New York: The Macmillan Company, 1925.

time required for giving the tests varies greatly. Thirty to sixty minutes are generally required; however, some group tests require two or three hours. The time consumed by individual testing also varies; the average is perhaps sixty minutes for the Terman-Merrill Revision of the Stanford-Binet. In giving nonverbal tests, from two to ninety minutes are required. Equivalent forms are available for most group intelligence tests. These forms are especially valuable in eliminating part of the practice effect when children are retested after short intervals of time. The cost of most group tests is small—a few cents per copy. In selecting a test, consideration and thought should be given to all items mentioned in the table, and a test should be chosen which fulfills the many demands of a particular testing situation.

## Inheritance of Mental Ability

Is intelligence inherited? This perennial question is still unanswered, although the methods used in contemporary studies are improved and refined. Present-day investigators have used many methods to secure relevant data: for example, the correlation technique, family history studies, co-twin control procedures, and foster-children experiments.

The first technique involves ascertaining the relationship between intelligence test scores for groups of individuals of differing degrees of blood relationship. The following coefficients are representative of recent investigations. Investigators report a coefficient of +.9 between the intelligence test scores of identical twins, while less resemblance is shown by a coefficient of +.6 for fraternal twins. Between the test scores of typical pairs of brothers and sisters, +.5 is reported; for cousins, +.25; and for parents and offspring, +.4. Thus, increase in amount of blood relationship is associated with increased similarity in intelligence test scores. This condition is alleged by some to show that, by the side of heredity, all other factors are dwarfed in comparison.[10] However, such relationships do not necessarily reveal the superior influence of heredity, since environment is usually much more similar for persons closely related than for those further removed. When factors such as heredity and environment are studied, it is almost impossible to control a sufficiently large number of items to enable one to state which factor is more important. Therefore, nearly all studies of nature-nurture, including correlation experiments, enable the pro-

---

[10] G. M. Whipple, ed., *Nature and Nurture, Their Influence upon Intelligence* (*27th Yearbook of the National Society for the Study of Education*, Part I). Bloomington, Illinois: Public School Publishing Co., 1928.

ponents of both factors to *find* a causal relationship according to their inclination.

Similarly, the results of another approach in the nature-nurture controversy may be interpreted. Writers have presented imposing arrays of statistics showing the frequency with which mental superiority, peculiarity, or defect persist in related stocks. The Kallikak-Jukes-Edwards families have been offered as *crucial evidence*. For example, it was found that two family lines traced to a soldier in the Revolutionary War differed conspicuously. One line established through a feeble-minded woman contained 480 direct descendants, among whom only 46 normal individuals were identified. In the line established with a normal woman, almost all were normal or superior.

Interesting here is the work of Terman,[11] who found that of 62 members in the Hall of Fame, 22½ per cent were related to 643 gifted children identified and studied in California. This finding leads one to recall Galton's famous analysis of 977 men of genius [12] who were found to have 535 eminent relatives, while 977 average men had but four relatives who were eminent. These data, and those recently obtained by careful anthropological studies, suggest the potency of direct family relationships in influencing behavior and accomplishment; they do not, however, present an especially strong case for the superiority of heredity over environment, since both Terman's and Galton's groups consisted of individuals coming typically from affluent, stimulating, and superior homes wherein ability is undoubtedly nourished. And, in the less fortunate groups, poverty, despair, and limited opportunity abound and persist.

A promising method of studying heredity was developed by Arnold Gesell,[13] who studied identical twins. Their development was so similar in emotional expression, in mental ability, and in certain motor acquisitions (such as stair-climbing) that Gesell concluded that environmental stimulation could not possibly account for the striking correspondence. Remarkable likeness persisted even when one twin member had undergone special training in stair-climbing or in vocabulary development. It appeared, therefore, that "inner growth" or "maturation" sets levels that special training did not enable the children to transcend.

Although Gesell's results are extremely interesting, they must

---

[11] L. M. Terman *et al., Genetic Studies of Genius: I. Mental and Physical Traits of a Thousand Gifted Children.* Palo Alto: Stanford University Press, 1925.

[12] F. Galton, *Hereditary Genius: An Inquiry into its Laws and Consequences,* 2nd ed. New York: The Macmillan Company, 1892.

[13] A. Gesell, "Maturation and the Patterning of Behavior," in *Handbook of Child Psychology* (rev. ed., C. Murchison, editor), Worcester, Mass.: Clark University Press, 1933. Chapter IV.

be viewed with reservation, since they are based upon observation of a relatively small number of cases studied for a short time. A related question arises: What differences in intelligence appear in identical twins reared for many years in decidedly different environs?

One investigator [14] reports the records of ten pairs of identical twins reared apart from birth or from infancy, and brought together and studied in maturity. In six pairs, no significant difference in test-intelligence was noted; in two pairs, twelve-point differences in intelligence quotients are cited; and the remainder differ by fifteen or seventeen points. These studies and other more recent follow-up studies of identical twins do not permit valid generalizations, for in some cases marked differences are reported while in others striking similarity is found. In addition, description of the environment is inadequate or incompletely reported in several studies.

The data upon identical twins have been used to support the theory that heredity is *the* important factor in determining the intelligence of boys and girls. In fact, many books in psychology and education have been inclined to overemphasize the force of heredity. Students of education are sometimes led to believe that an I. Q. is fixed and immutable.

## Influence of Environment

A number of studies have been conceived to ascertain the influence of enriched educational programs on the I. Q. Studies at the University of Iowa show substantial gains for orphanage children who are provided with nursery school experience. However, in some studies in other centers, gains are not reported; in still others, the gains are small and of little significance.[15] More important than these slight gains are the improved attitudes and emotional poise that seem to result from attendance in some nursery schools. Moreover, in several of these studies, it appears that the I. Q. which a child receives is determined to a considerable degree by the particular test that he takes, as well as the age at which he is tested. Test results of young children vary more than those secured from older children. Because of these considerations, it seems desirable for the student to view the child's mental age as a measure of *status attained* in the special abilities measured by the test. The teacher should not anticipate that the child will attain the same

---

[14] G. C. Schwesinger, *Heredity and Environment.* New York: The Macmillan Company, 1933. P. 230.

[15] This material is reviewed in the *Psychological Bulletin,* March, 1940, and in the *39th Yearbook of the National Society for the Study of Education,* Part I.

rating on other intelligence tests; nor should he anticipate that repetition of the same test will always bring the same result. Intelligence test results are modifiable; in the early years, ratings are shown to improve when various types of opportunities are provided. Similarly, changes are reported for school children. For example, a study of Negro children by S. D. Scruggs [16] reveals that, among elementary-school children, improvement in reading ability and general academic proficiency are associated with gains in I. Q. In fact, gains in intelligence test scores are shown to occur even in college by other studies, where steady increases have been reported in the averages of students during the four-year period. [17]

Again and again, it has been shown that changes of large magnitude also occur. [18] For example, in the *39th Yearbook of the National Society for the Study of Education,* one investigator reported a study containing I. Q. retests after an interval of at least two and one-half years for over 1100 children in three New York City schools in which a shift of 20 or more points occurred in 16 per cent of the cases. [19] Large shifts have also been repeatedly demonstrated by other studies; moreover, they have been found at all levels including college, wherein, to quote R. L. Thorndike, "The studies have agreed in finding that those students who remain through a college course tend to gain in intelligence score." [20] In addition, it has been pointed out that the interval between test and retest influences the accuracy of prediction. As the time element increases, the closeness of relationship decreases.

[16] S. D. Scruggs, "Effect of Improvement in Reading upon the Intelligence of Negro Children," *Bulletin of Education,* University of Kansas, May 1935. Cf. also: Madeline Semmelmeyer, "Promoting Readiness for Reading and for Growth in Interpretation of Meaning," in *Reading and Pupil Development* (compiled and edited by Wm. S. Gray) (Chicago: University of Chicago Press, 1940), p. 62.

[17] The results of recent studies are in striking contrast to those on which the following conclusions were based: "The maximal contribution of the best home environment to intelligence is about 20 I. Q. points, or less, and almost surely lies between 10 and 30 points. Conversely, the least cultured, least stimulating kind of American home environment may depress the I. Q. as much as 20 I. Q. points. But situations as extreme as these occur only once or twice in a thousand times in American communities." B. S. Burks, "Comments on the Chicago and Stanford Studies of Foster Children," *27th Yearbook of the N. S. S. E.,* Part I. Bloomington, Illinois: Public School Publishing Company, 1928, p. 309. Quoted by permission of the Society.

[18] The following statement is typical of many made during the early years of testing: "We can only say that the I. Q. is certainly constant within narrow margins." L. S. Hollingworth, *Gifted Children.* New York: The Macmillan Company, 1926. Pp. 156-158.

[19] Cf. comment by G. D. Stoddard, "Intellectual Development of the Child: An Answer to the Critics of the Iowa Studies," *School and Society,* Vol. LI (April 27, 1940), p. 531.

[20] R. L. Thorndike, "Constancy of the I. Q.," *Psychological Bulletin,* Vol. XXXVII (March, 1940), p. 168.

These data support the conclusion of another investigator: "The fact that rates of growth in mental abilities are variable is now well established by the studies of various investigators. In addition to the studies of our group, there are such studies as Honzik's covering the ages 21 to 72 months; Freeman and Flory's, for ages 8 through 17 years; and Wellman's, from pre-school to college." [21] The foregoing observation concerning the variability of the I. Q. is based upon the data for groups as well as upon careful case studies.[22]

Another study, by every criterion one of the most careful investigations in this field, dealt first with tests and retests of children during the first three years of life. The same children were given several individual intelligence tests at regular intervals until they were nine years of age.

The I. Q. changes evidenced by these children are of particular interest because the children have all had a high degree of testing experience under relatively constant conditions. Because such experiences should reduce spurious variations at a minimum, smaller than usual I. Q. changes might be expected. Actually, the changes seem, in many respects, to be similar to those of other studies. . . . a fourth of the group change 10 or more I. Q. points on retest made one year after the initial test; while an equal number change 17 or more I. Q. points over a three-year interval. . . . When the amount of change in I. Q. from one test to a later one is plotted against I. Q. at the first test, the scatters show no significant relation between I. Q. and stability of scores.[23]

This brings us to still another type of study which reveals an alteration in the I. Q.'s of children—studies of children in foster homes.[24] One surprising result of these studies is the frequency with which high I. Q.'s have been obtained. Leahy, for example, gives data for a group of children of ages five to fourteen, all of whom were adopted before they were six months of age.[25] The mean I. Q. is 110.5. Skeels cites an average I. Q. of 115.4 for 147 children adopted before they were six months of age.[26] Forty-one received I. Q.'s of 120 or above.

The extent of the deviation in the I. Q.'s of foster children and

[21] N. Bayley, "Factors Influencing the Growth of Intelligence in Young Children," *39th Yearbook of the N. S. S. E.*, Part II. Bloomington, Illinois: Public School Publishing Company, 1940, p. 77. Quoted by permission of the Society.

[22] N. Bayley, "Mental Growth in Young Children," *39th Yearbook of the N. S. S. E.*, Part II, p. 11.

[23] N. Bayley, "Mental Growth in Young Children," *39th Yearbook of the N. S. S. E.*, Part II, pp. 18 and 20. Quoted by permission of the Society.

[24] M. Skodak, *Children in Foster Homes; A Study of Mental Development.* Iowa City: University of Iowa Studies in Child Welfare, Vol. XVI, No. 1, 1939.

[25] Alice M. Leahy, "Nature-Nurture and Intelligence," *Genet. Psychol. Monog.*, Vol. XVII (1935), pp. 236-308.

[26] Harold M. Skeels, "Mental Development of Children in Foster Homes," *J. Consulting Psychol.*, Vol. II (1938), pp. 33-43.

those of their true parents is noteworthy; it suggests the operation of a number of related forces under circumstances which may be profitably analyzed. In attempting to account for these differences, one should recall that these children were adopted in infancy, and that their early, most formative years were spent in an environment in which their foster parents may have been more zealous than some true parents to provide an environment for the sturdy growth and development of the children whom they really "wanted." It is certainly justifiable to assume that affection, love, and concern, generously but judiciously bestowed on growing children, have very desirable effects upon wholesome nurture. In any event, it seems that a fine environment and cordial attitude affect I. Q.'s to some extent.

It would be logical, therefore, to assume that especially poor environments would retard development. And this seems precisely the result obtained in comparisons of younger and older children in several impoverished environments. Asher's study of Kentucky mountain children (1935), Sherman and Keys' study of isolated mountain children (1932), and Wheeler's account of East Tennessee children add corroborative evidence to the earlier studies of Canal Boat, Gypsy, and other sibling groups.[27]

These studies lead us to modify a rather prevalent concept about the constancy of the I. Q. Since these studies suggest that alterations in I. Q. occur at every age level, it would seem best not to attempt to predict future development of children from the results of a single intelligence test. If such information is used with other findings about child development, it may enable a teacher to offer the child guidance and counsel that are valuable. But it cannot be too strongly emphasized that individual development is variable, and that caution should be exercised in making predictions.[28]

### Distribution of Intelligence

The good teacher will attend to the differences in boys and girls and will make an effort to discover each child's limitations and abilities from observations of many types. One type of data may

[27] For an excellent summary, see the *Psychological Bulletin,* March, 1940, and C. L. Nemzek, "The Constancy of the I. Q.," *Psychological Bulletin,* Vol. XXX (1933), pp. 143-167.

[28] N. Bayley, "The Role of Intelligence," *Mental Health in the Classroom. 13th Yearbook, Department of Supervisors and Directors of Instruction, N.E.A.* Washington, D.C.: N.E.A., 1941. Pp. 53-54.

*The Harvard Growth Study* should be examined for crucial data on variability. Cf. *Predicting the Child's Development,* by W. F. Dearborn and J. W. M. Rothney. Cambridge, Mass.: Sci-Art Publishers, 1941.

be obtained from an intelligence test. If an intelligence test is given to 100 typical school children of the same age, some extraordinarily high and some very low scores will be obtained. In fact, such great disparity will be found between the highest and the lowest scores that, if the differences are changed into mental age units, a range of several years will occur. The slowest child of 100 ten-year-old pupils may be seven or eight and the brightest twelve or thirteen years old mentally. However, in any group, the difference between the most retarded child and the one just above him will be relatively small, and the interval between the highest child and the one just below him will be similarly small. Of course, many children will make similar scores, and if the scores are presented graphically, most of them will be found to cluster about a central point. If these scores are changed into mental ages and the mental ages are divided by the chronological ages, a distribution in I. Q.'s will appear according to the general characteristics of a normal distribution curve. It is valuable for the teacher to know as accurately as possible the mental maturity of each child in order that he may provide materials suitable for mastery and success.

Test scores for many types of school children have been found to be distributed roughly according to the normal probability curve —the idiot differs only in degree of retardation from the imbecile, and the imbecile stands just below the moron. Above the moron is the dull group, while the majority of the population will be found clustering somewhat closely about or in the interval 90-110. This large group is classified as "normal" or "average" by Terman—because they represent best the typical school child and include some 50 per cent of the total school population. Consideration of a typical distribution of intelligence test scores indicates that fewer cases appear as the scores become higher. Thus, at I. Q. 120 and above, we find, according to recent studies, approximately 12 per cent of our children, while four per cent reach or exceed I. Q. 130.

Pintner [29] notes a somewhat similar distribution for children of different age and grade levels. Of course, in an inferior social district, where homes and general cultural conditions are poor, a disproportionately large number of low scores will be obtained, but the wide range and the concentration of scores about a central point still will remain *the* typical features of the distribution. In a superior social district one will find an unusually large number of high I. Q.'s, but the range will be great and the scores will cluster about a central point. The teacher may expect, therefore, to deal

[29] R. Pintner, *Intelligence Testing*, 2nd ed. New York: Henry Holt and Company, 1931. Chapter X.

with children varying widely in ability, regardless of the nature of the district or the type of community in which he is working. The distributions in Table V illustrate the variability in the intelligence of school children. The Terman-Merrill data are perhaps the most valid representation.

TABLE V

PERCENTAGE DISTRIBUTION OF INTELLIGENCE QUOTIENTS
OF UNSELECTED CHILDREN

| Classification | I. Q. | Witty: 1000 Unselected Children Grades 1-8 | Madsen: 880 Elementary-School Children Grades 1-8 | Sandiford: Hypothetical Normal Population | Terman-Merrill 1937 Revision:* Unselected Population |
|---|---|---|---|---|---|
| "Near genius" or "genius" | Above 140 | 0.03 | 0.2 | 0.25 | 1.33 |
| Very superior............. | 120-140 | 8.5 | 9.8 | 6.75 | 11.30 |
| Superior.................. | 110-120 | 14.3 | 17.4 | 13.00 | 18.10 |
| Normal, or average....... | 90-110 | 56.9 | 51.6 | 60.00 | 46.50 |
| Dull, rarely feeble-minded. | 80- 90 | 10.8 | 12.4 | 13.00 | 14.50 |
| Borderline, sometimes dull, often feeble-minded..... | 70- 80 | 7.2 | 6.4 | 6.00 | 5.60 |
| Feeble-minded........... | Below 70 | 2.2 | 2.3 | 1.00 | 2.63 |
| Total.............. | | 99.93 | 100.1 | 100.00 | 99.96 |

*See M. A. Merrill, "The Significance of I.Q.'s on the Revised Stanford Binet Scales," *Journal of Educational Psychology*, 1938, Vol. 29, pp. 641-651.

A word should be said about the terms used for designating the various I. Q. groups in Table V. "Normal" was employed by Terman to refer to those children having I. Q.'s 90 to 110, and "genius" or "near-genius" for those having I. Q.'s 140 or above. These descriptive terms are unfortunate; one should bear in mind that they refer simply to one group of children who are *average* in testintelligence and to another who make extraordinarily high I. Q.'s. Normalcy, involving the reconciliation of emotional drives and obstacles to adjustment, and "genius," implying the product of several variables (including ability, drive, and opportunity) are not indicated by reference solely to an I. Q.

## Growth of Intelligence

Several growth curves have been constructed from intelligence test results. The curve which Pintner [30] believes is most representative is presented by Figure 1. This curve exhibits its most rapid rise during the first few years in children's lives. Common observation substantiates this, for the preschool child does make an ex-

[30] *Ibid.*

tremely large number and variety of adaptations and probably grows more rapidly at this time than during any later period. In this diagram, growth seems to cease at age 14 or 15. This age level is, of course, speculative; Pintner [31] stated that the point of cessation may lie anywhere between 14 and 22 years. Terman,[32] in standardizing the Binet test, used 16 years. He recommended that 16 years (presumably the upper limit of mental growth) be used as the divisor in calculating the I. Q. of persons of chronological age 16 or above. Recent investigations suggest that ability to learn

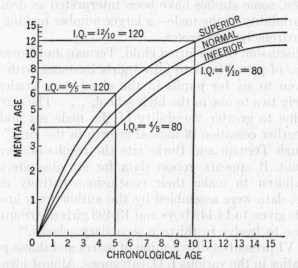

**Fig. 1. Hypothetical Growth Curves Which Give a Constant I. Q.** (From H. E. Garrett and M. R. Schneck., *Psychological Tests, Methods, and Results,* by permission of Harper & Brothers, publishers.)

persists at least until age 45, and that the capacity that has reached its zenith at perhaps 22 years continues to function until human beings are "very old," and thus enables them, if they will, to solve problems, to see relations, to deal with abstractions—indeed, to carry on all kinds of intelligent behavior. Therefore, the theoretical curve should not end with the plateau pictured, for if there be a decline among older folk, it is attributable to lassitude, lack of interest, ineffective work habits, and other factors that lessen efficiency in the old and the young alike. Finally, it is important to bear in mind that, although this curve represents growth for large groups, there are significant individual and group variations that alter its form in other cases.

---

[31] *Ibid.*

[32] L. M. Terman, *Measurement of Intelligence.* Boston: Houghton Mifflin Company, 1916.

## Sex Differences in Intelligence

With the introduction and general use of the intelligence test, it was found that the average intelligence test scores of the sexes were strikingly similar. Nevertheless, popular thought continues to attribute better ability to men than to women in many types of human endeavor.

Although many investigations have revealed very small differences only in the average test scores of boys and girls and of men and women, some studies have been interpreted as demonstrating greater variability of the male—a larger number making extremely low and extremely high scores.

In a discussion of the gifted child, Terman and Burks [33] assert: "The ratio of gifted boys to gifted girls increases with age, being about seven to six for pupils in the elementary grades, and approximately two to one in the high school. . . . The excess of boys may be due to greater variability of the male sex and (in later ages) to earlier cessation of mental growth in the girls."

Although Terman and Burks cite the results of seven studies, they do not, it appears, report data for an adequate number of bright children to make their conclusions entirely dependable. Therefore, data were assembled by the author from group intelligence tests given to 14,149 boys and 13,493 girls distributed through grades nine to twelve in thirteen secondary schools. [34]

Table VI presents a distribution of scores and shows percentages and sex ratios in the various I. Q. categories. Almost identical numbers of boys and girls are classified in the I. Q. interval 140 and above, and approximately equal percentages are found in the interval 130 to 139. It appears significant, further, that about two per cent of these secondary-school pupils have I. Q.'s 130 or above. The percentage of children in the amentia group (I. Q. 70 and below) is small, as is the percentage in the borderline category (I. Q. 70 to 79). Although larger numbers of boys than of girls are present in the sub-average groups, the differences between the sexes do not appear to be highly significant. The similarity of boys and girls in test-intelligence is clearly demonstrated by the fact that 48.2 per cent of the boys reach or exceed the median score of the girls.

Although this study deals only with secondary-school pupils, it

---

[33] L. M. Terman and B. S. Burks, "The Gifted Child," in *Handbook of Child Psychology* (rev. ed., C. Murchison, editor). Worcester, Mass.: Clark University Press, 1930. Chapter XIX, p. 776.

[34] P. A. Witty, "Relative Frequency of Gifted Boys and Girls in the Secondary School," *Educational Administration and Supervision*, Vol. XX, No. 8 (1934), pp. 606-612.

TABLE VI
DISTRIBUTION OF SCORES OF 27,642 HIGH-SCHOOL PUPILS (Witty)

| I. Q. Group | Number | | Percentage | | Ratio of Boys to Girls |
|---|---|---|---|---|---|
| | Boys | Girls | Boys | Girls | |
| 140 and above...... | 47 | 48 | .322 | .354 | .938 |
| 130 to 139.......... | 250 | 244 | 1.767 | 1.810 | .976 |
| 120 to 129.......... | 1,237 | 1,103 | 8.742 | 8.175 | 1.069 |
| 110 to 119.......... | 3,013 | 2,972 | 21.294 | 22.026 | .967 |
| 100 to 109.......... | 3,896 | 4,080 | 27.536 | 30.238 | .911 |
| 90 to 99.......... | 3,573 | 3,356 | 25.253 | 24.872 | 1.015 |
| 80 to 89.......... | 1,713 | 1,394 | 12.106 | 10.331 | 1.172 |
| 70 to 79.......... | 369 | 260 | 2.608 | 1.927 | 1.353 |
| Below 70.......... | 51 | 36 | .360 | .267 | 1.348 |
| Total............ | 14,149 | 13,493 | 99.998 | 100.000 | |

suggests the essential similarity of boys and girls in general intelligence. It is, of course, true that more boys than girls "drop out" of school. Thus, it may be that the data are not truly representative. Whatever the final outcome of this controversy may be, these data suggest that differences in the intelligence test scores of boys and girls are relatively small and insignificant.

## Racial Differences

An extensive and perplexing literature has developed from studies of the intelligence of different "races" in America. The procedure typically followed was to test samples of each "racial" group, calculate average scores, and make comparisons after consulting age equivalents or norms. This procedure was used in the analysis of the test scores of recruits in the United States Army during the First World War. Recent immigrants made relatively low average scores while older immigrant stocks fared much better. From these data, the conclusion was drawn that the intelligence of the Poles, the Italians, the Russians, and the Greeks was low, while that of the English, the Scotch, the Germans, and the native-born American was high.[35] The limiting effects of unfamiliarity with our language, a short period of life in a new world, and lack of acquaintance and experience with our customs and traditions were not taken into account. Nordic superiority became a generally accepted myth. Although these theories have been disproved, the

[35] C. C. Brigham, *A Study of American Intelligence*. Princeton, N. J.: Princeton University Press, 1923.

C. C. Brigham, "Intelligence Tests of Immigrant Groups," *Psychological Review*, Vol. XXXVII, No. 2 (1930), pp. 158-165.

dogma of race superiority still holds high rank among American superstitions.

It must be clear that if a test were flawlessly constructed it would be useful in making race comparisons when, and only when, the groups tested had had common interests and experiences. Garth,[36] who for years assigned I. Q.'s to the races, concedes that there is doubt whether the test data present a valid basis for comparison of Negroes, Mexicans, and Indians.

Negroes in America have been studied much more extensively than other racial groups. Their average scores are typically lower than those of whites; moreover, Negroes possessing allegedly larger amounts of white blood usually make higher average scores than those of suspected pure Negroid ancestry. Pintner expressed a rather generally accepted interpretation of these data:

> In the case of the Negro and perhaps in the case of the Indian we have a race of inferior intelligence as measured by our present intelligence tests and as compared with American whites. The greater the amount of white blood entering the various mixtures of the two races, the greater is the intelligence of the resulting progeny and this takes place because of the inheritance of mental ability.[37]

The statement that "the greater the amount of white blood . . . the greater the amount of intelligence" should be examined carefully. Psychologists are frequently unaware of the extent of miscegenation in the American Negro population. Anthropologists estimate that only about one-fourth of American Negroes are of unmixed ancestry.[38]

Few published studies deal with the relationship of Negro-white ancestry and intelligence.[39] Investigators have usually separated the Negro subjects into groups on the basis of skin color and compared their average intelligence-test scores. This method is of doubtful validity, because it has been demonstrated that the racial composition of the individual Negro cannot be determined accurately by estimates of pigmentation.[40]

[36] T. R. Garth, "Racial Minds," *Psyche.*, Vol. VIII, No. 3 (1928), pp. 63-70.

[37] R. Pintner, *op. cit.*, p. 520.

[38] M. J. Herskovits, *Anthropometry of the American Negro* (New York: Columbia University Press, 1930), p. 15; and E. A. Hooten, *Up From the Ape* (New York: The Macmillan Company, 1930), p. 589.

[39] P. A. Witty and M. D. Jenkins, "Intra-Race Testing and Negro Intelligence," *Journal of Psychology*, Vol. I (1936), pp. 179-192; P. A. Witty and M. D. Jenkins, "Case of 'B'—A Gifted Negro Child," *Journal of Social Psychology*, Vol. VI, No. 1 (1935), pp. 117-124.

[40] M. J. Herskovits, *Anthropometry of the American Negro* (New York: Columbia University Press, 1930), p. 227, and "On the Relation Between Negro-White Mixture and Standing in Intelligence Tests," *Pedagogical Seminary*, Vol. XXXIII, No. 1 (1936), pp. 30-42.

Nevertheless, several investigations are well-known and are still widely quoted. In one study, Negro school children were classified into four groups: "pure," "three-fourths Negro," "mulatto," and "quadroon," on the basis of "skin color, hair texture, and general facial and cranial conformation, the main emphasis being upon skin color." The average intelligence test scores were in direct relationship to the amount of Negro blood; the lowest was assigned the group designated "pure" Negro. A number of investigations yielded similar results when similar methods of study were employed.

These studies have been seriously challenged by anthropologists whose investigations have revealed little relationship between differentiating physical traits (such as skin color, breadth of nostril, and lip thickness) and intelligence. These results, repeatedly verified, led one investigator to observe:

> The relationship between test scores and physical traits denoting greater or less amounts of Negro blood is so tenuous as to be of no value in drawing conclusions as to the comparative native ability or relative intelligence of the Negro when compared to the white.[41]

The student should exercise great caution in accepting generalizations and assertions concerning the intelligence of the races, for great individual differences are present in every race. It is important, therefore, that we ascertain and develop these widely distributed abilities.

The student should anticipate that every racial group will contain some gifted children. As an example of this, one investigation [42] is convincing. Among 8,000 Negro children, *twenty-six* of I. Q. 140 and above were found—one, a child of surpassing test-intelligence. Great promise inheres in these children as well as in the gifted children in every other racial group. The social importance and cultural significance of this issue must not be forgotten.[43] In the words of Wallace: "For the combating of racism before it sinks its ugly fangs deep in our body politic, the scientist has a special responsibility. Only he can clean out the falsities which have been masquerading under the name of science in our colleges, our high schools, and our public prints. Only he can show how

---

[41] M. J. Herskovits, "On the Relation Between Negro-White Mixture and Standing in Intelligence Tests," *Pedagogical Seminary*, Vol. XXXIII, No. 1 (1926), p. 41. Corroboration of Herskovits' conclusions may be found in: J. Peterson and L. Lanier, *Studies in the Comparative Abilities of Whites and Negroes* (Baltimore: Williams and Wilkins, *Mental Measurements Monographs*, Vol. II, No. 5 [1929]).

[42] P. A. Witty and M. D. Jenkins, "Educational Attainment of Gifted Negro Children," *Journal of Educational Psychology*, Vol. XXV, No. 8 (1934), pp. 585-597.

[43] Ruth Benedict, *Race: Science or Politics*. New York: Modern Age Books, 1940. Cf. also: O. Klineberg, *Race Differences*. New York: Harper and Brothers, 1935.

groundless are the claims that one race, one nation, or one class has any God-given right to rule." [44]

In conclusion, the words of Franz Boas are fitting: "If we were to select the most intelligent, imaginative, energetic, and emotionally stable third of mankind, all races would be represented." [45]

## The Feeble-Minded and the Dull

Since the advent of the intelligence test, an increased amount of attention has been given the feeble-minded. The intelligence test proved useful as a means for identifying this group and for determining the degree of defect. After a considerable amount of experimentation, it was generally agreed that test ratings would *roughly differentiate* the following three groups:

|  | I. Q. |
|---|---|
| Moron | 50-70 |
| Imbecile | 25-50 |
| Idiot | 25 and lower |

Because of the degree of defect, children in the two lower categories seldom enter or remain in school. But the moron group, which contains the majority of the feeble-minded, presents a real problem, since most of the children in this group will attend school and will find the typical curriculum ill suited to their needs.

Estimates of the number of feeble-minded children in the public schools vary from about .5 to 4 per cent. Pintner stated: "In all probability, therefore, we may take this estimate of about 1 per cent of the population of countries like Great Britain or the United States as being feeble-minded in the sense that the degree of mental defect is so great as to make them practically useless in modern society." [46]

We have pointed out that the intelligence test is useful in identifying the feeble-minded.[47] However, its value and dependability must not be overestimated. For a number of years, investigators held that the mental status of 80 to 90 per cent of the feeble-minded was traceable to heredity; therefore, there appeared to be no cure for this condition. The attitude of workers has been altered somewhat during the past fifteen years, for it has been found that I. Q.'s are more changeable than we had previously assumed, and

---

[44] Henry A. Wallace, in an address delivered at the World's Fair, New York, October 14, 1939. Quoted by Benedict, *op. cit.,* p. 258.

[45] Franz Boas, *Anthropology and Modern Life,* rev. ed. New York: W. W. Norton and Company, 1932. P. 79.

[46] R. Pintner, *op. cit.,* p. 339.

[47] Note the somewhat larger proportion found in the Terman-Merrill study, p. 438.

it has been shown that impoverished conditions may depress the I. Q. Moreover, it has been asserted that children of feeble-minded parents sometimes attain normal or superior ratings on intelligence tests—when they are offered from infancy through early childhood the stimulation that a superior home affords. Thus, while the I. Q. is an essential item in identifying the feeble-minded, diagnosis should not depend solely upon its use; instead, it should be based upon a comprehensive study of many factors and conditions.

It is well to point out that by the time the slow-learning child becomes a candidate for observation in school, he is often 9 or 10 years of age. Both hereditary and environmental forces have already had abundant opportunity to produce marked and frequently lasting effects upon him. At these ages, attempts have been made to increase the mental level of the feeble-minded through physical therapy; tonsils have been removed, surgical operations performed, teeth drawn, and nutrition improved; yet the mental condition has been altered little.[48] These studies might lead one to emphasize the role of heredity if he were to overlook the fact that the feeble-minded child usually emerges from an environment characterized by poverty, depression, and restricted opportunity during his infancy and early childhood.

Our hope seems to lie in early identification and systematic and carefully planned training for this group. Every school administrator faces this problem, since there were estimated to be some 450,000 children mentally retarded to such a degree that they seem to require special education.[49] According to the White House Conference Report on Special Education (1931), less than 60,000 of these were enrolled in special classes. The opportunities provided for this group have been repeatedly shown to be inadequate. For example, in one study, 540 special classes, enrolling almost 12,000 children, were examined.[50] Investigation of the type of school, promotional schemes, and time and subject allotment showed that in most cases the instructional methods and subject matter resembled closely those of the regular elementary schools.

The typical class made the following time allotment for individual subjects: 1 hour for reading and related activities, 50 minutes for arithmetic, 20 minutes for spelling, and over 1.5 hours for

---

[48] R. Pintner, "Feebleminded Child," in *Handbook of Child Psychology* (rev. ed., C. Murchison, editor). Worcester, Mass.: Clark University Press, 1933. Chapter XX, p. 834.

[49] White House Conference on Child Health and Protection (Section III, Education and Training), Committee on Special Classes, *Handicapped and the Gifted.* New York: D. Appleton-Century Company, 1931.

[50] P. A. Witty and F. N. Beaman, "Practices in Special Classes," *Educational Trends* (Northwestern University), Vol. I, No. 1 (1932), pp. 4-15.

handwork. The remainder of the daily schedule was divided among subjects such as physical education, penmanship, and music. Thus, one finds the subjects of the ordinary elementary school transferred to the special class. There are exceptions, of course, and these exceptions are worthy of more detailed treatment, since they reveal an exceptional clarity and vision in enriching the opportunities for this group. Nevertheless, the data show strikingly the need for a scientific development of the curriculum and the formulation of more appropriate techniques for instruction. There is a special need for more intelligent adjustment of work to the intellectual maturity and interests of the adolescent subnormal child than has been prevalent in the past.

Several published accounts disclose marked progress in special education. For example, one student devised a curriculum based upon detailed study of the abilities and interests of each child. Expression through an activity program was one important feature of this work. Experiences were selected solely in terms of the needs of the children. They included: (1) projects to develop social competency and individual adjustment; and (2) activities associated with the special interests of each child.

At the end of a semester, this program was evaluated. This group made higher scores than comparable groups enrolled in typical formal classes on standardized tests and on other measures of attainment in subject-matter areas. Moreover, the group was distinctly superior in activities requiring co-operation, initiative, and self-direction.

In this type of program, there are certain objectives that the special class seeks to attain. First, it aims to provide a center for careful study and a program of *continuous* diagnosis for each child. Second, it seeks to offer experiences that will promote personality adjustment and social competency. Third, it aims to offer a series of genuinely pleasant and individually satisfying activities. Finally, it aims to lead each child as far as possible in his quest for economic security.

The final aim is sometimes overemphasized. In a properly balanced curriculum, children participate in activities which, as Martens [51] points out, will lead them to become self-respecting and self-reliant adults. Therefore, social adjustment and maximum individual growth supersede all other aims, values, or objectives. Materials for a program of this character are readily procurable. For example, representative activities are described in a symposium

---

[51] E. H. Martens, *Introduction to Group Activities for Mentally Retarded Children.* Washington: Office of Education, U. S. Department of Interior (Bulletin No. 7), 1933.

compiled by Martens:[52] "The child's immediate environment—the home and the community—constitute the subject matter of the first activity described. . . . The production and preparation of foods, child care, home and school beautification are vital elements of this general theme. Then we dip into the fields of social studies, natural science, music, literature, and vocational preparation, each one of which is important in the education of the whole child."

All the activities described in this monograph bring about a natural wholesome integration of school and life experience.[53] Few teachers will desire to follow these descriptions exactly; but most can benefit greatly by developing projects along similar lines. In fact, every teacher will profit from examining these suggestions for making school more vital, interesting, and worth while. For almost all teachers must deal with retarded children. To do so more intelligently and more sympathetically, they must understand the complexity of the problem, and they must have recourse to activities and materials that will enrich the experiences and nourish the abilities of these boys and girls.

### The Gifted Child [54]

Experimentation in the area of individual differences has been deeply influenced and enriched by the intelligence-testing movement. One of the most notable contributions has been the increased recognition and improved understanding of superior children that it has engendered. As early as 1924, a *Yearbook of the National Society for the Study of Education* contained reports of studies that led to the formulation of certain widely accepted theories concerning the nature and needs of gifted children. In the intervening period, our knowledge has been extended and deepened by supplementary evidence accumulating from genetic studies of this group.[55]

About 1920, the concept was advanced that an extraordinarily high I. Q. was associated with genius. L. M. Terman designated his volume, which described 643 children having I. Q.'s of 140 plus, *Genetic Studies of Genius*. In fact, he went so far as to state that "from the ranks of gifted children [I. Q. 140 plus] and from

[52] *Ibid.*

[53] One of the most helpful volumes that contains numerous additional suggestions is written by Christine Ingram, *Education of the Slow-Learning Child*. New York: World Book Company, 1934.

[54] Also see Chapter 18.

[55] G. M. Whipple, ed., "Intelligence: Its Nature and Nurture," *39th Yearbook of the N. S. S. E.* Bloomington, Illinois: Public School Publishing Company, 1940.

nowhere else our geniuses in every line are recruited." L. S. Hollingworth also made similar prognostications; she asserted, "Only the gifted can create," and "Individuals of surpassing intelligence create national wealth, determine the state of industry, advance science, and make general culture possible." [56]

These investigators now exercise greater caution in writing; however, one has recently advanced a rather startling hypothesis: [57]

It has now become clear from follow-up studies that children who test at 140 I. Q. are far from genius in any accepted meaning of that term. . . . It is necessary, therefore, to revise the idea that 140 I. Q. delimits genius. From subsequent observation of the mental products of tested persons, it seems reasonable to suggest that the degree of mental ability involved in producing works of genius falls as far above 140 I. Q. as the latter falls above the generality. At and above 180 I. Q., performance begins to appear that corresponds to the lexicographer's idea of genius.

Although Hollingworth believes that the child of I. Q. 180 possesses the potentiality for genius, other investigators are inclined to attach less significance to the I. Q. and to give more weight to other factors. For example, Terman writes: [58]

Our conclusion is that *for subjects brought up under present-day educational regimes, excess in I. Q. above 140 or 150 adds little to one's achievement in the early adult years.*

The data reviewed indicate that, *above the I. Q. level of 140, adult success is largely determined by such factors as social adjustment, emotional stability, and drive to accomplish.*

It seems clear that an extraordinarily high I. Q. in childhood is not necessarily an indicator of later attainment that may be regarded as the work of genius. What do these high ratings mean, if they do not indicate "genius"?

For two decades gifted children have been considered by many investigators to be those youngsters who earn extraordinarily high I. Q.'s. The demarcating line above the average may be drawn at several places on the distribution surface. All children having I. Q.'s above 125 are designated "gifted" by some investigators; others draw the line of demarcation at I. Q. 130. Terman has referred to children of I. Q. 140 plus as "genius or near-genius." The author of this chapter has studied a relatively small number

[56] These statements of L. S. Hollingworth will be found in her book *Gifted Children.* New York: The Macmillan Company, 1926. Cf. her position in *Children Above 180 I. Q.* Yonkers-on-Hudson, N. Y.: World Book Company, 1942.

[57] L. S. Hollingworth, "Review of Research," *39th Yearbook of the N. S. S. E.,* Part I, p. 62. Quoted by permission of the Society.

[58] L. M. Terman and M. Oden, "The California Gifted Group at the End of Sixteen Years," *39th Yearbook of the N. S. S. E.,* Part I, pp. 83-84. Quoted by permission of the Society.

of children of I. Q. 140 and above during the past fifteen years; his results resemble closely those of Terman, and corroborate his conclusions at many points.[59] The following description of gifted children may be considered fairly representative of the reports of the leading investigators.

Children of I. Q. 140 or above may be found to the extent of four or five in every thousand individuals in the public school. Many more extraordinarily bright boys and girls earn I. Q.'s 130 and higher.

These bright children are superior to their classmates of similar ages in size, strength, muscular control, and general health. Although much overlapping and similarity are found between gifted and unselected children in physical development, *every* careful study shows that the bright child typically is not a physical weakling. The notion that extremely bright children are physically retarded, unsocial, bespectacled, "booky" misfits has been disproved.

Gifted children usually are not one-sided in their development. Their academic records are generally superior. In the elementary school they do their best work on tests of reading and language, and their poorest in handwriting and in spelling. Their superiority in reading is especially noteworthy. Forty-five per cent of Terman's group learned to read before entering school. Terman [60] states regarding one child: "As early as twenty-one months she read and apprehended simple sentences; by twenty-six months her reading vocabulary was more than seven hundred words."

In all his school work, the gifted child succeeds, and typically he is modest and well-adjusted socially. Nevertheless, his general educational growth progresses at a rate such that in the upper elementary school he has knowledge and acquisitions which surpass those of children classified two or three grades above him. Almost every study shows that such gifted children are offered little that is mentally or educationally provocative in the subject matter of their grades.

Beyond doubt, these children possess unusual ability. To make

---

[59] P. A. Witty, "A Study of 100 Gifted Children," *Bulletin* (University of Kansas), Vol. II, No. 7 (1930). Cf. also P. A. Witty, "A Genetic Study of 50 Gifted Children," *39th Yearbook of the N. S. S. E.,* Part I.

Paul Witty and Viola Theman, "A Follow-up Study of Educational Attainment of Gifted Negroes," *The Journal of Educational Psychology,* January, 1943, Vol. XXXIV, No. 1, pp. 35-48.

Paul Witty and Viola Theman, "Case Studies and Genetic Records of Two Gifted Negroes," *The Journal of Psychology,* 1943, Vol. 15, pp. 165-181.

[60] L. M. Terman and B. S. Burks, "Gifted Child," in *Handbook of Child Psychology* (rev. ed., C. Murchison, editor). Worcester, Mass.: Clark University Press, 1933. P. 781.

it possible for this ability to become effective, it will be necessary
for us to alter a number of established school practices. Some of us
must change our standards of attainment and aim to develop a
program diversified in content and rich in opportunities for the
development of self-direction, self-criticism, and continuous reconstruction of experience. Surely schools should be reorganized in
ways such that these essentials for maximum child development
can be provided. Undoubtedly, many of the maladjustments of the
gifted are to be attributed to our attempt to force participation in
child society upon children with adult or very advanced minds. A
boy of ten who said that "flaunt" means "to display or show with
intent to show" and that "Mars" means "God of War; planet; also
a verb" was content to play neither with children of his own
chronological age nor with those of his mental age. Interests separated them. He found, however, a theater group and a book club
in which he could find joyful participation. Much of his preferred
activity was, and still is, solitary. Because children are so complex,
differences between them in interest and in emotional growth, as
well as in ability, are likely to be great. Teachers must learn to
respect individuality and to recognize the fact that an intelligence
rating constitutes only one item in ascertaining the needs of any
child.

The rating on an intelligence test is, however, an important
consideration in identifying a group of children whose capacity to
profit by our academic offerings is indeed great. This fact is established beyond question by these studies of gifted children.[61] For
example, at the time the author carried on a third follow-up study
of one group of gifted children, the majority of the young people
were in college. Almost half of the marks of the boys and 70 per cent
of the girl's marks were "A." Not a single failing mark was received
by a girl; two failures were assigned the boys. The marks of the 30
per cent who had graduated were distinctly above average. There
was no unemployment in the young people who were not in college.

Over 50 per cent of these gifted young people had to earn half
or more of their expenses in order to attend college. One may
logically question whether this is the most profitable manner in
which to spend their time. And in view of their unusual capacity
and potentiality, one may question the character and propriety
of the typical college offering. The answer to the first question is
clear. It would seem a desirable social investment if scholarships
were provided for *all* these bright young people whose educational
attainment and ability make it almost certain that they will gain

---

61 Paul Witty, "A Genetic Study of 50 Gifted Children," *39th Yearbook of the
N. S. S. E.,* Part II. Bloomington, Ill.: Public School Publishing Company, 1940.

measurably from attendance in college. How unfortunate that about 15 per cent of these young people have had to abandon their aspirations to complete college because of economic necessity!

These studies also disclose the need for curricula that will give opportunity for the full expression of the capacities of the most gifted persons enrolled in college. Many data make one doubt that this need is now being met in the American college. Thus, some studies show that the overlapping of educational attainment, objectively measured, is so great that about 20 per cent of the sophomores and 15 per cent of the freshmen reach or exceed the median score of seniors in certain colleges. Reasonably, Terman proposes that we "quit accrediting college courses and credit instead the individual student." [62]

Although the intelligence test does not enable us to identify "geniuses," it is nevertheless helpful when it is employed judiciously. It has made possible the identification of one type of child whose contribution to society might be very great. And it has made us aware of our responsibility as teachers for exploring the wide range of abilities within our groups and for attempting to provide appropriate individual and group experience.

There is a special opportunity for educators to attempt to develop curricula which will be so broadly conceived that every child will be challenged to develop to his maximum. Perhaps this is the goal we should seek in the case of the gifted child, recalling that the most gifted child is not far removed from the child just below him in ability, and that while such children differ in degree of mental ability, they are inextricably related to other children in other ways.

## Intelligence of Other Groups

Intelligence tests have been employed widely with other groups: for example, the delinquent and the physically handicapped. At one time, low intelligence was believed to be a causal factor in delinquency. In several studies of school children, delinquents were found to make lower average scores than "problem" children whose averages on intelligence tests were considerably below the norms. [63]

[62] L. M. Terman, "The Gifted Student and His Academic Environment," *School and Society*, Vol. XLIX (1939), pp. 65-73.

[63] Significant discussion of other factors involved may be found in the following: S. Glueck and E. T. Glueck, *One Thousand Delinquent Boys* (Cambridge, Mass.: Harvard University Press, 1933); C. R. Shaw, *Delinquency Areas: A Study of the Geographic Distribution of School Truants, Juvenile Delinquents, and Adult Offenders in Chicago* (Chicago: University of Chicago Press [Behavior Monographs], 1929); and W. I. Thomas and D. S. Thomas, *Child in America: Behavior Problems and Programs* (New York: Alfred A. Knopf, 1928).

It has been pointed out that these studies do not prove that low intelligence is the cause of delinquency. This fact is clearly shown in several studies in which the average scores of apprehended delinquents were the same as the averages of the boys and girls generally in the communities from which the delinquents came. Again and again, such studies reveal that the community which produces the delinquent is characterized by unfavorable conditions such as excessive poverty, unemployment, inadequate recreational facilities, and meager educational opportunities. All these factors and conditions doubtless contribute to delinquency. In studies of delinquents, as in investigations of other groups, the average intelligence of the group is seldom *the* important consideration. Our concern, then, should be centered in a patient and sincere attempt to understand each child and to provide for him the best possible conditions to insure his sturdy growth and development. Diagnosis of his nature and needs must be comprehensive; in such an appraisal, the intelligence test will be but one of many items, viewed in its proper relationship to the entire picture.

### Aptitude Testing

Recognition of the incompleteness of intelligence test ratings in predicting many types of development led to a search for more reliable instruments to gauge aptitude and proficiency. In a sense, the intelligence test may be thought of as an aptitude test—a measure useful in forecasting, within certain broad limits, a child's success in schoolwork. Here, again, we should point out that such an approach should never be narrowly conceived. In association with data secured from a comprehensive study of each child, the intelligence test is useful. Similarly, in a comprehensive study and appraisal of a child, an aptitude test may yield valuable information.

The widespread interest in this field is indicated by the fact that during the three-year interval 1932 to 1935 the scientific literature contained over two hundred titles on aptitude tests.[64] Since 1935, interest in the measurement of aptitude has continued.

The term *aptitude* is used in two ways—"one as a measure of a special ability (for example, the measurement of visual acuity), and the other as a prognostic measure (for example, the use of a special test to forecast success in an occupation)."[65] Some psychologists stress the second interpretation and distinguish between

---

[64] H. Toops and G. F. Kuder, Chapter III in *Review of Educational Research,* Vol. V, No. 3 (June, 1935).

[65] David Segel, Chapter IV in *Review of Educational Research,* Vol. XI, No. 1 (February, 1941), p. 42.

aptitude and proficiency. According to Hull, "an aptitude test is a test designed to discover what potentiality a given person has for learning some particular vocation or acquiring some particular skill." [66] Thus, a clerical aptitude test may be employed to test a girl who has had no training in this field but who wishes to know whether she possesses the capacity to become a successful clerical worker. A proficiency test, on the other hand, attempts to reveal how skillful a person actually is in a particular type of activity or job regardless of the amount of training he has had or the degree of ability he possesses.

The difference between natural aptitude and acquired ability is much more a matter of theoretical interest than of practical concern, for it is very difficult to estimate the relative influence of the two factors. In general, it may be said that tests labelled "aptitude" tests seek to predict accomplishment in relatively narrow fields such as manual dexterity, mathematical ability, stenographic ability, and so forth.[67]

Among the first aptitude tests were those of C. E. Seashore, who investigated thoroughly the basic abilities required in singing or in playing musical instruments. The Seashore Musical Talent Tests were devised to ascertain the extent or degree to which a group or individual possessed these basic abilities. The most important tests may be given by use of six Victor records arranged in two series: the first, designed for persons who have received considerable instruction in music; the second, for children or adults who have had little or no training. In each series, the following types of tests are found: pitch, loudness, time, timbre, rhythm, and tonal memory.

Although Seashore and his students have experimented extensively with these tests, they have reported correlations which suggest certain limitations of the tests. The tests appear to be most adequate in identifying those extreme cases who will profit little by training in music, as well as in designating students of exceptional promise. Grades of abilities within different groups—especially in the capable group—are less successfully predicted. The tests constitute, however, an important practical achievement in the field of music.

Many studies have been conducted in a search for the special

[66] Clark L. Hull, *Aptitude Testing*. Yonkers, N. Y.: World Book Company, 1928. P. 50.

[67] G. M. Ruch and David Segel, *Minimum Essentials of the Individual Inventory in Guidance,* Vocational Division Bulletin No. 202, U. S. Department of the Interior, Office of Education, 1940.

For further information concerning this test and other aptitude tests mentioned, see the chart of tests at the end of this chapter.

abilities underlying mechanical aptitude. A number of tests have been devised; of these the following are representative: the Stenquist Mechanical Aptitude Tests, the MacQuarrie Test of Mechanical Ability, and the O'Rourke Mechanical Aptitude Tests.

The Minnesota test, which is based on the Stenquist tests, contains: measures of discrimination secured through the use of various paper formboard designs and figures, and tests of spatial relations, interests, assembling, packing blocks, and sorting cards. Other mechanical aptitude tests include measures of finger dexterity, rate of manipulation, and other items. Various studies of the practicality of these tests have yielded somewhat conflicting results; yet, competent students are agreed that knowledge of the basic abilities measured by them constitutes a practical aid in effective counsel and guidance.

Measures of talent have been developed in an effort to select and guide students more effectively in the field of the arts. Among the most widely used of such tests are the McAdory Art Test and the Meier-Seashore Art Judgment Test. These tests examine the student's ability to recognize merit in acknowledged products of art. For example, in the Meier-Seashore test, pictures of 125 pairs of art products are presented; one in each pair is the work of a master. The student is asked to examine each pair of samples and to select the best product. These tests mark simply a beginning in the analysis and study of artistic appreciation. Nevertheless, they represent, with tests of literary appreciation, a beginning in an important area.

For years there has been an effort to develop tests that will predict outstanding success in athletics or sports. The Brace Motor Ability Tests and the Rogers Physical Capacity Tests are examples. In the Rogers tests, a strength index is obtained from measures of grip, and so forth; an athletic index from success in the 100-yard dash, the broad jump, and so forth; and a skill index from ability to throw a baseball, football, or basketball. These tests, like other predictive measures, are of value chiefly in supplementing and extending other types of data that may be assembled in an effort to understand and guide pupils.

Prognosis tests in special subject fields have also been developed. Readiness for reading is one of the abilities most thoroughly investigated. For secondary-school students, instruments such as the Orleans Algebra Prognosis Test and the Symonds Foreign Language Prognosis Test have been constructed to predict success in particular subjects. The relationship of scores on these tests to success in particular fields is sufficiently high to make them of value when they are employed in conjunction with other measures.

In addition to these tests, there are others which aim to predict success in special fields such as medicine, teaching, and engineering. The Moss Medical Aptitude Test is of this character; it appears to have value in decreasing the failures in medical schools when it is used with other measures. Tests in the fields of teaching and selling have proved of very limited value. Comparatively few of these tests appear to have been carefully validated. Before attempting to use an aptitude test, the student should seek to determine what has been reported concerning the validity of the test, the kind of group upon which it has been standardized, the number of cases employed, and so forth. At the present time most of these tests are very rough measures; hence, the student must be cautious in interpreting their results. However, as one item in a complete appraisal of pupil growth, the aptitude test is often revealing. Undoubtedly, the future will bring important extension, development, and refinement of technique in this area. We shall be able then, as in the case of the intelligence test at the present time, to evaluate aptitude tests more adequately.

## Summary Statement

The intelligence testing movement appeared as a conspicuous luminary in 1916. By 1920, it had penetrated far and deeply into American educational practices; and from 1920 to 1930, its influence was. apparent in almost every school system. In many professional publications which made their appearance during the latter period, intelligence testing occupied high rank among topics considered of significance. In these discussions, students of education were advised of three main uses for mental tests: for diagnosis, prognosis, and classification of school children. The intelligence test was treated as an accurate means of predicting a pupil's growth. Accordingly, expectancies in educational accomplishment were set forth both for general academic proficiency and for specific subject mastery as well. Moreover, since it was believed that the intelligence test yielded a measure of inborn ability, test results were employed for classifying pupils into "homogeneous" groups. These and many other practices illustrate the far-reaching results of the movement in education.

During the past ten years, intelligence tests have been subjected to careful study, and experimental data now enable one to appraise them with considerable fairness and impartiality. Today we are aware of the limitations as well as the values of these tests. It is evident that many of the high hopes and claims of mental test enthusiasts have not been fulfilled. For example, we are fully

TABLE

REPRESENTATIVE TESTS OF INTELLIGENCE

(Key to symbols appears

| Name of Test | Age Level | Group (G) or Individual (I) | Time Required for Administering |
|---|---|---|---|
| | | | VERBAL TESTS |
| American Council Psychological Examination | Grades 9-12............. | G | 60″ |
| | College Freshman......... | G | 60″ |
| California Tests of Mental Maturity | Kgtn.-Grade I............ | G | |
| | Grades 1-3.............. | G | 45″ for short forms; |
| | Grades 4-8.............. | G | |
| | Grades 7-10............. | G | 90″ for long forms |
| | H. S., adults............ | G | |
| Carnegie Mental Ability | High School and College... | G | 65″ |
| Henmon-Nelson Tests of Mental Ability | Elem. Exam.: Grades 3-8............. | G | 30″ |
| | H.S. Exam.: 7-12......... | G | 30″ |
| | College Exam.: College.... | G | 30″ |
| The IER Intelligence Scale CAVD | 3 years to adult......... | G and I | No limit |
| International Group Mental Tests | Kindergarten to adult..... | G | 3¼ hrs. |
| Kuhlmann-Anderson Intelligence Tests | Grades 1-12; ages 6-18 yrs... | G or I | 40″-60″ |
| McCall Multi-Mental Scale | Grades 2-8.............. | G | 25″-30″ |
| Minnesota Pre-school Scale | Ages 18 months to 6 years. | I | No limit |
| National Intelligence Test A and B | Grades 3-8.............. | G | 25″-35″ |
| Ohio State U. Psychological Test | College Freshman......... | G | 2 hrs. |

* For more detailed information concerning these and other tests, see the following refer-
The Mental Measurements Yearbook, 1941); C. K. A. Wang, *An Annotated Bibliography of*
** From review by P. R. Farnsworth in *1940 Mental Measurements Yearbook*, O. V. Buros

VII

AND APTITUDE WITH SALIENT DATA*

on page 130.)

| Number of Forms | Types of Scores | Coefficient of Reliability | Publisher | Year of Publication |
|---|---|---|---|---|

OF INTELLIGENCE

| Number of Forms | Types of Scores | Coefficient of Reliability | Publisher | Year of Publication |
|---|---|---|---|---|
| 1 yearly<br>"  " | Point scores, % rank<br>(same) | <br>.95 | ACE<br>" | 1933 on<br>1924 on |
| 1 (three editions)<br>1 (three editions) | Age and grade norms, M.A. and I.Q. | .94<br>.90-.96<br>.95-.97<br>.94<br>.92-.97 | CTB | 1936-39<br>"<br>"<br>" |
| 1 | Point scores, % grade norms | .95 | HMC | 1932 |
| 3<br>3<br>2 | Age, grade norms, % rank, M.A. (same for each) | .88-.94<br>.88-.94<br>.89 | HMC | 1932-36<br>1932-35<br>1932 |
| 1 | Point scores, age, grade norms, % rank | .79-.85 | TCBP | 1927 |
| 2 | Point scores; means, S.D. for various groups | .78-.97 | PUP | 1926 |
| 1, in 9 series, a test for each grade | Age norms, Median M.A., I.Q. | None given | ETB | 1927-1939 |
| 2 | Age, grade, T, Brightness scores, M.A. | .89-.94 | TCBP | 1925 |
| 2 | Point scores, % scores, M.A., I.Q., S.D. | .89 | ETB | 1932 |
| 3 | Age, grade norms; M.A., I.Q., letter ratings | A: .70-.92<br>B: .75-.95 | WBC | 1920 |
| 1 yearly | Norms for college freshmen, centile rank | | OSU | 1924 on |

ences: O. V. Buros, *The 1940 Mental Measurements Yearbook* (Highland Park, New Jersey: *Mental Tests and Scales* (Peiping, China: Catholic U. Press, 1939).
ed.., Highland Park, New Jersey: Mental Measurements Yearbook, 1941.

TABLE

REPRESENTATIVE TESTS OF INTELLIGENCE
(Key to symbols appears

| Name of Test | Age Level | Group (G) or Individual (I) | Time Required for Administering |
|---|---|---|---|
| | | **VERBAL TESTS** | |
| Otis Self-administering Tests of Mental Ability | Intermediate Exam.: Grades 4-9............. | G | 20″-30″ |
| | Higher Examination: H.S. and College........ | G | 35″-40″″ |
| Revised Stanford-Binet Scale (Terman and Merrill) | Ages 2 yrs. and over...... | I | 60″-90″ |
| Terman Group Test of Mental Ability | Grades 7-12.............. | G | 40″ |
| | | **NONVERBAL TESTS** | |
| Army Beta | Adults................... | G | 40″-50″ |
| Arthur Performance Scale | 6 yrs. and over.......... | I | 35″-90″ |
| Detroit First Grade Test | Beginning 1st grade; 5-9 to 7-10 years.......... | G (10-12 maximum) | 20″-30″ |
| Detroit Kindergarten Test | Kindergarten............. | I | 7″-12″ |
| Pintner-Cunningham Primary Mental Test | Kindergarten, Grades 1 and 2......... | G | 15″ |
| Pintner-Paterson Performance Scale | 4 yrs. and over.......... | I | 45″-90″ |
| Porteus Maze Test | 3-14 years, and adult...... | I | 15″-20″ |
| | | **TESTS OF SPEC** | |
| Detroit Mechanical Aptitude Examination, Revised | Jr. and Sr. H.S. (ages 12-20).................... | G | 40″ |
| Luria-Orleans Modern Language Prognosis Test | Grades 7-13; H.S., College.. | G | 85″ |

VII (*Continued*)

AND APTITUDE WITH SALIENT DATA

on page 130.)

| Number of Forms | Types of Scores | Coefficient of Reliability | Publisher | Year of Publication |
|---|---|---|---|---|
| OF INTELLIGENCE (*Continued*) | | | | |
| 4 | Age norms, M.A., and I.Q. | .90-.95 | WBC | 1922, 1928 |
| 4 | (same) | .89-.92 | | " " |
| 2 | M.A. and I.Q. | .90-.98 | HMC | 1937 |
| 2 | Point scores, age and grade norms | .89 | WBC | 1920 |
| OF INTELLIGENCE | | | | |
| 1 | Point scores, % rank, letter ratings | .987 | CHS | 1920 |
| 2 | Point scores, M.A., I.Q. | | CHS | 1925-1930 |
| 1 | Point scores, % scores, M.A., I.Q., letter ratings | More reliable than average teacher's judgment | WBC | 1920, 1921, 1937 |
| 1 | Point scores, age norms | | WBC | 1922 |
| 1 | Point scores, M.A., % rank | .88-.93 | WBC | 1923 |
| 1 | M.A. median, M.A., % rank | .97 | CHS | 1917, 1923 |
| 1 | M.A. | .95 | CHS | 1915, 1916, 1924, 1933 |
| IAL APTITUDE | | | | |
| 2 (1 for girls; 1 for boys) | Age and grade norms for each sex | Girls: .87 Boys: .76 | PSPC | 1928-1939 |
| 1 | No norms | About .75 | WBC | 1928-1930 |

TABLE

REPRESENTATIVE TESTS OF INTELLIGENCE

(Key to symbols appears

| Name of Test | Age Level | Group (G) or Individual (I) | Time Required for Administering |
|---|---|---|---|
| | | | TESTS OF SPECIAL |
| McAdory Art Test | All grades, College, Art School................. | G | 90″ |
| ·MacQuarrie Test for Mechanical Ability | Grades 6-12.............. | G | 30″ |
| Meier-Seashore Art Judgment Test | High School, College...... | G | 45″-50″ |
| Minnesota Mechanical Aptitude Test | Jr. high school to adults... | | |
| Minnesota Mechanical Assembly Test | Jr. H.S. boys; can be used with older groups....... | I (or small group) | About 1 hr. |
| Moss Medical Aptitude Test | Beginning medical students | G | About 1½ hrs. |
| Orleans Algebra Prognosis Test | Grades 7-9 students who have had no algebra..... | G | 90″ |
| Orleans Geometry Prognosis Test | H.S. students who have studied no geometry..... | G | 80″ |
| Revised Minnesota Paper Form Board Test | Jr. high school; can be used with older groups....... | G | About 15″ |
| Seashore Measures of Musical Talent | Grades 5-16, adults....... | G | 60″-80″ |
| Stenquist Mechanical Aptitude Tests | Grade 5 to adult.......... | G | I—45″ II—50″ |
| Turse Shorthand Aptitude Test | High school and up....... | G | 45″-50″ |

VII (*Continued*)

AND APTITUDE WITH SALIENT DATA

on page 130.)

| Number of Forms | Types of Scores | Coefficient of Reliability | Publisher | Year of Publication |
|---|---|---|---|---|
| APTITUDE (*Continued*) | | | | |
| 1 | Age and grade norms | .79-.93 | TCBP | 1929 |
| 1 | Age norms | .90 | PC | 1925 |
| 1 | Percentile rank median scores | "Reliable enough for most purposes"** | BR | 1929-1930 |
| (Battery of tests) | | .81 | MAC | 1930 |
| 1 | Percentile norms for boys, girls, engineering and art students | Jr. H.S. boys: .94 Others: .68-.79 | MAC | 1930 |
| 1 form each year | Percentile norms | .93 | CPS | 1930 on; new form each year |
| 1 | | None given | WBC | 1928-1932 |
| 1 | | None given in Manual | WBC | 1929 |
| 2 | Norms for various ed. groups, engineering school students, and adults | .85-.90 | PC | 1934 |
| 1 (Series A for unselected groups; Series B for musicians— prospective or actual students of music) | Percentile norms | .84-.88 | RCA | 1919-1939 |
| 2 (Tests I, II) | T scores, percentile scores | I: .79 II: .65 | WBC | 1921 |
| 1 | | | WBC | 1937-1940 |

TABLE VII—(*Continued*)

KEY TO SYMBOLS FOR PUBLISHERS

ACE—American Council on Education
744 Jackson Place
Washington, D. C.

BR—Bureau of Research
University of Iowa
Iowa City, Iowa

CHS—C. H. Stoelting Company
424 Homan Avenue
Chicago, Illinois

CPS—Center for Psychological Service
Washington, D. C.

CTB—California Test Bureau
3636 Beverly Boulevard
Los Angeles, California

ETB—Educational Test Bureau
720 Washington Avenue
Minneapolis, Minnesota

HMC—Houghton Mifflin Company
432 Fourth Avenue
New York City

JBL—J. B. Lippincott Company
East Washington Square
Philadelphia, Pennsylvania

MAC—Marietta Apparatus Company
Marietta, Ohio

OSU—Ohio State University Press
Columbus, Ohio

RCA—RCA Manufacturing Company
Camden, New Jersey

PC—Psychological Corporation
522 Fifth Avenue
New York City

PSPC—Public School Publishing Co.
Bloomington, Illinois

PUP—Princeton University Press
Princeton, New Jersey

TCBP—Teachers College Bureau of Publications
Columbia University
New York City

WBC—World Book Company
Yonkers-on-Hudson
New York

aware that a single test is not a reliable measure of the individual's mental ability. In this chapter we have noted some of the hazards in predicting mental growth from test results, and the fallacies and dangers involved in certain educational practices have been cited. In addition, we are now able to see how unwarranted and false were some of our assumptions associated with race or sex differences in intelligence. Moreover, we have seen the limitations of the test scores used independently in predicting special ability or aptitude. Despite these limitations of intelligence and aptitude testing, its use still occupies a significant role in educational work. When test results are considered in connection with other data in arriving at an estimate of a child's nature and needs, they are of undisputed value. Treated in conjunction with developmental data covering physical, emotional, and educational growth, they help us understand children. Hazards in their use are numerous; but, notwithstanding these facts, tests may assist the teacher in arriving at a sound basis for intelligent diagnosis, intelligent counselling, and intelligent guidance of school children.

## QUESTIONS AND EXERCISES FOR DISCUSSION AND STUDY

### A. Meaning of Intelligence Testing

1. Formulate your own definition of intelligence, emphasizing what you consider the most important factors in intelligent behavior.

2. Trace briefly the intelligence testing movement, noting particularly the contributions of the following: Wundt, Galton, Binet, Terman, Thorndike, Pintner and Paterson, Terman and Merrill.

3. Examine as many as possible of the following types of intelligence tests: verbal, nonverbal, group, individual. Be able to describe one of each type, especially the Terman-Merrill revision of the Binet. What are the advantages and disadvantages of each type of test?

4. From your examination of tests and from your reading, what do you think intelligence tests really measure? What factors essential to success do they fail to measure?

5. What are the values and dangers in the use of intelligence tests? Should they be administered and interpreted by school psychologists or by the classroom teacher? Give reasons. Should the I. Q. of children be known by the children themselves; by their teachers; by their parents?

### B. Influence of Heredity and Environment upon Intelligence

1. Why do the following studies fail to prove that heredity has a more important influence upon intelligence than environment?

a. High correlation between increase in blood relationship and increased similarity in intelligence test scores.

b. Frequency of mental superiority, peculiarity, or defect in related stocks, as, for example, in the Kallikak-Jukes-Edwards families.

c. Similarity of test-intelligence of twins.

2. Summarize briefly the findings of the following people concerning the constancy of the I. Q. and the effect of the environment upon intelligence: Bayley, Freeman and Flory, Wellman, R. L. Thorndike, Skodak, and Sherman and Keys.

3. In what ways and to what extent may a child's environment and his physical or emotional condition affect his I. Q.? (Read especially: Rockwell, "Intelligence Testing—Its Basic Assumptions and Unanswered Questions," and Bayley, "The Role of Intelligence.")

4. Formulate what you consider to be a sane tentative conclusion as to the relative influence of heredity and environment upon intelligence.

### C. Distribution and Growth of Intelligence

1. How is intelligence distributed in a typical school population? Observe, if possible, some pupils in the classroom and on the playground, and note the wide range in ability. Check your judgment of the intelligence of a few individuals at the upper and lower limits with intelligence test scores and with the teacher's judgment.

2. Trace briefly the growth of intelligence, indicating the rate of growth at different age levels. Cite examples of children whose mental growth has been irregular.

3. What conditions foster mental growth? What, therefore, is the responsibility of the school in promoting mental development?

### D. Sex and Race Differences in Intelligence

1. Summarize briefly evidence for and against the contention that men are superior to women in intelligence. Give the conclusion you draw from the evidence:

2. Summarize briefly the data presented by the following for and against the contention that the white race is superior in intelligence: Brigham, Pintner, Herskovits, Witty and Jenkins.

3. Why does the prevalence of lower intelligence test scores among Negroes, Indians, and immigrant groups fail to prove that these races are inferior to white groups?

4. Formulate your conclusions as to what your attitude should be toward race superiority.

### E. The Mentally Retarded, the Gifted, and the Delinquent

1. Describe the physical, mental, and emotional characteristics of: the feeble-minded child; the gifted child.

2. What criteria can be used in identifying the feeble-minded; the gifted?

3. Does an extraordinarily high I. Q. signify genius? According to Terman, what factors determine "success" above I. Q. 140?

4. What are the advantages and disadvantages of special classes or schools for: the gifted; the dull; the feeble-minded?

### F. Aptitude and Aptitude Testing

1. What is meant by aptitude? Distinguish between special aptitude and intelligence.

2. If possible, examine a few special aptitude tests. Describe and evaluate two or three.

3. What are the values, limitations, and dangers in the use of tests of special aptitudes?

### SELECTED REFERENCES FOR FURTHER READING AND STUDY

#### A. General Background

Witty, P. A., editor, *Mental Health in the Classroom*, 13th Yearbook, Department of Supervisors and Directors of Instruction, N. E. A., Washington, D. C., 1941.

————, and C. E. Skinner, editors, *Mental Hygiene in Modern Education*. New York: Farrar and Rinehart, 1939.

#### B. Nature and Growth of Intelligence; Intelligence Testing

Bayley, N., "The Role of Intelligence," in *Mental Health in the Classroom*, 13th Yearbook, Department of Supervisors and Directors of Instruction, N. E. A., P. A. Witty, editor, Washington, D. C., 1941, Chapter III.

Buros, O. V., *Mental Measurements Yearbook*, 1938, 1940. Highland Park, New Jersey: The Mental Measurements Yearbook, 1939, 1941.

Pintner, R., *Intelligence Testing*. New York: Henry Holt and Company, 1931.

Rockwell, J. G., "Intelligence Testing: Its Basic Assumptions and Unanswered Questions," *Educational Method*, Vol. XIX (Nov., 1939), pp. 19-31.

Terman, L. M., and M. M. Merrill, *Measuring Intelligence*. Boston: Houghton Mifflin Company, 1937.

Witty, P. A., "Toward a Reconstruction of the Concept of Intelligence," *Educational Method*, Vol. XIX (Nov., 1939), pp. 3-11.

## C. Influence of Heredity and Environment upon Intelligence

Thorndike, R. L., "Constancy of the I. Q.," *Psychological Bulletin*, Vol. XXXVII (March, 1940), pp. 167-186.

Whipple, G. M., "Intelligence: Its Nature and Nurture," *39th Yearbook of the National Society for the Study of Education*, Parts I and II. Bloomington, Ill.: Public School Publishing Company, 1940.

————, "Nature and Nurture, Their Influence upon Intelligence," *27th Yearbook of the National Society for the Study of Education*, Part I. Bloomington, Ill.: Public School Publishing Company, 1928.

Witty, P. A., editor, "Intelligence in a Changing Universe," *Educational Method*, Vol. XIX (Nov., 1939), pp. 1-62.

## D. Sex and Race Differences in Intelligence

Benedict, Ruth, *Race: Science or Politics*. New York: Modern Age Books, 1940.

Wellman, B. L., "Sex Differences," in *Handbook of Child Psychology*, rev. ed., C. Murchison, editor. Worcester, Mass.: Clark University Press, 1933. Chapter XV.

Witty, P. A., "Relative Frequency of Gifted Boys and Girls in the Secondary School," *Educational Administration and Supervision*, Vol. XX, No. 8 (1934), pp. 606-612.

————, and H. C. Lehman, "Racial Differences: The Dogma of Superiority," *Journal of Social Psychology*, Vol. I, No. 3 (1930), pp. 394-418.

## E. The Feeble-Minded and the Dull

Doll, E. A., "I. Q. and Mental Deficiency," *Journal of Consulting Psychology*, Vol. IV, No. 2 (March-April, 1940), pp. 53-61.

Ingram, Christine, *Education of the Slow Learning Child*. Yonkers, N. Y.: World Book Company, 1935.

Martens, Elise, *Introduction to Group Activities for the Mentally Retarded*. Washington, D. C.: Office of Education, U. S. Department of the Interior (Bulletin No. 7), 1933.

————, *Teachers' Problems with Exceptional Children: III. Mentally Retarded Children*. Washington, D. C.: Office of Education, U. S. Department of the Interior (Pamphlet No. 49), 1934.

Pintner, R., "Feebleminded Child," in *Handbook of Child Psychology*, rev. ed., C. Murchison, editor. Worcester, Mass.: Clark University Press, 1933. Chapter XX.

Tredgold, A. F., *Mental Deficiency*, 6th ed. Baltimore: Williams and Wilkins, 1937.

Whipple, G. M., "Intelligence: Its Nature and Nurture," *39th Yearbook of the National Society for the Study of Education*, Parts I and II. Bloomington, Ill.: Public School Publishing Company, 1940.

White House Conference on Child Health and Protection (Section III, Education and Training), Committee on Special Classes, *Handicapped and Gifted*. New York: D. Appleton-Century Company, 1931.

Witty, P. A., and L. P. Thorpe, "Personality Development in the Feebleminded and the Gifted," in *Mental Hygiene in Modern Education*, P. A. Witty and C. E. Skinner, editors. New York: Farrar and Rinehart, 1939. Chapter XIII.

### F. The Gifted Child

Hollingworth, Leta S., *Gifted Children*. New York: The Macmillan Company, 1926.

Terman, L. M., *et al.*, *Genetic Study of Genius*, Vols. I and III. Palo Alto: Stanford University Press, 1925.

————, and B. S. Burks, "The Gifted Child," in *A Handbook of Child Psychology*, rev. ed., C. Murchison, editor. Worcester, Mass.: Clark University Press, 1933. Chapter XIX.

Witty, P. A., "A Study of One Hundred Gifted Children," *University of Kansas Bulletin in Education*, Vol. II, No. 7 (1930).

————, "Evidence Regarding the Nature of Intelligence from the Study of Superior Deviates," *Addresses and Discussions Presenting the Thirty-Ninth Yearbook, Intelligence: Its Nature and Nurture*, N. S. S. E., pp. 23-30. Bloomington, Ill.: Public School Publishing Company, 1940.

————, "Some Considerations in the Education of Gifted Children," *Educational Administration and Supervision*, Vol. XXVI (Oct., 1940), pp. 512-522.

### G. The Delinquent Child

Brown, A., "Conduct Disorders and Delinquency," in *Mental Hygiene in Modern Education*, P. A. Witty and C. E. Skinner, editors. New York: Farrar and Rinehart, 1939. Chapter XVI.

Frank, Lawrence, "Fundamental Needs of the Child," *Mental Hygiene*, Vol. XXII (July, 1938), pp. 353-379.

Healy, W., and A. Bronner, *Delinquents and Criminals: Their Making and Unmaking*. New York: The Macmillan Company, 1926.

Shaw, C. R., and others, *Delinquency Area*. Chicago: University of Chicago Press, 1929.

### H. Aptitude and Aptitude Testing

Bingham, Walter, *Aptitudes and Aptitude Testing*. New York: Harper and Brothers, 1937.

Hull, Clark L., *Aptitude Testing*. Yonkers, N. Y.: World Book Company, 1928.

# CHAPTER 7*

# Individual Differences and School Adjustments

## Individual Differences in Learning

The classroom teacher needs little argument to convince her of the fact of individual differences among pupils. She observes differences as she stands before the class and notices individual characteristics of physical size and personality in pupils of approximately the same chronological age. Some pupils are short, others are tall. Some are frail, others appear strong. Some seem to be happy and light-hearted, others are moody and sad.

Take a cross section of any age group living in your locality and line them up at scratch for any test, measurement, or event designed to reveal innate or acquired abilities. Ask them to run, jump, throw a ball, read, write, compute, appreciate the arts, or memorize. The resulting performance will show a wide range of varying degrees of achievement. In addition to objective achievement levels, what are the feeling reactions of the respective contestants? This feeling response is very important to consider, since it is the emotional component of the personality and may affect performance in many activities.

No two persons—not even identical twins—are so equipped by nature as to develop and react identically to the same situation. It is essential, therefore, to recognize and to make provision for these inevitable individual differences. Such provisions are exemplified in progressive education by vocational guidance and in industry or business by alert personnel management.

## Differences revealed by tests

If a general ability test, such as an intelligence test, were administered to an average class, the intelligence quotients might

---

* For the point of view expressed in this chapter, the author is indebted to *Visual Outline of Educational Psychology,* by Guy T. Buswell (New York: Longmans, Green and Company, 1939).

range from 80 to 130. The largest differences appear among the extremes, but a considerable number of the children will have I. Q.'s approximating 100. The phenomenon of similarity is provided for by group teaching, but wide differences among individuals are not so easily met by ordinary methods and materials. For the teacher, the major problem brought about by individual differences is to make education or the curriculum fit the many needs, interests, and capabilities of the individuals who comprise the group. It is generally agreed that the school should provide opportunities for the full development of the individualities and capabilities of all of the children. In a sense, individual variation among pupils is an asset for the modern teacher.

If one were to take a typical, unselected class of fourth-grade children and measure them on any one of the measurable abilities which the school is supposed to be teaching, one would find that the abilities of a group of thirty-five children range all the way from the average second-grade ability to an ability equal to the average for pupils finishing the eighth grade.

Although these differences in ability have long been recognized, the tendency remains to operate the schools too much as though all pupils were alike and were able to make equally good responses to a given quality of teaching, irrespective of mental capacity, health, aptitude, social background, and interest.

Most teachers are likely to present material on the level of the larger middle group of the class. As a result, many pupils in the best one-fourth of the class are probably working below their capacity to do schoolwork and often becoming bored. Pupils in the least able fourth of the class are struggling along, missing a large part of what they ought to learn, simply because the work is not adapted to their level of comprehension and achievement.

## Range of differences

Chart I presents a graphic representation of the achievement on a battery of tests of pupils in Grade 4B of a school in a large city school system. The ages of pupils in this class range from eight years, four months to thirteen years, five months. The achievement of these pupils ranges from below average achievement for the second grade up to the level of achievement usually found at the middle of the sixth grade. In reading comprehension, the range of individual differences is from second to ninth grade, and in arithmetic computation from third to seventh grade. Similar interpretations may be made for other tests.

The outstanding fact about a chart of the status and achievement of individuals in a class is the range of differences. Of equal importance is the fact that many of the individuals have approximate, or similar, status and achievement. Traditional methods of group teaching have tended to overemphasize the similarities and to ignore the differences. The modern methods of teaching combine group instruction and individual instruction as parts of the educative process. Provision for individual differences means that not all children will be reading the same book at the same time or attempting to master identical factors and skills at the same time.

CHART I

THE RANGE OF SOME INDIVIDUAL DIFFERENCES IN A 4B CLASS

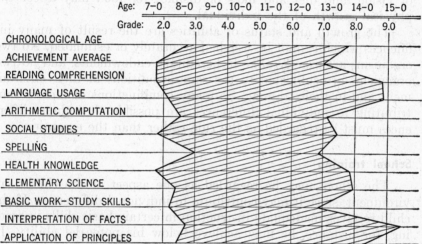

Individual differences and the need for school adjustments are often vividly indicated when a standardized test of intelligence, reading, or arithmetic is administered. It is not unusual to discover that the most capable pupils in a group achieve test scores five or even six grade levels above the least capable pupils. In a fifth-grade class to which an intelligence test was administered, the highest mental age was 14 years and the lowest was 8 years. Some pupils in the fifth grade can read only 50 words per minute, whereas other pupils may read more than 250 words per minute. Some pupils may complete three arithmetic exercises while other pupils are completing one arithmetic exercise of the same difficulty.

## Nature and Causes of Individual Differences

Differences exist in almost any characteristic or trait or ability that might be mentioned. Even identical twins differ in such specific traits as rate of reading, ability to do arithmetic, and the like. These differences may be even more pronounced in the emotional and personal characteristics of the individual.

## Environment and heredity

While many factors contribute to individual differences, individual differences are generally attributed to factors of heredity and environment. A child may inherit defects in vision or in hearing and in certain characteristics of physical stature. Environmental circumstances, such as exposure to a sudden and intense bright light, extreme strain, or an accident, may result in defects of vision, and diet and likes or dislikes for food may affect the physical growth of the individual.

The growth and status of abilities are the result of many influences which cannot be weighed accurately or estimated. No two organisms are exactly alike in hereditary endowments, and no two organisms are subjected to the same conditions in their environment and in their training. So many combinations of factors contributing to individual differences are possible that these differences must be regarded as the rule rather than the exception.

## School training

The school may be regarded as one aspect of the child's environment, since it may contribute to individual differences. If the child receives inadequate instruction in certain basic skills in reading, for instance, he may achieve below his potential ability. In such a case, remedial treatment in reading can help him to master the basic skills and to function at a reading-achievement level commensurate with his ability. The same generalization about remedial treatment applies to any area of learning, such as arithmetic and language, where instruction has been inadequate. The school, however, can do little to remedy or change differences caused by heredity and environment, such as intelligence and physique.

The differences among children occur very early in the life of the child. Gesell [1] and others who have studied infants have found relatively wide differences in the ages at which infants respond to movements and noises. Such investigators have found that some children learn to speak simple words and to walk within the first year of life while other children may not attain these skills until much later.

---

[1] Arnold Gesell and Helen Thompson, *The Psychology of Early Growth.* New York: The Macmillan Company, 1938.

The differences in the mental ability of individuals are often larger than most of us realize until we study these differences. Individuals are often classified into groups according to the degree of mental ability which they possess. One classification, adopted by Terman and often used, is: *genius, very superior, superior, above average, below average, inferior, border-line,* and *feeble-minded.* Children of the genius group find it very easy to make rapid progress through the entire range of the curriculum. Those who are deficient mentally or feeble-minded frequently cannot master any of the usual curriculum in elementary education.

## The Distribution of Individual Differences

An interesting fact about individual differences of any complex characteristic such as academic aptitude or mechanical aptitude is that when an unselected sample from a homogeneous population is measured by application of a standard unit, the measure of such a group of individuals—when fitted into a frequency distribution—tends to approximate the normal probability curve. In other words,

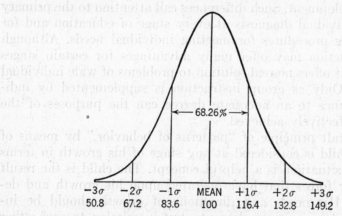

|  | $-3\sigma$ | $-2\sigma$ | $-1\sigma$ | MEAN | $+1\sigma$ | $+2\sigma$ | $+3\sigma$ |
|  | 50.8 | 67.2 | 83.6 | 100 | 116.4 | 132.8 | 149.2 |

**Fig. 2. Frequency of I. Q.'s for the Stanford-Binet Tests of Intelligence, Forms L and M.**

the individual differences as indicated by scores on a mental test are about equally distributed above and below the average score. This can perhaps be best illustrated by a graphic representation of the normal curve.

Practically all tests of mental ability or achievement which are constructed in accordance with the best principles and practices provide for a distribution of scores similar to that indicated by the normal frequency curve. It is interesting to note, however, that in actual practice teachers and administrators are generally much more sensitive to or aware of pupils who are low in ability as compared with pupils who have unusual or high ability. This awareness is reflected in studies of retardation of pupils and in the acceleration and enrichment of pupil programs of study. Such awareness is probably stimulated by the fact that both parents and administrators are disturbed if a pupil fails to meet certain so-called minimum grade standards set up by the school, but are relatively unconcerned with the unusual pupil who achieves these standards.

### The Need for the Study of Individual Differences in Many Characteristics

The principle of individual differences is very important in the guidance of pupils. No two pupils need exactly the same assistance or present to the teacher identical problems of adjustment. In the case of one pupil, for example, home training and other environmental factors may have developed certain skills to a high degree. Another pupil of approximately the same mental ability may be quite deficient in some phase of reading or arithmetic or personality development. Such differences call attention to the primary need for individual diagnosis at every stage of education and for some definite procedures for meeting individual needs. Although group instruction may offer many advantages for certain stages in learning, it offers no real solution to problems of wide individual differences. Only as group instruction is supplemented by individual guidance to an adequate degree can the purposes of the school be effectively achieved.

The Gestalt principle of "patterns of behavior," by means of which the child is considered at any stage of his growth in terms of the total situation, is a helpful concept. The child is the result of the many forces that have operated upon his growth and development. His needs and directions of growth should be interpreted, not as separate elements, but in relation to each other in terms of a continuously changing pattern in which he responds to larger, or total, situations as well as to parts, or elements, of situations.

In the development of a personality, there must be integration in continuity of action. A pupil personality involves a large number of different factors and characteristics. These must be organized, co-ordinated, and integrated so that the individual will function in a consistent way. In normal wholesome development there is integration or good adjustment. Disintegration or maladjustment may result if the child suffers from disease or a vicious environment.

### School Adjustments to Individual Differences

Schools have long recognized the need for organizing pupils into groups for instructional purposes. Many plans have been tried. Often pupils have been grouped together on the basis of mental age and intelligence quotients. Experience has shown that these factors when considered alone are seldom satisfactory. In grouping pupils, the modern concept is that not only chronological age and mental maturity, but also physical maturity, social maturity, and emotional maturity should be considered. One psychologist, Willard Olson, calls the composite of these age and maturity factors *organismic age*. Even with the best schemes of classification of pupils, some plan of individualization of instruction is desirable and necessary.

*Homogeneous grouping.* The children who enter the first grade at the age of six are heterogeneous in ability. A first-grade child with a mental age of five years may be sitting next to a first-grade child with a mental age of eight years. Often, they are given the same assignments and required or expected to do the same work. The grouping of children in classes or schools so that class groups are relatively homogeneous in mental ability has helped to solve this problem. Individualization of instruction has helped even more.

Ability grouping should be a means for bringing about effective instruction for children of all levels of ability. The content of the courses and the methods of instruction should be adapted to learning capacities. In certain of the academic subjects, bright children need less drill and can interpret and see relationships in what they learn more quickly than children who are less bright. They profit from a method permitting them to work independently and to exercise their own initiative and originality. Children of less aptitude need more direct help from the teacher. Frequently they need more drill in academic subject matter. The degree to which teachers will need to adapt their teaching methods depends upon the potential abilities of the pupils in any given class group and the nature of the subjects or curriculum. There are, for example, phases of teaching reading, arithmetic, and language that require more drill and review than are necessary in history or geography. Furthermore, a need may exist for more intensive work in teaching a subject at the beginning than at a later stage of the work.

### Plans for Individualized Instruction

Many experiments have been carried on in which successful procedures have been evolved for the individualization of instruction. These are as important at the high-school level as they are at the elementary-school level. They include such plans as the Dalton Plan, Winnetka Technique, Project Plan, and Contract Plan. Each of these may be described briefly as follows.

## The Dalton Plan

Three fundamental concepts are inherent in the orthodox form of the Dalton Plan. The first is freedom of movement and choice of materials; second is co-operation, or the interaction of group life; and third is economy of forces, or the budgeting of time.[2] According to the Dalton Plan, the school should be organized on the basis of a unit technically known as a "house." A "house" includes a cross section of the entire school enrollment. The second feature of the plan is that the traditional classrooms must be transformed into subject-matter laboratories. In these laboratories, the pupils of all grades work simultaneously on their several tasks, either individually or in groups. As equipment, these laboratories require movable tables, libraries of reference books, filing devices, maps, charts, visual aids, and other apparatus for independent study. The third feature is the abandonment of a fixed schedule of classes. According to Miss Parkhurst, the principle of the budgeting of time is dependent upon this last feature.

Each pupil receives a job book consisting of a set of mimeographed assignments or guide sheets. The unit or contract is for one day's work, which each pupil must plan daily by referring to the bulletin board. During the first fifteen minutes of the morning session, the pupil meets in his "house" with his "house teacher" to plan for the best utilization of his day. The remainder of the morning session is spent in various laboratories, according to the pupil's plan, and this session closes with a conference time when subject-matter specialists meet certain assigned classes. The afternoon session is devoted to scheduled periods of art, music, physical education, and industrial or household arts.

## The Winnetka Plan

At Winnetka, Illinois, the pupil's work on essential skills and knowledges is individualized. In this work, lectures and recitations are abandoned entirely in favor of self-instructive practice exercises and diagnostic tests. The self-instructive practice exercises enable the pupils to attain a definite goal, and the diagnostic tests indicate

[2] Helen Parkhurst, *Education on the Dalton Plan.* New York: E. P. Dutton and Company, 1922.

either that the goal has been attained or that further practice is necessary.[3] The individual pupil works on each goal or unit only until he has mastered it. For each goal to be attained, several series of practice exercises are provided. Diagnostic practice tests are also provided in several equivalent forms for each goal. When a pupil satisfactorily masters one goal, he proceeds to the next; but if he fails to master the goal, the scoring of the test makes self-evident the additional practice that he needs to pass the mastery test.

The materials must be prepared in such a manner that the goals are clear to the pupil, in order that he may so instruct himself as to attain mastery of the goal. If ordinary textbooks are to be used, they must be supplemented with mimeographed assignment sheets, supplementary explanations, and practice materials. These mimeographed instructions are bound into a so-called "assignment booklet."

In their administrative setup, the group and creative activities of the junior high school in Winnetka do not differ from conventional practice as much as the individual instruction technique differs from the usual classroom procedures. The extra-classroom activities and the elective choices in manual arts, fine arts, and music are provided in many conventional secondary schools; however, Winnetka does provide for a high degree of integration and correlation among the various departments of the curriculum.

## The Project Method

Although many teaching procedures have the names of "project" and "problem" attached to them, the real project method suggested by Kilpatrick is seldom found, particularly in the secondary school. Kilpatrick suggests four types of projects.[4] They are: "producer's project," "consumer's project," "problem project," and "drill project." The first type, the producer's project, is to make, to construct, or to produce something. A toy house or a poem may be the thing produced. The consumer's project includes projects in which the purpose is to use, or consume something, or to appreciate the product of others. The problem project is to solve a problem; it may be a simple problem like drawing a doll, or it may be a difficult one like describing how the Greeks lived. The aim of the drill project is to acquire some skill; it may involve adding two and two, recognizing and spelling a word, or finding the standard deviation

[3] C. W. Washburne, "A Program for Individualization," *Twenty-fourth Yearbook, National Society for the Study of Education,* Part II. Bloomington, Ill.: Public School Publishing Company, 1925.

[4] W. H. Kilpatrick, *Foundations of Method.* New York: The Macmillan Company, 1925. Chap. 21.

of a statistical distribution. Even on group projects, individualization of instruction is possible through the division of labor in the planning and execution of group or individual assignments and obligations.

### The Contract Plan

One of the outstanding school systems to sponsor the contract plan is the Scarsdale, New York, public school system. This method, or plan, has for its prime purpose the individualization of instruction. It has appropriated some of the features of both the Dalton and the Winnetka plans. Insofar as the assignments, or contracts, are for a period of a month, and as the curriculum is divided into as many contracts or units as there are school months, the contract plan is similar to the Dalton Plan. It is similar to the Dalton Plan and to the Winnetka Plan in the self-instruction materials, diagnostic tests, and mastery tests, which are called *cumulative power tests*. The Summit, New Jersey, Junior High School has adapted for its use a contract plan modeled on the plan employed in Scarsdale, New York, and on the practices recommended by H. L. Miller.[5]

### The activity program

The modern activity program has been introduced increasingly during recent years into public and private schools. This program permits greater flexibility in adaptations to individual differences than any of the other plans which have been discussed. In the modern activity school, projects on such units as transportation, communication, farming, and the like have taken the place of stereotyped question-and-answer recitations. In this newer educational approach, children participate in planning their activities; they engage in trips and in research and expressional activities.

The core of the usual activity program has these central ideas: first, that children should be treated as individuals; second, children's interests and needs should be considered in shaping the curriculum; third, children should learn by actual participation in many activities; fourth, children should practice democracy and should learn to solve the same kind of problems that they will meet after they finish school. Today, in a typical activity school, children

---

[5] Ralph I. Underhill, "The Scarsdale Plan," *Journal of the National Education Association*, Vol. 18 (March, 1929), pp. 77-78. Ralph I. Underhill, "The Experiences of Scarsdale with Individual Instruction," *New York State Education*, Vol. 18 (March, 1931), pp. 677-678, and H. L. Miller, *Creative Learning and Teaching* (New York: Charles Scribner's Sons, 1927).

treat teachers as friends instead of as masters. In place of fixed desks and seats are chairs and workbenches. In addition to text-books, pupils use newspapers, magazines, and reference books, and take excursions or trips. Instead of studying subjects in separate capsules only, as reading, spelling, and arithmetic, they study them combined into projects.

Thus, having had their interest aroused by pictures and books on aviation which a teacher has brought into their classroom, pupils may decide to study airplanes. They form committees, go to libraries, museums, and airports to find out what the kinds of airplanes are, what they carry, and how trips are arranged. Later they report to their classmates, draw pictures, write and produce plays. In the same way, they study boats, farming, or Washington, D. C. In doing these things, they have been learning to read, write, count, and multiply.

In an activity school, children also spend part of their time dancing, singing, playing musical instruments, and telling stories. Instead of doing calisthenics, they play games. The result of all this is that a modern activity school is noisy, but most pupils are too busy to be mischievous. When one is naughty or sulky, he is sent, not to a busy and distraught principal, but to a mental hygienist, who tries to find out what is wrong.

Because the activity school is not standardized, it makes great demands on its teachers, who, besides being well-trained and having wholesome personalities, must be resourceful and creative. Teachers cannot leave their pupils' progress in reading, writing, and arith-metic to projects and chance, but must provide their charges with concentrated individual drill in those subjects when necessary. Activity-school teachers have also recently given much attention to testing their pupils and evaluating the activity program's results.

The author [6] compared some 500 youngsters, carefully matched in intelligence, family background, caliber of their teachers, and so forth, in matched activity and traditional schools. As has almost every examiner before him, he found that the activity pupils were equal or superior to conventional pupils in reading, spelling, lan-guage, and arithmetic achievement. To test previously unmeasured intangibles, he devised new measures, and he used observation of pupils as well as pencil-and-paper tests. The results were that activity pupils scored higher than those in traditional schools in knowledge of current affairs and of people, honesty, co-operation,

---

[6] J. Wayne Wrightstone, *Appraisal of Newer Elementary School Practices.* New York: Bureau of Publications, Teachers College, Columbia University, 1938.

leadership, ability in creative writing and art, critical thinking, and breadth of interests.

In summary, the usual procedures in an activity program may be roughly described in a series of steps, which are not mutually exclusive and which do not follow any unvarying sequence. The steps are: (1) stimulation or identification of interest; (2) planning in terms of the pupils' questions, problems, and methods of work; (3) investigation and research to obtain facts, regardless of their source or subject-matter allocation; (4) integration of the content into meaningful reports, exhibits, and so forth; (5) culmination and sharing of a solution to the problems or projects; and (6) evaluation or appraisal of the outcomes of the project.

## Adjustments to Varying Needs of Pupils

While there are many adjustments that can be made on a group basis once and for all in a given year for a given grade, many adjustments must be made on an individual basis and perhaps from day to day. No simple formula or device has been discovered or formulated that provides automatic means of discovering or applying needed pupil adjustment. Observation, tests, and judgment establish a point of departure from which adjustment to the needs of individuals may begin after the grosser and more obvious adjustments have been made on a group basis.

There is little flexibility in the programs of many schools. Certain periods of the day are assigned to the hearing of recitations, and fixed time schedules are followed rather closely. In some of the more progressive schools, individual instruction, units of work, or group projects which combine several of the subjects for instructional purposes are used. These require somewhat more flexible schedules than traditional practices. Such flexibility, however, is the exception rather than the rule in the average classroom.

Regardless of the various plans which encourage individualized instruction, the classroom teacher must be fundamentally responsible for making adjustments to the varying needs of the pupils. Such schools as those using the Winnetka, Dalton, Project, and Contract plans do facilitate such adjustments to the varying needs more effectively than schools where the traditional plans of mass instruction are employed. Regardless of the particular plan, however, any teacher can make certain adjustments to individual differences among pupils.

### Adjustments to low ability

Many teachers make adjustments to low ability by several devices. One of these is the assignment of extra drill, for example, in arithmetic skills, in reading, and in work-study skills in the social studies. A second adjustment to low ability is for the teacher to make similar assignments and to set less extensive standards for mastery. Thus, for a low-ability pupil, the teacher might assign in arithmetic more work of a computational sort and rather simple problems in arithmetic reasoning. For high-ability pupils, more complicated assignments with more complex problems in arithmetic reasoning would then be assigned. For the low-ability pupil, the standard of achievement would be less extensive than for the brighter pupil. For some pupils of especially low ability, it is necessary to develop markedly different courses of study or curricula. In these differentiated curricula, special aptitudes and abilities of the pupils are sought and attempts are made to provide as concrete and specific experiences for the pupils as are possible.

### Adjustments for special disability

Contrasted with adjustments to low ability are adjustments made for special disabilities in ordinary schoolwork. The special disabilities may arise because the individual has failed to master a particular skill or concept at a particular time and thus finds himself handicapped in more advanced work. Teachers generally have found that adjustments for these disabilities may be made by providing special attention to the pupil during a study period or a free period or by helping the individual after school. In reading, for example, the pupil may have some difficulties or disabilities in eye movements, vocabulary, or even in temperament that hold up his growth. Such cases call for experimentation and observation in order that the teacher may locate the cause, whether it be in a physical or intellectual skill or in the temperament or environment of the child. In the same class of adjustments may be the correction of deficiencies in school subjects caused by skipping or absence. The usual adjustment is to provide the individual with make-up work that will supply the loss or to give the extra drill in the minimum skills and abilities necessary for further work.

### Adjustments for high ability

Adjustments to unusual proficiency are usually necessary for the so-called bright, or gifted, pupils. The adjustments most frequently applied by good teachers for unusual proficiency are to require a minimum amount of drill or study in the case of able pupils who far exceed the standards set for average pupils, and to enrich the programs of such individuals by adding activities or subjects beyond the regular curriculum, by increasing the number and variety of applications of principles involved, and by adding advanced materials or problems in the ordinary subjects.

## Adjustments for health

Adjustments to health and physical defects may be made by giving special attention and supervision to pupils where it may be desirable to have frequent medical inspection, and to maintain close co-ordination with parents and clinical agencies in the community. For certain health and physical defects, classroom adjustments may be made, such as; seating in the front of the classroom for the hard of hearing and for those whose eyesight is poor. Special lighting may be provided for the partially sighted pupils. Rest periods for the undernourished and part-time schedules for pupils whose vitality is low are other adjustments that might be made.

## Social adjustments

Very often social adjustments are desirable and necessary. For some pupils, adjustments for social growth may be made by assigning activities that will correct deficiencies in the home training or in social background, such as training in cleanliness, neatness, respect for others, and etiquette. For some pupils, assignment to activities in the classroom, such as special duties or monitorial service, may help to develop social characteristics. Some pupils it may be necessary to transfer to a new environment in the same school or in another school in order to provide for individual differences in social adjustment.

## Role of the principal

In one elementary school, the principal provides a remedial teacher who specializes in diagnostic and remedial work for children who show low achievement for their grade in reading and arithmetic. This teacher is made available from the regular allotment of teachers assigned to the school by distributing among the other teachers the pupils who would normally be assigned to her. Another teacher's schedule was arranged to permit her to conduct a testing program. Some problem cases were referred to the Bureau of Child Guidance. Lacking adequate cumulative records, the principal and a committee of teachers designed a record card and formulated a case record for case studies made by teachers of those pupils in each class who showed inferior or superior achievement in certain fields.

The principal, also, has a health program in which the school nurse, teachers, and home co-operate in order to remedy defects in vision, adenoids, tonsils, and teeth. Several of the free clinics in the city also co-operate.

### Role of the teacher

The administrative devices, such as the ones which have been discussed, exist to assist a teacher in adjusting the work to the needs of the individual or the group. The role of the teacher in adjustment activities is very important. The other machinery of adjustment is ineffective to the extent that the teacher does not make use of it and co-ordinate it with her own classroom instruction. She must act as the guide and counselor of the pupil for whose benefit the adjustment is planned. Other agencies should function primarily through the teacher or with her knowledge and approval. The concept of adjustment rests upon the assumption that every teacher will have a rather complete, intimate, and sympathetic knowledge of each pupil.

### A Case of School Adjustment to Low Ability and Overageness

The case of an overage boy with low-average achievement in school subjects and related skills is illustrated by Chart II. He has an I. Q. of approximately 85. This pupil achieves a rating on tests in reading, arithmetic, and spelling at about third-grade level.

CHART II

AN OVERAGE BOY WITH LOW-AVERAGE ACHIEVEMENT IN A
FOURTH-GRADE CLASS

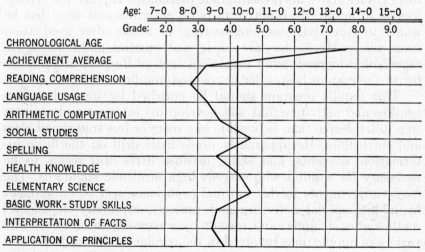

Language and health knowledge are also low. On the other hand, the pupil achieves between fourth- and fifth-grade levels in social studies, health knowledge, and elementary science. His achievement is low in basic work-study skills and such aspects of reflective thinking as interpretation of facts and application of principles. He is reported to have no physical defects. He wishes to go to a vocational high school and to become a radio repairman.

This boy is three and one-half years overage for a normal 4B class. His abilities are decidedly nonacademic, and his interests tend toward mechanical activities. Remedial measures might be of slight help in raising his achievement in academic subjects and skills. His achievement in social studies and elementary science indicate that the teacher might use these subjects to develop further proficiency in reading, arithmetic, and language. More fundamental adaptations of curriculum are required. This boy should be placed in a special group in a junior or a vocational high school, where his program could be adapted to his interests and capacities in mechanical training. It is more important from the points of view of civic efficiency and personal adjustment that the boy be well adjusted to his social group and situation, and that he develop such interests and capacities as will allow him to become a self-supporting citizen, than that he kept in a traditional academic class with academic subject matter.

## A Case of School Adjustment to High Ability

The boy for whom data are presented in Chart III is of unusually high intelligence. In his achievement average, he is two or more grades above his present grade placement. He receives private lessons in music. He is active in pupil activities and says that he wants to enter business, engineering, or music after graduation from college. His hobbies are music, mathematics, and reading. He reports that he reads adult magazines such as *Harper's* and a number of the current best-seller fiction and non-fiction books.

This pupil's program should be enriched by unusual opportunities and activities that will develop his interests and abilities to a fuller degree than is possible in a more or less traditional class and curriculum. He apparently needs little drill on the basic information, concepts, and skills, because little drill seems to be necessary for a pupil who exceeds high academic standards. The major adjustments for his unusual proficiency will be enrichment by adding special activities and projects, especially in science, mathematics, reading, and music; by increasing the number and variety of applications involved in the regular school subjects; and

CHART III

AN UNDERAGE BOY WITH HIGH-AVERAGE ACHIEVEMENT IN A
SEVENTH-GRADE CLASS

| | Age: | 7-0 | 8-0 | 9-0 | 10-0 | 11-0 | 12-0 | 13-0 | 14-0 | 15-0 |
|---|---|---|---|---|---|---|---|---|---|---|
| | Grade: | 2.0 | 3.0 | 4.0 | 5.0 | 6.0 | 7.0 | 8.0 | 9.0 | |
| CHRONOLOGICAL AGE | | | | | | | | | | |
| ACHIEVEMENT AVERAGE | | | | | | | | | | |
| READING COMPREHENSION | | | | | | | | | | |
| LANGUAGE USAGE | | | | | | | | | | |
| ARITHMETIC COMPUTATION | | | | | | | | | | |
| SOCIAL STUDIES | | | | | | | | | | |
| SPELLING | | | | | | | | | | |
| HEALTH KNOWLEDGE | | | | | | | | | | |
| ELEMENTARY SCIENCE | | | | | | | | | | |
| BASIC WORK—STUDY SKILLS | | | | | | | | | | |
| INTERPRETATION OF FACTS | | | | | | | | | | |
| APPLICATION OF PRINCIPLES | | | | | | | | | | |

by encouraging special reports or projects that stress independent
work and study.

## Adjustments by Special Agencies

In larger communities, child guidance clinics have been formed.
The personnel of the clinic normally includes a full-time or part-
time psychiatrist, a physician who is usually a specialist in mental
and nervous maladjustments of children, an educational psychologist, and psychiatric social workers or visiting teachers. Children
are referred to the clinic by teachers for examination, diagnosis,
and prognosis. The clinic personnel recommends treatments and in
many cases assists in the actual treatment of the individual.

In other communities, usually smaller ones, a school counselor
is employed. The school counselor, a qualified psychologist with
educational training, acts as diagnostician for maladjusted children
who show symptoms of scholastic deficiencies, behavior abnormalities, and emotional disturbances. In some instances, the work of
the counselor is limited to diagnosis and prescription, the corrective
treatment being applied by the classroom teachers. In other instances, the counselor undertakes the remedial instruction of some
of the more difficult cases.

Some communities, although they are rare, employ only a visiting teacher or psychiatric social worker. The visiting teacher's
services are devoted principally to the treatment of children who

present problems of scholarship or conduct of a baffling, erratic, troublesome nature, or who exhibit other personal and social maladjustments which the regular staff of the school finds itself unable to understand or to deal with unaided.

## Summary

Individual differences in learning are apparent even to the casual observer. The varieties of needs and differences are almost infinite, whether in physical size, in personal and social adaptability, in temperament, or in achievement in academic skills and abilities. Wide ranges of differences exist in every class, despite attempts at homogeneous or ability grouping.

The nature and causes of individual difference are many and varied. Some of the causes which are considered most influential are heredity, physical environment, sex, race, culture or "social climate," health, temperament, and previous educational experiences.

Various plans have been evolved for making school adjustments to individual differences. These include the Dalton Plan, the Winnetka Plan, the Project Plan, the Contract Plan. In addition to these, various guides have been formulated from the experiences of teachers with adjustments to low ability, adjustments for special disabilities or for deficiencies in school subjects, adjustment to unusual proficiency or high ability, adjustment to health and physical defects, and adjustment for personal social adaptability.

The school is increasingly accepting responsibility for "fitting" its program to the different needs of individual pupils. This it does in several ways, each of which has an important place in a modern school system.

Activities in a classroom provide a fertile field for diversified levels and kinds of achievement for individual pupils. In a unit of study planned for the class as a whole, each pupil may proceed at his own rate of progress in academic learning; he may find expression for his interests in creative design; he may take part wholeheartedly with the rest of the group in social activities. Every progressive elementary or secondary teacher can today make of his classroom a workshop in which individual interests and abilities are given free play.

Special reading disabilities, for example, require specialized methods of teaching, and reading clinics have been set up to afford these. Personality difficulties and behavior problems, also, may need to be diagnosed and treated by persons who know the intricacies and interrelationships of human conduct. Child guidance clinics offer service in this direction.

Since functional relationships exist among the concomitant

factors of educational, personal, social, and other relationships, integration of personality depends first upon the discovery of the multiple causes of tension, or maladjustment, for the individual. The discovery and diagnosis of difficulties in intellectual and academic factors are aided materially by valid and reliable tests and measures.

Records and reports play an increasingly important role in adjustment. Without records and reports, guidance tends to become haphazard to the degree that the counselor forgets, lacks, or ignores relevant data about the individual and his history, or fails to have available successive portraits of changes in his growth. Besides this function, records and reports must grow from the philosophy and the purposes of the school, so that they reflect valid and reliable periodic evidence of the growth and development of each pupil in the avowed objectives of the school. Tests, records, and reports thus become a means to the teacher, first, for guiding the individual to integrate his personality; and, second, for adjusting school and related environmental factors in such a way as to facilitate integration and desirable growth in personality.

Every child should learn to be a good citizen and to grow in those characteristics that are considered a mark of good citizenship, but each in his individual ways and at his own rates of growth. Every child should learn to read, write, and figure sufficiently well to get along in his individual way of life. Every child should learn to make a living as well as to enjoy a living. Every child should function physically, socially, and spiritually in his most effective individual way.

## QUESTIONS AND EXERCISES FOR DISCUSSION AND STUDY

1. In what subjects will students of high mental ability have a greater chance of success than students with low mental ability?

2. Explain why some students who obtain high marks in elementary school turn out to be only average or poor in high-school work.

3. What courses would you recommend for a student with high I. Q. who wishes to enter an engineering college?

4. Formulate a plan that you consider would provide an adequate system of guidance for a high-school student.

5. Indicate reasons for favoring or not favoring classification of pupils on the basis of I. Q.

6. Would you recommend that, if a pupil is very good in several subjects, he should spend all of his extra time on subjects in which he is poor?

7. Are individual differences in pupils generally increased or decreased by the training which they receive in schools: (a) in perceptual-motor skills? (b) in complex intellectual tasks?

8. Can an unusually poor environment lower the I. Q. of a child of good mentality, or can an unusually rich environment make a normal child out of a mental defective?

9. Are there essential physical, emotional, and mental differences between bright, average, and dull children?

10. If an individual is superior in one trait or in practicing a given ability, is he likely to be superior in others?

11. Are differences within an individual among his various abilities significantly large?

12. What are the major differences in learning among bright and dull children?

13. What are the values of such adjustments as one might find in the Dalton, Winnetka, or Project plan?

14. Should a boy who is socially 14 years old but who has a mental age of about 10 years be retarded in the fifth grade rather than promoted to junior high school?

15. Should a child who is physically 10 years old but who has a mental age of 14 years skip several grades in school?

## SELECTED REFERENCES FOR FURTHER READING AND STUDY

Bain, Winifred E., *Parents Look at Modern Education.* New York: D. Appleton-Century Company, 1938. (Chapters II-IV show how children differ at various age levels.)

Baker, Harry J., *Characteristic Differences in Bright and Dull Pupils.* Bloomington, Illinois: Public School Publishing Company, 1927.

Barthelmess, Harriet M., and Philip A. Boyer, "An Evaluation of Ability Grouping," *Journal of Educational Research,* Vol. 26, pp. 284-294, 1932.

Burnham, W. H., "Success and Failure as Conditions of Mental Health," *Mental Hygiene,* Vol. 3, pp. 387-397, 1919.

Courtis, S. A., "Maturation as a Factor in Diagnosis," *Thirty-Fourth Yearbook of the National Society for the Study of Education,* Chapter X, pp. 169-187. Bloomington, Illinois: Public School Publishing Company, 1935.

Freeman, Frank S., *Individual Differences.* New York: Henry Holt and Company, 1934. (Especially Chapters IX and X.)

Gilliland, A. R., and E. L. Clark, *Psychology of Individual Differences.* New York: Prentice-Hall, Inc., 1940.

Jennings, H. S., *The Biological Basis of Human Nature.* New York: W. W. Norton and Company, 1930.

Martens, Elise H., *Parents' Problems with Exceptional Children.* Washington, D. C.: U. S. Government Printing Office, 1932. (Office of Education Bulletin, 1932, No. 14.)

Miller, W. S., "The Classification of 6A Pupils into Ability Groups," *Proceedings of Minnesota Society for the Study of Education,* 1924.

Parkhurst, Helen H., *Education on the Dalton Plan.* New York: E. P. Dutton and Company, 1922.

Pintner, Rudolph, *Intelligence Testing.* New York: Henry Holt and Company, 1931.

Reed, H. B., *The Influence of Training on Changes in Variability in Achieve-*

ment. *Psychology Monographs*, Vol. 41, No. 185. Princeton, N. J.: Psychological Review Company, 1931.

Turney, A. H., "Status of Ability Grouping," *Educational Administration and Supervision*, Vol. 17, pp. 21-42, 110-127, 1931.

Whipple, Guy M., ed., "Adapting the Schools to Individual Differences," *Twenty-Fourth Yearbook of the National Society for the Study of Education*, Part II. Bloomington, Ill.: Public School Publishing Company, 1925.

Woodrow, H., *Brightness and Dullness in Children*. Philadelphia: J. B. Lippincott Company, 1919.

INDIVIDUAL DIFFERENCES AND ADJUSTMENTS 155

annet, Psychology Monographs, Vol. 41, No. 185. Princeton, N.J.: Psycho...

Williams, Guy Mar...... Adapting the Schools to Individual Differences. Twenty...

Part II. Bloomington, Ill.: Public School Publishing Company, 1925.

Woodhour, H., Brightness ..........  Philadelphia: J. B. Lippin-

cott Company, 1919.

# Part IV

# THE LEARNING PROCESS AND EVALUATION OF LEARNING OUTCOMES

## CHAPTER 8

# General Aspects of Learning

### The nature and definition of learning

The interest of the educational psychologist in learning centers around the conditions under which learning takes place most easily and most rapidly. The attention at present concentrated on remedial education indicates that we are still far from having complete knowledge of the optimum conditions of learning under many circumstances; otherwise, it would not be necessary to devote so much energy to elaborate programs of re-doing what has been done before.

Countless definitions of learning have been given. The tendency of modern psychologists is to try to define learning in objective, experimental terms. The following definition epitomizes points of emphasis in many of these definitions: *Learning is a process of progressive behavior adaptation.*

### The dynamics of learning [1]

Common sense makes a distinction between purposive and non-purposive behavior—between the aimless and diffuse expenditure of energy and the calculated carrying out of a planned and projected program of action. But it is difficult to maintain this distinction in the light of exact logic, or to substantiate it by detailed experimentation on behavior. For example, the cat which is confined within the puzzle box, and which, being hungry, can smell the food outside that it will get if it releases itself, has, as we say, a *motive* for getting out of the box. But much of the behavior that ensues, in the light of this supposedly clear want, is trial and error, and if viewed without knowledge of the entire situation, is apparently purposeless.

*Goal-seeking,* or some ultimate purpose in behavior, is one of the

---

[1] Also see Chapter 9.

outstanding dynamic factors in learning. Kilpatrick, for example, regards purposeful activity as the essential basis of intellectual life and as the foundation of intelligent learning. (See the articles in the *Journal of the National Education Association,* Volume 24, Number 9, December, 1935.) As has just been said, however, it is difficult to divide all behavior into purposive and non-purposive by any set of criteria yet devised.

Countless puzzling phenomena in the animal world further complicate the formation of a decisive judgment on the exact nature of purpose. Nobody really knows whether the insect which lays its eggs in only one type of environment and which seeks that environment with considerable accuracy, has even a vague notion of what we call "goal-seeking" in a human being. Thus, if we attempt to differentiate purpose in human beings and other animals, we must do so on some basis other than the merely utilitarian nature of behavior. Even in the case of human beings, the demonstration of purpose depends upon the introspective report of the behaving organism rather than upon the classification of the behavior itself.

One way of looking at purpose as a dynamic factor of learning is to regard it as the incipient or partially completed portion of an imminent behavior cycle. Viewed in this fashion, the difference between the purposive portion of an act and the remainder of the same act is largely chronological.

*Mind* is another dynamic factor. There are also many ways of considering the mind. Some regard it as a reservoir of convertible energy in a conative (action) state of being. A simpler way of saying the same thing would be to call it a powerful force trying to move in some direction of lowered resistance or emergent attraction.

An even less tangible definition of mind can be given in terms of metaphysics. Such a definition would imply that the mind is qualitatively different from the body in its basic and elementary construction. Many of the philosophical physicists of the ancient world, such as Democritus, lacking the mass of experimentation which is now at our disposal, were inclined to view the mind in this way.

A third, and somewhat more objective, method of describing mind as a dynamic factor of learning is to treat it as a form of behavior, particularly behavior that is progressively effective, altering, and alterable. Guthrie [2] so defines mind in his *Psychology of Learning.*

There does appear to be a powerful energizing force behind

[2] E. R. Guthrie, *The Psychology of Learning.* New York: Harper and Brothers, 1935. P. 4.

behavior. The log lying on the hillside, rotting under the influence of the sun and rain, is changing its appearance, structure, and position, but we do not say that it is learning. Neither do we say that the log has a mind or that the changes being produced in it are the result of some mental operation. Rather, we reserve the description of behavior governed by mental processes for that which is an active adjustment to changing external circumstances. Even so, some mechanists are not willing to recognize any difference between this type of mental behavior and the physical alterations taking place in the log lying on the hillside.

*Drive,* or emotional reinforcement, is a third and final dynamic factor in learning. As has been pointed out in another discussion, there is evidence for believing that human beings possess strong inclinations toward certain types of behavior. These tendencies, as described by Thorndike, have been listed and described. Such basic wants and desires provide the primary motivation for the beginning of complicated behavior cycles. As these cycles develop, they are progressively reinforced by individualized habits grounded in glandular and physiological reaction.

The emotional reinforcement of behavior, viewed purely from the external side, is rather easily understood. But it is given far too little attention by both parents and teachers. Emotional responses become associated with a variety of situations in exactly the same way that other responses become so associated. Conditioned emotional responses are common, and constitute the only basis upon which we can hope to build a program of motivating school subjects.

### The mechanism and process of learning

We may begin our discussion of the mechanism of learning with a consideration of the so-called "reaction hypothesis." Simply stated, the reaction hypothesis holds that there is no reaction without stimulation. This is not a reciprocal statement, however, and there may be stimulation without reaction under a variety of circumstances. According to the reaction hypothesis, it is impossible to have purely spontaneous conduct. It is to be noted that the exciting stimulus may be internal as well as external. Thus, we see that all learning begins with an excitatory situation.

What happens when the organism is stimulated? Theoretically, it would be possible for stimulation to produce a generalized response of unco-ordinated and undifferentiated nature and with few regulatory characteristics. As a matter of fact, this is what does happen in some diseased conditions of the nervous system and certain abnormal mental states. Ordinarily, however, the reaction which the organism gives to adequate stimulation is relatively co-ordinated, integrated, and differentiated.

The outstanding characteristic of the systematic nature of response is the feature of *association*. This is the process by which events contiguous in time or space tend to recall each other. The phenomenon has long been known to analytical observers of human conduct. "Once bitten, twice shy," "the burnt child dreads the fire," and numerous similar maxims illustrate man's recognition of this basic process in learning.

Although association has been recognized as a process for hundreds of years, the exact mechanism by which it takes place has not been and still is not surely known. Early psycho-philosophers believed that the association was between ideas, and that the mechanism was some undefined metaphysical affinity. Even today, with our substantial knowledge of neurology and physiology, the exact working of this interesting occurrence is partially conjectural.

It must not be supposed that the associative is the only kind of learning, but it appears to be the predominating one in the case of certain school subjects—a fact that accounts for the emphasis given to this type of learning in the present chapter.

Association probably takes place by a process known as conditioning. Guthrie[3] has described conditioning as follows: *"A combination of stimuli which has accompanied a movement will on its recurrence tend to be followed by that movement."*

The phenomenon of conditioning is a fundamental mechanism of adjustment and one of the basic principles upon which learning depends. As has been said, just how or why it happens is something that is still clouded in mystery. In the past it has been believed that reacting mechanisms responding to stimuli (so-called "unconditioned" stimuli) which naturally excite them have a tendency to draw into their neural channel by some sort of attraction "casual" incoming impulses. This theory, known as the "theory of drainage," held that such an attraction resulted in lowered resistance along the pathway followed, thus making it easier for the same path to be followed on future excitation of approximately the same combination of sense organs. Plausible as this theory may sound to those who are not highly trained in the neural phases of learning, it has been severely questioned by both experimental and theoretical psychologists.

Thorndike, although admitting the phenomenon of conditioning, feels that it is relatively specialized and not to be regarded as

[3] E. R. Guthrie, *The Psychology of Learning*, p. 26. Reprinted by permission of Harper and Brothers.

a formula for the explanation of all learning. The following quotation states this point of view.[4]

It has been assumed by many in a rather vague way that there is some connection between the discussion of associative shifting as given by Thorndike in his own classic treatise and the conditioned reflex, but the exact nature and extent of this relationship has never been made entirely clear, particularly with an experimental basis. It happens that Thorndike has interested himself in the problem and put forth a discussion which attempts to settle the issue. In general, his conclusions may be summarized as follows:

1. The conditioned reflex, while adequately demonstrated experimentally, is a special, if not an unnatural form of learning in which the variables are controlled to a far greater extent than in everyday life, and, consequently, the learning is modified accordingly, being of a special variety.

2. The phenomenon of the conditioned reflex is not the general pattern for learning but exhibits certain peculiar features of its own which are not generally characteristic of learning. For example, in associative shifting of the usual sort reward of a satisfying sort plays a considerable part. This is not true in the formation of the conditioned reflex.

3. In associative shift the change is likely to take place somewhat gradually. In fact, it must be gradual in some cases. This is not true in the case of the conditioned reflex where the change is of the all-or-none variety and occurs comparatively rapidly.

4. Ordinary associative connections diminish in strength (forgetting) with the passage of time. The reverse is the case of the conditioned reflex, since the phenomenon of temporary extinction passes away with time and conditioning again begins to function.

5. The chronological position of the conditioned stimulus is of more importance in the case of the conditioned reflex than in the case of the ordinary associative shift.

A number of principles of conditioning have been so well established, however, as to make it worth while to call them to the student's attention.[5] No better statement of these principles in summary form has been given than that by Guthrie, which is herewith reproduced.[6]

---

[4] Francis F. Powers and Willis L. Uhl, *Psychological Principles of Education*. New York: D. Appleton-Century Company, 1933. Pp. 390-391.

[5] The higher thought processes (for example, Spearman's "eduction of relations" and "eduction of correlates") go so far beyond simple conditioning that it is difficult or impossible to explain the higher thought processes on the basis of conditioning. See C. Spearman's *The Nature of Intelligence and the Principles of Cognition* (New York: The Macmillan Company, 1923) and *The Creative Mind* (New York: D. Appleton-Century Company, 1931). In spite of the cogent objections of Thorndike to regarding the conditioned response as a basic explanation of all learning, and the splendid work of Spearman in elucidating the higher mental processes, the work on the conditioned response offers some of the most exact experimental work ever done in the field of the mechanics of human behavior.

[6] E. R. Guthrie, *The Psychology of Learning*, pp. 33-36. Reprinted by permission of Harper and Brothers.

1. The simple conditioned reflex is most readily established when the substitute stimulus is given shortly before the original stimulus (the stimulus used in the laboratory to elicit the reflex to begin with).

2. Simultaneous and backward conditioning are possible, but less effective than forward conditioning.

3. A substitute stimulus which has, to use Pavlov's language, been conditioned to a response loses this effect when it is repeatedly given without reinforcement from the original stimulus. This Pavlov calls *temporary extinction*.

4. This loss of effect can proceed farther than the zero point, and the "extinguished" stimulus will have an inhibiting effect on the response.

5. Temporary extinction may disappear after a period of rest, or after disturbance from a new irrelevant stimulus.

6. When extinction is carried out repeatedly, recovery is progressively diminished, until it fails to take place.

7. Having conditioned $S_1$ to a response, $S_2$ may be conditioned by being presented with $S_1$, $S_3$ by being presented with $S_2$, and so on. In my opinion this is not an important generalization, since the essential condition of associative learning is the association of the new stimulus *with the response, not with the original stimulus.*

8. A response involving wide-spread bodily action is more readily conditioned than a response confined to a few local effectors.

9. There seems to be evidence that among children conditioned responses are formed more readily as age advances, and more readily in the more intelligent.

10. One attempt to form a conditioned response during sleep has been failure. Conditioning failed in another experiment by Harlow and Stagner (1933) when skeletal muscles were paralyzed by curare, though smooth muscle reflexes were conditioned at the same time. An active response, in other words, is the essential of conditioning, not merely the association of the stimuli.

11. The certainty of conditioning seems to depend on the number of pairings of substitute stimulus and response.

12. Negative or inhibitory conditioning is possible, achieved by presenting a stimulus and not insuring the response, or by distracting the response, or by inhibiting the response, or by presenting the substitute stimulus after the original stimulus. The signal has a positive inhibiting effect on the response. In many cases such inhibition is clearly accompanied by conflicting responses.

13. Retention of conditioned responses over a period of years has been reported.

14. A conditioned inhibiting stimulus has an after-effect which may last as long as fifteen minutes. Such after-effects are in some cases additive.

15. When a substitute stimulus has been conditioned, other stimuli to the same class of sense organs may be found to elicit the response. This is called *generalization*.

16. If the substitute stimulus is presented some time before the original stimulus, this delay interval finally characterizes the conditioned response.

17. Similar stimuli (as two tones of about the same frequency) may be discriminated by following one but not the other with the response.

18. A point of resemblance can be reached at which this discrimination will fail and previous conditioning will be lost and a general disturbance of behavior appear.

19. The same disturbances in behavior can be produced by delaying the original stimulus in practice.

20. A stimulus acting separately and the same stimulus acting as an element of a pattern may have radically different effects; the combination may act as a conditioner and the element as an inhibitor; or the element may act as a conditioner and the combination as indifferent. When we refer to a "stimulus" we must ordinarily mean a combination of stimuli in which the pattern is essential. Humphrey . . . conditioned a response to a tone and found that when the tone was made part of a melodic phrase the conditioning effect was absent. Josiah Royce illustrated this point many years ago by pointing out that a man's response if we step on his foot and then apologize will be quite different from the response we elicit if we apologize and then step on his foot.

## Types of learning: the products

We have considered learning as a process and some of the mechanisms by which it takes place. We now come to a consideration of the learning products which may result from learning activity. These products are: (1) skills and habits, (2) social competence, and (3) abstract and creative thinking. We shall consider each separately. While we have definite rules for the achievement of each of these learning products, accomplishments are so varied that some psychologists have held that there are three general kinds of intelligence—the mechanical, the social, and the abstract.

1. *Skills and habits.* All of us have noted at one time or another the difference between the poised and well co-ordinated adult and the awkwardly clumsy adolescent. The difference lies primarily in the skill with which adults automatically handle themselves; this skill, in turn, results from faithful adherence to training habits. But there are clumsy adults as well as skillful ones. It is possible to ingrain habits of awkwardness and slovenly posture and to make more difficult the task of acquiring co-ordination and balance.

The development of skill calls for a correct initial performance. The difficulty with most amateur typists is that they have tried to develop a technique of their own instead of taking some lessons at the beginning. Correct initial technique and practice are the simple formula by which skilled activities reach a high level. This view is borne out not only by experimentation but by observation of outstanding athletic performance.

With respect to artistic skill, creative skill, and talent, individual differences in learning and accomplishment may be explained by the statement that probably people differ in the basic ingredients which go to produce skilled acts. Artistic accomplishment is really skill, plus imagination, plus practice.

2. *Social competence.* Social competence is probably the most practical single learning product. The egocentric nature of childhood makes it necessary that the child learn many, if not the greater part, of the things that make up what we call "social adjustment." As in the case of individual differences in mechanical aptitude, people may differ somewhat in general sociability. But the most glaring ineptitudes in social adjustment appear to be caused not by any natural lack of sociability, but rather by failure to grasp and practice the behavior necessary to secure this adjustment.

The acquisition of social competence is dependent upon the advanced development of the psychological factors of observation and attention and the direction of these faculties to the minutiae of human conduct. Biologists would be loath to admit that human emotions are much less violent than they were thousands of years ago. There has been a vast change, however, in the responses of people to emotionalized behavior on the part of others. Yet all emphatic and widespread reactions carry with them concomitants that are obvious to the practiced eye. No small part of social adjustment consists in the ability to recognize these cues and to react to them skillfully.

3. *Abstract thinking.* Psychologists have always met with difficulty in their efforts to define the essential nature of abstract thinking, which presents many problems to one who attempts to subject it to experimentation. These difficulties are reflected in the efforts of teachers to develop in pupils the ability to do abstract and creative thinking. The philosophical concept of universals is involved—*chairness* as against an individual chair—and along with it the doctrine of ·psychological emergence. The experience of a learner with a wide variety of objects of roughly similar nature from the perceptual standpoint normally leads through a process of psychological synthesis, the elements of which are only vaguely understood, to a generalized "picture" exhibiting emergent characteristics of some or all of the original component experiences. These synthesized concepts are customarily verbalized. Abstract thinking, in turn, proceeds by permutations and combinations of the words. Furthermore, the words may be learned by themselves with their meaning dependent upon definition and other words, rather than upon direct sensory experience and a process of induction. This possibility has led to problems of verbalism and superficial learning that have deeply concerned some who have given

special attention to it.[7] Since abstract thinking takes place in large part through the mechanism of words, the importance of a large vocabulary, resting upon an adequate sensory experience, becomes obvious. Likewise, the value of correct reading habits, particularly higher-level reading habits, takes on augmented significance.

## The principles of learning

That the process of learning in both animals and human beings possesses features of regularity and system will be denied by no one who has examined the problem. Tremendous progress has been made in the last two decades, furthermore, in clarifying the nature of the process and the resulting products. But when one comes to describe the learning process by a series of laws and principles, the problem of verbalization is considerable, since the process itself is extremely complicated and the scientific recording of all the variables and conditions of a learning experiment well-nigh impossible. When we stop to consider that the alteration of what may appear to be a minor factor in the learning condition may completely change the final result, the importance of this obstacle becomes manifest. In addition to the difficulty of objectively recording all the aspects of a situation is the problem of terminology. Even a complex and highly inflected language lacks words to describe the multitudinous phases of human reaction. A further difficulty in formulating a statement of principles of behavior is the absence of a common denominator among experimenters: since research scientists pay attention to different phases of the same situation, they naturally state their results differently. Nor does it help to say that we can solve the problem by stating everything in strictly objective terms. This method of solution is quite satisfying theoretically, but when put into actual practice, it often results in an absurd quantity of details. With the foregoing qualifications in mind, it is our purpose to state certain principles of learning that appear to be fairly well established. The discussion will follow in general the point of view of Thorndike.

All animals appear to learn most effectively when they are "in the mood." This is a principle of learning borne out both by common sense and by experimentation. It is sometimes known as the *law of readiness*. Readiness does not connote mere desire to learn: there is much more to psychological readiness. Readiness involves physiological maturity of certain of the structures to be

---

[7] Alfred Korzybski, *Science and Sanity*. Lancaster, Pa.: Science Press Printing Company, 1941.

C. K. Ogden, *The Meaning of Psychology*. New York: Harper and Brothers, 1926.

used. The walking of the young baby, in spite of his desires and sometimes frantic efforts, awaits the development of the mechanism that makes the learning of walking structurally possible. Regardless of the psychological desire to learn or the maturity to do so, such factors as fatigue and physiological unreadiness must not be overlooked.

A second learning principle is illustrated by the common saying, "Practice makes perfect." This principle has been called the *law of exercise*. The law of exercise does not guarantee that mere countless repetitions of any given reaction will serve to fix it, although the erroneous belief that it does has led in some schools to the institution of drill methods diametrically opposed to the principles of efficient learning. Except in the case of motor learning, mere *practice* by itself is not a potent factor in learning. Even in the learning of skills, effective learning requires much more than mere practice. At this point it is well to call attention to the fact that the several optimum conditions of learning implied by the principles being stated usually must be present simultaneously in order to insure the best learning. For example, repetition or exercise of a reaction does not result in optimum learning when the organism is in a state of unreadiness. In other words, the principles of learning that are being stated now are really descriptions of the various phases of effective learning and are in no sense alternative principles by which learning may take place.

It is common knowledge among both teachers and students that subjects which a pupil dislikes thoroughly, because of either the content itself or of some situation connected with or following the learning, are likely to be poorly mastered. The same truth has been expressed as the *law of effect:* learning responses that have been accompanied or followed by satisfying states or conditions, which the organism strives to maintain or attain, tend to be repeated and mastered more easily (selected and learned). The learning is "stamped in," however, because of the functional consequences of the activity rather than because of the effect of the feeling and emotional concomitants of the learning.

The converse statement of this principle is not equally true. Annoyers are much less effective than satisfiers. Annoyers do not weaken learning "connections" as much as satisfiers strengthen them. Learnings that are accompanied or followed by annoying consequences (states or conditions that the learner attempts to avoid or supersede) are not necessarily weakened. In fact, many studies have shown that learning responses may be established when the after-effects are unpleasant. Thus, the principle of effect requires many additions and amendments to the bald statement that pleasant effects reinforce and unpleasant effects detract from learning.

In addition to the three principles just stated, certain qualifying circumstances enter into many learning situations. Some investigators believe that learning experiences which are first or last have a tendency to gain a certain ascendency. This belief has been stated in the so-called laws of *primacy* and *recency*. Another qualifying circumstance is the emotional tone of the learning itself. There is some evidence that strongly emotionalized situations contain more fixative power than weakly emotionalized situations. This has been called the *law of intensity*.

It is necessary that teachers bear in mind the principles and qualifying circumstances of learning situations. When we come to translate the above principles into classroom practice, we find that it is easy to do so as far as statement is concerned but sometimes very difficult in practice. Encompassing all of the three major points in one thought, we find that optimum learning takes place when the learner is in a state of psychological and physiological readiness, when he repeats at intervals the learning series which is to be mastered, and when that series is accompanied by an emotionally satisfying experience. The major task of the school and the teacher is to arrange the learning situation so that these conditions prevail.

## The role of insight in learning

There are several puzzling major problems of learning about which leading authorities are still disagreed—and violently so. One of these controversies concerns the extent to which insight plays a part in learning.

Roughly classified, there are two "schools" of thought on the major process of learning itself. One school explains learning by what its critics call "machine theory." According to this mechanistic theory of learning, the entire process can be explained as a series of complicated connections among the receiving, transmitting, and reacting structures in the body. This point of view discounts completely spontaneous ideation and gives very little attention to learning syntheses and emergents.

The second school, while admitting certain of the experimental facts of the first, adds to its explanatory mechanism the factor of insight on the part of the learner. "Insight" is not easy to define. It connotes a grasp on the part of the learner of an entire situation, particularly of the interrelationship of parts of the situation to each other. It minimizes the role of habit in learning and the mechanical phases, stressing the units in the nervous system and similar explanatory principles. It holds that the learner, and only the learner, is aware more or less clearly of the *why* of his action. A quotation from Köhler [8] will give, in the words of one of the outstanding exponents of insight, the point of view.

If habit and reproduction are not to be regarded as the main motors of so-called mental life, what shall we say are the real ones? To this question there is one answer, not well formulated but implicitly accepted, which we may call the layman's belief. It is the layman's belief that, in general, he himself directly feels *why* at one time he has one attitude, and later on another; also that, for the most part, he knows and understands directly *why* he is inclined to do one thing in a certain particular situation and *why* a definitely different thing under subsequent different conditions. In his view, then, he is experiencing directly and truly much of that dynamical context, the development of which constitutes mental life. Opposed to this belief and altogether foreign to it, we have the view of most learned psychologists at the present time. From their viewpoint, one is inclined to do one thing now and then another, because, in the first instance, certain nerve paths are most available and, in the second instance, certain other paths are most open. Fortunate those people in whom the most permeable nerve paths in practise are usually the right and appropriate ones! From the psychologist's point of view it would be a pure mystery if a person's behavior should ever be determined, as the layman believes, directly by the concrete properties of the actual situation. The layman's belief is in full agreement with everyday experience; the learned view harmonizes with what we suppose to be the viewpoint of natural science. I shall confess at once that I choose the layman's belief whole-heartedly. In the treatment of sensory process *gestalt* psychology prefers the data of naïve description to the findings of prejudiced introspection. Following this line, the theory of the sensory field has begun to have a much more intimate contact with the natural sciences than it ever had when it imitated a self-made ideal of these disciplines. Similarly if, with regard to the total field, we adopt the view of common experience, what is *called* the viewpoint of natural science will soon be given up, in place of which we shall substitute the theory of dynamics. At the start of our present discussion, therefore, the obvious, almost the vulgar, will have to be said. It is not our fault that, to a deplorable degree, the obvious has disappeared from learned psychology, so that we have to rediscover it. Later in the course of this analysis the obvious aspects of common experience will assume the function of expressing certain fundamental properties of physical dynamics in the nervous system. This is exactly the contrary of the prevailing opinion.

It is quite apparent that adherence to either the extreme mechanistic explanation of learning, or the extreme insight explanation, would actually make some difference in school organization and teaching practice. Obviously the machine theory explanation heavily stresses external factors in the form of the stimuli in the situation, while the insight explanation emphasizes inner factors in the form of complicated states of awareness in the learner by which he tells why he is doing what he does, as Köhler puts it.

---

[8] From GESTALT PSYCHOLOGY, by Wolfgang Köhler, published by Liveright Publishing Corporation, 1929, pp. 349-350.

Naturally, the teacher who wishes to be psychologically sound in setting up classroom situations is concerned about the extent to which the learner is able to make an intuitional contribution to the process.

*Attention and minimal cues.* One way to reconcile. the apparently diametrically opposed theories of trial and error and insight is to emphasize two principles of learning which both schools of thought grant, and which may possibly be more important than either school has ordinarily considered. These two phenomena are *attention* and *minimal cues.* The phenomenon of attention may well be closely related to that of insight. The inattentive and indifferent animal confronted with any learning problem is far more likely to drift through a trial-and-error series than is the animal which is highly motivated and attentive. True, it can be contended that the starving rat turns in a more dynamic behavior series than the full rat and, biologically speaking, attends to what he is doing. But when a less biological definition of attention is given, this is not so likely to be the case. Chess, for example, is a game in which relationships play a considerable part. Of two opponents of comparable mental ability playing a game of chess, the one who attends to the game more closely will win the majority of times. In other words, the discernment of relationships is partially, if not wholly, a function of attention.

The theory of minimal cues also plays its part in reconciling mechanistic and intuitional theories of learning. Psychologists who employ the mechanism of conditioning as an explanatory theory in learning grant that the conditioned response can be attached to parts of the entire situation and, occasionally, small parts at that. Gestalt psychologists grant that a configuration is not a psychologically flat phenomenon, but that certain features of the configuration emerge, and that these emergent properties tend to move to meet the learner, so to speak. In these two phenomena we have our possible reconciliation. For, the so-called learning without practice, or problem-solving without practice, may be nothing more than the attention on the part of the learner, animal or human, to minimal cues. Response to these minimal cues may, in its incipient stages, be sub-observational, and the final response which appears to be spontaneous and *de novo* may be merely the external manifestation of an elaborate internal change.

If this eclectic theory of insight happens to be correct, the implications for the school teacher are emphatic and obvious. Our classroom practice should strive harder than ever to secure attention and to teach the principles of concentration by disregarding of distracting stimuli and raising the threshold for such stimuli. In conjunction with this effort supervised practice would be given in careful response to the details of learning situations.

## Forgetting

Everyone is familiar with the annoying possibilities of forgetting. The psychological nature of forgetting, however, still retains some mystery. To begin with, it is not an "all-or-none" process. We forget parts of a learning series and remember others, and we cannot tell why we have forgotten the part we have lost and remembered the parts that we have kept. We meet Mr. Jones today, forget his name tomorrow when we see him, and recall it the day after tomorrow when we see him again.

We can look at the phenomenon of forgetting in either of two ways: as a passive process or as an active one. Regarding it as passive, forgetting is the dimming of learning, usually through the mere lapse of time. This theory really holds that forgetting is a negative process and that the basic explanation of the phenomenon probably lies in a fading image of a weakening neural connection. But this theory is unsatisfactory when applied to many everyday phenomena. For example, it does not explain why we forget parts of a learning series and remember other parts. Also, it does not explain why we remember Mr. Jones' name one day and not the next.

To consider forgetting a really active process is more plausible and fits more easily observed phenomena. This may be termed the interference theory of forgetting. According to it, the principal cause of forgetting is the interference of other learning. While it is true that this other learning takes time, and therefore time is a factor in both theories, nevertheless the interference theory serves to explain situations that cannot be explained by the passive theory. This interference theory implies that there is considerable advantage in having some kinds of knowledge pretty well compartmentalized. If one had to memorize "The Ride of Paul Revere," for example, in a thousand different forms, with only slight changes between the forms, memory of any one of them would be a more difficult mental process than learning a completely different poem of the same number of words.

Practically all students of forgetting grant that it occurs most rapidly in a comparatively short space of time after the first complete mastery of the learning series. This basic principle of forgetting contains definite implications for school practice. Many teachers are satisfied when they have an individual or class up to one correct performance of a learning exercise. A review of the same exercise may not come until the end of the semester. This is incorrect. Reviews should follow soon after the period of complete fixation and with decreasing frequency.

## Unlearning and relearning

From the standpoint of psychology, there is no such thing as "correct" learning. Learning is simply a process that takes place, and it cannot be right or wrong. But when learning must meet certain defined objectives, then it is possible to say that it is right or wrong.

It is frequently necessary, when learning does not meet defined objectives, to undo it and replace it with other learning. Relearning, or reconditioning of the learner, is a lengthy and unsatisfactory process in many cases. Even though we do not know exactly what happens in the nervous system when learning takes place, we do know that learning has a certain psychological inertia, and persistence and replacement by a different but similar process is quite difficult.

Experience has shown two things to be of value in the process of reconditioning. The first is that reconditioning can take place when a stronger motivating stimulus is present during the reconditioning series than accompanied the original series. For example, Watson's baby, who had learned to cry at the sight of a rabbit or other furry object, learned not to cry when a furry animal was introduced at a distance with a piece of candy in the proximate environment. This simple but fundamental experiment gives important clues for much emotional and attitudinal reconditioning.

The second significant principle of reconditioning is that relearning discrete parts of a series is likely to be less profitable than relearning the entire series. This may appear at first glance to result in some waste of time through overlearning, but in actual practice the time spent in connecting transition points would be still more costly.

## School conditions affecting learning

The organization of the school represents an important factor in the production of optimum learning. It is doubtful whether the average administrator and teacher fully realize the extent to which the nature of the school environment is a potent factor in the learning of every child. While it is impossible to list all of the school conditions that affect learning and to discuss each fully, it is our purpose here to treat the three principal items.

The organization of the school exerts a crucial influence in learning. That nothing is more confusing to the child's mind than inconsistency is amply illustrated in home life: we are all familiar with the sort of child produced by parents who are always disagreeing on policies of discipline concerning him. We find exactly the same thing within the school. While it is not desirable to have teachers entirely standardized in their outlook, it is desirable and necessary to have a definite policy and atmosphere permeate the entire staff. The principal of the school actually exerts more influence upon the effectiveness of the learning in his school than any single teacher. The policy of the school should be clearly stated and understood by the staff and students alike.

The personality of the teacher is a second vital school condition affecting learning. Learning is largely a matter of morale and motivation, and these can be seriously impaired in the pupil by the personality of the teacher. It was pointed out in Chapter 2 that the teacher must sincerely like young people and must have the ability to get along with them. In addition, the teacher must know his or her subject well enough to set up the learning sequences in a sound fashion, taking full cognizance of the general level and spread of ability among the individuals of the class.

A third school condition that affects learning is the machinery employed for getting parental co-operation with the school. Some children get too much comfort at home for the difficulties they are encountering at school. This situation tends to set the parent against the teacher, with the child as the middle man doing the manipulating. Other children, on the contrary, are treated with undue harshness at home. In this case the task of the school, in order that more effective learning may take place, is to build up morale and restore self-confidence.

## QUESTIONS AND EXERCISES FOR DISCUSSION AND STUDY

1. Define learning and describe the conditions under which you think it takes place best.

2. Do you believe that most things that people do have a purpose? Explain.

3. Why is the mind so difficult to define and describe? What is your own notion of the nature of mental activity?

4. What is the reaction hypothesis? Upon what mechanical and chemical laws does it depend?

5. Explain the theory of neural drainage and give some arguments for and against the likelihood of its being the best explanation of the phenomenon of conditioning.

6. Name and discuss some of the differences between conditioning and association as presented by Thorndike.

7. Name as many of the principles of conditioning as you can, and illustrate each.

8. What are the three principal products of learning, and why is each important?

9. To what extent do you agree with the description in this chapter of the nature of artistic accomplishment? If you disagree, on what basis do you rest your argument?

10. What three principal laws of learning are given in the chapter? Apply each to a practical school situation.

11. What is meant by the theory of "insight"? Do you feel that it is a valuable principle in explaining learning situations that you have observed?

12. Name three reasons why reconditioning is important in education.

## SELECTED REFERENCES FOR FURTHER READING AND STUDY

Betts, Evelyn Wylie, *Time-limit Vs. Work-limit in Learning.* Baltimore, Md.: The Williams and Wilkins Company, 1934.

Bode, Boyd H., *How We Learn.* Boston: D. C. Heath and Company, 1940.

Butler, Frank A., *The Improvement of Teaching in Secondary Schools.* Chicago, Ill.: University of Chicago Press, 1939.

Davis, Robert A., *Psychology of Learning.* New York: McGraw-Hill Book Company, 1935.

Edwards, A. L., and H. B. English, "Effect of the Immediate Test on Verbatim and Summary Retention," *American Journal of Psychology,* July, 1939.

Frederick, Robert W., Ragsdale, Clarence E., and Rachel Salisbury, *Directing Learning.* New York: D. Appleton-Century Company, 1938.

Gifford, W. J., "The Nature of Learning," Chapter XI in *An Introduction to Modern Education,* by C. E. Skinner, R. E. Langfitt, *et al.* Boston: D. C. Heath and Company, 1937.

Gottsdanker, R. M., "Experimental Study of Fixation of Response by College Students in a Multiple-choice Situation," *Journal of Experimental Psychology,* November, 1939.

Griffith, Coleman R., *Psychology Applied to Teaching and Learning.* New York: Farrar and Rinehart, 1939.

Gurnee, H., "Effect of Collective Learning Upon the Individual Participants," *Journal of Abnormal and Social Psychology,* October, 1939.

Guthrie, E. R., "Effect of Outcome on Learning," *Psychological Review.* September, 1939.

————, *The Psychology of Learning.* New York: Harper & Brothers, 1935.

Herrick, C. J., "Awareness in the Inductive Solution of Problems Using Words as Stimuli," *Archives of Psychology,* 1939.

Hilgard, Ernest R., and Donald G. Marquis, *Conditioning and Learning.* New York: D. Appleton-Century Company, 1940.

Hill, C. J., "Goal Gradient, Anticipation, and Perseveration in Compound Trial-and-error Learning," *Journal of Experimental Psychology,* December, 1939.

Husband, R. W., "Intercorrelations Among Learning Abilities," *Pedagogical Seminary and Journal of Genetic Psychology,* December, 1939.

Katona, George, *Organizing and Memorizing: Studies in the Psychology of Learning and Teaching.* New York: Columbia University Press, 1940.

Knight, F. B., "Techniques of Learning." (In National Commercial Teachers Federation, *Fifth Yearbook.*)

Köhler, Wolfgang, *Gestalt Psychology*. New York: Liveright Publishing Corporation, 1929.

Lorge, I., "Thorndike's Contribution to the Psychology of Learning of Adults," *Teachers College Record*, May, 1940.

McConnell, T. R., *et al.*, *The Psychology of Learning. Forty-First Yearbook, National Society for the Study of Education*. Bloomington, Ill.: Public School Publishing Company, 1942. Part II.

McGeoch, John, *The Psychology of Human Learning*. New York: Longmans, Green and Company, 1942.

Millard, C. V., "Adapting Instruction in Basic Skills to the Child's Level of Maturity," *National Elementary Principal*, July, 1939.

Munn, N. L., "Relative Effectiveness of Two Conditioning Procedures," *Journal of General Psychology*, July, 1939.

Powers, Francis F., and Willis L. Uhl, *Psychological Principles of Education*. New York: D. Appleton-Century Company, 1933.

————, *et al.*, *Psychology in Everyday Living*. Boston: D. C. Heath and Company, 1938. Chaps. 13-17.

Race, Henrietta V., *Psychology of Learning Through Experience*. Boston: Ginn and Company, 1938.

Salisbury, F. S., *Human Development and Learning*. New York: McGraw-Hill Book Company, 1939.

Sand, M. C., "Effect of Length of List Upon Retroactive Inhibition When Degree of Learning is Controlled," *Archives of Psychology*, 1939.

Sandiford, P., "Nature of Learning," *School* (elementary and secondary editions), February-March, 1940.

Schmeidler, G. R., "Retroaction and Proaction in Serial Learning," *American Journal of Psychology*, October, 1939.

Sherman, M., "Emotional Disturbances and Reading Disability." (In Chicago University, *Recent Trends in Reading*.)

Sisson, E. D., "Retroactive Inhibition: The Temporal Position of Interpolated Activity," *Journal of Experimental Psychology*, August, 1939.

Skinner, C. E., and associates, *Readings in Educational Psychology*. New York: Farrar and Rinehart, 1937. Part III.

————, ————, *Readings in Psychology*. New York: Farrar and Rinehart, 1935. Chaps. 12-15.

————, P. L. Harriman, and others, *Child Psychology*. New York: The Macmillan Company, 1941. Chaps. 4, 5, and 9.

Smith, Henry L., *Relation of Retention to Speed of Learning*. Bureau of Cooperative Research, Indiana University, 1939.

Thorndike, E. L., *Human Learning*. New York: D. Appleton-Century Company, 1931.

————, *The Psychology of Wants, Interests, and Attitudes*. New York: D. Appleton-Century Company, 1935.

Ward, Lewis B., *Reminiscence and Rote Learning*. Columbus, Ohio: Psychological Review Company, 1937.

# CHAPTER 9

# The Dynamics of Learning

In psychological theory no question is more perplexing than that of motive. Traditional psychology had much to say about instincts as the basic drives to action. Until relatively recently, teachers were told that the educational process was essentially one of modifying and guiding the child's instincts. Now, the instinct hypothesis has been devastatingly criticized.[1] Objective psychology has substituted physiological reactions for the old dualistic theory of instinct.[2] The learner is regarded as a sort of stimulus-response mechanism, and the purpose of education is to effect the proper conditionings. Since this view becomes sterile and pedantic when it is pushed to its logical extreme, various dynamic theories have been advanced. For example, the popular appeal of Freud, Adler, and Jung depends in part upon their emphasis on motive.[3] Salesmen, advertisers, propagandists, and teachers have a practical concern with this problem. They must know how to direct appeals that will bring about certain desired responses, or they fail in their work. Therefore, their interest in the problem of motivation is immediate and practical rather than theoretical.

Since a review of all the various theories of motivation would lie far beyond the scope of this book, only a single point of view will be discussed:[4] a simple theory that underlies modern educa-

---

[1] L. L. Bernard, *Instinct*. New York: Henry Holt and Company, 1924.

[2] For example, F. H. Allport, *Social Psychology*. Boston: Houghton Mifflin Company, 1924. See especially Chapters II and III.

[3] For a convenient review, see R. S. Woodworth, *Contemporary Schools of Psychology*. New York: Ronald Press Company, 1931. Chapter 5, "Psychoanalysis and Related Schools."

A clearly written non-experimental account of the dynamics of behavior will be found in J. A. Hadfield, *Psychology and Morals*. New York: Robert M. McBride and Company, 1926. An unusually helpful account of various points of view is to be found in G. Murphy and F. Jensen, *Approaches to Personality*. New York: Coward-McCann, 1932. See especially Chapters IV, V, and VI.

[4] In this connection the following books should be read:

Bernard Hart, *The Psychology of Insanity*, 4th ed. New York: The Macmillan Company, 1931.

R. B. Raup, *Complacency, the Foundation of Behavior*. New York: The Macmillan Company, 1925.

Eugenio Rignano, *The Psychology of Reasoning*. New York: Harcourt, Brace and Company, 1923.

174

tion and mental hygiene. The justification for this point of view is that it has practical value in actual classroom work with boys and girls. Following the account of a theory of motivation will be given a review of important experimental findings on motives and learning. A final section in this chapter will deal with the educational implications of theory and experiment for classroom procedure.

## A Theory of Motivation

Teachers are curious to know not only what their pupils do, but, also *why* they act in certain ways. Since, by definition, science deals with descriptions of observable data, this question must be answered theoretically, for no one has ever seen a motive. We assume that certain acts are the results of motivation. If, for example, a pupil makes a "bright remark" in class, the teacher might assume that he is desirous of attracting attention. When in out-of-school learning a boy enthusiastically tackles the problem of building a model airplane that will win in a contest, the inference is that this activity meets a felt need. His lethargy in learning to calculate the volume of solids in the arithmetic class is assumed to be the result of the fact that such knowledge does not relate to his felt needs. The point being made is that a discussion of motivation leads us into inferences and speculations. Nevertheless, every teacher has observed the vast difference between the zest with which some out-of-school activities are undertaken and the reluctance with which, say, the learning of the fourth declension is approached in the Latin class at the close of the day.

## Definition of motive

A *motive* is anything that initiates, sustains, and directs an activity. Subjectively, it is recognized as a want or need. Objectively, it is inferred as the driving force behind an act. In other words, although motivation is a difficult problem to formulate in a systematic account of human psychology, everyone knows how it feels to have a great many unsatisfied wants or needs. Even an idle perusal of a mail-order catalog or the advertising section of the daily paper may arouse a multitude of motives. Each year new designs in automobiles make people dissatisfied with their old car and desirous of owning a new one. Correspondence schools advertise skillfully to make us want to increase our incomes by learning a new vocation, by acquiring facility in speaking a foreign language, or by achieving social prestige. In the windows of stores we behold displays of clothing, furniture, or other goods that frequently arouse in us the desire to purchase them. When we respond to these situations by experiencing wants or needs, we are motivated. The dictionary contains many synonyms that designate the subjective aspect of motivation: *wants, desires, drives, cravings, urges, wishes, appetites, needs*—these are a few of the commonly used words applied to the subjective aspect of motives.

### The primary motive

Observations of infant behavior justify the inference that the basic drive or motive is that of regaining or maintaining the optimum physiological balance.[5] Uncomfortable clothing, cold, hunger, and thirst are familiar illustrations of conditions that upset the balance and induce crying. The primary motive, therefore, appears to be a biological need for optimum complacency. Complacency, however, should not be understood as meaning immobile posture and vegetative existence. On the contrary, the healthy infant kicks, squirms, and cries. Restraint of free movement seems to induce a strong upset in the infant's equilibrium. When the very young infant sleeps about twenty hours a day and spends the rest of the time in ceaseless activity, parents know that the health regimen is probably satisfactory. Basically, motivation is the life process itself. The goal or end-result is the restoration or the maintenance of the optimum conditions for normal, healthy growth and development.

### "Unconscious" motivation

Certain schools of psychology make a great deal of the so-called "unconscious mind." [6] Apparently, the notion is that many human motives arise from the depths of the unconscious mind and cause people to do things without knowing why they act. This hypothesis is wholly unnecessary and leads to elaborate theories far beyond any useful or sensible requirement. The infant, of course, is unable to verbalize its impulsion to get food when it is hungry or to secure help when a pin is sticking into it. Nevertheless, its cries usually bring someone who will restore the optimum balance. In a sense,

---

[5] ". . . the original nature of man reduces to nothing more than the presence of life processes." See Shaffer, *The Psychology of Adjustment*. Boston: Houghton Mifflin Company, 1936. Pp. 40 and 32-40; also Chapter IV, "Motivation."

[6] For an account of conflicting views of the "unconscious mind," see *The Unconscious: a Symposium*. New York: Alfred A. Knopf, 1929. See especially Chapter IV, "The Unconscious of the Behaviorist," by J. B. Watson, for an objective account.

In this connection see also William Healy, *Personality in Formation and Action*. New York: W. W. Norton and Company, 1938.

therefore, the motives of the infant are unconscious. An older infant will reach out to grasp a bright, shiny object or will exhibit signs of pleasure when being dressed for an outing. Of course, the infant has no interest in or concern about the introspective components of such behavior, nor has it any ability whatsoever to analyze and to report on the subjective aspects of its actions.

Motives are unconscious only in the sense that many of them are unverbalized. The intelligent, sophisticated adult may develop some interest in trying to analyze and to verbalize the reasons for certain of his acts. Obviously, many adults have no interest at all in the reasons for their behavior. Animals and young children, not being students of psychology, act on unconscious motives. The rebellious pupil may not know that his hostility toward the school arises from the fact that he is unable to make a satisfactory adjustment. There is, however, no justification for assuming the existence of an unconscious mind. As soon as we become introspectively aware of the reasons for a given act, the motivation is conscious. For example, when the high-school pupil maps out a course of action that will lead to entrance into a certain vocation, his motivation is conscious. If he throws an eraser at another boy, he may not fully understand that his act was in part the consequence of boredom.

It should be clearly recognized that many of the dynamic processes underlying school learning have not been verbalized and that, in a large sense, much motivation is "unconscious."[7] The skillful teacher is alert to seize upon every opportunity to utilize felt needs and to create desirable felt needs. These are largely unverbalized by the pupils. They are experienced as upsets in complacency, and lead to activities that will restore the optimum balance. For example, a high-school senior encountering Blake's "The Tiger" in her literature book might be greatly perplexed about the meaning of the poem. Let us assume that she reasons out an interpretation which, according to the teacher, is probably correct. That activity, initiated and sustained by a felt need, would lead to a thrill of satisfaction when the balance was restored. Of course, if she had read Dewey's *How We Think*,[8] she might have some conscious awareness of the nature of her motivation. More probably, the dynamics of this act would be wholly "unconscious."

---

[7] Words which connote controversies are placed within quotation marks. The use of these terms does not imply either the acceptance or the rejection of any particular point of view.

[8] John Dewey, *How We Think*, rev. ed. Boston: D. C. Heath and Company, 1933. This book should be read by every student of education, as it provides a psychological foundation of method.

### Learned motives

The preceding discussion of literary interpretation has gone far afield from the account of physiological drive as the primary motive. As a matter of fact, there is an essential unity in both types of motivation. First, something has to occur that upsets the optimum balance. In the case of the infant, it is something that disrupts the physiological rhythms. For the older child, it may be something that interferes with the "mental" complacency; that is, it may be a problem situation, a doubt, or a perplexity. Although the degree of difference between physiological and "mental" complacency is great, essentially there is no division. The second step is the same in both cases—namely, to undertake activity that will restore the balance. This activity, usually of the trial-and-error variety, may eventually bring success. If so, the tension is reduced and the response tends to be repeated when a similar situation is encountered later.

Some psychologists have been interested in drawing up neat lists of motives that supposedly govern human behavior. In a few textbooks, literally scores of motives are listed, whereas in other books all behavior may be reduced to a few basic motives or even to one motive. Much more important than the question of how many motives there are is it to discover how motives are acquired in the life history of the individual. It has already been pointed out that the primary motive is that of regaining or maintaining the optimum physiological balance, a condition which the sophisticated adult experiences as complacency. The infant soon learns that its satisfactions depend upon its adjustments to other people—that it must know how to secure attention. This learning is done in a "mechanical," "unconscious" way. Cries bring someone who attends to the infant's needs; hence, cries become the learned signal to gain attention.

The dynamic nature of the learning process is inherent in the biological impulse to maintain or regain complacency. Although at the beginning of human life the complacency is wholly physiological in nature, the normal child soon begins to acquire an increasing number of "mental" needs. To take possession of brightly painted toys, to gain attention, to play, to go out in the baby carriage—these are homely examples of "mental" needs. Every parent knows something about the needs expressed by the youngster at Christmas time. When a youngster is taken through the toy department or past the candy counter, there is seldom any doubt about the reality of dynamic motives. Both real and fancied needs are multiplied to an enormous degree throughout the life history of an individual. Highly paid advertisers exercise skilled techniques in creating new needs by appeals in magazines, newspapers, and radio programs. Although the promise is held out that the newest purchase will bring complacency, no sooner is the goal reached than new desires are aroused.

Although psychology has been slow to recognize the dynamic nature of human behavior, philosophers, especially those interested in ethics, were concerned about this problem over two thousand years ago. Aristippus of Cyrene, for example, taught that the way to achieve optimum complacency is to extract the greatest possible pleasure from each succeeding moment. Epicurus modified this teaching to mean that the greatest good is lifetime happiness. Antisthenes, on the contrary, stated that the greatest complacency is to be achieved by cultivating the life of reason and despising sensory gratifications. This emphasis was expanded and systematized by the Stoic philosophers, especially Epictetus and Marcus Aurelius. Novelists and playwrights have likewise been concerned about the dynamics of human behavior and the nature of motivation. Even though the dynamics of behavior have been neglected in certain systems of psychology, theoretical and practical interest in the problem has never been absent.

Owing to the nature of individual differences, it is impossible to draw up a complete list of dependable human motives which may be utilized in education. Such a list would be an oversimplification. Certain personality needs are, however, generally recognized, and they furnish leads for more effective classroom work. Under each of the following categories there would be literally scores of specific motives characteristic of the social conditioning of any single individual.

1. *Competition.* In our social order competition for rewards receives a great deal of emphasis. Adler upholds the view that the urge to be superior is the basic motive in human behavior.[9] Certainly parents and teachers put pressure on children to achieve the maximum and to win out in competitive endeavor. Greenberg, May and Doob, and others have adduced evidence to indicate that, while human beings naturally strive for goals, striving with others (co-operation) or against others (competition) are learned forms of behavior. Every observer recognizes the fact that public school children work more efficiently in competitive situations than in

---

[9] Alfred Adler, *What Life Should Mean to You.* Boston: Little, Brown and Company, 1931. Also see Mark A. May and Leonard Doob, *Research on Competition and Cooperation,* Bull. 25, Social Science Research Council, New York, 1937, and Margaret Mead, *Cooperation and Competition among Primitive Peoples* (New York: McGraw-Hill Book Company, 1937).

co-operative situations under current conditions. Perhaps this should not be.

2. *Group approval.* Outstanding achievement in activities of interest to the group is hailed with mixed feelings of admiration and envy. In the modern school each child has an opportunity to have his accomplishment estimated upon the basis of effort and capacity. Thereby he has some chance to gain the commendation of his teachers and to escape from a sense of frustration.[10] Group athletics furnish opportunities for co-operative, noncompetitive activity whereby group approval may be experienced by all participants. Interscholastic athletics and the traditional system of school marking, however, deprive a great many children of the opportunity to gain in self-confidence by experiencing group approval.

Both the competitive and the group-approval motives are intimately related to the emotional nature of the learner. When these drives are blocked and satisfactions are denied, the personality tends to be disrupted. Some children will resort to any extreme to avoid defeat or to escape censure. When teachers rely too much upon these motives, they may unwittingly encourage cheating, personality conflicts, hostility, and delinquent behavior. The principal contribution of the guidance emphasis in education is that it points out the necessity for adjusting the task to the capacity of the individual learner. Thus the child is not placed in situations where no measure of success or of social approval is possible.

3. *Sense of achievement.*[11] Experimental studies clearly show that knowledge of progress is a powerful incentive in learning. When the child is aware of desirable accomplishment, and particularly when he is given judicious approval, he has a powerful incentive for tackling more difficult problems. Few teachers realize how purposeless and aimless the traditional curriculum seems to many pupils. At the college level there is a great difference between the motivation of successful students in vocational curricula and that of students taking the general academic course. Link goes so far

10 For a general discussion and a list of additional readings about the important topic of frustration, see S. H. Britt and S. Q. Janus, "Criteria of Frustration," *Psychological Review*, Vol. XLVII, No. 5 (1940), pp. 451-470.

See also N. R. F. Maier, *Studies of Abnormal Behavior in the Rat* (New York: Harper and Brothers, 1939); and Allison Davis and John Dollard, *Children of Bondage* (Washington: American Council on Education, 1940). These two references deal, respectively, with effects of frustrations upon animals and human beings.

11 On the basis of an experiment conducted by him, Abel concluded that it is the goal and not its attainment which stimulates learning, since the former creates in the individual the restlessness and energy which initiates activity, whereas the latter brings about quiescence from striving. (L. B. Abel, "The Effects of Shift in Motivation upon Learning of a Sensori-Motor Task," *Archives of Psychology*, No. 205. New York: Columbia University Press, 1936.)

as to point out that an educational program which deprives the learner of a sense of genuine achievement related to the felt needs of life is disastrous for personality development.[12]

4. *Interest.* It is axiomatic that we learn best that in which we are most interested. A neglected phase of educational research is the study of out-of-school learning, which is invariably characterized by great interest on the part of the learner. Common observations, however, supply plenty of evidence to establish the generalization that interest is the most potent determinant of effective learning. Repeatedly, studies have shown that a great deal of school learning is soon lost, while we remember those things which we have found to be useful in present activities. Since few adults ever have occasion to extract cube roots, to conjugate *potior*, to make a word-by-word study of a Shakespearean play, or to enumerate the important battles of the Civil War, those items are quickly forgotten. When a skillful teacher discovers the interests of her pupils and seeks to relate them to the class work, the period is transformed from a routine procedure into a genuine learning situation.

## Experimental Studies of Motivation

### Competition

The classic studies on the effects of competition were undertaken by Moede.[13] In one experiment, he studied the ability of boys twelve to fourteen years of age to bear pain. The strength of an electric shock was gradually stepped up until the subjects demanded that it cease. When observers were present, the boys would endure much more pain than they would when alone. The threshold for pain was greatly raised when two boys were pitted against each other in a competition to discover which could take the more pain without calling a halt.

In another important experiment, Moede took the measure of strength of grip under two conditions.[14] First, the boys squeezed the dynamometer while alone; later, they squeezed it in front of the group. The boys with lowest scores were stimulated to do better when they appeared before the group, but the superior boys tended to make lower scores in group performance. The implication is that the superior boys were less stimulated by a competitive urge than were the inferior. Possibly, the superior lost interest because of the ease with which they surpassed the inferior boys. When the

---

[12] H. C. Link, *The Return to Religion.* New York: The Macmillan Company, 1936.

[13] W. Moede, *Experimentelle Massenpsychologie.* Leipzig: Hirzel, 1920.

[14] *Supra.*

boys were paired for competition, the superior boys tried to surpass their opponents and the inferior boys attempted to make the best scores possible.

Maller's experimental investigation of competition is important for education.[15] For materials he used simple addition of single digits. His subjects were 1,583 pupils in grades five, six, seven, and eight. First, the pupils were tested without any special motivation in order to discover their normal accomplishment level. Second, they were tested under four different types of motivating conditions: (1) unmotivated; (2) working for self; (3) working for the group; and (4) free choice. He reported that these pupils did better when they were motivated than they did when no motivation was used. They worked harder, however, to earn a high individual ranking and a prize for themselves than they did to gain a high standing and a prize for their group.

The most interesting results were obtained when the pupils had free choice. He found the following arrangement to represent the order of strength of motives when choice was allowed: (1) working for own sex (boys against girls, girls against boys); (2) working for self; (3) working for the team; (4) working for the class; and (5) working for a group arbitrarily selected by the teacher. Nevertheless, Maller's investigation includes many contradictory and perplexing results and does not furnish a basis for drawing up dogmatic laws of competition.

Out of the great number of similar investigations on the effects of competition, one more is selected for mention here. Vaughn set up an experiment in which ten subjects practiced six weeks on marksmanship.[16] During a three-week experimental period, the subjects were given various types of motivation. Finally, there was a three-week period in which they continued to practice but without any special motivation. The three motives used were: (1) to get the highest score; (2) to earn the highest score on the basis of a handicap; and (3) to make the greatest relative improvement. The results showed that each participant did best under those conditions that were most favorable to him. The crack riflemen did their best in competition for the highest score; the poor shots did best in working for greatest relative improvement; and the average shots achieved most under the handicap contest.

[15] J. B. Maller, *Cooperation and Competition: an Experimental Study in Motivation, Contributions to Education 384.* New York: Teachers College, Columbia University, 1929.

[16] James Vaughn, "An Experimental Study of Competition," *Journal of Applied Psychology,* Vol. XX, No. 1 (1936), pp. 1-15.

See also C. M. Diserens and James Vaughn, "Experimental Psychology of Motivation," *Psychological Bulletin,* Vol. XXVII, No. 1 (1931), pp. 15-65.

Experiments are lacking to show what may be the mental hygiene effects of excessive use of the competitive motive. There is some evidence in the literature to indicate that the gratification of success is not wholly dependent upon winning in a competition, but rather upon the achievement of a particular goal set by an individual. In athletics a, competitor may be disappointed by his poor showing even though he wins, and the defeated contestant may be gratified by his display of improvement. Owing to our excessive stressing of competitive activity, some mental hygienists believe that avoidance of competition is a symptom of an inferiority attitude. The modern school has made a serious effort to tone down the emphasis upon competitive activity and to stress co-operation. Most thoughtful teachers believe that the best way to guide children toward the goal of wholesome personality is to adjust each task to the level of capacity of the child. Thereby, the gifted children do not gain recognition with a minimum expenditure of energy, and the backward children are not discouraged by competition in which they are foredoomed to fail.

Greenberg's experiment seems to have important implications for education.[17] She brought two children together before a table on which was a pile of blocks. When very young children were placed in this situation, there was no evidence of competition. No child tried to grab all the blocks or to belittle the activity of the other children. With older groups of children, however, there was definite evidence of aggressive behavior. In part, the increase in competitive motivation was attributable to the growth of ability to use the blocks purposefully and constructively. In part, no doubt, the development of competitive activity was dependent upon the influence of home and school training. Since the social order is organized on a competitive basis, adults tend to train children to be aggressive. Like other experimenters, however, Greenberg found great individual differences and many confusing results. There does seem to be evidence that the school might do much more in educating pupils in co-operative undertakings, as there is no reason for continuing to assume that competition is the most powerful incentive in ideal learning situations.

## Social facilitation

The classic investigations of group influences upon mental activity were made by Mayer, who used fourteen boys about twelve years of age as his subjects.[18] In brief, he arrived at three conclu-

---

[17] P. J. Greenberg, "Competition in Children: an Experimental Study," *American Journal of Psychology*, Vol. XLIV, No. 2 (1932), pp. 221-248.

[18] August Mayer, "Ueber Einzel—und Gesamtleistung des Schulkindes," *Archiv für die Gesamte Psychologie*, Vol. I (1903), pp. 276-416.

sions: (1) test scores were markedly improved when the boys worked as a group; (2) fewer errors were made in group work than in individual work; and (3) the scores in group work were more uniform than those made in solitary performance. Although a sense of rivalry entered into the motivation, the principal factor was social facilitation (the awareness of the presence of others engaged in the same tasks). Many other investigations have confirmed the hypothesis that group work is much more stimulating than work done in solitude. Some evidence has been found to substantiate the belief that a spirit of rivalry may develop spontaneously in group activities.

Husband, however, discovered that success in solving problems in algebra was not increased when the pupils worked together.[19] Pupils who were adept in working out the solutions proceeded to obtain the answers, while the less able pupils looked on. In solving codes and jigsaw puzzles, the pupils tended to work co-operatively. It is of interest to note that friends were much more successful in obtaining solutions for jigsaw puzzles and codes than were strangers.

There are great individual differences in responsiveness to group influences. In some instances, there is a marked decrement in the quality of work, even though the amount of work may be increased. Many investigators have found that social facilitation is most potent in the case of slow learners. There is reason to believe that most pupils work better in a group when the task is of a mechanical type or a drill lesson, but that in complicated acts involving thought the presence of others is a handicap. Nevertheless, introspective reports by high-school and college students indicate that many of them are encouraged to work harder, to achieve greater improvement, and to persist in learning activities when they have a feeling that others are engaged in the same quest.

### Rewards and punishments

Hurlock's experiments have an important bearing upon the problem of motivation.[20] Using three equated groups, she was able to determine the relative efficacy of praise, blame, and ignoring results. Older children were found to respond more to praise than

---

[19] R. W. Husband, "Cooperative versus Solitary Problem Solution," *Journal of Social Psychology,* Vol. 11, Second Half, (1940), pp. 405-409.

[20] E. B. Hurlock, "The Value of Praise and Reproof as Incentives for Children," *Archives of Psychology,* Vol. 71 (1924). See also E. B. Hurlock, "An Evaluation of Certain Incentives Used in School Work," *Journal of Educational Psychology,* Vol. XVI, No. 3 (1925), pp. 145-159.

An important discussion pertinent to this topic is: L. Chase, *Motivation of Young Children, University of Iowa Studies of Child Welfare,* Vol. V (1932).

to blame. Girls were less responsive to both praise and blame than boys were. The brightest children were relatively more responsive to blame whereas the dull were influenced most by praise. The Negro pupils reacted slightly more strongly to praise and the white pupils to blame. Throughout the results, however, there were a great many significant individual differences.

In another experiment, Hurlock showed that the long-time effects of praise and blame are unequal.[21] Using four groups of pupils who worked on addition tests over a five-day period, she found that continued praise tended to facilitate improvement. The effects of reprimands tended to diminish. When she ignored the errors and the successes, the indications of improvement were lacking. The fourth group was the control or standard of comparison. In short, she found that praise is better than blame, but that blame is better than ignoring results. Here, as in most other experiments on learning, there were great individual differences, although the five-day experimental period was too brief for conclusive results. What the relative effects of praise and blame might be on older students has not yet been experimentally determined.

Leuba compared performance when no incentive was used with that when prizes were offered.[22] Even though the value of the prizes was small, the children worked more effectively when they had an incentive. Children whose initial scores were in the lowest quarter made the greatest relative gain. Scholastic honor societies, money prizes, recognition by the faculty, degrees *cum laude*—these are a few incentives which are thought to have great value in stimulating better performance in learning. Just what their effects may be has not been experimentally ascertained. There are some grounds for assuming that rewards are more stimulating for the dull and the slow learners than for the bright and studious. At least, Leuba's findings support that assumption.

## Some Implications of Theory and Experiment

### Motivation is a complex affair

Both Wood [23] and Sears [24] have demonstrated that college students work better under motivation than they do when incen-

---

[21] *Supra.*

[22] C. L. Leuba, "A Preliminary Experiment to Quantify an Incentive and Its Effects," *Journal of Abnormal and Social Psychology*, Vol. XXV, No. 3 (1930), pp. 275-288.

[23] T. W. Wood, "The Effect of Approbation and Reproof on the Mastery of Nonsense Syllables," *Journal of Applied Psychology*, Vol. XVIII, No. 3 (1934), pp. 657-664.

[24] R. R. Sears, "An Initiation of the Repression Sequence by Experienced Failure," *Journal of Experimental Psychology*, Vol. XX, No. 6 (1937), pp. 570-580.

tives are lacking. They also discovered that the effects of incentives soon wore off. Apparently, if one relies upon a single incentive, initial improvement is effected, but shortly the incentive loses potency. Teachers must be judicious and tactful in using praise and censure. If commendations are given in extravagant fashion, they become meaningless. Repeated scoldings make some children tense and rebellious, whereas other children gradually become indifferent to blame.

All the experimental investigations of motives have clearly demonstrated the existence of great individual differences. Consequently, no set of rules can be drawn up for use in motivating the improvement of learning. There is, however, one important exception to this statement. In general, when the learner is aware of his progress, he works more efficiently than he does when he is ignorant of his status. Symonds and Chase have conclusively demonstrated this fact.[25] Nevertheless, short-time fluctuations in the learning curve are to be expected; hence, if a day-by-day record is kept, the pupil might become discouraged and confused. For example, a golf player who keeps a chart of daily progress will constantly be made aware of plateaus and actual losses of skill.

Some students of psychology and psychiatry have repeatedly attempted to reduce human motivation to a few fundamental principles. Although these views are interesting to read, they represent attempts to oversimplify the problem. Through social conditionings, the individual acquires an infinite variety of motives. No useful purpose is achieved in trying to reduce them to a small number of basic drives. The emphasis should be upon the enormous complexity of human motives rather than upon futile efforts to reduce the matter to a few dogmatic "laws of action." The skillful teacher appeals to many different motives in order to get her pupils to do their best work. Furthermore, she arranges situations that will arouse new and more desirable motives.

### Motives are not mysterious "forces"

Once educators believed that the child inherited a number of motivating forces called "instincts." A child who collected stamps, for example, was thought to be impelled by the collecting instinct. Fighting and going to war were thought to be manifestations of the pugnacity instinct. An instinct of gregariousness was thought to be the reason why we like to be in a group. In general, the instincts were regarded as unlearned or inherited forces. Some of

---

[25] P. M. Symonds and D. H. Chase, "Practice versus Motivation," *Journal of Educational Psychology*, Vol. XX, No. 1 (1929), pp. 19-35.

them, being useful for social adjustments, were considered as worthy to utilize in education; others, being pernicious and dangerous, were to be modified or stamped out by the school. Among the prominent upholders of this doctrine were McDougall [26] and Freud.[27] Since a new emphasis has developed, it is worthwhile to analyze briefly the reasons why the instinct view has been given up.

First, a comparison of the writings of advocates of the instinct hypothesis was made by Bernard.[28] He found that no two writers agreed on the same list of instincts. Second, the notion that "forces" were inherited had no scientific justification. Third, nearly all the so-called instincts were known to be the result of learning. The instinct hypothesis neglected entirely the great importance of social conditions. Fourth, it represented a mechanistic point of view. Neither human beings nor animals show any indication that mysterious "forces" direct their behavior in mechanical fashion. Among human beings, at least, the evidence is that behavior is highly complex and variable. Fifth, it was reasoning in a circle. Imagine that you were asked why men go hunting and that you replied, "There's a hunting instinct." Then, if you were asked, "How do you know?" your reply would be, "See; they are going hunting." Clearly, that sort of reasoning is fallacious.

## Motives are not merely physiological drives

The human infant is a physiological organism with vast potentialities for physical growth and social development. Obviously, the physiological drives are uppermost in the period of infancy, and they furnish the basis upon which all other drives are developed. It is questionable, however, whether every adult motive can be usefully or actually traced back to its origin in the physiological processes of the infant. Reacting against the fallacies inherent in the instinct hypothesis, some theorists have tried to analyze every motive down to its supposed organic basis. Thereby they become just as dogmatic as the upholders of the instinct doctrine. Their explanations are far-fetched and do violence to common experience. For example, to trace the relationship between a wish for a new car and the physiological drives might eventuate in an interesting piece of casuistry, but it would serve no practical purpose for educational procedure.

[26] See, for example, William McDougall, *The Energies of Men* (New York: Charles Scribner's Sons, 1933); and his *Social Psychology* (Boston: Luce, 1911), Chapter II.

[27] Sigmund Freud, *General Introduction to Psychoanalysis*. New York: Boni & Liveright, 1920.

[28] L. L. Bernard, *op. cit.*

Simply, a motive is any activity in progress. When the goal has been reached and a measure of complacency has been attained, the motive has vanished. If a difficult translation exercise in French arouses determination to get a satisfactory rendition in English, the pupil has a motive. Once the translation has been effected, that motive has gone. Since, however, the normal individual is never wholly complacent, either physiologically or "mentally," there are innumerable activities constantly in progress. Therefore, motives are continuously operative. A false and futile problem is raised by those who would reduce motivation wholly to physiological drives or to "mental forces."

## Attention and attitude

People attend to anything that interests them—that is, which has stimulus value. When we are thirsty or hungry, an intrusive feeling of bodily discomfort upsets our entire balance; but after satiating the need, we have little immediate interest in food or drink. If a person has habituated himself to experience a thrill of satisfaction upon working out a crossword puzzle, his attention may be attracted by the puzzle section of his daily paper. For those who have not learned to get this type of satisfaction, the page may have absolutely no interest. An attitude is a more or less permanent set to pay attention whenever certain situations arise. One of the most important tasks in education is to teach children how to find interest and satisfaction in desirable situations and to create the appropriate attitudes.

1. *Some ways of securing attention.* Intelligent teachers try to relate the class activities to the felt needs of the learners. Consequently, they arouse in their pupils intrinsic motivation to pay their maximum attention to the task in hand. Observations of out-of-school learning clearly demonstrate the great difference between the way a group of boys perfect their skill with air-rifles and the manner in which they achieve mastery of sentence diagramming.[29]

The school must not, however, content itself with using motives that are already present. If education merely utilized the motives that are already potent determinants of behavior, no progress would be possible. The aim is to set up learning situations that will create new and more desirable types of motivation. For example, the pupils who enjoy "The Lone Ranger" should not have a steady diet of western thrillers in their literature class. Neverthe-

[29] See S. L. Pressey and F. P. Robinson, *Psychology and the New Education*, rev. New York: Harper and Brothers, 1944. Chapter V.

less, by capitalizing upon their enjoyment of adventure stories, an alert teacher can lead them on to find pleasure in higher types of literature. The guiding principle is to discover what worthy interests already exist, and then to set up situations that will lead to higher types of satisfactions. In this way, the level of attention-getting situations is raised and the number of worthy interests is increased.

It cannot be emphasized too strongly that most of the experimental studies on motivation have been done in artificial situations and have covered only short periods of time. Therefore, they have a minimum contribution for classroom work. More studies of out-of-school behavior would contribute much to educational practice. Teachers profit by observing what situations elicit the spontaneous attention of pupils in real life situations. Without turning the schoolroom into a circus or pushing the matter to an absurd extreme, teachers can greatly increase the efficiency of curriculum mastery and the enthusiasm for improvement by incorporating these familiar observations into classroom activity.

2. *The development of attitudes.* Studies indicate that detailed factual mastery is soon lost in the years beyond school. Attitudes and emotionalized ideals may have a more lasting influence in the life of the pupil. For instance, long after the details of *Silas Marner* are forgotten, there may remain a distaste for reading English classics. In many schools, attitudes are the incidental by-products of instruction. The primary aim of such schools is merely to bring each pupil up to a given level of curriculum mastery. Spontaneous activities of intrinsic interest are, therefore, relegated to an *extra*curriculum status. Whether the pupils are interested, indifferent, or wholly uninterested is a secondary matter in such a school. In the future, the school must, on the contrary, seek more purposefully to develop proper attitudes and thus secure outcomes that are more abiding and dynamic.

One of the most important attitudes for effective learning is a justified feeling of self-confidence. Therefore, the school should emphasize success experiences for the young learners and guidance for each pupil. Where such a program is successfully instituted, much of the traditional hostility toward the school has vanished. Evidently, the pupils in some schools are led to look upon the teacher as an inexorable taskmaster who sets impossible goals and who condemns them to frustration and inferiority. Teachers who have had experience in different types of good and bad schools are almost unanimous in agreeing that pupils have better attitudes in the more socialized, humanized, democratic school systems.

Even though experimental studies show that higher types of

mental activity are most efficient in solitary work, the fact remains that the democratic school must emphasize the development of socialized attitudes. Children must be taught to work co-operatively and for the benefit of the social group. Historically, the school has placed too much emphasis upon "rugged individualism." A growing understanding of and appreciation for the religious and the political beliefs of other people must be developed during the days of school. Through the experience curriculum, children must be taught to accept responsibility for the care and proper use of community property. They must be led to acquire the proper attitudes that are basically essential for the democratic way of life. These attitudes must be developed through experience, not through exhortation.

All learning is, of course, an active, dynamic, adjusting process. Hence, we literally do learn by living or, as we say, through activity.[30] That statement should not be misconstrued to mean that pupils must run about the room or be otherwise in constant motion. Such an opinion is a ridiculous and unfounded notion. The statement means that the human mind should not be looked upon as a sort of receptacle to be poured full of facts by the teacher or as a glorified sponge that soaks up learning. *Pupils learn most effectively when they are engaged upon purposeful tasks that will lead to desirable satisfactions when the goals have been attained.* Whereas it is possible to force motivation by mechanical devices and tricks, the ideal motivation upon which to base education is the felt need of the learner, which, when satisfied, will lead on to higher and more desirable types of felt needs.

### QUESTIONS AND EXERCISES FOR DISCUSSION AND STUDY

1. A clear understanding of motivation is the most difficult as well as the most important topic in educational psychology. Why is this statement true? Why are there so many elaborate theories of motivation? Why do most of the experimental investigations deal with short-time studies conducted under somewhat artificial conditions?

2. Observe as many young infants as you can, and try to infer the reasons for the various types of behavior they exhibit. In formulating a theory of motivation, seek to obtain the simplest possible explanation to fit the facts ("Occam's razor" or the law of parsimony).

3. What techniques were used by your favorite teacher to interest you in schoolwork? Wherein did some of your teachers fail to obtain the best possible degree of motivation?

4. Practice alone is not sufficient to make perfect; there must be practice with zeal. Give some illustrations from your own school experience to show that repetition without adequate motivation is ineffective for learning.

---

30 *Vivendo discimus* (We learn by living).

5. Interview a number of children, asking them what they want for Christmas or for their next birthday. Find out whether there is any great difference with age. Some psychiatrists have reported that they can infer a great deal about the motivation of children by asking, "If you could have three wishes granted, what would you ask for?" Try this technique on some young children. Does it give you any insight into motivation?

6. Make a study of advertisements to determine how successfully they motivate you to experience strong motives. Some advertisements make no appeal to you. Why? Do you find some advertisements that no longer have any interest, but which would once have motivated you strongly? Explain the difference.

7. College students in vocational curricula are said to do better work than those in the academic (A. B.) course. Why might that be true? Is there any way to relate the general cultural courses to the felt needs of the learners? Give some examples of ludicrous attempts to relate the curriculum to the present needs and interests of the pupils. Is there any need to go to such extremes?

8. Some writers emphasize the wish for security. List as many specific desires for security as you can think of. Is it true that we have an infinite complexity of motives, or do we have a few, such as the wish for security, for new experience, for response, and for recognition? Think of some specific wishes to gain various types of recognition.

9. Is there any real danger in using money prizes, medals, honor rolls, and other tangible forms of recognition to motivate pupils to learn well? Explain clearly the difference between extrinsic and intrinsic motivation. Give some examples from daily life.

10. Contrast the difference between out-of-school learning and in-school learning. What can the teacher learn from observing the activity of a group of children who are learning how to build and fly model airplanes?

11. What do studies indicate about the permanence of school learning? (See, for instance, C. E. Skinner, editor, *Educational Psychology*, pp. 312-323.)

12. The Jesuits made a great deal of use of the competitive and rivalry motives in education. (See Thomas Hughes, *Loyola, and the Educational System of the Jesuits*.) Are there any dangers in excessive use of these motives? Are they not the leading motives which create interest in interscholastic athletics? What are the effects of competition and rivalry?

13. Why have the laboratory studies of human and animal motivation contributed so little to actual classroom procedures? What type of experiments would you suggest?

14. Make a list of specific motives that you have acquired recently. Do any of them upset your complacency because they are unsatisfied? What plans have you made to obtain satisfaction of them?

15. Make a list of various tricks and devices that have been used to attract your attention and to arouse your interest. Why is it questionable to employ these methods in education? What would you substitute?

16. What school subjects are essential to master but are unrelated to the immediate felt needs of the pupils? How would you obtain adequate motivation in such cases? Can you think of any subjects that have neither immediate nor relative connection to the felt needs of life? What would you do if you had to teach those subjects?

### SELECTED REFERENCES FOR FURTHER READING AND STUDY

Benson, C. E., *et al.*, *Psychology for Teachers*, rev. ed. Boston: Ginn and Company, 1933. Chapter VI.

Guthrie, E. R., *The Psychology of Human Conflict*. New York: Harper and Brothers, 1938.

Holt, E. B., *Animal Drive and the Learning Process*. New York: Henry Holt and Company, 1931.

Murphy, G., L. B. Murphy, and T. M. Newcomb, *Experimental Social Psychology*. New York: Harper and Brothers, 1937.

Powers, F. F., and others, *Psychology in Everyday Living*. Boston: D. C. Heath and Company, 1938. Chapter VI.

*The Psychology of Learning, Forty-first Yearbook*, Part II, National Society for the Study of Education, 1942. See especially Chapters VIII and IX.

Shaffer, L. A., *The Psychology of Adjustment*. Boston: Houghton, Mifflin Company, 1936.

Skinner, C. E., editor, *Readings in Educational Psychology*. New York: Farrar and Rinehart, 1937.

————, *Readings in Psychology*. New York: Farrar and Rinehart, 1935. Chapters XV and XXI.

Thomson, M. K., *Springs of Human Action*. New York: D. Appleton-Century Company, 1927.

Thorndike, E. L., *Human Learning*. New York: D. Appleton-Century Company, 1931.

————, *Psychology of Wants, Interests, and Attitudes*. New York: D. Appleton-Century Company, 1935.

Tolman, E. C., *Purposive Behavior in Animals and Men*. New York: D. Appleton-Century Company, 1932.

Valentine, W. L., editor, *Experimental Foundations of General Psychology*. New York: Farrar and Rinehart, 1938. Chapter VI.

Woodworth, R. S., *Dynamic Psychology*. New York: Columbia University Press, 1918.

Young, P. T., *Emotion in Man and Animal*. New York: John Wiley and Sons, 1943.

————, *Motivation of Behavior*. New York: John Wiley and Sons, 1936.

————, *The Psychology of Emotion*. New York: John Wiley and Sons, 1942.

# CHAPTER 10

# Transfer of Training

## The Problem of Transfer

Without doubt the transfer of training problem is complicated by terminology. Few would be so rash as to say that training, or even the effects of training, in some given line of activity is picked up and moved, or bodily transported to some other activity, function, or part of the organism. Yet that is the connotation which the term seems to bear. Thus, we find *transfer* defined by the *Standard Dictionary* as follows: "To convey, remove, or cause to pass from one person or place to another; transport; shift." In other words, the expression *transfer* of training undoubtedly implies a physical movement or shifting of training, or its effects, at least—a hypothesis which certainly can gain scant logical or physiological support. It would seem that the psychologically untenable meanings of the basic terminology, combined with experimental data of a somewhat ambiguous or equivocal nature, have led many psychologists to abandon all apparent interest in the topic.

When the problem is approached, however, not from the standpoint of an actual transference of training, but rather from the broader point of view of trying to determine what, if any, are the effects on the behavior of the individual in one situation which result from his having passed through a process of training or learning in another and previous situation, it would appear altogether worthy of study and investigation. In fact, much of our problem seems to have arisen out of the fact that too many have tried to set up separate theories of transfer of training, or have tried to establish special delimiting laws for this as a separate aspect of behavior, and in consequence have implied that problems involving transfer of training lie beyond the pale of the ordinary principles governing human behavior. Transfer should not rest on an assumption of peculiar or atypical human reactions. On the contrary, we should realize that in studying transfer of training we are merely concentrating our interest, attention, and analyses on certain perfectly normal aspects of human behavior. The student's ideas with respect to this problem should be in conformity with generally accepted principles governing psychological response, and he would do well to avoid any notion that presents transfer as an unusual or rare type of human activity to be interpreted in terms of some special set of laws or data.

## Historical antecedents

It is little wonder to us, however, that current discussions of transfer have difficulty in adhering to acceptable psychological principles when we go back and consider the antecedents of the present problem. It is an historical fact, of course, that these discussions grew out of the older hypothesis of *formal discipline*. According to this idea, anything which "improves the mind" in any way improves it generally, or in all ways. It is this school of thought that for centuries has advocated certain activities because they were "good mental discipline," or "good mind training." A learning exercise was supposed to be valuable if it was difficult or even distasteful to the individual. Accordingly, for hundreds of years Latin, mathematics, grammar, and the like were taught not so much for the purpose of having students learn them as such as for giving the students mental training, or for "disciplining their minds" or "sharpening their wits."

That this point of view was well rooted in the history of human thought is seen when we notice Plato [1] in his *Republic* quoting Socrates as saying with respect to arithmetic and geometry:

> Arithmetic has a very great elevating effect, compelling the soul to reason about abstract number, and rebelling against the introduction of visible or tangible objects into the argument. . . .

> And have you further observed that those who have a natural talent for calculation are generally quick at every other kind of knowledge; and even the dull, if they have an arithmetical training, although they may derive no other advantage from it, always become much quicker than they would otherwise have been?

> The knowledge at which geometry aims is knowledge of the eternal, and not of aught perishing and transient. . . . Geometry will draw the soul toward truth, and create the spirit of philosophy, and raise up that which now is unhappily allowed to fall down. . . . As experience. proves, anyone who has studied geometry is infinitely quicker of apprehension than one who has not. . . . There is an infinite difference between them.

---

[1] Plato, *The Republic*, rev. ed., trans. by Benjamin Jowett, with a special introduction by William Cranston Lawton. New York: P. F. Collier and Son, 1901. Book VII.

At a slightly later period we find that Quintilian, the great Roman educator, jurist, and rhetorician, took much the same position, as we see in the following statement: [2]

As regards geometry, it is granted that portions of this science are of value for the instruction of children: for admittedly it exercises their minds, sharpens their wits and generates quickness of perception. But it is considered that the value of geometry resides in the process of learning, and not as with the other sciences in the knowledge thus acquired.

Both Plato and Quintilian present about as clear a statement of the disciplinary approach to learning as one could find. At the same time, for fear we get the idea that such notions represent only an earlier period of thought, it probably is well for us to note the great percentage of people, even well-known educators, who still justify not only the contents of their courses but also their pedagogical techniques in disciplinary terms. Of course, we all are more or less familiar with the rationalizations of many athletic coaches, who would have us believe that football, or track, or baseball, or some other organized sport, "sharpens the mind," or "makes a boy keen and alert," or "teaches a boy how to meet emergencies," or "trains a boy how to meet the problems of life." Others are like a certain professor of manual arts who laid claim to an integral place in the curriculum of his institution because he said that his subject taught precision, and accuracy, and thoroughness, and, consequently, caused students to do better work in all their subjects. Such claims frequently are evidences of scholastic "growing pains," the rationalized and experimentally unsubstantiated attempts to elevate a field of work to academic respectability.

It should be recognized, however, that at their worst these younger and, in many instances, exceedingly valuable branches of training are but emulating some of the older and more classically accepted fields of thought. Thus, we have the chairman of the department of physics in a certain state university who, when discussing the purposes of college physics, claimed that it made a student a better citizen, gave him poise and judgment in social situations, and, in order to clinch his arguments, made a statement about as follows: "If I were driving along a country road and should see an automobile wreck ahead of me, and if in this wreck there was one person who had had physics and four who had not, I'd be able to tell immediately which one of the five had had physics because of the way in which he would conduct himself, his better self-control." Then there was the college president who

---

[2] B. I. Bryan, "The Psychology of Quintilian," master's thesis, Peabody College, 1929.

called his faculty together to discuss the institution's curriculum, and, reflecting his own training, emphasized the importance of Greek and Latin. By way of illustration he said that, if he knew of a garage worker in town who had had Greek and Latin, he would want to take his car to this man because he would be a better automobile mechanic by virtue of the fact that he had had Greek and Latin. In fact, this general approach is so common that we probably should not be grossly at error if we should say that formal discipline, in a greater or less degree, is still the commonly accepted educational assumption.

In a way, this is not to be considered strange. When psychologists and experimental educators have come along and set up their experiments and concluded that there is little or no transfer of learning, or have proscribed it by concluding, as did one recent author,[3] who said that the amount of transfer is between zero and 20 per cent, positive or negative, they have flaunted their ofttimes artificially derived data in the face of common, ordinary experience and observable fact. In fact, this datum of everyday life would seem to be almost adequate by itself to support the theory that, in some fashion or other, there is transfer of learning. Let us look at certain very commonplace examples.

### The Case for Transfer

If there is little or no transfer, why is it that educational methods are so difficult to change; why is it that each generation tends so strongly to pattern its pedagogical procedures after those of its teachers, even though it presumably was not being taught methods by these teachers but only subject-matter content? Why is it that many college professors teach with rather evident success large numbers of courses which they themselves never had as students? Why is it that a student will build up an emotional attitude (that is, a habit) against the teacher of English, say, and it will affect all of his study habits to the extent that he fails all his other courses? Why is it that a stenographer who has learned to type on the conventional keyboard can switch to the new Dvorak keyboard and become expert so quickly? Why does a person who has learned to read English, his native language, find that it takes him less time to learn to read German, say, than it took him to learn to read English in the beginning? Why have so many of the outstanding business executives in America risen to their positions of authority

---

[3] Peter Sandiford, "Transfer of Training," in *Encyclopedia of Educational Research,* ed. by W. S. Monroe. New York: The Macmillan Company, 1941. Pp. 1306-1313.

through the channels of lowly, closely supervised work which has offered no apparent training in directing the work of others? Why is it that so many baseball managers do not permit their players to play golf during the regular season and thus acquire a "swing" which is quite different from that of a batter striking at a pitched ball? Why is it that a boy who has learned to swim "dog-fashion," say, does not have to go through the whole process of learning to swim all over again when he begins to learn the breast stroke? Why is it that an electrician may never have seen an electric iron of a given type and yet may be able to repair it quite satisfactorily when it is brought to him? Why is it that the practice attendant upon taking two or three of our so-called intelligence tests usually results in an increase in a child's intelligence quotient, even if computed from a test different from any which he has taken? Why does an experienced cook usually make fewer failures when trying new recipes than does the novice?

We could go on almost indefinitely, pointing out the fact that we are forced to recognize the existence of some condition in practical, ordinary situations whereby the influence of learning in one situation is felt in some manner in the learning of another situation. Probably what we should recognize is that the individual never makes any response, never has any experience, that does not modify him in some way. As a matter of fact, there probably is no better illustration of the verity of this transfer hypothesis than the process of learning itself, the process of the progressive alteration or modification of the individual so that responses in subsequent situations are influenced or modified in some way by the previous activities and experiences of the organism. If this is borne in mind, and if, for the time being, at least, we do not concern ourselves with the applied and somewhat teleological aspects of transfer, that is, whether transfer is directed toward a positive or a negative goal, it should be evident that a special theory of transfer actually is superfluous in a consideration of the fundamentals of the problem. When this point of view is taken, the data, both experimental and anecdotal, which establish transfer as a reality appear to be too extensive and obvious to cite. Thus, we are not concerned with whether or not there is transfer, but with the conditions under which transfer, especially transfer of certain types, can be anticipated.

### The Experimental Evidence

Many so-called studies of transfer of training have failed to obtain any measurable evidence of transfer because they have taken a group of subjects, reduced the responses of all subjects to an average, and thereby completely obliterated all individual effects that might have been noted. In this connection, we must recognize two facts: first, that the same stimulating situations do not affect different individuals in the same way, and consequently combining individuals' responses may do nothing but obliterate significant tendencies; second, whereas a situation may result in what is called "positive transfer" for a given individual in one instance; it may result in negative transfer in another instance and in a third instance may yield no measurable results at all.

For several years the writer has been having students learn to use the touch system in learning to typewrite. The learning extends over 30 days, the practice on each day being divided into three ten-minute periods, with a two-minute intervening rest period. On the 6th, 12th, 18th, and 30th days, an interference factor is introduced during the second ten-minute practice. First, the $g$ and $h$ keys are reversed. This lasts only for the one ten-minute period, and in the third period of the day the keyboard is returned to normal. In the second period of the 12th day, the $l$ and $s$ keys are reversed; then at the beginning of the third period, the keyboard is changed back to normal. On the 18th day, the same general procedure is carried out, but this time with the $e$ and $i$ keys. On the 30th day the reversal involves the $g$ and $h$, $l$ and $s$, and $e$ and $i$ keys, all at the same time. In Table VIII one will notice certain summary results of the learning activities of twelve of the students who have taken the experiment. Figures 3, 4, 5, and 6 are graphic portrayals of the records of students $B$, $C$, and $K$, and a larger group of 16.

An examination of these figures and the table will show that the shifting of the $g$ and $h$ keys produced very different effects on the learning of the different students. Thus, student $A$ lost almost a hundred letters during the period of interference, but came back in the third period, after interference, to only a little less than the efficiency achieved in the first period. Student $B$, however, actually showed an improvement with interference, as did students $C$ and $G$. On the other hand, where students $B$ and $G$ did less well in the third period than in the second, student $C$ improved markedly in the third period. It would seem that we might say that some negative transfer, or "carry-over," ranging from slight to marked, is noted in the third-period data of students $A$, $E$, $K$, and $L$, with $B$ and $G$ occupying equivocal positions. In contradistinction to this, however, the third-period data of students $C$, $D$, $F$, $I$, $J$, and possibly $H$ apparently indicate that practice with the $g$ and $h$ keys reversed should not be expected to show any transfer effect. Furthermore, the composite or average scores for 16 subjects indicate

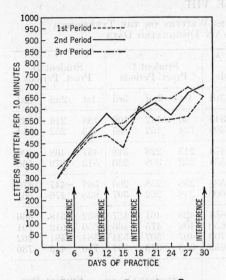

Fig. 3. Subject *B's* Learning Curves in Typewriting for First, Second, and Third Ten-minute Practice Periods on Designated Days.

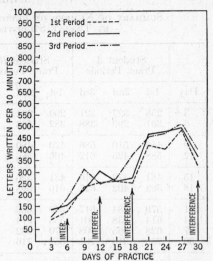

Fig. 4. Subject *C's* Learning Curves in Typewriting for First, Second, and Third Ten-minute Practice Periods on Designated Days.

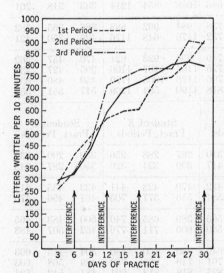

Fig. 5. Subject *K's* Learning Curves in Typewriting for First, Second, and Third Ten-minute Practice Periods on Designated Days.

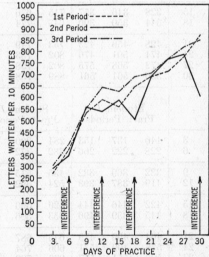

Fig. 6. Combined Group of Sixteen Subjects' Learning Curves in Typewriting for First, Second, and Third ten-minute Practice Periods on Designated Days.

TABLE VIII

SUMMARY OF NUMBER OF LETTERS WRITTEN ON THE TYPEWRITER
BY TWELVE STUDENTS ON DESIGNATED DAYS

| Day | Student A Pract. Periods | | | Student B Pract. Periods | | | Student C Pract. Periods | | | Student D Pract. Periods | | |
|---|---|---|---|---|---|---|---|---|---|---|---|---|
| | 1st | 2nd | 3rd | 1st | 2nd | 3rd | 1st | 2nd | 3rd | 1st | 2nd | 3rd |
| 3 | 258 | 327 | 321 | 290 | 291 | 343 | 90 | 142 | 106 | 188 | 214 | 243 |
| 6 | 391 | 299 | 388 | 382 | 403 | 399 | 124 | 152 | 185 | 453 | 252 | 614 |
| 9 | 459 | 510 | 586 | 470 | 489 | 474 | 243 | 228 | 318 | 437 | 468 | 420 |
| 12 | 588 | 425 | 612 | 496 | 586 | 534 | 252 | 308 | 250 | 513 | 379 | 566 |
| 15 | 481 | 472 | 610 | 431 | 526 | 538 | 258 | 258 | 266 | 568 | 447 | 470 |
| 18 | 562 | 402 | 627 | 616 | 598 | 600 | 248 | 262 | 397 | 625 | 476 | 561 |
| 21 | 579 | 584 | 617 | 550 | 630 | 654 | 423 | 461 | 457 | 632 | 518 | 466 |
| 24 | 614 | 538 | 601 | 553 | 574 | 650 | 408 | 475 | 466 | 650 | 612 | 791 |
| 27 | 628 | 665 | 708 | 570 | 682 | 700 | 497 | 507 | 534 | 584 | 591 | 762 |
| 30 | 759 | 316 | 761 | 652 | 716 | 652 | 313 | 373 | 394 | 786 | 443 | 736 |

| Day | Student E Pract. Periods | | | Student F Pract. Periods | | | Student G Pract. Periods | | | Student H Pract. Periods | | |
|---|---|---|---|---|---|---|---|---|---|---|---|---|
| 3 | 159 | 154 | 151 | 420 | 424 | 464 | 602 | 813 | 849 | 181 | 182 | 177 |
| 6 | 242 | 168 | 238 | 515 | 469 | 581 | 685 | 826 | 685 | 294 | 277 | 298 |
| 9 | 255 | 268 | 254 | 675 | 667 | 615 | 1111 | 988 | 1003 | 297 | 287 | 315 |
| 12 | 348 | 298 | 309 | 733 | 622 | 646 | 1058 | 854 | 1214 | 333 | 318 | 261 |
| 15 | 328 | 346 | 357 | 715 | 676 | 738 | 984 | 962 | 888 | 386 | 365 | 382 |
| 18 | 344 | 350 | 390 | 643 | 774 | 732 | 1176 | 648 | 1176 | 426 | 350 | 421 |
| 21 | 428 | 456 | 423 | 753 | 749 | 749 | 956 | 923 | 921 | 470 | 457 | 362 |
| 24 | 474 | 501 | 476 | 802 | 753 | 725 | 1164 | 1107 | 1106 | 395 | 427 | 433 |
| 27 | 472 | 568 | 575 | 802 | 758 | 796 | 1126 | 1005 | 1179 | 450 | 480 | 531 |
| 30 | 530 | 561 | 561 | 889 | 758 | 818 | 1190 | 584 | 1209 | 517 | 351 | 552 |

| Day | Student I Pract. Periods | | | Student J Pract. Periods | | | Student K Pract. Periods | | | Student L Pract. Periods | | |
|---|---|---|---|---|---|---|---|---|---|---|---|---|
| 3 | 140 | 137 | 153 | 284 | 300 | 310 | 267 | 288 | 256 | 330 | 200 | 233 |
| 6 | 228 | 222 | 266 | 382 | 372 | 417 | 399 | 324 | 326 | 350 | 287 | 348 |
| 9 | 332 | 369 | 332 | 435 | 515 | 432 | 470 | 423 | 441 | 433 | 435 | 414 |
| 12 | 419 | 387 | 393 | 524 | 392 | 584 | 556 | 577 | 705 | 467 | 456 | 475 |
| 15 | 422 | 446 | 444 | 526 | 596 | 565 | 389 | 685 | 740 | 500 | 483 | 465 |
| 18 | 445 | 359 | 496 | 453 | 506 | 569 | 600 | 711 | 776 | 462 | 507 | 483 |
| 21 | 464 | 459 | 479 | 645 | 687 | 649 | 730 | 750 | 780 | 504 | 443 | 603 |
| 24 | 578 | 499 | 571 | 606 | 764 | 791 | 740 | 800 | 780 | 489 | 568 | 603 |
| 27 | 505 | 551 | 577 | 836 | 720 | 825 | 818 | 813 | 901 | 481 | 542 | 524 |
| 30 | 614 | 406 | 595 | 920 | 303 | 901 | 906 | 782 | 894 | 515 | 454 | 601 |

that, where interference of this nature is introduced, one should anticipate a lowering of efficiency during the time of interference but no "carry-over" or transfer effects in the learning which im-

mediately follows. As has been indicated, of course, this average
condition very definitely is not descriptive of the learning of certain
individuals.

During the second period of the 12th day, students $B$, $C$, and $K$
improved in the number of correct letters they could write, despite
the change of the letters $l$ and $s$. All other students in this group
lost in efficiency, and the average score for 16 subjects showed a
marked drop. During the third period, students $A$, $D$, $G$, $J$, $K$, and
$L$ not only improved over their second-period results, but also did
better than they did on the first period of the same day. So we
might say that these six students show that there was no transfer
from the interference experiences of the second period to the
normal responses of the third period. Before this is carried to a
generalization, however, we should note that the learning of students $C$ and $H$ not only was less effective in the third than the
second period, but also that there may be some evidence to indicate
that the transfer effects were so pronounced as to prevent the
students from regaining their first-period efficiency. In addition to
these two, student $B$ did less well during the third period than
during the second, though the apparent "carry-over" was not sufficient to pull her down below her first-period record. Still further,
students $E$, $F$, and $I$ improved somewhat during their normal third
periods, but they did not attain to the level of efficiency they
reached in the first period before their interference experiences of
the second period. On top of this we should remember that the
composite results for the group of 16 reveal none of their idiocratic
tendencies. They merely indicate that reversing the $l$ and $s$ keys
will result in a lowering of efficiency during the particular period
in which it is experienced, but that one should not expect a measurable transfer effect on the learning that immediately follows.

Somewhat comparable data are noted for the 18th day, where
the $e$ and $i$ keys were changed. On the 30th day, however, during
the second period of which the $g$ and $h$, $l$ and $s$, and $e$ and $i$ keys
were reversed, a more evident interference effect is noted. Thus,
all students except $B$, $C$, and $E$ did worse, usually much worse,
during the second period. In fact, exclusive of these three, the 81
practice periods with a normal keyboard so affected the learning of
thirteen students during the second ten minutes of the 30th day
that they were only 67 per cent as efficient, on the average, as
during the first period. Nevertheless, when these three students are
considered separately, we find that they were 10 per cent more
efficient, on the average, when the keys were reversed than they
had been previously. The latter condition, of course, is completely
adumbrated by a statement that, on the average, the 16 students

were only 71 per cent as efficient during the second as during the first period.

When the transfer or "carry-over" from second-period interference to third-period practice is studied, we seem to conclude, in general, that such carry-over was quite negligible, the third-period average being 99 per cent of the first-period average. In this connection, students D, F, I, J, and K failed to do as well during the third period, following second-period interference, as they did during the first period before the interference experience. At the same time, student C, who seemed to be more affected, probably confused, by the prospects of a change of keys than by the reversals themselves, showed no measurable persistent effects of the interference experience in her third-period work. Although their results are somewhat less pronounced, something of the same trend (no transfer) is noted for students E, G, H, L, and probably A. In other words, there are two groups of students whose learning activities point to diametrically opposite conclusions with respect to transfer, yet both trends are lost in the group average.

From a somewhat different approach, an analysis of individuals' records is rather interesting. Student D, for example, showed a marked lowering of efficiency during interference practice on the 6th and 12th days. In both instances, however, there seemed to be no "carry-over" from second-period experiences to third-period activity, these third periods showing greater efficiency by 36 per cent and 10 per cent, respectively, than was noted in the first periods. On the 18th and 30th days, however, D was not able to do as well during the third periods as during the first, the percentage losses in efficiency being 10 and 6. So in two situations D's third-period data point to no measurable transfer effect from second-period experiences, and in two other situations there appears to be evidence of some "carry-over" from one series of activity to another.

When the results from the third period are compared with those of the first, student F did better on the 6th and 18th days, and worse on the 12th and 30th days. Student H gained slightly on the 6th and 30th days, lost slightly on the 18th, and lost markedly on the 12th. Student K lost appreciably on the 6th day, slightly on the 30th, and showed a pronounced gain on the 12th and 18th days. Of course, other very obvious variations are evident, but these should suffice to illustrate the point that the nature and extent of transfer effects are not a kind of constant commodity even for an individual. There is evidence of transfer, abundant evidence it would seem, but the evidence is strong in indicating that one would be most unwise to talk only in terms of group trends and to eliminate either individual tendencies or variations in tendencies.

## The Control and Direction of Transfer

Up to this point our main attention has been given to what might be called basic or background considerations. It must be realized, however, that few problems have more practical bearing on the program of the school than does this one of transfer. Furthermore, in school the problem immediately becomes one of the control or direction of transfer. Manifestly, it is not possible for a child to learn everything that he will be expected to know during the time he is in school, nor is it possible for him to learn to meet all the divergent types of situations and problems that do and will arise in his life. If we may think of education as training in and for complete living, we recognize at once the concern of the educator with any process or procedure that will enable children to gain the most for both in- and out-of-school living from the system of education through which they pass. Since the educator always has assumed that there must be transfer of some type, and since we have found this to be a perfectly tenable conclusion from a psychological point of view, it is immediately pertinent to know how the greatest amount of desirable transfer can be brought about.

One of the most certain ways of securing the type of transfer desired is to make an avowed, unequivocal attempt to obtain it. Without doubt we have many studies, for example, the fairly recent one by Gordon,[4] in which there is very little evidence of measurable transfer, either positive or negative, but in which there is little logical reason to suppose that such transfer would be discovered by the techniques employed. In this study, for example, Gordon administered five verbal tests: one each in reading, sentence completion, disarranged sentences, vocabulary, and analogies. Then she gave an experimental group of 53 subjects 23 periods of practice on short, multiple-choice, verbal analogies. At the end of the time, she found that with no apparent attempt whatsoever to tie up this practice with improvement in any particular field of response, no improvement was noted, except, as one might anticipate, in verbal analogies themselves. To be sure, a study such as this re-emphasizes that which has been quite apparent in the field for many years, namely, that we should not expect mere improvement in one field of learning to be accompanied by concomitant

[4] M. A. Gordon, "General and Specific Factors in Transfer of Training through Verbal Tests," *Archives of Psychology*, 1938, No. 227.

changes or improvement in a variety of dissimilar fields. At the same time, it would seem that its practical value is very small, both from the point of view of research techniques and from that of results obtained.

In contradistinction to a study of this type, we find a research such as that conducted by Woodrow,[5] who studied the effect of teaching students *how* to memorize materials. A group of 106 college sophomores was used as a control, no training or practice in memorizing being given this group. On the other hand, the group was administered a test involving six different forms of material for memorization, both at the beginning of the study and at the end, something like five weeks later. The other subjects in the experiment were divided into a practice group and a training group. Of these Woodrow says, "They were both given practice, between the initial and final end-tests, in two forms of memorizing, namely, learning poetry verbatim and learning nonsense syllables in columns of pairs. To the practice group this drill was given, as has been customary in experiments on transference, in a routine fashion without any explanation of principles, discussion of methods, or comparison of the methods to be used in different kinds of problems. To the training group some practice was given with the same materials utilized by the practice group but, in addition, instruction was given in the technique of memorizing. The total time consumed by each group, apart from the end-tests, was 177 minutes divided into periods occurring twice a week for four weeks."

The practice group devoted 90 minutes to the memorization of poetry and 87 minutes to the memorization of nonsense syllables. The training group, on the other hand, spent 76 minutes in listening to a presentation of the best methods of memorizing, another 76 minutes in actually memorizing poetry, and 25 minutes in memorizing nonsense syllables. Of the practice of the training group, Woodrow says that the memorizing was "done with the purpose of attempting, as far as possible, to apply the rules that had been learned."

When the final end-tests were given, it was found that mere practice, or undirected drill, as, for example, practice such as was used by Gordon in the study previously mentioned, yielded thoroughly equivocal results, there being a few seeming gains in efficiency and a few seeming losses, but all changes were relatively small and, taken together, truly unpredictable. On the other hand, the training group, which, it will be remembered, had less actual practice than the practice group, showed effects "which are uni-

---

[5] H. Woodrow, "The Effect of Types of Training upon Transference," *Journal of Educational Psychology*, 1927, Vol. 18, pp. 159-172.

formly large and positive." In other words, when the learning was of such a type that the subjects developed habitual tendencies to respond as a result of several different types of stimuli, or when there was a conscious, predetermined attempt made to teach in such a manner as to cause transfer of a particular type, this transfer actually did appear.

At the present time we hear much about the necessity for courses of study having a functional value in the lives of the children who take them. One of the unfortunate by-products of this point of view is that some educators apparently think that certain courses, or organizations of subject matter, have greater inherent transfer value than do other courses. This is a regrettable position, however, because there are few if any types of subject matter which, if left to themselves, or if put in the hands of a teacher who does not organize her work properly, can be expected to have much "carry-over" or much out-in-life value. Conversely, there are few courses, indeed, which cannot be presented from a functional point of view, a point of view aimed to make the material learned in the class-room function in out-of-school situations.

An informal illustration may serve to show how a desirable principle can be studied, or even taught for many years, and yet have little effect in a non-scholastic situation. Several years ago the writer was teaching in the summer school of a certain college. On the morning of July 3rd, he happened to see a group of students clustered around the flagpole on the campus. He walked up to them and found that they were faced with the problem of buying enough rope to raise the flag, but in order to do this they had to know the height of the pole. This they had not been able to determine. Finally, the writer saw a stick, measured its length, propped it next to the pole, and then measured the shadows of the stick and the pole, after which, of course, there was nothing but a simple proportion to figure in order to determine the height of the pole. The interesting thing, however, was that after the students had been told how high the pole was, and their subsequent purchase of rope had confirmed the estimate, one of the older students came to the writer and said, "I just wish you'd tell me how you figured how tall that pole is.. I've been teaching arithmetic for 40 years, and I can't figure how you found out." The tragedy of the situation was that this man had been teaching this identical principle most of the time but had been teaching it solely as a textbook situation, apparently never having approached it as something which can and will "carry-over" in normal life situations. The weakness here, then, was a methodological weakness, not one inherent in the subject matter itself. Thus, we come back again to our earlier thesis that, if a teacher wishes to have a transfer from one situation to another situation, she must organize her work with this definitely in mind; she must teach for transfer if she is going to attain her goal.

Another point to consider in regulating the nature of transfer effects that may be obtained from one situation to another is that, though ideals and principles have a place in the teaching program, though rules may be presented with profit, at least in instances, there must be an adequate and diversified illustration of these generalizations if there is going to be a profitable transfer from the first to subsequent learning situations. Too often we have mere detached generalizations made so that children studying them have no basis for applying them in actual situations. It is often similar to the following condition. A nine-year-old boy who had been going to Sunday School one day brought home a lesson paper which had on the front a picture of a group of boys playing baseball, which one of the boys had left to guide an elderly woman across the street. The boy's father noticed the picture and thought he would like to see just what the child did learn from it. Accordingly, he asked the boy what the picture meant. Without hesitation the child said that it meant that you could not hit a baseball unless you held the bat in the correct position. He had been taught a few conventional generalizations about moral behavior, but these generalizations had not been sufficiently illustrated in actual life experiences to enable the child to apply the generalization himself. His informal teaching with respect to batting form apparently was more specific and effective.

Years ago Judd [6] reported an experiment that illustrated the same point. He and Scholckow, an assistant, used two groups of fifth- and sixth-grade pupils. Each was supposed to throw a dart at a small target under water. The greatest difficulty one experiences in this is to take proper account of the deflection of light through refraction, which results in the target seeming to be removed from where it actually is. One group of boys was given a fairly complete theoretical discussion of the principles of refraction, and the other group was given no instruction of this type at all. At first the practice was carried out with the target 12 inches under water, and there was no apparent difference in the efficiency of the two groups. In fact, Judd says, "Theory seemed to be of no value in the first tests. All the boys had to learn how to throw the dart, and theory proved to be no substitute for practice."

After this, the position of the target was changed so that it was

---

[6] C. H. Judd, "The Relation of Special Training to General Intelligence," *Educational Review*, 1908, Vol. 36, pp. 28-42.

only four inches under the water. In this instance the practice of the group without theoretical training resulted in errors that were "large and persistent." The group with theory, though, adapted its technique to the new situation rather quickly. It is interesting to note, however, that the theoretical instruction did not prove especially valuable until it had been supplemented by actual illustrative practice. In this connection Judd says, "The theory is not a substitute for direct experience; it is rather a frame in which experiences may be properly held apart and at the same time held together. The boys who did not have the theory had experiences, but one experience got in the way of another and there was disconcerting confusion."

Another research that pointed in the same general direction as that conducted by Judd and Scholckow, but with more direct application and meaning for school learning activities is Gates'[7] investigation involving transfer in spelling. Two experiments were conducted, both of which yielded somewhat comparable results. For our purposes, the second experiment will be reviewed. This involved 823 pupils in each of two groups, known as the "Generalization Group" and the "Control Group." Both groups were given an initial and a final test of 100 words. In addition, another test was given on words not studied by either group but the spelling of which was related to certain rules taught to the Generalization Group.

The results from our point of view are quite interesting. The Generalization Group, as can be seen from Table IX, did slightly though very little better than the Control Group on the 100 words that both had studied. This was true on 13 of the 14 comparisons. In only one instance, however, was there a statistically significant difference between the groups. In other words, where both groups had a comparable direct study experience, generalization in the study of rules resulted in only a very, very small positive advantage, if any advantage at all. More interesting than this, though, as will be noticed in the table, is the difference between the two groups in the spelling of new words, but words related in principle to certain rules that had been taught to the Generalization Group. This apparently is the test of transfer, and it can be seen that in every instance the Control Group did less well than the other group. Six of the 12 differences are more than three times their standard errors, and two others are more than 2.5 times their standard errors. This would indicate that in eight of the 12 comparisons there is less than one chance in 100 that the obtained

[7] A. I. Gates, *Generalization and Transfer in Spelling*. New York: Teachers College, Columbia University, 1935.

difference is not significant. So we see that when generalizations, or principles, or rules, are taught along with specific learning activity, they do not supplant the latter, but they do put the child in a more favored position for meeting other comparable experiences.

TABLE IX

RELATIVE EFFICIENCY OF STUDENTS TAUGHT SPELLING
WITH AND WITHOUT THE LEARNING OF GOVERNING RULES (Gates' Data*)

| Grade | 100 Studied Words | | | | 51 New Words Applying Rules | | | |
|-------|-------|-------|-------|-------|-------|-------|-------|-------|
| | Group | | Diff. | $\Sigma_{diff.}$ | Group | | Diff. | $\Sigma_{diff.}$ |
| | Gener. | Control | | | Gener. | Control | | |
| 3A | 81.3 | 82.4 | −1.1 | 3.4 | 15.1 | 12.6 | 2.5 | 1.6 |
| 3B | 77.5 | 75.7 | 1.8 | 3.2 | 15.7 | 12.7 | 3.0 | 1.7 |
| 4A | 91.1 | 89.6 | 1.5 | 1.1 | 18.5 | 15.1 | 3.4 | 1.7 |
| 4B | 90.7 | 88.8 | 1.9 | 1.4 | 23.5 | 18.4 | 5.1 | 1.8 |
| 5A | 90.3 | 86.3 | 4.0 | 2.1 | 25.2 | 20.0 | 5.2 | 1.5 |
| 5B | 93.9 | 92.9 | 1.0 | 1.1 | 26.8 | 21.3 | 5.5 | 1.7 |
| 6A | 93.2 | 91.5 | 1.7 | 1.3 | 27.2 | 23.1 | 4.1 | 1.8 |
| 6B | 91.1 | 88.9 | 2.2 | 1.7 | 27.7 | 22.6 | 5.1 | 2.0 |
| 7A | 92.4 | 91.6 | 0.8 | 0.9 | 28.7 | 24.4 | 4.3 | 1.4 |
| 7B | 94.4 | 92.4 | 2.0 | 0.8 | 30.2 | 24.1 | 6.1 | 1.4 |
| 8A | 97.4 | 95.6 | 1.8 | 0.6 | 32.4 | 27.4 | 5.0 | 1.4 |
| 8B | 93.9 | 90.9 | 3.0 | 1.2 | 32.9 | 27.0 | 5.9 | 1.4 |

*A. I. Gates, *Generalization and Transfer in Spelling*. New York: Teachers College, Columbia University, 1935.

Results such as these obtained by Woodrow, Judd and Scholckow, and Gates have been reaffirmed in a variety of investigations and stand out in some of the more thorough reviews or digests of the literature, as, for example, those by Orata,[8] Brownell,[9] Hamley,[10] and Bayles.[11] The latter of these makes a summary generalization that is exceedingly pertinent to this discussion:

If we would make training transfer, our teaching must accomplish two objectives more or less simultaneously: First, it must bring the student to understand as many widely useful relationships, principles, or generalizations as possible; second, it must whet the student's realization that his previous training has wide possibilities for transfer, but that transfer is never automatic. It must

[8] P. T. Orata, *The Theory of Identical Elements*. Columbus, Ohio: Ohio State University Press, 1928.

[9] W. A. Brownell, "Theoretical Aspects of Learning and Transfer of Training," *Review of Educational Research*, 1936, Vol. 6, pp. 281-290 and 337-339; 1939, Vol. 9, pp. 268-273 and 312-318.

[10] H. R. Hamley, "Formal Training; a Critical Survey of Experimental Work," *British Journal of Educational Psychology*, 1936, Vol. 6, pp. 233-249.

[11] E. E. Bayles, "An Unemphasized Factor in Current Theories Regarding Transfer of Training," *Journal of Educational Psychology*, 1936, Vol. 27, pp. 425-430.

bring a realization that transfer comes only if and when one senses for one's self that transfer is possible. One becomes able to make the greatest transfer of previous training when, and only when, as a matter of habit, one is on the alert to recognize previous relationships, principles, meanings, or generalizations which may be used in the new situations that are always at hand.

So, by way of summary, we would appear to have justification to speak of transfer of training in the sense of modification of the individual through experience. Then, if the schools wish to utilize the principles of transfer, they must be thoroughly alert to the facts of individual difference and variation. Lastly, in order to obtain desirable transfer, there must be a planned arrangement of materials and development of instructional methods aimed at obtaining specific effects. In other words, we must teach for transfer if we wish to find it in most profitable form.

## QUESTIONS AND EXERCISES FOR DISCUSSION AND STUDY

1. Do you think that the term *transfer of training* has led to a confusion in thinking on the problems involved? What evidence have you?

2. How do modern concepts of transfer of training differ from the conventional formal-discipline concepts? Find five instances from your ordinary personal contacts and/or popular reading in which a formal-discipline concept is held.

3. How could the very common, or frequent statistical, as opposed to individually analytical, studies of transfer overshadow important data with respect to the problem?

4. In the data from the typing experiment, what do you consider the two most important facts relating to transfer?

5. Could the formal-disciplinist account for data such as are shown for student *B*, Figure 3?

6. What is there in Gordon's experimental set-up that would be likely to result in the type of results she finally obtained? Contrast this with Woodrow's procedure.

7. What does the expression "functional value in the lives of children" mean to you when applied to a course? What are two courses that you have had which do not conform to this standard? Two that do? Why do you so brand each course?

8. Should rules be taught in grammar? In arithmetic? In morals? In etiquette? In swimming? Why do you take the position you do?

9. Summarize Gates' findings in a sentence of not over 50 words.

10. In Bayles' statement two principles are set forth. Do you know of any illustrations that conform, or any that do not conform, to these principles?

## SUGGESTED REFERENCES FOR FURTHER READING AND STUDY

Bruce, R. W., "Conditions of Transfer of Training," *Journal of Experimental Psychology*, Vol. 16, 1933, pp. 343-361.

Davis, R. A., *The Psychology of Learning*. New York: McGraw-Hill Book Company, 1935. Chap. 10.

Dorsey, Mattie, and L. T. Hopkins, "The Influence of Attitude upon Transfer," *Journal of Educational Psychology*, Vol. 21, 1930, pp. 410-417.

Eaton, T. H., "Mental Discipline," *Journal of Higher Education*, Vol. 2, 1931, pp. 493-501; Vol. 3, 1932, pp. 31-38.

Eurich, A. C., and H. A. Carroll, *Educational Psychology*. Boston: D. C. Heath and Company, 1935. Chap. 17.

Judd, C. H., *Education as the Cultivation of the Higher Mental Processes*. New York: The Macmillan Company, 1936.

————, *Psychology of Secondary Education*. Boston: Ginn and Company, 1927. Chap. 19.

Orata, P. T., *The Theory of Identical Elements*. Columbus, O.: Ohio State University Press, 1928.

Starch, D., H. M. Stanton, and W. Koerth, *Psychology in Education*. New York: D. Appleton-Century Company, 1941. Chap. 8.

Thorndike, E. L., "Mental Discipline in High School Studies," *Journal of Educational Psychology*, Vol. 15, 1924, pp. 1-22, 83-89.

Webb, L. W., "The Transfer of Training," Chapter 13 in *Educational Psychology* (edited by C. E. Skinner). New York: Prentice-Hall, Inc., 1936.

# CHAPTER 11*

# Perceptual-Motor and Associational Learning

For convenience in discussion, some psychologists refer to three levels of learning. The first, or simplest, level may be described as "reflex." This reflex may be "native" and unconditioned, or conditioned. Such reflexes function automatically. Simple reflex acts, such as drawing the hand away from a hot object, illustrate this. Even an apparently simple reflex-arc pattern, however, is highly complex in character when studied in detail, and such a pattern is modified by the general or specific situation in which it occurs. The second level of organization consists of connections that involve more conscious perceptual-motor learning. Consciously perceived stimuli result in a more consciously planned response, such as turning the head at the sound of a phone bell and subsequently answering the phone. Other connections may be called third-level organizations of learning. These so-called "higher" responses are heavily weighted with mental content and involve various degrees of thinking.

## Perceptual-Motor Learning

Different names have been applied to different kinds of learning. One of the simplest kinds of learning is *perceptual-motor* learning. In this type of learning, perceptual stimuli or situations initiate motor responses. In infants it may be illustrated by their reaching for a brightly colored object. On the adult level it may be illustrated by learning to play a musical instrument, to drive a car, or to typewrite.

The term *perceptual-motor* implies two aspects in this type of learning. The perceptual aspect comprises the stimuli that reach the individual through the sense organs. The motor aspect com-

---

* For the point of view expressed in this chapter, the author is indebted to *Visual Outline of Educational Psychology*, by Guy T. Buswell (New York: Longmans, Green and Company, 1939).

prises the motor, or muscular, responses to respective stimuli. Concomitant with such learning are various feelings, emotions, attitudes, and meanings which are a part of the total learning configuration. These concomitant learnings are dynamic in that they influence perceptual-motor learning.

### Elementary perceptual-motor learning

Many simple examples of perceptual and motor learning may be observed in young children. These include reaching for objects, imitating sounds, using a spoon in eating, and removing the paper in which a toy or other object is wrapped. It is readily seen that the ability to adjust to a changing environment is closely related to the individual's capacity to perceive situations and make the various responses required.

Studies of young children which have been made by Gesell and others indicate rapid maturation in the early years of life, especially in perceptual-motor learning. The normal child develops in motor, language, adaptive, and social behavior from month to month. In motor development, at one month the average child lifts his head occasionally when lying face down; at two months he holds his head erect momentarily; at five to six months he sits if propped up; at eight months he sits without support; at twelve months he walks with support; at eighteen months he walks confidently without support and begins to feed himself with a spoon.

### Perception in motor learning

In motor learning, the value of sensation is that it marks perception and initiates an appropriate co-ordination with motor learning activities and with related intellectual and emotional concomitants. As the individual matures, more complicated skills result from a better integration of activities. Motor skills are most necessary in making physical adaptations to the environment. In the school, for example, this development of motor skills may be observed in activities on the playground, in the gymnasium, and in woodwork, sewing, and cooking, penmanship, and countless other activities.

Motor co-ordination is necessary to a well-adjusted individual because good co-ordination reduces fatigue and helps the individual to use his energies more economically and effectively. Poor motor control or co-ordination may indicate a need for training in specific activities involved in penmanship, drawing, dancing, and the use of tools.

## Maturation and learning in development [1]

In the development of a person, the processes that are called "learning" and "growth," or maturation, are so closely related that it is difficult to separate them, except for convenience in discussion. In the young child who cannot as yet sit up, stand, or talk, the difficulty may be that the child has not yet reached a stage of maturation, or mental and physical development, that will permit him to learn efficiently how to perform these perceptual-motor skills. The same may be true of a second-grade child who is attempting to learn whole arm movement in handwriting. He may be unable to develop the skills required because his level of physical and mental growth, or maturity, may not give him adequate equipment for effective learning. The same effect of immaturity is often found in such skills as playing tennis or other games, reading rapidly, and learning certain skills and concepts in arithmetic or history.

Motor co-ordination and learning are closely associated with the physical and mental maturity of the individual. Frequently teachers and parents fail to recognize this fact and attempt to force the growth of an individual. Under the best conditions of learning, performance of motor acts would not be encouraged until such time as the individual arrives at the proper stage of development. For example, parents who try to force a very young child's rate of growth in learning to walk do not realize that the child's muscular, or motor, development is not yet ready for this task. The situation is the same in such school activities as handwriting, which is a form of sensorimotor learning. Many children of the first and second grades have not developed sufficient muscular, or motor, co-ordination; therefore, the teaching of handwriting to such children becomes an undesirable educational activity at these grade levels. Naturally, individual differences exist among individuals, and the teacher or parent must decide from observation when the best time for teaching certain motor skills is at hand.

The same holds true of the more complicated motor skills that are involved in typewriting and learning to play a good game of tennis. To become a good typist, for example, it is necessary to have proper co-ordination between the sensory or perceptual stimulus and the muscular or motor responses involved in planning the layout of the material on a sheet of paper and the consequent movements involved in manipulating the keys of the typewriter. All learning requires activity on the part of an individual. The organization or guidance of motor activities and learning may help

---

[1] Also see Chapter 4.

to produce a much more efficient rate of learning, but only provided that the maturity of the individual is at an appropriate stage.

## Classes of perceptual-motor learning

Many school subjects and activities require various degrees of perceptual-motor learning. In some activities the perceptual factors are relatively simple and the motor responses are also relatively simple, as in sawing a piece of wood or in tossing a ball to a companion. In other activities the perceptual factors are relatively simple but the motor responses are relatively difficult, as in drawing a curved design exactly to scale. In still other activities the perceptual factors are relatively difficult but the motor responses are relatively simple, as in tracing a path through a difficult maze or selecting the proper size of bolt or screw from an assortment in order to assemble a simple machine. Again in some activities both perceptual and motor aspects are relatively difficult, as in playing a difficult musical composition. These examples illustrate some of the combinations of perceptual and motor factors. In addition, all of these situations involve many mental and emotional factors which vary according to the type of activity and its degree of complexity.

Various classes of perceptual-motor learning are commonly found in school. A first general class may be called the development of new perceptual-motor skills. Many of these new skills, however, are learned early in the life of the child because the child has attended nursery school or because the parents have guided the growth of the initial development of the perceptual-motor skills. For many pupils the development of the skills of handwriting, of playing a musical instrument, and of working in the laboratory require relatively new perceptual-motor skills. The adjustment of the microscope in the science laboratory is another example of a possible perceptual-motor co-ordination which for most individuals is entirely new.

A second general class involves the integration of motor skills already developed with new stimuli, or perceptual, factors. In this kind of perceptual-motor learning, the situation requires that the motor skills already mastered are to be related to a new stimulus. An example of this type of perceptual-motor learning may be found in tracing star outlines, in which situation the learner sees his hand, pencil, and star outline by looking in a mirror. It is also present in learning to fly a plane, to throw a forward pass in football, and to operate a card-punch business machine. In these

illustrations the motor co-ordination required for performance has
to a large degree been learned in previous simple and somewhat
similar activities. The essence of this kind of perceptual-motor
learning is to integrate, or form a new synthesis of, motor responses
in order to meet the needs of a new situation.

When learning to ride a bicycle, for example, we bring to that
situation all the sensorimotor abilities that we have acquired in
learning to walk and to maintain our equilibrium. In a like manner,
games of motor skill such as playing quoits and darts call upon
perceptual-motor skills which an individual may have acquired in
other games. As a consequence, learning is more rapid than it
would be if the individual had to begin with the fundamental
perceptual-motor skills. Likewise, when an individual studies
algebra after mastering the concepts of arithmetic, his initial progress is more rapid because of his previous experiences. In reading,
although it is mainly learning of the associational and intellectual
type, various motor skills involved in the movement of the eyes
and the perception of words and letters are important factors.

Another class of responses may be described as an extension or
refinement of the skills in the second class. The distinguishing characteristics of the third class of perceptual-motor responses are the
dexterity and accuracy of performance. This class may be illustrated by skilled work in assembly of parts of a machine, expert
office machine operation, and the co-ordination of a well-trained
football team in charging the opponent's line. In this kind of
response, basic motor skills have been established for a variety of
situations, and the emphasis is upon speed and accuracy.

## Processes of growth and learning

The process of growth which is assumed to work in perceptual-
motor skills may be generally described as follows. An interest,
need, or drive develops in a person. This leads to a feeling of restlessness, which in turn expresses itself in the form of various
activities and behaviors. Many of these responses may be ineffective and inappropriate to attaining the goal which inspires the
interest or need or drive. Thus, in learning to typewrite, the student
hits many wrong keys. Preliminary or exploratory activities of
this kind are termed "trial and error." The individual is trying
with his own biological and psychological equipment to achieve as
effectively as possible a goal or purpose.

During the exploratory period, many associations and connections are established in the individual. Some of these are satisfactory and some are unsatisfactory. Those which are satisfactory

tend to be retained and those which are unsatisfactory tend to be dropped. Gradually a pattern of behavior is established, so that each movement provides the necessary and desirable cues to initiate the next movement or component of behavior. In this way a person learns effectively to typewrite, to play a piano, or to play tennis in terms of his potential abilities.

Some of the steps in the process of developing perceptual-motor skills may be briefly summarized. Only through activity or actual performance can these skills be learned. The first step consists in making exploratory or trial-and-error responses or movements to the sensory situation faced. This step stresses activity or movement rather than thinking about the situation. The second step grows out of the first. From many movements or responses made, certain "accidental" ones will tend to become selected and stamped in because they result in motor responses that provide a more successful movement or satisfactory solution to the problem or situation. These successful responses are gradually built up as habits or skills. A third step in this kind of learning consists in recalling and reproducing the perceptual and motor activities that were parts of the initial successful movements. In the effort to reproduce the sensations or "feel" that accompanied the selected movement, the most effective learning procedure is to re-enact the successful motor responses and related emotional and intellectual concomitants until speed and accuracy are achieved. A fourth step in this type of learning involves repeated exercise until the successful response is established as a habit and can be maintained by the individual at a level commensurate with his optimum ability. The application of established principles of teaching will facilitate the learning of adequate motor responses.

In developing any skill or ability, a person reaches a level of achievement or maturity that represents his optimum capacity, and he cannot appreciably improve this level of optimum achievement, no matter how hard he tries. In speed of reading, for example, a limit is reached beyond which it is difficult to improve. In a like manner, there are limits at various stages of development to the speed with which the pupil can add, multiply, subtract, and divide, operate a typewriter, or sew with a needle. The limits of learning for sensorimotor materials vary from person to person: some people have very high limits and some persons have limits that are low, while most persons have moderate or average limits.

### Curves of growth

If curves were drawn representing the growth of learning, they would show a trend as follows. The initial progress is slow, but later progress is made at a rather rapid rate. When the limits of the learner's ability have been reached, the curve tends to flatten out. The gradual improvement or progress in the mastery of a set of skills may be indicated by means of a graph called the *learning curve*. The use of a graphic method permits a comparison of the growth curves for individuals and emphasizes the fact that individual differences or variations in rate of growth do appear. It is valuable at times to make a composite curve of growth showing successive measurements obtained from a group of individuals. In both individual and group curves, the same general trend may be observed in the mastery of easy as well as of difficult skills. The explanation for this is that, in different learning situations, most individuals eliminate errors rapidly at first and then more and more slowly.

## Guides for motor learning

For the prospective or "practicing" teacher, various generalizations may be drawn to help in guiding instruction in perceptual-motor learning.

(1) Detailed analysis of the learning process should come after some facility in a skill has been established, because, if introduced prematurely, such part-by-part approach will divert attention from a co-ordinated response to the whole situation.

(2) The suggestions and guidance should be adapted to the level of development that the learner has reached at a given time.

(3) The teacher's suggestions and guidance should be adapted to needs that are indicated by systematic and objective tests and observations.

(4) At first, accuracy in perceptual and motor performance should be emphasized; later, dexterity should be sought.

(5) Although explanations are valuable and necessary at times, the learner's guidance can most effectively be served by expert demonstrations.

(6) In teaching complicated perceptual-motor skills, the whole method is generally more effective than the part method, in which attention is focused on separate and isolated elements of the total performance.

## Associational Learning

Associational learning uses as its medium numbers, words, and concepts that are largely abstract or symbolic in form and nature. Associational learning is one of the basic processes in the curriculum of the school. This type of learning comprises associating meanings with words and concepts, recognizing and recalling relationships between and among numbers, and mastering the facts in various school subjects or courses.

## Associating experiences

*Association* is the process of relating experiences to each other. Experiences, both real and vicarious, become more meaningful as they are related to previous experiences of the learner. Present experiences recall, through the process of association, other experiences; hence, the present experiences take on a new meaning. Although association may not result in a good memory, memory is an essential part of associational learning. This is true because memory is the process of strengthening or reinforcing associations. Associational learning may be the deliberate recall or recognition of past experiences, as well as the behavior called "automatic memory," which is caused by many associations. The general concept of memory involves what might be called various degrees of associative learning which apply to a varying extent to such aspects of learning as retention, recall, and recognition.

It is important to consider forgetting as well as remembering. These are not necessarily opposites. What is retained, recalled, or recognized from the past is rarely, if ever, a duplicate of a previous experience. As a matter of fact, it can easily be demonstrated that several persons who observe a very objective demonstration will vary in their memory of even the essential facts, objects, or persons involved in the demonstration. The degree of accuracy varies with each person. Everyone tends to fill in the gaps with inferences that seem reasonable, that is, with experiences or events that such gaps might possibly have included or what he should like to have them include. This means that our memory of the past is a personal version, and one that usually contains some unconscious and inevitable inaccuracies or amendments to the actual facts.

## Steps in associational learning

When associational learning is analyzed into its component parts, it may be described as follows. The first step is *sensation,* which records and fixes to some degree the fact that is perceived. The second step is the *strengthening of the association or connection* between the new fact, concept, or meaning and the previously acquired facts, concepts, or meanings. The third step is *memory or duration* of the new learning. The fourth step is the *modification and extension of the association* by means of new and relevant experiences. The fifth step is the *diminution of earlier associations* involving facts or concepts that are not used or reviewed in any consistent or purposeful manner.

Associations occur under certain conditions, which are the subject of the laws of learning. Many associations that may be relatively meaningless and that may tend to hinder the desired educational growth of the pupil are occurring simultaneously in the child. These offer many possibilities for making connections. The problem of the teacher is to stimulate and guide the pupil so that he will make meaningful and effective associations.

## Laws of learning

From the very early days of psychology it has been recognized that a stimulus or situation, whether simple or complex, tends to encourage the recall of past experiences that are similar in whole or in part to the present situation. The fact that some elements of a new situation recall the corresponding elements of an older situation is called the *law of similarity.* Another fact to be observed about learning is that we tend to contrast the past with the present situation, as when day suggests night, or when hot suggests cold. This suggestion or recall of an opposite is called the *law of contrast*. A third tendency is for a part of a present situation to recall the whole situation of something past, or for the whole situation being experienced to recall some particular thing out of past experience. This tendency to connect past with present situations, or ideas and concepts that are closely related or in close succession in space or time, is called the *law of contiguity*. The consensus among psychologists is to consider the three primary laws of learning as fundamentally one law of the contiguity of experience. The elements of likeness or similarity, and unlikeness or contrast, are thus regarded as variations of the larger concept of relationships involved in contiguity.

The associations formed by any one of the three primary laws of learning are related to the so-called "secondary laws of learning" formulated by Thorndike. These are the laws of recency, vividness, and frequency. The *law of recency* refers to the fact that the strength and completeness of an association after it is once made depend upon the freshness of the association, the newly learned connections being more nearly perfect than those learned in the past. Of course, the factor of use of a connection may overcome the advantage of recency. The *law of vividness* refers to the fact that the intensity of the stimulus or the emotional tone of the situation in which the association is made affects the strength, permanence, and completeness of the association. When the emotional tone of the situation touches the pupil, and especially if it attaches to the material to be learned, he is very likely to make the whole situation a permanent association. The *law of frequency* refers to the fact that unless opportunities arise for exercising the association learned, it will disappear.

Failure to recognize the complex nature of a learning situation is common. A teacher may feel that she has performed her duty when she has provided each child in the classroom with a textbook. Actually, many other factors of learning are involved in the situation. These include, among other things, physical defects in sight or hearing, the emotional set of the learner, the simplicity or complexity of the concepts or material to be learned, and like factors. Less tangible and less observable factors that are effective in modifying the associations are the accumulated habits of the child, his attitudes, the adaptability of his personality, his memory, and his powers of concentration. The teacher must recognize these individual differences. Interest, also, is an active factor. Repeated failures in a subject may result in such a dislike for it that associations are made with great difficulty. It is clear that any defects of the physical organism, such as defective motor control, tend to interfere with or to block the associations that depend upon such factors.

## Meaning

The ease and readiness with which associations are formed also depend upon the knowledge of their meaning. Mere rote associations generally fail to elicit active interest and are soon forgotten. Associations that the teacher prefers to have pupils establish should be presented in the light of the individual's interests and experiences. It is important that the associations desired to be presented to the child be adapted to his age, needs, and particular interests. An association that has significant meaning to a child of ten may have no significance to an adolescent of sixteen years of age, and vice versa.

## Gestalt theory

In relatively recent years, a contribution of the Gestalt psychology has been made to the effect that all mental phenomena have a configuration. The Gestalt point of view on the process of associational learning is not an emphasis on or explanation of how separate ideas or situations are associated, because these have not occurred other than as parts of a total situation or configuration. Ideas and situations are generally regarded as not separate or isolated, because they are always parts of an experience or series of experiences having a definite pattern, or configuration, by which they possess meaning and significance to a learner. To illustrate this theory, the date of 1492 serves to stimulate the association of other facts about Columbus' discovery of America because the whole situation with many details is suggested and recalled by a part of the experience. Even in Gestalt psychology, however, contiguity of experience is an essential component in establishing the unit of learning, or configuration.

Objects and ideas should be presented through several different senses, when possible, and should be carefully associated in their relationships. This is the basis for recommending not only the usual verbal materials but also visual and auditory aids such as pictures, motion pictures, and radio. Studies have shown that the more associations and relationships that are developed for a concept, the more meaningful and the more lasting is that concept. Associations generally should not be considered as ends in themselves, but rather as means for solving more complex problems. Uncritical and isolated associations may lead to erroneous knowledge or belief. Many erroneous meanings and connections may be attributed to the tendency of the learner to make only partial and incorrect associations.

## Primary and Concomitant Learnings

Among others, Kilpatrick [2] has insisted upon a distinction between primary and concomitant learnings. *Primary* learnings are the more definite and tangible outcomes of any particular learning experience. Thus, the process of learning the multiplication combinations may be directed toward the objective of gaining skill in multiplying effectively in a problem of mathematics. During such a learning experience the pupil will have *concomitant* learnings, such as accuracy in technique, self-reliance, attitudes toward the teacher, and attitudes toward himself and his associates. These concomitant learnings involve attitudes, appreciations, and general emotional tones usually associated with personality.

It is important to recognize that the teacher may influence the pupil not only in his primary learnings but also in his so-called concomitant learnings. Some educators argue that the concomitant learnings are the basis of character education and are, therefore,

[2] William H. Kilpatrick, *Foundations of Methods*. New York: The Macmillan Company, 1925.

more important than the more tangible and obvious primary learnings.

## Motivation

All learning may be influenced by intrinsic and extrinsic motivation. Intrinsic motivation can establish within the individual a recognition of need that will develop into an interest or a drive by which the individual voluntarily learns. Adroit teachers can stimulate such interests and drives by many devices, principally by setting up situations that lead pupils to suggest the desirability of achieving certain goals.

Extrinsic motivation, however, uses various devices, some of which are on the borderline of intrinsic motivation. Praise and blame, for example, are effective when they come from persons whom the learner respects. Although many investigations indicate that praise is the most effective of incentives tested, other studies may be cited to show that it is not always effective for some pupils. Another device used is rivalry, especially between groups, and self-rivalry, or competition with one's past record. Self-rivalry may be illustrated by the use of graphs of progress of results on objective standardized tests. Closely associated with the methods of praise and blame are rewards and punishments. Generally speaking, if punishment is inflicted when the reason is not clear or acknowledged, it may breed antagonism and a desire to avoid the form of learning with which it may be associated. Rewards in the form of money are rarely desirable forms of motivation. Rewards of an intangible sort related to satisfaction or esteem are most desirable. All of these various sources of motivation rest upon the wish of individuals for social approval, for mastery or dominance, for personal satisfaction, or for giving pleasure to another individual.

## Summary

Psychologists have set up three levels in the organization of learning and behavior. From simple to more complicated levels, they are called successively conditioned response, perceptual-motor learning, and associational learning. Each of these types of learning may be subdivided into various classes, or categories.

In most types of learning, the same general growth curve seems to be followed. Initial learning of a new task is rapid, and then learning or skill develops more and more slowly.

Associational learning involves the major law of contiguity of experience, in which the law of similarity and the law of contrast are included.

The Gestalt theory of learning has made an important contribution in that it contends that any idea or situation cannot exist in isolation but is always part of some definite pattern or configuration.

Primary learnings are acquired with concomitant learnings as a necessary partner in the learning process. Concomitant learnings relate mainly to dynamic aspects of personality and character development.

While intrinsic motivation is most desired, certain extrinsic devices sometimes prove valuable in stimulating learning. These sources of motivation rest upon a desire for social approval, for mastery, or dominance, and for pleasure to self or another individual.

## QUESTIONS AND EXERCISES FOR DISCUSSION AND STUDY

1. To what extent is it possible to identify and to separate the contributions of maturation and learning in the development of a child?

2. Discuss the factors responsible for the characteristics of a curve of learning to typewrite or to master skills of a game.

3. How does perception take place?

4. Do all pupils in a class give exactly the same meaning to a new perception? Explain.

5. Explain the generalization that every perceptual experience has a feeling tone.

6. Explain and illustrate several skills in reading that are mainly perceptual types of learning.

7. List some factors that are essential to clear perception.

8. How are associations formed in most school learning experiences?

9. Explain how learning facts about a unit on transportation may utilize principles of the Gestalt psychology.

10. How would you test the associational process in the subject of elementary science?

11. Explain how association is a factor in memory, and also how association can be a factor in forgetting.

12. How can teachers help students to form associations abundantly and effectively?

13. Explain the psychological principle involved in the statement, "A kind word is better than a dozen threats."

14. Describe a classroom situation in which the laws of similarity, contrast, and contiguity are illustrated.

15. Describe a situation in which you illustrate primary and concomitant learnings.

### SELECTED REFERENCES FOR FURTHER READING AND STUDY

Carter, Harold D., "Emotional Correlates of Errors in Learning," *Journal of Educational Psychology*, Vol. 27, pp. 55-67, 1936.

Coffey, Hubert S., and Beth L. Wellman, "The Role of Cultural Status in Intelligence Changes of Preschool Children," *Journal of Experimental Education*, Vol. 5, pp. 191-202, December, 1936.

Courtis, S. A., "Maturation as a Factor in Diagnosis," *Educational Diagnosis, Thirty-Fourth Yearbook*, National Society for the Study of Education, Chap. X, pp. 169-187, 1935.

Gesell, Arnold, and Helen Thompson, *The Psychology of Early Growth*. New York: The Macmillan Company, 1938.

Goodenough, Florence L., and Russell C. Smart, "Inter-Relationships of Motor Abilities in Young Children," *Child Development*, Vol. 6, pp. 141-153, June, 1935.

Guthrie, E. R., *The Psychology of Learning*. New York: Harper and Brothers, 1935.

Jersild, A. T., *Training in Growth and the Development of Children*. New York: Bureau of Publications, Teachers College, Columbia University, 1931. *Child Development Monographs*, No. 10.

Koffka, Kurt, *Gestalt Psychology*. New York: Harcourt, Brace and Company, 1935.

Leuba, C., "An Experimental Study of Rivalry in Young Children," *Journal of Comparative Psychology*, Vol. 16, 1933, pp. 367-378.

McGeoch, John, *The Psychology of Human Learning*. New York: Longmans, Green, 1942.

McNemar, Quinn, "Practice and General Motor Ability," *Journal of General Psychology*, Vol. 14, pp. 464-66, April, 1936.

Newman, H. H., Frank N. Freeman, and K. J. Holzinger, *Twins: a Study of Heredity and Environment*. Chicago: University of Chicago Press, 1937.

Stuart, Herman N., "A Study of Sensori-Motor and Conceptual Thinking in Children Between the Ages of Nine and Eighteen," *Journal of Experimental Education*, Vol. 4, pp. 147-53, December, 1937.

Thorndike, E. L., *The Fundamentals of Learning*. New York: Columbia University Press, 1932.

Wheeler, R. H., and F. T. Perkins, *Principles of Mental Development*. New York: The Thomas Y. Crowell Company, 1932.

White, M. M., "Some Factors Influencing Recall of Pleasant and Unpleasant Words," *American Journal of Psychology*, Vol. 48, pp. 134-139, 1936.

# CHAPTER 12

# Reflective Thinking and Problem Solving

## The "stroboscopic" point of view [1]

A stroboscope is an instrument used in the study of the successive phases of motion by means of periodically interrupted light. By means of it, the mechanical engineer is able to observe the movements in machinery far too rapid for the human eye otherwise to see. For a permanent record to use in prolonged study, he might prefer a complete series of photographs covering every phase of the particular motion being investigated. Ultra-rapid motion picture cameras have been developed for such purposes, and it is now possible to obtain records of the motion of a high-velocity bullet as it leaves the barrel of a rifle. These techniques for obtaining static views of dynamic events are fairly new in the fields of engineering and physics. The "stroboscopic" point of view is a very old one in psychology; and, although it is of some help in describing the dynamics of reflective thinking and reasoning, it leads to egregious mistakes.

The principal advantage of this point of view is that from it we can analyze and describe each successive move in a complete act of reflective thinking. Imagine that we have an ultra-rapid camera with which we can take a sequence of "stills" while an acquaintance solves a problem. By a careful scrutiny of each "still" picture, we might be able to select five or six that would represent significant episodes in the quest for a solution. A more thorough analysis might enable us to find illustrations of some points discussed in a conventional textbook on traditional methods of teaching boys and girls to think. At least, we might learn something about the structure of the thought process.

---

[1] The author is indebted to the interesting discussion in Part Four of R. W. Holmes, *The Rhyme of Reason*. New York: D. Appleton-Century Company, 1939.

### A couple of problems for an obliging acquaintance

In order to obtain the "still" pictures, suppose we commence by playing an ancient game. We must choose nine books, each of a different size. Then we designate three places on the desk A, B, and C, respectively. Now we place a large book on A, and then put a smaller one on top. Our acquaintance is told, "The object of this game is to move the books from A to C without placing the larger book on the smaller book." No doubt, he makes the appropriate moves without an error. Then we place three books on A, with the smallest on top, a larger one below, and the biggest on the bottom. The rules are the same throughout the game: a larger book must never be placed on a smaller book. Possibly, he makes one false move here, but the likelihood is that he succeeds on the first attempt. Hence we proceed with four books, then with five, and so on, one book at a time, until he has moved the nine books piled up in order of size on A to C, never placing a larger book on a smaller one.

For our second problem we might have him "work something out in his head." Suppose, therefore, we give him the "brain-teaser" about the germs which reproduce so rapidly that their number is doubled each minute. Were two of these germs placed in a bottle, by the end of an hour they and their offspring would completely fill it. Now, how long would it be before the bottle was half-full? He would be likely to reply, "Thirty minutes"; but, of course, he would be wrong. We urge him to reflect a bit, and then he gives us the correct answer, "Fifty-nine minutes."

### An analysis of the thought process

Our "stills" would be very numerous, since a high-speed camera can take as many as about four thousand in a half-second. If we were not bewildered by the mass of pictures, we might be able to locate a few important episodes. First, there is an upset in the complacency of our acquaintance; he takes a participant attitude toward the problem. Perhaps his forehead is wrinkled and his posture is intent. Second, he seems to engage in some trial-and-error behavior, as when he tries to move the nine books from A to C, or when he "talks out" his solution for the puzzle about the microbes. Third, he may check all overt responses for a time while he "goes over the problem in his mind." At length, he "sees through" the "brain-teaser," and relaxes with a laugh.

A more formal analysis of the "stills" might enable us to classify them according to principal stages in the process. First, there is a situation for which our subject has no prepared reaction; hence he either hesitates while he surveys the difficulty, or he jumps to a conclusion. Second, we may find evidence, both in the pictures and in his subjective report, that he attempts to diagnose the difficulty. Third, he may report that he makes use of hypotheses, as in working out the rule for the book game. Fourth, he might tell us that he imagined the consequences of some of these courses of action, and then discarded all but the most appropriate one. Fifth, he seems to resolve the difficulty by overcoming it with the rule or principle that he has discovered.

A great deal of attention has been devoted to investigating the successive episodes in a complete act of reflective thinking. No one would question the importance of learning how to think clearly or of teaching pupils how to become "cold, clear logic engines." Even a hasty survey of the beliefs and actions of our neighbors indicates that few of them are able to think clearly. They dose themselves with patent nostrums, "correct" serious eye defects by exercises prescribed by quacks, unquestioningly accept as truth whatever they read in print, and invest their life-savings in "get-rich-quick" schemes. In the field of social relations and international affairs, their judgments are formed by prejudices and ignorance. Many of them are fully aware of their inability to think clearly; hence they will purchase books or attend classes purporting to train their minds.

If it were possible to analyze each step in a complete act of problem solving, it would be a relatively simple matter to devise techniques for teaching boys and girls to think clearly. In fact, we could introduce a course into the curriculum and entitle it "How to Think." The only difficulty is that such a course would not accomplish its objective. For many years educators firmly believed that certain studies, like mathematics or languages, disciplined the mind and trained pupils in clear thinking. When educators finally admitted science into the curriculum, they were mollified by the idea that training in scientific procedures would contribute something to disciplining the mind. During the last few decades, millions of pupils have had courses in science and have learned the "steps in the scientific method." The outcome has been disappointing in that the younger generation seem to be about as confused in their thinking as their elders. Huxley's dictum about making the mind a "cold, clear logic engine" is still far from realization. As a matter of fact, very few people would elect to choose such a fate either for themselves or for their children. A course in the structure of thought would be for most people a boring and useless study.

## The dynamic point of view

Mentally alert educators have long suspected that there is something wrong with the methods used in teaching pupils to think. In the first place, they are very certain that there is no technique whereby "the mind can be strengthened." Of course, few present-day teachers believe in the old "faculty psychology," but many teachers resent the introduction of new courses or new methods into the school: in faculty meetings they still speak of the superiority of the "disciplinary subjects" like mathematics and languages, particularly if they happen to teach these courses. The notion of formal discipline in education is hard to scotch. In the second place, educators are becoming acquainted with the growing body of experimental literature about the thought processes of efficient adults. There seems to be little evidence to show that clear thinkers, when confronted by new problems, follow an orderly, systematic, step-by-step course in achieving a solution. As a matter of fact, the thought processes of gifted adults appear to be quite disorderly and unsystematic. None of the orderly "steps in a complete act of reflective thinking" can be found without doing violence to the facts. In the third place, educators now tend to regard the thought processes as a part of the total behavior of the individual in the changing environment. Thinking does not take place in a vacuum; it is merely an aspect or phase of the total process of adjustment to situations. Like many other activities, it is an improvable function.

The static "stroboscopic approach," therefore, is inappropriate, and it has led to unfortunate blunders in methods and in curriculum making. A "still" picture of a friend is a disappointing possession. It may suggest a characteristic action; perhaps the photographer caught a revealing expression; but the "still" is lifeless. A whole series of pictures might be more revealing, but they cannot represent the vitality of a person. Similarly with our analytical discussion of the thought processes, we secure nothing but "stills" which deceive us into believing that thinking is a static matter.

## An example of the dynamics of thinking [2]

Here is the sort of problem our parents encountered in their study of algebra—a fact which may explain the distaste some of them acquired for this subject:

---

[2] From L. Hogben, *Mathematics for the Million.* New York: W. W. Norton and Company, 1937.

I have 1,872 tacks, nails, and screws mixed together in a box. There are three times as many tacks as nails, and three times as many nails as screws. How many of each do I have?

We might solve the problem by hit-or-miss methods, but that would keep us at the task for too long a time. Some people would dismiss the problem by saying, "I never could succeed at figures!" Suppose that we accept this problem as a challenge to our wits and try to achieve a solution. It is probably as dry and as difficult for the prospective teacher as many of the problems that he may later on have to assign to his pupils. The procedure in working a solution may teach us something about the dynamics of problem solving.

First, we shall work more efficiently if we make use of algebraic symbols—which are nothing more than a shorthand. It is clear that $n$ (nails) equals $\frac{1}{3} t$ (tacks), and that $s$ (screws) equals $\frac{1}{3} n$ (nails). It is also clear that $t$ plus $s$ plus $n$ equals 1,872. If we do not obtain this equation, we have not read the problem carefully. It may be that we never thought of using symbols other than $x$ and $y$ in solving problems by algebra. In that case, we are victimized by fixed habits. Second, it is evident that the following equation can be written:

$$t + \tfrac{1}{3} t + \tfrac{1}{3} \left( \tfrac{1}{3} t \right) = 1,872.$$

The sense of this equation may be more difficult to grasp, but it will be apparent when the problem is reread. If it is not clear then, at any rate we have an excellent illustration of an upset in complacency. Third, it is possible to write this equation now:

$$t \left( 1 + \tfrac{1}{3} + \tfrac{1}{9} \right) = 1,872,$$
$$\text{or, to simplify, } \tfrac{13}{9} t = 1,872;$$
$$\text{hence, } t \text{ (tacks)} = 1,296.$$

Since there are one-third as many nails, I have 432 nails; and since I have a third as many screws as nails, I have 144 screws. Last, we can check the accuracy of the solution by adding 1,296, 432, and 144, which total 1,872.

## The two attitudes toward problem solving [3]

Some readers perused this illustration merely because it "was included in the assignment." They took the spectator attitude, a sort of passive waiting until something should be done. The artificiality of the problem did not appeal to them any more than

[3] See E. F. Heidbreder, "Problem Solving in Children and Adults," *Journal of General Psychology*, 1928, Vol. 35, pp. 522-545.

much of the work presented in the classroom elicits the interest of boys and girls. On the other hand, there is some little evidence to indicate that learning may take place even when the pupils have the spectator attitude. When the teacher demonstrates a technique, at least the procedure is likely to "turn out right," whereas if the pupils attempt a new technique, the results may be confusing. More specifically, it has been suggested by some educators that competent demonstrations for which careful preparations have been made by the teacher may help to initiate the desired train-of-thought process in pupils. Recently there has been some interesting discussion about the value of laboratory work in the elementary sciences, the objection being that correct procedures are not grasped by the pupils when only individual laboratory work is given at first.

There could be little doubt, however, that the participant attitude is the more dynamic and fruitful. The participant may blunder at first, and perhaps he may never reach a valid solution; but at least he is growing in experience as a result of his activities. He tries out various hypotheses, looks for relationships among the parts of the situation, welcomes "hunches," and even jumps to conclusions. If he has learned how to control his thought processes, he will delay making an overt response until he has weighed and considered the matter. For instance, to revert to the problem of the marvelous microbes, a common response is "a half-hour," but that answer is a snap judgment which an experienced thinker would correct in a few moments.

### The dangers of oversystematization

In "The Purloined Letter," Poe presents a clear picture of a systematic thinker. The Prefect thoroughly investigated every likely place of concealment. Describing his methods to Dupin, he said:

> I took the entire building, room by room; devoting the nights of a whole week to each. We examined, first, the furniture of each apartment. We opened every possible drawer; and I presume you know that, to a properly trained police-agent, such a thing as a *secret* drawer is impossible. . . . We have accurate rules. . . . The cushions we probed with fine long needles. From the tables we removed the tops. . . . We examined the rungs of every chair. We opened every package and parcel. We removed every carpet, and examined the boards with the microscope. . . . I am not more sure that I breathe than I am that the letter is not at the Hotel.

Dupin, not being a victim of oversystematized thinking, located the letter in the most obvious place in the room, a rack just beneath the mantelpiece.

Efficient teachers will not try to inculcate fixed habits of thinking or routinized procedures for meeting "typical" problems. The attempt to teach fixed habits, which is the direct outcome of the fallacious and one-sided "stroboscopic" analysis of thinking, is stultifying. The pupil must be taught to integrate certain principles into his experience and to achieve a flexible mastery of them. Under routine drill in formal grammar in which little or no real thinking is required, the pupil acquires a great many fixed habits, but he seldom acquires a more effective command of his language as a result. If, however, he is to learn how to vary the awkward "high-school" style of sequence (subject-verb-object) in sentences, he must acquire a "flexible" mastery of grammar. Then he can vary the style by opening one sentence with an adverb. Once he is taught to think in terms of word relationships, he will be able to punctuate more intelligently. Likewise, he will be able to apply his grammar in thinking out the meaning of such a line as this from Browning:

Irks care the cropful bird?

The first problem here is to locate the verb, and then to add the words that have been omitted to preserve the meter. When this has been done, the line begins to take on real meaning.

In general, the safest rule is to tone down the emphasis upon the tool operations in any field of knowledge. When we teach "fundamentals" too assiduously, we tend to rely upon thoughtless drill and to expect large results from mechanical repetition. Of course, some drill work is necessary. Nevertheless, unless the tool operations are really understood, the drill is not worth very much, and almost the same results could be obtained from a parrot. High-school teachers of geometry are chastened when they collect the first set of "originals" from their classes. Apparently, the pupils have done nothing more than to memorize the theorems in a mechanical fashion, without the slightest understanding of the practical applications. Many a textbook in algebra is overloaded with formal problems in rare types of factorization. Few college students can square 412 in their heads; and yet if they understood the applicability of the familiar $(a+b)^2$ they could easily do it. The problem can be simplified into $4^2$ (adding four 0's) plus $12^2$ plus 12 times 400. Unfortunately, very few persons who have passed a high-school course in algebra or geometry ever use this knowledge again. One reason why these courses do not function in our lives is that all the class time was taken up in drill upon "fundamentals."

Another safe rule is to disregard the old injunction about "proceeding from the simple to the complex."[4] Of course, the curriculum must be adjusted to the maturity and the experience of the learner. It would be foolish to try to teach the calculus in the primary grades. On the other hand, there is good evidence to indicate that relatively complex material may be introduced at the outset of a course of study. In modern language study, we could do just as well if we commenced by hearing the language spoken and by recognizing the familiar English roots in many of the printed words. Instead of this meaningful approach, the traditional educator insists upon a dreary year of drill upon grammatical rules and vocabulary. He is obsessed by the dogma about proceeding from the simple to the complex. An ingenious psychologist taught some of his subjects to recognize Chinese characters in a series of graded difficulty; other subjects he taught to recognize complex characters at first, and then to learn simpler and simpler ones. He found that those who proceeded from the simple to the complex did not benefit, and that it was just as effective to commence with the hard characters.

Now, it would be a very thoughtless person who would not seriously question some of the statements made in the two foregoing paragraphs. First, exception was taken to the value of drill lessons as contributory to developing the ability to think. Repetition may be of inestimable value. It may afford an opportunity for the true factors in learning to become operative. It does help to consolidate the material into the experience of the learner when it is done with zeal and understanding. On the other hand, drill should be avoided whenever better methods are available. For instance, suppose that a pupil writes *accross*. We might *drill* him on the correct spelling, or we could have him prefix *a* to the following words:

> bout
> cross
> far
> cross
> new
> *etc.*

He should tell what changes are thus effected in the words and observe that the first consonant remains unchanged. If the difficulty is that he persists in omitting the commas to set off nonrestrictive clauses, we might *drill* him upon the rule. A better approach would be to have him read some sentences aloud and to

---

[4] See C. Hull, "Quantitative Aspects of the Evolution of Concepts," *Psychological Monographs*, 1920, Vol. 28, No. 123.

note the difference, if any, when a nonrestrictive element is omitted; then he should read some sentences which contain restrictive elements, and observe the alteration of meaning when they are left out. In short, drill has its place, but it is not a very effective procedure in teaching pupils how to think.

Second, the dogma about beginning with the simple and proceeding to the complex was challenged. The curriculum is still too largely based upon the "stroboscopic" analysis of the psychology of the learner. The educator who is educationally alive speaks a great deal of the *experience* curriculum. This is entirely at variance with an earlier type of curriculum. For instance, the efficient teacher of history may be quite willing to begin the course in his department with a study of contemporary events. Earlier teachers often insisted upon "giving the pupils a background" first; thus, they usually commenced with ancient times, and then gradually worked down to the present. In teaching effective writing and speaking, they began with grammar and formal rhetoric and insisted upon observance of all the minutiae of "good usage." The mentally alert English teacher of today is more likely to commence by trying to arouse a felt need to write or say something worth while. It might appear logical to spend weeks in drilling on the "fundamentals" of algebra. In fact, there are enough complexities in such topics as fractional exponents and imaginary numbers to occupy a semester or two in high school. A more thought-provoking approach to algebra, however, might be to start out with the assumption that algebra is merely a form of language. On the very first day, the class might well begin by using the language of algebra to express some relatively simple problems and to solve them.

## The occasion for thinking

We think when we are confronted by a situation for which we do not have a prepared response and which we are unwilling to meet in an impulsive way. When we first sat behind the wheel of the family car, we had a great deal to learn. There were very few prepared reactions which we could use in starting the car and shifting the gears. Perhaps our teacher pointed out the various gear positions and showed us how to shift correctly. At first, we had to move slowly, lest we confuse reverse and second. We tried to recall the diagram which he used to illustrate his instructions. With added experience, however, we acquired a complex series of prepared reactions, and then we could devote our attention to the scenery or to the actions of other drivers.

Thinking, then, involves a sort of delay in the response. During this interval the whole situation is surveyed, past experience is brought to bear upon the difficulty, and a tentative decision is made. Some logicians have defined thinking as an "as·if" type of behavior. Possible courses of action are weighed and considered and then one mode of response is selected. A radio announcer speaks of the ease with which anyone may borrow money "to clean up your bills or to take that restful vacation. Salaried people need no endorsers. Call at your nearest —— Finance Office and see how easy it is to borrow three hundred dollars." Here is a persuasive appeal to act on impulse, and it evidently pays large dividends to the "loan sharks." If we delay our visit until after we have analyzed the opportunity, we may decide not to go at all. The interest rate is "only" three per cent, but it is three per cent each month on the total amount borrowed. The hesitancy about visiting the —— Finance Office gave us time to do some "as if" behavior. Our calculations, done either "in our heads" or on scratch paper, show us that we would have to pay $444 back to the company; hence we may decide to forego this opportunity.

We are all familiar with the type of behavior described by the adjectives *heedless, thoughtless,* and *impulsive.* In this type of action there is little or no delay, the situation is not carefully scrutinized, and the past experience of the person is not brought to bear upon the difficulty. A sixth-grade pupil, obviously a retardate, described his methods of solving problems in arithmetic as follows: "If there are lots of numbers, I add them up. If there are only two long numbers, I subtract. If there are just two numbers and one is a very small one, I divide if they come out even. If they don't come out even, I multiply." No doubt, this apocryphal story may seem too far-fetched and absurd to illustrate the point. When we consider the haste with which adults respond to "get-rich-quick" appeals, or the difficulty which the average person has in working simple problems in arithmetic, we might conclude that the boy has many companions in his retardation. Possibly, far more of our own behavior would be aptly described as heedless than we should care to admit.

Unfortunately, mathematics really is a badly taught subject, and most adults have never learned to think correctly in terms of mathematical symbols. There appears to be no evidence to indicate that mathematics requires a special endowment; on the contrary, when school marks are intercorrelated, it is found that there is no indication of a special ability in mathematics. Most of the instruction is formalized, and fixed habits are acquired. When problems arise in everyday life situations, there is a minimum of transfer from the artificial instructions given in school. Realizing this fact, many people buy books on "mathematics simplified" to make up for their deficiencies. They know that they are inefficient and handicapped because they cannot think in terms of mathematical symbols. They have learned from costly experience that they make snap judgments in financial matters, that they cannot balance their checking accounts, and that relatively simple operations in arithmetic confuse them.

Except for a relatively few basic skills which must be mastered by drill, the entire curriculum should be a prolonged series of experiences in thinking. Even the difficulties of English spelling may be presented in such a way as to involve thinking. Possibly the drill upon number combinations, the achievement of reasonable legibility in handwriting, and a relatively small amount of "factual information" might be exceptions. Of course, some skills have to be improved by repeated practice, and certain facts have to be mastered by rote learning. In the efficient school, however, these phases of the curriculum will be reduced to the minimum essentials. Wherever it is feasible, the school should present the curriculum as a series of graded occasions for thinking.

## Some examples of problem-solving situations

It would be a great mistake to believe that mathematics is the subject *par excellence* for giving the pupils sound training in the experience of thinking. As a matter of fact, nearly every subject in the curriculum lends itself to this objective. For one example, consider the short poem entitled "Memorabilia" which Browning wrote:

> Ah, did you once see Shelley plain,
>     And did he stop and speak to you,
> And did you speak to him again?
>     How strange it seems and new!
>
> But you were living before that,
>     And also you are living after;
> And the memory I started at—
>     My starting moves your laughter!
>
> I crossed a moor, with a name of its own
>     And a certain use in the world no doubt,
> Yet a hand's-breadth of it shines alone
>     'Mid the blank miles round about:
>
> For there I picked up on the heather
>     And there I put inside my breast
> A moulted feather, an eagle-feather!
>     Well, I forget the rest.

Is this incomprehensible? Not in the least, if we are willing to give the poem some thought. We shall first need to enlarge our experience a bit. Robert Browning was an intense admirer of Shelley, whom he had never met personally but whose poems he considered to be among the very best. The "you" in the first verse gives us a clue; Browning meets a person who had seen Shelley and had talked with him. Of course, he is excited; but the stranger laughs, perhaps contemptuously—possibly, in view of what we know of Shelley's life, hatefully. Then Browning shifts to an allegory, in which the symbolism is rather clear. If a hint or two are in order, let it be said that the moor symbolizes a dismal waste place, like the personality of this man who could not reverence the memory of Shelley, and that the feather represents another item which Browning can add to his memorabilia of Shelley. The achievement of a satisfactory interpretation of this poem is an excellent opportunity for problem solving.

For another example, assuming that all of us are students of psychology, let us try to figure out why the Communists have no liking for psychoanalysis. We might begin by reading Freud's *Civilization and Its Discontents* to learn what his social philosophy is, and then compare his views with the philosophy of collectivism. If that is too unstimulating a problem, we might try to find out why the majority of our English scientific terms come from Greek rather than from Latin roots. In fact, a reading of Kittredge and Farley's *Words and Their Ways in English Speech* would set us to thinking about many interesting problems connected with familiar words and their changing meanings. We might even try to find out why school and college marks are not always a reliable basis upon which to predict success or failure in after-school life. Of course, there are so many occasions for thinking that there is no need to multiply examples here. Every phase of the curriculum abounds in occasions for experiences in problem solving.

### Thinking is not a mysterious process

A belief hard to explode is the prevalent notion that thinking is a mysterious, recondite process. In the first place, thinking does not take place *in vacuo*. There are no general rules the observance of which will enable us to think clearly at all times and under all circumstances, no matter what the specific problem may be. On the contrary, each situation has its own peculiar characteristics, and it demands a different type of adjustment from that which would be appropriate to any other situation. For instance, each one of the following situations demands a radically different type of thinking:

*a.* Underline the word unlike the other four:

> spondee
> tribrach
> ballade
> choriambus
> ditrochee

*b.* RUN is to DEER as what is to FISH?

*c.* The following item from Binet's Intelligence Scale is no longer appropriate: State three differences between a king and a president. Why?

*d.* What is the meaning of these lines, quoted from Bassanio's Casket Speech?
Look on beauty and you shall see 'tis purchased by the weight,
Which thereby worketh a miracle in nature,
Making them lightest that wear most of it.

*e.* Factor $a^2 + 10a + 24$.

*f.* Is it true that German scientists have made more contributions than the scientists of any other nation? Defend your answer.

In the second place, the ability to think necessitates a background of information germane to the problem about which the thinking is to be done. Thus, in situation *a,* one must have a knowledge of some of the rare types of meter in English versification to see that *ballade* (a French lyrical form) is the misfitting term. In *b* the situation is relatively familiar to all of us; hence problems like this are often presented in intelligence tests. In *c* one has to apply a background of experience in recent social history. Example *d* might baffle a person who has forgotten that Shakespeare delighted in plays upon words of double meaning and that *lightest* denoted *fairest* as well as *a minimum of weight* three centuries ago. Even for the person who has taken a single semester of algebra, *e* is easy enough. The only difficulty is to decide upon the factors of 24 and to determine the correct signs. In obtaining an answer to *f,* a procedure might be suggested: arrange lists of eminent scientists of various nationalities, and then compare the tabulations. Obviously, the solution in each of these little problems requires a different sort of background and a different procedure.

In the third place, thinking always involves a problem. If the pupil is to do any thinking, he must be confronted by a situation for which he does not have a prepared response and to which he is eager to make a satisfactory adjustment. Some situations that are full of problems for an adult leave the pupil unmoved. Consequently, the intelligent teacher attempts to present the curriculum in such a way as to meet the needs and interests of the learner. All of us find pleasure in thinking about our own difficulties and in figuring out the best ways of solving them. Abstract and hypothetical issues leave many of us in a state of indifference and unconcern. For example, few people would honestly admit that Michelangelo's "Figure of Adam" disturbs them. Whether the finger of God has just touched Adam's finger or whether it is about to touch Adam is a question which would "leave them cold." "What a pedantic controversy!" some would remark. Indeed, they might very well be justified in deriding a concern about this question. The point is, however, that many of the "problems" in school are likely to be regarded as just as artificial and far-fetched by the pupils as this one may have seemed to the reader.

On the other hand, this illustration does bring out one point in the strategy of teaching pupils. At least, the "problem" is a definite one and it may be presented in concrete terms. The art teacher can bring a reproduction of the fresco into her class for all to see. Sometimes, particularly in the problem-solving attack upon social issues, the discussion rambles along, the terms are not defined, and the original question is soon forgotten. If the problem situation is meaningful to the pupils, it becomes the teacher's responsibility to direct the activity toward a solution and to keep the pupils "on the track."

In the fourth place, problem solving involves the location, organization, and evaluation of data. It cannot be repeated too often that pupils do not think *in vacuo;* there are always facts and hypotheses derived from their past experience. Sometimes the data may be drawn from past experience right away; at other times the information must be found in books or in laboratory activities. Among the common errors in problem solving are the following: insufficient or inaccurate data, inflexible habits of meeting various difficulties, failure to observe similarities and differences among the data, and snap judgments. The lack of adequate data may arise from the immaturity of the pupil, from "blind spots" in his experience, from restricted experience, or from low intelligence. One of the most hopeful signs in curriculum revision is that the difficulty of school experiences is now being established by scientific investigations of pupil maturity. Also at the present time, a great deal of attention is being devoted to the diagnosis and treatment of individual subject-matter disabilities; hence some of the "blind spots" are being eliminated. Special provision is being made for the handicapped pupil through the establishment in the larger communities of special opportunity classes, and there is some encouraging evidence to show that better opportunities are being given to children living in economically and socially substandard environments.

Ability to organize data into meaningful relationships is largely dependent upon native intelligence, and great individual differences exist within a single classroom. Nevertheless, the teacher of today does not accept the notion that intelligence is a mysterious faculty that develops in a vacuum. Even the slowest learners can benefit by experiences in problem solving. The basic requisite is that the problems for retardates be well within their range of experience. Likewise, all pupils are able to learn some of the techniques for evaluating their conclusions. Under the guidance of the teacher, they can experience without harmful effects the outcomes of inappropriate solutions and achieve the thrill of satisfaction that comes when a real problem is correctly solved. Of course, throughout the process the teacher must be fully aware of the existence of great individual differences. Some pupils have but one talent, others have five, and a few have ten talents.

## Conclusion

When mental activities are analyzed and described in isolation from one another, we may gain a great deal of interesting and valid information about the "structure of the mind." We may also be led to consider that thinking is something which is actually separable from the other aspects of experience. The truth is, however, that this point of view is nothing but a "stroboscopic" picture of the real dynamics. We cannot "teach pupils to think" in general. There is no set of precepts or "master principles" that can be universally applied. The occasion for thinking arises when we are confronted by an unavoidable situation for which we have no prepared reaction. Then we manipulate either the materials of the situation or the symbols thereof until we have devised a plan of action. Since no two situations are exactly alike, there is very little that we can learn in the way of specific techniques that may be applicable to all of them. The curriculum should be a prolonged series of experiences in meeting innumerable problems and in achieving a more or less satisfactory adjustment to each of them. The aim of the educational process is to enrich the experience of the pupil so that he may learn how to find data, organize them appropriately, and evaluate the possible consequences of various courses of action that he might take.

The procedures that are most inimical to the development of proficiency in reflective thinking and problem solving are two: overemphasis of rote learning and an overeagerness to stimulate thinking by assigning artificial problems. In some schools, the major emphasis is upon "subject-matter mastery": the teachers are obsessed by the idea that the pupils must "get the facts," and they are extremely critical of problem-project trends in education.

One of the most unfortunate by-products—that is, misuses—of the new standardized achievement tests is that they focus attention upon the "need" for bringing every pupil up to the norm for his grade and assumed capacity. Consequently, there seems to be an increase in the use of drill lessons, with the only improvement being that more attention is now paid to motivation. The result is a stultifying type of education that might be more appropriate for parrots than for boys and girls. Equally disastrous is the belief that problems can be "assigned" and that "the problem-solving approach" is the panacea for all educational ills. Such a belief leads to the absurd notion that facts are unimportant, that we must only teach pupils to think. Actually, facts are all-important; without facts we cannot think at all. Thinking is nothing more than the utilization of past experience in meeting a situation for which we have no prepared response. Like other abilities, it is amenable to improvement under the guidance of teachers.

## QUESTIONS AND EXERCISES FOR DISCUSSION AND STUDY

1. Is it true that there is no such thing as a distinctive ability in mathematics? (Read E. Dexter, "Does Mathematics Require Special Endowment?" *School and Society*, Vol. XXXIV, 1936, pp. 220-224.) Can you find any evidence to support the notion that facility in mathematics is a "primary mental ability"?

2. Is it correct to say that a knowledge of the formal structure of thought will not suffice to make us clear thinkers? Skim through a few textbooks on college logic and report upon your findings. Would a mastery of higher mathematics benefit us more in daily situations?

3. What do you think about the desirability of introducing a special course in which the emphasis would be upon the canons of clear reasoning? Are there not some general principles that could be applied to a great variety of practical situations?

4. A large corporation has signs posted about its plants admonishing all employees, "Think!" Do you believe that this is a good way to stimulate people to be reflective? Can you devise a better plan?

5. Have you ever been told that a certain subject would teach you to think clearly? If so, what subject? Did the advice work? Have you ever seen an advertisement of a correspondence course that would teach you "how to unlock the hidden resources in your personality"? What is your opinion of these courses?

6. Could a person be a proficient thinker in one area—say, in mathematics—and be an inefficient thinker in other areas? (Laplace is an outstanding example. Is he typical or an exception?)

7. Can a general habit of open-mindedness be taught? If so, how would you proceed to teach it?

8. Illustrate the point that it is dangerous to teach nothing more than specific habits. Are some specific habits necessary? Give some examples. How

does the process of integrating knowledge into one's experience differ from that of acquiring specific habits? Explain.

9. Give some examples of instances showing that mastery of fundamental principles is no guarantee of the likelihood that one will use them in meeting problems.

10. Give some examples of genuine problems that have challenged you. Can you recall some attempts made to interest you in problems that "left you cold"? Is there any value in working on problems that do not meet your felt needs at the time? Answer carefully.

11. It is often said that the teacher cannot do the pupil's thinking for him. All that she can do is to provide a situation, or sequence of situations, in which he must utilize his past experiences and thus, through the enrichment of his present experience, get ready for richer subsequent experiences. Do you agree? What circumstances might interfere with this outcome?

12. Is it true that when the dynamic nature of reflective thinking is investigated, it is found to be orderly or disorderly? (See E. L. Thorndike and C. B. Upton, "An Experiment in Learning an Abstract Subject," *Journal of Educational Psychology*, Vol. VI, 1922, pp. 321-329.) Try solving a simple puzzle and see whether your thinking proceeds by clear-cut steps or by what might be defined merely as a "participant activity." Should we teach children to think in terms of logical steps?

## SELECTED REFERENCES FOR FURTHER READING AND STUDY

Dewey, John, *Logic—the Theory of Inquiry*. New York: Henry Holt and Company, 1938.

Gates, A. I., and others, *Educational Psychology*. New York: The Macmillan Company, 1942. Chapter XIV.

Hartmann, G. W., *Educational Psychology*. Chapter IX. New York: American Book Company, 1941.

Skinner, C. E., editor, *Readings in Educational Psychology*. New York: Farrar and Rinehart, 1937. Chapter XIII.

————, and others, *Educational Psychology*. New York: Prentice-Hall, Inc., 1936. Chapter V.

# CHAPTER 13

# Imagination, Creative Thinking, and Appreciation

In Dickens' novel *Hard Times,* Mr. Thomas Gradgrind says, "Teach these boys and girls nothing but facts. Facts alone are wanted in life. Plant nothing else, and root out everything else." The Grandgrind spirit persists into the present time, and in many schools there is still an excessive emphasis upon subject-matter mastery. As Fletcher has pointed out,[1] some teachers are completely absorbed by the task of "putting the curriculum across"; hence, they neglect the expressive or creative aspect of the educational process. No doubt, two rather obvious reasons account for this neglect. First, we live in an acquisitive social order, in which the emphasis is upon possession and achievement rather than upon creation and esthetic experience. Second, educational psychology has been concerned with scientific experiments dealing with the mechanical phases of the learning process, and consequently the nature of creative processes has been somewhat neglected. Even the physical arrangements of the average classroom suggest a theory of education based upon passive absorption of facts rather than creative and expressive activities.

In the school that is alive to progress, the teacher will not be concerned primarily with the merchandising of subject matter. On the contrary, the emphasis will be upon the dynamic nature of learning itself. The teacher will stimulate and guide the psychological activities of the pupils, and will not be "a mere clerk in the storeroom of accumulated knowledge." [2] The great task is to discover the backgrounds, aptitudes, interests, and capacities of each individual pupil, and then to utilize this information in promoting the intellectual and emotional development of the learner.

---

[1] J. M. Fletcher, *Psychology in Education.* Garden City, N. Y.: Doubleday, Doran and Company, 1934. Pp. 302-306.

[2] Glenn Frank, in H. L. Miller, *Creative Learning and Teaching.* New York: Charles Scribner's Sons, 1927. P. vii.

## Creative Imagination

Experimental investigations, as well as everyday observations, show that young children have great powers of creative imagination. In the average school, with its great emphasis upon fact learning and drill lessons, these powers are not used as a point of departure. On the contrary, the procedure is one that will almost inevitably make the child matter-of-fact, unimaginative, and stodgy. The child-centered school, on the other hand, sets up an educational program that utilizes these creative powers and fosters their further development. As Rugg says, no psychological finding of our age has had more far-reaching influence in vitalizing the educational process than the discovery of the fact that children have creative ability and that the school can help the child to develop these powers.[3]

### Creative imagination in play

Many parents have had the disappointing experience of giving an elaborate toy to a child and then finding that the toy is soon discarded. Children seem to like toys that can be manipulated in such a way as to produce a variety of happenings. The toy itself may be simple and inexpensive, but it must furnish a stimulus for some type of expressive or creative activity. For example, an elaborate and expensive electric train set shortly loses its play value because it has limited possibilities for manipulation. Objects that can be manipulated in various ways, that can be taken apart and put together, and that can be endowed with complex patterns of meaning serve as toys for young children. An arrangement of dining-room chairs may, for instance, become a train, a bus, or an airplane. Blocks may serve to build castles and palaces. If, on the other hand, the meaning is already suggested by an elaborate toy representative in the last detail, such as a completely furnished doll house, the possibilities for creative imagination are so meager that the object soon loses its play value.

Check-list studies indicate that young children are interested in dramatic, active forms of play.[4] The materials of play are secondary to the possibilities for manipulating and giving meanings to almost any sort of material. Techniques and rules are also secondary to creative imagination. In the play of young children,

---

[3] H. O. Rugg and Ann Shumaker, *The Child-Centered School*. Yonkers, N. Y.: World Book Company, 1928. P. 228.

[4] See especially H. C. Lehman and P. A. Witty, *The Psychology of Play Activities*. New York: A. S. Barnes and Company, 1927.

rules are of no importance; the joy comes from expressive activity itself.[5] Only when the competitive motives have been developed do definite techniques and rules become important considerations in play. The young child seems to enjoy those activities in which successes are experienced and in which surprising results are obtained. The presence of other children engaged in similar activities may suggest new outlets for expressive behavior and increase the child's pleasure in his own play.

The disparity between the spontaneous play of the preschool child and the educational program in the typical school is obvious. In school there is still a tendency to make a false separation between play and work. According to some people, the school is a place for work; hence, the program must be serious and adult-controlled. Play is still regarded by some persons as non-purposeful, idle, time-wasting activity. Like Mr. Gradgrind, they have no patience with educators who would utilize the play motive in education. There is no real dividing line between work and play. What is work to one individual may be play to another. The play spirit may enliven work, and play may become work when it no longer satisfies spontaneous interests. The program should be based upon the psychological nature of the learner; then this false separation between play and work will not exist.

## Creative imagination in stories

As all parents know, young children enjoy hearing fairy tales, adventure stories, and pleasing jingles. Some tales, such as "The Three Bears," may be requested over and over again. Each time a familiar story is reread, it seems to furnish additional stimulus for creative imagination and identification. As in the case of play, the line of development proceeds from the active and dramatic to the subdued and factual. When children begin to read, they prefer highly imaginative, illustrated stories that furnish a great deal of stimulation to creative imagination. Later, sex differences and individual preferences are indicated. Then, as a rule, boys prefer stories of adventure and discovery, whereas girls like sentimental love tales.[6] In both sexes, the dominant motive is to find gratifying opportunities for identification with heroes or heroines who have attained those goals desired by the reader. Stories, therefore, furnish a vicarious satisfaction for unsatisfied desires.

---

[5] Jean Piaget, *The Moral Judgment of the Child.* London: Kegan, Paul and Company, 1932.
[6] A. M. Jordan, *Children's Interests in Reading.* Chapel Hill, N. C.: University of North Carolina Press, 1926.

## Creative imagination in moving pictures

Observations of child behavior in the motion-picture theater are illuminating.[7] When exciting scenes are displayed, the children applaud, shout encouragement, or become tense. It is apparent that powerful identifications have been established. Occasionally, the plot of a motion picture furnishes suggestions for a new type of play. In one community most of the boys were observed to practice assiduously with long whips after they had seen a picture in which the hero overcame his enemies by flicks of his whip. Recently a glorification of the "G-Man" stimulated young boys to obtain "Junior G-Man" badges and to create play activities in which they tracked down spies. Among girls, at a later age, sentimental trash is read to satisfy the longing to know more about the "secrets of the movie stars." The girls do not need much encouragement to purchase the cosmetics and the styles of clothing endorsed by movie favorites. Boys appear to be somewhat more delayed in reaching the level of romantic identifications, and they continue to prefer adventure pictures.

## Creative imagination and the radio

During the great popularity of the "Buck Rogers" programs, the members of a high-school physics class broke much apparatus by trying to duplicate those fantastic experiments. Textbook experiments seemed dull and commonplace as compared to those outlined in the radio programs. In some households the children listen to broadcasts for over two hours a day, particularly between the hours from six to eight in the evening. At this time there is a great variety of adventure thrillers, some of which have maintained their popularity for several years. In some cases the radio stories furnish leads for new forms of expressive activity in children's play. In a great many instances, these spontaneous interests may furnish important leads for educational guidance and direction. In many schools, however, they are utterly ignored, and sometimes they are actually discouraged. The alert teacher tries to utilize these interests as a starting point in education, seeking to lead the pupils to develop higher and more discerning interests.

In play, movies, and reading interests there appears to be a clear line of development. At first the interest is in highly imaginative activities, with few sex differences indicated. Later, girls commence to develop an interest in activities which enable them to

[7] M. V. Seagoe, "The Child's Reactions to the Movies," *Journal of Juvenile Research,* Vol. XV (1931), pp. 169-180.

secure identifications with romantic themes. Boys become more interested in opportunities to gain distinction as conquering heroes and adventurers. Both sexes engage in these spontaneous activities in order to secure vicarious gratifications for motives which are denied satisfaction in humdrum reality. These activities afford an outlet for creative imagination when it finds no opportunity for expression in their education.

Undoubtedly, some of these activities are of questionable value. A few of them may be actually pernicious in their effects upon the developing personality; many of them may be of indifferent educational value. Two courses of action are open. One is to forbid children to engage in forms of activity which adults consider harmful or time-wasting. Thereby many conflict situations are created: children may satisfy their impulses furtively without the knowledge of their parents and teachers, or they may openly rebel against restrictions. The second way is to become familiar with the normal interests and incentives of children, and then to plan a guidance program that will direct these impulses into more educative outlets. There is no reason for believing that creative imagination may not have just as much a place in the mastery of arithmetic as in listening to a radio thriller. Of course, if such is the case, present methods of organizing and teaching arithmetic should undergo radical alterations. In schools where such reorganizations of subjects or activities of the curriculum have been undertaken, the results are gratifying, both in the heightened accomplishments of the pupils and in their enthusiasm for obtaining more education.

### Creative Thinking and Invention

#### The "stages" of creative thought

On the occasion of his seventy-fifth birthday, the eminent Helmholtz performed an invaluable service for psychology by describing his methods of discovering new facts and principles in physics, physiology, and psychology. He said: [7a]

> Often enough "happy thoughts" crept quietly into my thinking without my suspecting their importance at first; and then it was often impossible later on to recall under what circumstances they had come; they were simply there and that was all I could say. Sometimes they arrived suddenly, without any effort on my part, like an inspiration. So far as my experience goes, they never came to a fatigued mind and never at the writing desk. It was always necessary, first of all, that I should have turned my problem over on all sides to such an extent that I had all its angles and complexities "in my head" and could run

---

[7a] Adapted, by permission, from R. S. Woodworth, *Experimental Psychology.* New York: Henry Holt and Company, 1938. P. 818.

through them freely without writing. To bring the matter to that point is usually impossible without long preliminary labor. Then, after the fatigue resulting from this labor had passed away, there must come an hour of complete physical freshness and quiet well-being, before the good ideas arrived. Often they were there in the morning when I awoke, but they liked especially to make their appearance while I was taking a walk.

The illustrious mathematician Poincaré has written an analysis of his own mental processes in creative ability [8] which fully substantiates the conclusions of Helmholtz. Rossman's study of the methods of thought employed by inventors also confirms the theory that at least three "stages" of creative thought may be distinguished: [9] first, there is a period of preparation; then comes a time of "incubation"; finally there is a sudden illumination or flash of insight. Wallas has described a fourth "stage" which he calls verification.[10]

1. *The "stage" of preparation.* Nearly all creative thinkers report that they have to go through a laborious period of getting ready. A small minority of poets and painters reported that they wrote or sketched on the spur of the moment, but most of them were fully aware of a long time of preparation.[11] The characteristic feature of the time of preparation is that the problem is studied from all points of view, or that all the material is gathered for an artistic production, but there seems to be a blocking or inhibition in the mental processes. A recent study by Lowes reveals the arduous preparation that Coleridge made for his unfinished poem "Kubla Khan." [12] Apparently, the material was collected simply because of Coleridge's interest in Oriental legends. Every student is familiar with the fact that Coleridge had a vivid dream in which all these bits of knowledge seemed to combine themselves into a poem.

The preparatory period in creative thinking may be non-purposeful, as it probably was in the case of Coleridge. Because of interest in learning for its own sake, the individual may accumulate a vast amount of erudition on various subjects. From this source may come the flashes of insight which, on some occasions, may find expression in works of art or scientific discoveries. This period of

[8] Henri Poincaré, *Science and Method.* New York: Charles Scribner's Sons, 1915.

[9] J. Rossman, *The Psychology of the Inventor.* Washington, D.C.: Inventors Publishing Company, 1931.

[10] Graham Wallas, *The Art of Thought.* New York: Harcourt, Brace and Company, 1926.

[11] C. Patrick, "Creative Thought in Poets," *Archives of Psychology,* 1935, No. 178; and "Creative Thought in Artists," *Journal of Psychology,* Vol. 4 (1937), pp. 35-73.

[12] J. L. Lowes, *The Road to Xanadu.* Boston: Houghton Mifflin Company, 1930.

preparation may be purposeful, as in the case of an individual who learns all that he can about a given field of knowledge in order to find a basis for new discoveries or original ideas. Before writing "The Legend of Sleepy Hollow," Irving became thoroughly familiar with the folklore of the Hudson River country. Candidates for advanced degrees are counseled to discover a problem for their dissertations by first becoming thoroughly acquainted with all the literature in their chosen field.

At this point conventional education often leaves off. Most of the emphasis is placed upon preparation—that is, upon the passive absorption of facts and the learning of basic skills. Recitation periods, examinations, and drills are provided to achieve this objective. In other words, the *laissez-faire* school tends to emphasize the "intake" side of the learning process. The use to which the curriculum may be put by the individual pupil is not taken into account. Sometimes there is a tacit acceptance of the untenable doctrine of formal discipline.[13] Of course, factual knowledge and skills are essential for the pupil; but it is important to teach the pupil how to use them in expressive activities. Any adequate education, therefore, takes into account the other "stages" of the creative process.

2. *The "stage of incubation."* A most interesting characteristic of the creative thought process is that there seems to be a time of "incubation." Two examples from Patrick will indicate how creative artists go through a time of apparent inactivity before they get the "flash of inspiration":

I have an idea in the back of my mind for a long time, sometimes a week or two. I don't think constantly about it, but it keeps coming back.

I may get an idea for a poem from something that I see, which may be with me for a long time. For instance, I saw a nun leaning over a pool of flamingoes, and I got the idea of both being in captivity. I was a whole year trying to write that. I knew that it would be a sonnet or lyric, but that was all.[14]

It is a familiar observation that a prolonged period of hard work sets up a great many blockings and inhibitions. Shifting from one phase of the work to another may bring retroactive inhibitions [15]

---

[13] Formal or mental discipline is the doctrine that the learning of certain subjects "trains the mind." Learning to reason in the field of mathematics, for example, is supposed to train the "faculty of reason" so that it will function in all sorts of situations. While there is some truth to the doctrine, it needs many amendments, as has been shown in Chapter 10. The more scientifically valid concept which fits the facts is known as "transfer of training."

[14] C. Patrick, "Creative Thought in Poets," *Archives of Psychology*, 1935, No. 178, p. 30.

[15] *Retroactive inhibition* is the name used to denote the interference of a more recently learned activity with one learned previously. If, for instance, a pupil learns

and confusions. A sort of "plateau effect" may appear, but a period of rest or recreation may bring one back to the task with renewed zeal. In the better school, therefore, there will be a stimulating variety in the classwork, and the teacher will set up learning situations in which "plateaus" are reduced to a minimum. Anecdotes about the methods of work used by creative geniuses reveal that many of them do not follow in general a slavish, mechanical routine. On some occasions they may work uninterruptedly for hours, whereas on other days they may work but a few moments. All evidence points to the conclusion that the period of incubation cannot be forced or mechanized. There is evidence, however, that the idea recurs again and again during this period, and that under appropriate conditions it is definitely related to a specific goal.[16] The school, therefore, should attempt to maintain conditions favorable to this end.

3. *The illumination.* A famous archeologist related that for a long time he labored in vain to decipher the inscription on a broken fragment. One night he dreamed that an Assyrian priest appeared and showed him the whole inscription. So vivid was the dream that he awakened and wrote down the translation. The next day, upon resuming his study, he found that the translation was plausibly correct. This anecdote illustrates a characteristic of creative thinking that has frequently been noted. The illumination seems to come with amazing suddenness, to give a sense of elation, and to mystify individuals who are untrained in psychological analysis. If the individual has the requisite technical skill or scientific training, he can utilize these flashes of insight in creative productions. Writers like Emerson and Hawthorne kept journals or commonplace books in which they jotted down all their inspirations. A familiar characteristic of these illuminations is that they are soon lost unless some immediate record is made. When notes are taken, they may serve as leads for new scientific research or as the basis for original works of art.

4. *The verification.* The final "stage" in a complete act of creative thinking is to give it expression in some tangible form. The trained scientist organizes the "inspiration" into hypotheses for laboratory testing and verification. The writer expresses his ideas in some appropriate literary form, and the painter puts the "illumination" on canvas. Sometimes, of course, the results are disappoint-

---

a group of facts in geography and then immediately learns how to get the volume of solids, he may be unable to recall the most recently learned information in geography. Retroactive inhibition, then, is the tendency of a later learning to impair an earlier learning.

[16] C. Patrick, *op. cit.*

ing and fall far short of expectation. As a result of prolonged self-training, a musician reports: [17]

I had at times curious experiences of having glorious sounds leap unexpectedly into my mind—original melodies and complete harmonies such as I could not conjure forth at will, and exalted qualities of tone such as I had never heard nor before imagined. . . . I shall never forget the disappointment I experienced when I first wrote down a composition and played it. Could it be that this rather uninteresting collection of sounds was the same as the theme that sounded so glorious in my mind?

Readers of the lives of great scientists know that most of them had to make many attempts before they finally obtained a solution of their problems.[18] Most original manuscripts of great literature show that the authors spent much time in careful revision and reorganization. "Hunches" may be wrong; therefore, they have to be tested and evaluated. At this point the thought processes are reflective and critical. Consequently, it is essential to have a thorough knowledge of the field and an adequate mastery of technique. Many persons have "good ideas" but no skill in expressing them. For that reason, the school must teach pupils how to find an appropriate medium for self-expression and how to weigh the relative value of their "inspirations."

### Experimental study of creative thinking

Patrick asked a group of artists to try to find some inspiration in passages of Milton's *L'Allegro,* and a group of poets to get inspiration from a mountain landscape picture.[19] Since the products were uniformly excellent, she concluded that the artists and poets were not hampered by the demands of the experimental setup. Most of them said afterward that they had worked in their customary manner. Groups of non-artists and non-poets furnished a basis for comparison. All her subjects, both the gifted and the non-gifted, worked in about the same general way and gave evidence of following the four steps in creative thinking. Apparently, the difference between excellence and mediocrity of creative ability is one of degree, not of kind. This finding indicates that the school may do a great deal to encourage all pupils to acquire some facility in creative thought.

Platt and Baker have reported that chemists follow these four

---

[17] Henry Cowell, "The Process of Musical Creation," *American Journal of Psychology,* Vol. XXXVII (1926), pp. 235-236.

[18] See, for example, standard lives of Thomas Edison and Dr. Ehrlich.

[19] C. Patrick, *op. cit.* (Every serious student ought to read these important investigations.)

steps in inventive thinking:[20] first, they get their minds "soaked full of data on a problem"; then they have a period of intermission or relaxation. Next, "an apparent solution or proper method of attack" emerges when they "are not formally working on the problem," and have no papers before them. This thing occurs only when the "mind is completely saturated with the problem." Finally, the solution is reached or the problem is regarded as too difficult. Meinecke's analysis of the thought processes of a young inventor fully supports these conclusions.[21] On one occasion, after a prolonged and futile attack upon a problem, while the inventor was taking a walk, suddenly the correct method of procedure occurred to him. Hastening back to his laboratory, he was soon able to bring his work to a successful completion.

## Social facilitation and creative thinking

Co-operative undertakings seem to facilitate creative endeavors. The creative adult familiarizes himself with the previous work done in his field, and sometimes he associates himself with others who are engaged in the same task. Thereby he may get new leads to the solution of his problem and find further incentive to keep at the task. As a rule, creative thought is close to reality, and its end results are given to the social group. The inventor must be thoroughly familiar with the needs of society and with the field in which he is working, otherwise his inventions might be bizarre and purposeless. The poet and the artist must, of course, have strong powers of imagination, but they must also possess a sound knowledge of human nature, if they are to win an audience. Sometimes, to be sure, the creative genius may be far in advance of his age; but, unless a later age finds social value in what he has accomplished, he is either forgotten or regarded as a deluded eccentric. In other words, creative endeavor should always have a bearing upon the social group. When the social situation fosters and encourages creative activity, then great advances in art, literature, and inventions logically follow. Some environments and some epochs in history appear to have stifled creative thought.

Creative thinking should not be confused with idle, purposeless daydreaming. As a matter of fact, most creative thinking is purposeful and deliberate. The inspirations are consciously sought so that a more adequate solution for a perplexing problem may be

[20] W. Platt and B. A. Baker, "The Relation of the Scientific 'Hunch' to Research," *Journal of Chemical Education*, Vol. 8 (1931), pp. 1969-2002.

[21] Reported by R. S. Woodworth, *Experimental Psychology*. New York: Henry Holt and Company, 1938. P. 820.

found or so that more appropriate media for self-expression may be discovered. The new experiences are then shared with the social group. For instance, the traditional way of painting shadows was to represent them by blacks and grays. The impressionistic group, however, looked more closely and discovered that shadows may be more appropriately represented by various hues, and they sought to call this discovery to the attention of all who look at their paintings. There is no such thing as a genius who is not recognized at some time or in some locality as having made a worthy contribution to society. Idle daydreams may have expression in bizarre, eccentric activities, but their social value is either slight or nil.

The school must attempt to set up situations that will facilitate the development of purposeful imagination. Consequently, the pupils should be encouraged to look for new solutions to problems and to find adequate media in which to express their ideas. If the teachers are not impatient and hasty in judging by adult standards of technical excellence, the pupils will not be stifled and inhibited in creative activities. The emphasis should be upon co-operative endeavors and the sharing of new discoveries. One of the best ways in which to keep the thought processes on a sound course of development is to encourage the expression of new ideas. Then the teacher and the other pupils have opportunity to correct any tendency towards bizarre expression and purposeless goals. The dividing line between idle fantasy and creative thought is, indeed, thin, and unless ideas are shared, there is a real danger of acquiring freakish, purposeless, and useless notions. In school, therefore, appropriate situations should be provided for the stimulation of sane and wholesome creative thoughts. More important still, the pupils should be given ample opportunities to express themselves and thus to have bizarre trends corrected at the outset.

The presence of other pupils engaged in similar activities greatly facilitates the responses of the individual. He is encouraged to persist in his activity, and he finds opportunity to gain new insights from the experiences of his classmates. If, however, his accomplishments are judged in terms of adult perfectionist standards, or if he is compared with pupils of greater ability, he may become discouraged. His pleasure in sharing his own experiences with others in the social group may be lost. Therefore, the teacher must not uphold standards that are beyond the possibility of attainment by the pupil, nor should he compare the performance of one pupil with that of another. The desirable procedure is to point out to each pupil just how he is improving in creative performance and to suggest new attacks that might hasten the improvement. Eventually, of course, each pupil comes to realize his limitations; but he is not discouraged by the abrupt realization of incapacity for out-standing creative activity.

## Appreciation

It is a mistake to think of appreciation as a passive, absorptive response. On the contrary, appreciation is an active, dynamic reaction. Scientific experiments have demonstrated the fact that there are measurable amounts of muscular reactions in such acts as listening to a symphony orchestra, looking at a painting, or silently reading a book. In a sense, the individual "puts himself actively into the situation." This sort of behavior is called *empathy*. It is an active projection of oneself into something. In a sense, empathy is the basis for all meaning.[22] Certainly, it plays a large part in appreciation. Unless the pupil can put himself into the situation, he cannot appreciate it; in fact, the situation has no meaning at all for him. Every motion-picture goer has observed with amusement and interest the behavior of children when exciting scenes are shown. Their appreciation is exhibited in explicit, active ways. Adults, on the other hand, have learned to subdue their reactions to implicit, almost imperceptible degrees. Nevertheless, both children and adults respond actively to all situations that arouse their appreciation. The only difference is that adult behavior has been conventionalized and subdued.

### Emotion and intellect in appreciation

Although appreciation is usually accompanied by pleasurable emotions, the experience also includes understandings. To say that one likes something but is unable to explain why is the statement of a sentimentalist. One who really appreciates something has a background of experience that enables him to discern qualities of excellence and to detect all the elements of a given situation. Thereby he is able to have a sense of relative values. For example, in listening to Tschaikowsky's *Symphony No. 4 in F Minor,* he is able to recognize the composer's debt to Beethoven and to follow closely the themes in each of the four movements. Because of his background of understanding, he is able to converse lucidly about the "capricious arabesques" of the third movement, as well as about other parts of this symphony, the life and times of the composer, and other symphonies. If he appreciates this music, he can clearly tell what it means to him. If he does not like it, he can

---

[22] M. Schoen, *Art and Beauty.* New York: The Macmillan Company, 1932. Pp. 132 f.

analyze the qualities that displease him. In other words, the individual who appreciates music has understandings as well as emotional responses.

The necessity for knowledge as a basis for real appreciation can scarcely be overemphasized. Take, for instance, the following lines from the opening scene of *Macbeth*:

> Fair is foul, and foul is fair.
> Hover through fog and filthy air.

The entire meaning of the couplet is lost unless the pupil realizes that this *credo*, in which the three Witches join, is an old folk-belief about evil spirits: that not only are their moral standards the exact reverse of those of human beings, but also their aesthetic preferences likewise are the opposite of human preferences. To be sure, a complete understanding may sometimes destroy appreciation, as in the case of the pupil who learns that *Gulliver's Travels* and "The One-Hoss Shay" were intended to be biting satires. That fact, however, does not justify the nonintellectual, sentimental teaching of appreciations. Unless there is a basis of understanding, there cannot be any genuine appreciation.

## Teaching appreciations

The normal procedure in teaching appreciations is to give the pupil experience in creative undertakings. Unfortunately, many programs of education had little or no place for creative activity. The factual, drill-lesson approach was used in all subjects, whether fractions or poetry, spelling or drawing. Consequently, creative impulses were considered to have no place whatsoever in the school. Activities arising from the spontaneous interests and the felt needs of the pupils were relegated to a place outside the curriculum. The so-called "appreciation" lesson was nothing more than a variant of the drill procedure. Although the past tense is used here, this method of procedure has by no means entirely passed away. Wherever it still lingers, there can be no real guidance in the development of appreciations.

Appreciation implies that we enter into some degree of coincident thinking and feeling with a creative genius. To do so, we must have some basis of experience in creative activity ourselves. That does not mean, however, that we cannot appreciate music unless we can compose or play like a virtuoso. The activity necessary in true appreciation may give us some creative experience. The youngster who contrasts paintings of sunsets with the vivid colors

of the setting sun thereby learns a great deal about appreciation.
The part that creative thinking plays in all our activities is seldom
realized. For instance, we believe that we can read the following
sentence with full understanding: *The man rode down the street.*
Each reader, however, has a different mental image of the man, of
the street, and of the object or animal ridden. In other words, reading itself is a creative activity, and when it is rightly taught, it
involves appreciations as well as mechanical skills in eye movements.

For an illustration of how appreciations might be taught, consider how to present the familiar "Bugle Song" from *The Princess:*

> The splendor falls on castle walls
> And snowy summits old in story:
> The long light shakes across the lakes,
> And the wild cataract leaps in glory.
> Blow, bugle, blow, set the wild echoes flying,
> Blow, bugle; answer, echoes, dying, dying, dying.
>
> O hark, O hear! how thin and clear,
> And thinner, clearer, farther going!
> O sweet and far from cliff and scar
> The horns of Elfland faintly blowing!
> Blow, let us hear the purple glens replying:
> Blow, bugle; answer, echoes, dying, dying, dying.
>
> O love, they die in yon rich sky,
> They faint on hill or field or river:
> Our echoes roll from soul to soul,
> And grow forever and forever.
> Blow, bugle, blow, set the wild echoes flying,
> And answer, echoes, answer, dying, dying, dying.

One high-school class regarded this poem as a clear invitation
to do an interesting bit of creative reading. By group discussions,
they obtained a mental image of the scene, the speaker, and the
listener. Two members, talented in art, painted a picture of the
background, which greatly helped in visualizing the material of the
first stanza. After much debate, the class agreed that the speaker
was a young man addressing his bride. She, they imagined, was
first elated by the beauty of the landscape and the sound of the
bugle; but, as they stood there, the darkness fell and the echoes
died away. Then she became depressed at the thought that everything is fleeting and transient, perhaps even their love. He, therefore, assures her that the one abiding reality is love, which is
passed from one generation to the next. What does it matter if
Tennyson may not have had in mind such a meaning? The whole

class had an enjoyable half-hour, and most of them gained in the experience necessary for creative reading.

It would be a great mistake to assume that appreciations cannot be taught in any other courses than art, music, and literature. As a matter of fact, practically any subject in the curriculum may, *if properly taught,* result in worthy appreciations. In shorthand and typing, proper assigned readings and class exhibits may lead into an appreciation of our economic order and of the cultural advantages that it has made possible. Geometry, often taught in a factual and unimaginative fashion, should include special lessons to give the pupil an appreciation of carefully reasoned thought. In fact, if the curriculum were presented rightly, appreciations, as well as factual knowledge, would be the outcome, and nearly every subject would give ample stimulus to creative thinking. In the past, insufficient attention has been paid to the possibility of conserving and developing worthy appreciations. In fact, when factual drills are emphasized, the outcome may be an actual distaste for a given subject. All subjects should be taught in such a way as to give the necessary skills and the understandings basic to efficient living, but all of them should culminate in a genuine appreciation of our cultural inheritance.

### QUESTIONS AND EXERCISES FOR DISCUSSION AND STUDY

1. In subjects where drill is necessary, how should it be initiated and directed so that desirable attitudes will not be destroyed? Which is the easier type of lesson to teach, the appreciation or the drill?

2. In what ways can understandings contribute to appreciation? Show how you would use understandings to develop appreciation in one of the ordinary school subjects.

3. Find in your own experience several examples of loss of factual knowledge in a subject you once knew fairly well. Perhaps the passive subjunctive of a fourth-conjugation Latin verb or a fifth root might be examples. Even though the facts seem to be forgotten, does anything remain? Do you have a continued liking for the subjects in question?

4. Show how the old-fashioned school judged pupils' literary and artistic output by adult standards of technical excellence. Is that a good way to inculcate a desire to improve the form of a creative production? Explain.

5. How much attention was given in your elementary school to creative activities? Were you interested in perfecting your techniques so that you could express yourself more adequately?

6. What appreciations should be the outcomes of a course of study in American history? Could the course be presented in such a way as to inspire a pupil to read extensively in after-school life about American history? Have you kept up your own reading in the subject? Why, or why not?

7. What sorts of toys do young children continue to use in their play? What can we learn about creative imagination from studying the spontaneous play interests of young children?

8. What sorts of movies and radio programs do children like? Try to collect a list of preferences from children you know, and then classify the findings in terms of the ages of the children.

9. Try to recollect the type of books you read when you passed through "the reading craze"? How old were you at that time? Were the books principally imaginative or factual? Why do you now read less than you did at that time?

10. Do inventions and inspirations just "spring into the mind"? How might one prepare himself to have many "illuminations"?

11. Can pupils be compelled to write an "original composition"? Justify your answer.

12. What is the proper role of the teacher in an appreciation lesson? Explain in full with illustrations. Can appreciations be *taught?* Explain.

## SELECTED REFERENCES FOR FURTHER READING AND STUDY

Downey, J. E., *Creative Imagination*. New York: Harcourt, Brace and Company, 1929.

Fletcher, J. M., *Psychology in Education*. New York: Doubleday, Doran and Company, 1934. Part Two.

Hart, J. K., *Creative Moments in Education*. New York: Henry Holt and Company, 1935.

Hartman, G., and A. Shumaker, editors, *Creative Expression*. New York: John Day Company, 1932.

Lowes, J. L., *The Road to Xanadu*. Boston: Houghton Mifflin Company, 1927.

Mearns, H., *Creative Power*. New York: Doubleday, Doran and Company, 1929.

Mursell, J. L., *The Psychology of Secondary School Teaching*. New York: W. W. Norton and Company, 1932. Chapter VIII.

Schoen, M., *Art and Beauty*. New York: The Macmillan Company, 1932.

———, *The Psychology of Music*. New York: Ronald Press Company, 1940.

Skinner, C. E., editor, *Readings in Educational Psychology*. New York: Farrar and Rinehart, 1937. Chapter XII.

———, editor, *Readings in Psychology*. New York: Farrar and Rinehart, 1935. Chapter XIX.

*Supervision and the Creative Teacher* (a collaboration), Fifth Yearbook of the Department of Supervisors and Directors of the National Education Association. New York: Bureau of Publications, Teachers College, Columbia University, 1932.

Taba, Hilda, *Dynamics of Education*. New York: Harcourt, Brace and Company, 1932.

Wallas, G., *The Art of Thought*. New York: Harcourt, Brace and Company, 1926.

# CHAPTER 14

# Psychology of the School Subjects

## Introduction

Since the rise of psychological research in tests and measurements several decades ago, many principles and hypotheses of the learning process as applied to various subjects have been formulated and tested. Selected findings of psychological and educational research that seem to warrant application in modern school practices have been summarized in this chapter. Only major factors, or high spots, can be indicated, since it would require a separate volume to discuss and to illustrate the psychology of learning in the various subjects in the elementary and the high school.

## Psychology of art

The pupil's growth in art from infancy through adolescence may be characterized in three stages of development. The first includes the years from four to about the age of nine, the second stage is from the age of nine to fourteen, and the third stage is from the age of fourteen to eighteen. Although this division is arbitrary, it serves for practical purposes. These stages are used to characterize the "average" pupil rather than the child who is artistically gifted and who usually attains maturity levels in art at much earlier age levels than the typical child.

In the first stage, two forms of graphic expression characterize the period from the nursery school through the third grade. One of these might be called *graphic reproducing,* and includes the drawing of outlines of commonly experienced objects. These drawings are crude in the preschool years, but show more and more mature representation from year to year. The other development might be called *elementary composition,* and appears in the form of simple graphic expressions of experience involving more than a single concept or object.

In the first stage, artistic expression and activity are stimulated by free play and simple experiences and are characterized by uninhibited imagination toward objects that are of interest. Imagery in the child is generally more vivid than in later years, and there is little evidence of self-consciousness regarding technical rules and standards. Hurlock [1] reports an increase in embarrassment with increasing discrimination of detail as children grow older. While still in this first stage, a child may attempt to depict almost any idea or object, sometimes one which may be highly imaginative, original, and personal. For this age Mellinger [2] found that children preferred colored to black and white pictures, and realistic, rather than conventional, portrayal.

During this period the child is usually not interested in naturalistic drawings. He frequently depicts his interpretations or meanings of an object rather than attempting a drawing in proportion. Distortion is usual for a child at this period. Objects in his drawing that have most meaning for him are generally made more prominent. A flower or man may be drawn larger than a car or a house.

The role of the teacher is primarily one of guidance. The teacher can occasionally help the child with a technical problem in art when the child is mature enough and ready for such help. The teacher can provide a range and wealth of materials and activities, such as trips in the community and audio-visual aids, to enrich the child's experiences and concepts and thus provide suggestions for and stimulation to his artistic activities.

In the stage of nine-to-fourteen-year-olds, Murphy [3] reports that children showed increased interest and effort in drawings of adventure and of remote peoples and places. Interest in drawings of explorers and materials associated with battles and heroic exploits were frequently observed and may have been stimulated by the curriculum of the schools. During this age span, also, the children showed an interest in occupations, tools, and other materials of everyday use in the lives of historic peoples. Some observers report that self-consciousness and embarrassment in artistic expression begin to appear. At this age span more requests for craft activities and avoidance of painting activities were observed, especially on the part of children whose paintings did not receive general approval. About eleven years of age marks a point where many

---

[1] E. B. Hurlock and J. L. Thomson, "Children's Drawings: an Experimental Study of Perception," *Child Development*, Vol. 5, 1934, pp. 127-138.

[2] B. E. Mellinger, *Children's Interests in Pictures*. Contributions to Education, No. 516. New York: Teachers College, Columbia University, 1932.

[3] M. Murphy, *Observations of the Interests and Behavior of Children during Visits to Art Museums*. New York: Brooklyn Museum, Educational Division. Unpublished.

children show dissatisfaction with their artistic products and strive to attain more adult results and standards. The art interests and activities of children from twelve to fourteen increasingly tend to approximate those of adults.

## Psychology of Foreign Languages

Several theories of instruction in the foreign languages are proposed in modern education. The differences among these theories are mainly in the emphasis placed upon the four major objectives of foreign language study. Some years ago the Modern Foreign Language Study [4] issued a report in which the reading aim of foreign languages was emphasized as most important for students in secondary schools. This emphasis on the reading aim of foreign language indicated a need from the beginning of instruction for a type of reading which is intended "to increase the pupil's reading vocabulary, to give him valuable content experience, and to increase his ability in the reading process by affording him abundant opportunity for practice on pleasing, interesting and easy material." [5]

### "Extensive reading" theory

Extensive reading of a foreign language requires not only the acquisition of a fairly large reading vocabulary, but also knowledge and understanding of the content by means of related experiences. The procedure generally is to provide much sight reading with definite questions based on the reading material. In addition, short stories about the institutions, history, customs, and modern life of the people whose language is read are used extensively. The amount of the language that is read, using this approach, exceeds by two or three times the amount that is read under the more traditional grammatical-analysis approach to the study of a foreign language.

Emphasis on the reading objective has resulted in new methods of teaching as well as in new processes of learning. The difference in skills is vividly illustrated by studies of eye movements in the reading of a foreign language. Buswell [6] made an extensive investigation of eye movements in foreign-language reading by means of photographic records. The findings of this study indicate that the

[4] Algernon Coleman, *The Teaching of Modern Foreign Languages.* New York: The Macmillan Company, 1929.

[5] Helen M. Eddy, "Course of Study in French for High Schools," *Extension Bulletin,* University of Iowa, May 1, 1924, No. 105, p. 33.

[6] G. T. Buswell, *A Laboratory Study of the Reading of Modern Foreign Languages.* New York: The Macmillan Company, 1927.

students who were taught a modern foreign language by the direct method, which stresses natural reading habits, achieved in a two-year period of study the fundamental habits and skills of reading that are more or less characteristic of the mature reader of the English language. In contrast, the students who were taught by an indirect method, which stresses grammar and syntax, tended to have the skills and habits of reading that are more or less characteristic of the immature reader of English. Evidence from the studies by Buswell and others indicates clearly that attention to analytical and grammatical details tends to retard the development of reasonable speed in reading a foreign language and in comprehending adequately the content of what is read. The analogy may be drawn between teaching a child to read the English language by stressing grammatical analysis versus the procedure of natural reading by stressing the comprehension of meanings of language units with analysis and grammar applied at a reasonable period after the basic skills and techniques of the reading process have been established.

### "Organic" language theory

A recent study in the psychology of foreign language has been made in the Stanford Language Arts Investigation and is reported by Kaulfers.[7] In this study an emphasis was placed on a so-called "organic" conception of language. In this approach to language instruction, language abilities were developed from the beginning by means of content and activities that were rich not only in the direct language outcomes, but also in related or concomitant outcomes. In a sense, this study was a return to the fourfold aim of language, namely, the ability to read, to write, to speak, and to understand a foreign language when spoken. The major characteristics of the approach were the provision of a student-centered program, the socialization of activities of the language class, the individualization of the instruction, and the provision of a highly flexible time allotment in the curriculum. Some of the activities that were associated with this approach were cultural programs in the foreign language, creative activities in language arts through such means as puppet shows, dramatizations, topical outlines, and translation of foreign literature. The correlation between language arts and other subjects, such as social studies and English, was an essential characteristic.

The findings of the study indicate some very clear gains for this

---

[7] Walter V. Kaulfers, *Modern Languages for Modern Schools.* New York: McGraw-Hill Book Company, 1942.

approach to the learning of a foreign language. As compared with previous conditions and results of teaching, from two to three times as many students continued the study of a foreign language beyond the required two years. Data obtained from various inventories showed that students maintain a high degree of interest. Results from the application of attitude scales indicated very marked gains in the development of tolerance toward people of the foreign countries whose language was being studied. Special tests proved considerable gain in knowledge and understanding of the culture of the country. All of these gains were obtained without detracting from the achievement of the direct language as measured by the Co-operative Test ratings in reading, vocabulary, and grammar.

### Vocabulary and pronunciation

As in all language study, the student must learn meanings of the words most commonly met in reading or speaking a foreign language. In order to meet this need, the Modern Foreign Language Study has sponsored word counts in French, German, and Spanish. These counts of words provide guidance for the language teacher in building up the reading or speaking vocabulary of the students so economically that they will encounter few difficulties in word meaning when they begin more continuous reading or speaking of a language. In oral reading of the foreign language, pronunciation becomes an important factor, although it may not be so necessary if the major purpose of language study is to develop silent reading. Recently there has been a tendency to place more stress on oral reading than was recommended in the Modern Foreign Language Study. The development of skills of pronunciation can become exceedingly dull and boring unless drill is tied up with vital and worthwhile activities in the foreign language. For this purpose, the cultural values, the use of short language units that have interesting content, and the use of anecdotes, proverbs, and the like may be highly recommended.

### Psychology of History and the Social Studies

History and other social studies differ from most other subjects in that a concept of time is necessary for a full comprehension of social political, civic, and economic processes. The concept of time is developed in the child in a manner similar to that of his other concepts. However, the time concept involves the ability to project the self in terms of past, present, and future. The young child's ability to understand time is limited because of his lack of maturity and experience. As the child grows older, he refers to many things as past. Those which he connects with his experiences usually involve the idea of past, present, or future, while he often refers in an indefinite time pattern to those which he regards in an impersonal way. The concept of time is essential for history, since history is largely based on concepts and situations in the "past."

## Concepts grow from experiences

Concepts are the means by which we interpret present experiences in the light of past experiences. They represent the generalized meanings that we have acquired from our experiences, and are the bases for our interpretation of present events or situations. Each individual manages a situation according to the meanings that he has previously acquired. It is important, then, that children secure desirable concepts in the social sciences, since so many of the problems of today relate to these sciences.

## Developing concepts and information in the social studies

The objective most commonly emphasized in the social studies is the acquisition of basic social concepts and related information. The learning process involves not only the building of new concepts, but also the reconstruction of the ideas already held. Children in the first three grades, especially, while they have considerable social information, have, also, many misconceptions. It has been demonstrated that children in the intermediate grades and high school and even college students have serious misconceptions of basic facts in the social studies and their implications.

Teachers cannot reason that, because pupils use certain terms, they understand them, for it has been found that children frequently use terms the meanings of which they only vaguely or even inaccurately conceive. Meltzer [8] found that the concepts, or meanings, for the term *socialism* ranged from: "does lots of social duties," "goes to parties," "has to do with government," "is for working class," to such meanings as: "wants equal rights for workers; no rich classes," "want all to have an equal share of money, queer, usually foreigners," "want government control of fundamental industries and a more equal distribution of wealth." [9]

It would be a serious error, therefore, to assume at any time that a pupil's social concepts are complete and accurate. The true

[8] Hyman Meltzer, *Children's Social Concepts: A Study of Their Nature and Development.* Contributions to Education, No. 192. New York: Teachers College, Columbia University, 1925.

[9] *Ibid.,* p. 21.

status of the concepts of a child must be ascertained and dealt with fittingly if his optimum growth is to be assured. Continual, careful, and appropriate enrichment of the experiential background is the only guarantee of growth and development.

The general period of ages nine to fifteen is particularly productive for the acquisition of meanings. As experience accumulates, language develops, and mental age increases, the number and richness of concepts increase correspondingly. In reality, throughout adolescence there is a continuous increase of insight, imagination, concentration, problem-solving behavior, and related mental activities, all of which improve the ability to acquire and enrich concepts.

The significant generalizations justified by the research in this aspect of child growth in the social studies may, then, be summarized as follows: First, the learning process involves both the construction of new concepts and the reconstruction of those already held. Second, social concepts vary in difficulty, and so must be adapted, in the learning process, to the maturity of the child. Third, the general period of ages nine to fifteen is particularly productive for the acquisition of social meanings. Fourth, throughout adolescence the ability to acquire and enrich concepts is continuously developing.

### Developing civic attitudes and beliefs

It is a matter of common knowledge that most teachers of history and the other social studies have been principally concerned, in their teaching activities, with pupil achievement in the intellectual outcomes—concepts, facts, and skills—while they either treat civic beliefs and attitudes in a haphazard manner or ignore them.

In contrast with this typical attitude of teachers, research workers in the field of social studies are placing increasing emphasis on civic attitudes and beliefs. Much of the significant research now in progress in the social studies pertains to the so-called "intangible" attitudes and beliefs of pupils. These may be termed the dynamic outcomes of learning as distinguished from the intellectual outcomes, such as academic knowledges and skills. It is not intended here to suggest that attitudes and beliefs and the intellectual outcomes—knowledge and skills—are in categories that are mutually exclusive: on the contrary, they are intrinsically related.

While attitudes are deeply rooted psychologically, they can, nevertheless, be changed. The experimental evidence [10] indicates

---

[10] For a more detailed summary of research studies on "attitudes," see the article by Ross Stagner in *Encyclopedia of Educational Research*, pp. 69-74. New York: The Macmillan Company, 1941.

that certain specific attitudes are readily engendered and readily modified. Generalized attitudes, however, seem to be much more stable and to have their origin to a greater extent in home and community influences than in the school. It has been shown experimentally that the greatest changes in attitude occur when the teacher is conscious of the problem of attitude. The presentation of a relatively small amount of social stimulus material may produce a marked shift in attitudes. Pronounced shifts were produced, for example, after studying social insurance, capital punishment, and labor unions. In one case, a short lecture brought about a significant change in the direction of a more favorable attitude toward the League of Nations. On the other hand, it has been shown that there is a strong tendency for generalized attitudes to stay put.

While the research is inconclusive at many points in this area, the following generalizations seem to be well founded. First, the dynamic factors of attitudes and motives derived from civic beliefs are the mainsprings of civic action. Second, while attitudes have deep psychological roots, they can, nevertheless, be modified. Third, there are developmental levels of attitudes ranging from specific attitudes toward particular experiences to those representing the highest forms of mental organization. Fourth, specific attitudes are readily engendered and readily modified, while the higher-level generalized attitudes are more stable. Fifth, the greatest changes in attitudes as a result of teaching occur when the teacher is conscious of the problem of attitude. Sixth, children's social attitudes are similar to those of their parents.

### Acquiring work-study skills

The range of work and study skills required for successful achievement in social studies is very wide, as revealed in the studies by Price,[11] Thomas, [12] and Wrightstone.[13] They may be classified as follows:

1. *Visual skills and activities,* such as reading and the study of maps, charts, diagrams, and statistical tables.

[11] Roy A. Price, "The Use of Activities in Social Studies: A Critical Study of the Effectiveness of Fifty-Two Pupil Activities as Judged by Teachers and Students." Cambridge, Mass.: Harvard University, 1938. Unpublished doctor's thesis.

[12] Katheryne Colvin Thomas, "The Ability of Children to Interpret Graphs," *Thirty-Second Yearbook of the National Society for the Study of Education,* pp. 492-494. Bloomington, Ill.: Public School Publishing Company, 1933.

[13] J. Wayne Wrightstone, "Growth in Reading Maps and Graphs and Locating Items in Reference Books," *School Review,* Vol. 42, pp. 759-766, 1939.

2. *Listening skills and activities,* such as listening to radio programs, dramatizations, lectures, and sound motion pictures.

3. *Oral skills and activities,* such as giving reports or floor talks, recitation, and participation in group discussions.

4. *Writing skills and activities,* including writing up dramatizations and written reports of various kinds.

5. *Drawing skills and activities,* such as drawing pictures, cartoons, diagrams, charts, and maps.

6. *General skills and activities,* such as collecting stamps or coins, constructing models, and making field trips and local surveys.

The ability to read graphs and maps and to find items of information in reference books grows gradually and continuously from grade four through grade twelve. There is evidence that for pupils in any grade who have a mental age of fourteen, and especially through grade eight, the acquisition of work-study skills is very rapid, but decreases proportionately thereafter. Also, the ability of pupils to develop skills in reading maps and graphs and in finding information in references seems to improve rapidly as ·they grow older up to the chronological age of thirteen (the average for grade eight) and more slowly thereafter.

From the experimental studies in this area, five generalizations may be made that should be useful to teachers. First, it appears that pupils need guidance and direction in acquiring proper work and study skills. Second, there is a relationship between the intelligence and maturity of pupils and their ability to master certain types of skills. Third, the interpretation of graphs, except the most simple forms, requires skills too complex to be mastered by the average pupil below the fourth or fifth grade. Fourth, the process of learning or acquiring work-study skills is gradual and continuous. Fifth, ability to accomplish certain objectives in the social studies may be seriously affected by deficiencies in work-study skills.

### Developing powers of critical thinking [14]

The development of powers of critical thinking is one of the major objectives of the social studies. Through the elementary and high school, teachers should help children to develop the ability to recognize problems; to find, select, and reject evidence bearing upon them; to draw inferences and conclusions; and to test these in new situations. Evidence is at hand to demonstrate clearly that

---

[14] See Chapter 12.

children reason at an early age, that reasoning continues to develop throughout childhood and adolescence, and that the thought processes of children are not qualitatively different from those of adults. Long before the pupil starts to school, he begins to reason with the data at hand. He even attempts to make generalizations and to apply them in the solution of his problems. There is ample experimental evidence that the ability to generalize from appropriate facts and experiences is definitely present in the later primary period. At the high-school and college level, evidence from studies indicates that the powers of generalizing and inferring, as well as of applying concepts and principles to new situations, are a more permanent part of the equipment of an individual than is the memory of more specific facts and information.

Newlun [15] studied the effect of teaching the skills of summarizing. On the basis of experimenting in three schools for twelve weeks, he concluded: (a) that fifth-grade pupils can be taught to make creditable summaries; (b) that such training is probably more effective than conventional study methods; (c) that such training is unlikely to affect achievement in reading; and (d) that such training does not interfere with achievement in other directions. Simpson [16] undertook to determine the effect of specific training on ability to read historical materials. The scores from 606 pupils from the fifth, sixth, and seventh grades in and near Pittsburgh were utilized as the basis for conclusions. He found: (a) that reading ability improved following training in answering questions, in evaluating, in outlining, and in summarizing; (b) that organization of materials should precede attempts to answer questions; (c) that outlining was the most effective single method used; and (d) that specific training in answering questions, evaluating, outlining, and summarizing was more effective than the usual classroom procedure. Weaver,[17] in two carefully reported experiments, indicated that, on the basis of test scores, in American history extensive reading is certainly as effective as is intensive reading. He suggested that too much written work is required in history. Thus it appears that time spent in written work might better be spent doing serious reading. However, a moderate amount of well-planned written work might aid the learner in perceiving relationships and clarification of meanings.

---

[15] Chester Otto Newlun, *Teaching Children to Summarize in Fifth Grade History.* Contributions to Education, No. 404. New York: Teachers College, Columbia University, 1930.

[16] Robert Gilkey Simpson, "The Effect of Specific Training on Ability to Read Historical Materials," *Journal of Educational Research,* Vol. 20, pp. 343-351, 1929.

[17] Robert B. Weaver, "Relative Value of Intensive Study and Extensive Reading in United States History," *School Review,* Vol. 39, pp. 217-226, 1931.

## Psychology of Language

### Usage

Language is affected by the social as well as the mental growth of the individual. Studies by psychologists have shown that at the age of eighteen months simple sentences consisting of a noun and a verb have appeared. As the average child grows older, he uses simple sentences with simple phrases and, still later, more complex and compound sentences. The fact that language development is associated with mental ability is the finding of a study by Smith,[18] who concludes that the significant trend in the development of a sentence with increase in age is an increasing tendency toward the use of longer and more complete as well as more complex sentences. Studies of errors in usage reveal that verbs are most difficult, followed closely by errors in the use of pronouns and of double negatives. These errors persist at all grade levels because the complexity of forms of expression increases from grade to grade.

### Spelling

Present studies of the development of children in spelling indicate that children should learn the spelling of words for which they will have actual use. Although the basic word lists are valuable as guides, the word which the child needs in connection with other activities should be taught when the need for it arises. Individual differences in spelling needs and abilities should be recognized by the teacher. Adjustments to individual needs or difficulties should be made by the use of methods that provide for individual differences, and by the development of children's ability to learn new words as they need them.

### Composition

In written composition, children should learn those types and rules of writing which the social and school situations require. The findings in this field indicate that the teacher should provide the children with occasions for spontaneous writing, for inspirational writing, and for systematic training in writing techniques. Among students in high school there are many differences in specific writing abilities: one student may have poor spelling ability,

---

[18] M. E. Smith, *An Investigation of the Development of the Sentence and the Extent of Vocabulary in Young Children, University of Iowa Studies in Child Welfare,* Vol. 3, No. 5, 1926.

inferior writing ability, and faulty sentence structure. An intelligent teaching program will be based upon the abilities of each pupil in the class, and the materials, methods, and activities to be employed will utilize the needs and abilities of each pupil. The English teacher should make an inventory of the English abilities possessed by pupils as well as of their deficiencies which may need remedial treatments.

## Penmanship

In handwriting, or penmanship, research has shown that manual dexterity develops slowly, and that a complex form of skill like handwriting is a slow growth. In the primary grades, the type of writing and the requirements of speed and quality should be adapted to young children's ability. Manuscript writing in the primary grades has been found to make the beginning of writing easier because letter characteristics of manuscript approximate those of book print. Although it was generally felt that sufficient skill in writing should be reached by the end of the sixth grade, recent studies have shown that it is advantageous to continue instruction beyond this grade if improvement in handwriting is a necessary and desirable objective. Speed of writing at the sixth-grade level is usually not adequate for use in the junior and senior high school. In the second place, the writing of sixth-grade pupils is not yet mature. Often the writing of junior and senior high-school pupils deteriorates. To prevent this, some instruction or guidance in writing should be continued through the school years, especially in the case of poor writers.

## Psychology of Mathematics

Investigations by MacLatchy [19] and Woody [20] provide an indication of the average pupil's knowledge of counting, measuring, and number processes before formal school instruction in arithmetic is begun. These studies reveal that, even before children enter school, many of them have attained considerable ability in counting, in reading simple numbers, in telling time, in knowing the common units of measurement, and in dealing with simple exercises in addition and subtraction. Such experiences in number and arithmetic are gained in the home, on the playground, and

[19] Josephine H. MacLatchy, "Number Abilities of First Grade Children," *Childhood Education,* Vol. 11, pp. 344-347, 1935.

[20] Clifford Woody, "The Arithmetical Backgrounds of Young Children," *Journal of Educational Research,* Vol. 30, pp. 188-201, 1937.

in other community experiences of young children. The degree of mastery of number concepts and relationships varies among the individual pupils and seems to have a fairly close relationship to the mental age and home background of the pupil.

## Mental age and achievement in arithmetic

Washburne [21] and the Committee of Seven have carried on extensive studies to determine whether or not there are minimum mental-age or readiness levels at which it is most efficient for the child to learn various arithmetic processes. On the basis of five years of investigation, the committee concluded that there are stages in a child's mental growth before which it is generally ineffective to teach various arithmetic processes. They recommend, for example, that the easier addition facts should not be taught until a child has reached a mental age of 6 years, 5 months. At the other end of the scale, they have indicated that effective mastery of denominate numbers should not be attempted until a child has reached a mental age of 14 years. These studies have been criticized and defended, but certainly they provide some guidance to teachers regarding the adaptation of arithmetic to the different mental abilities of pupils.

## Problem solving in arithmetic

Various studies have been carried on regarding the most effective methods of learning problem solving in arithmetic. Hanna [22] made one of the most extensive studies about such learning. He experimented with three groups of pupils in Grades 4 and 7 in order to determine which methods would be most effective for the different ability groups in problem solving. The dependencies method ("To find the answer I must know this fact," "To know this fact I must find this," and so forth) was especially effective with pupils of low mental ability, and it was equally good with the individual method for pupils of average and higher ability. The individual method, in which the pupil uses any method that he desires, was also fairly effective with average and above-average pupils. The conventional formula method ("What is called for?") proved to be less effective. Other studies have emphasized the correlation between reading ability and problem solving.

---

[21] Carleton Washburne, "Grade-Placement of Arithmetic Topics," *Twenty-Ninth Yearbook of the National Society for the Study of Education*, 1930, pp. 641-670.
[22] Paul R. Hanna, "Methods of Arithmetic Problem Solving," *Mathematics Teacher*, Vol. 23, pp. 442-450, 1930.

## Use of crutches

Brownell [23] has carried on a number of studies that have contributed to the psychology of arithmetic learning. One of the most interesting of his investigations is a study of the effects of the use of a crutch in adding proper fractions. In this study, the group using the crutch did approximately as well as the non-crutch group. Both groups made the same kinds of errors; thus, the crutch was not effective in reducing the number or kinds of errors. Most interesting of all was the finding that the group using the crutch tended to drop it despite the teacher's effort to preserve its use. The results of this study indicate that a crutch may be an aid to learning for the child in one stage of his development, but that it will be eliminated almost automatically as higher stages of development are reached.

## Functions of arithmetic

In the modern curriculum, arithmetic has comprehensive functions: (a) the computational function, where the emphasis is placed upon the development of essential computational skills; (b) the informational function, which emphasizes the understanding of such institutions as banks, insurance, and taxation, where the social uses of number are extensive; (c) the sociological function, which emphasizes an understanding of the problems faced by institutions that use numbers extensively; and (d) the psychological function, which emphasizes quantitative thinking and relationships or methods in dealing with situations involving number experiences.

## Stages of growth

For convenience in discussion, it is possible to trace successive stages of growth in the average child in mastering arithmetic. Brueckner [24] has defined such stages, and they are here summarized in outline form. In the first stage, the child acquires a readiness for number by a variety of experiences with simple number concepts and a simple arithmetic vocabulary. These come from incidental experiences with number in daily life and are characteristic of the average child in the preschool years, the kindergarten, and the early part of Grade 1.

[23] W. A. Brownell, "Borrowing in Subtraction," *Journal of Educational Research*, Vol. 33, pp. 415-424, 1940.

[24] L. J. Brueckner, "The Development of Ability in Arithmetic," *Thirty-Eighth Yearbook of the National Society for the Study of Education*, Part I, 1939, pp. 280-281.

The second stage is characteristic of the average child in Grades 1 and 2. At this stage, the child grows in ability to read numbers, to count, and to group and to compare objects and in knowledge of the basic number facts of addition and subtraction. If the curriculum is planned so that the number and arithmetic activities are related to social situations, many simple applications of number in measurements and social practices help the pupil to acquire a rich background of meaning for numbers.

The third stage is characteristic of the average pupil in Grades 3 and 4. During this time the pupil masters the arithmetic processes that deal with whole numbers, and his understanding of social arithmetic is extended. At the end of, or as part of, this stage, the pupil will have mastered the addition and subtraction facts, as well as the easier multiplication and division facts. An understanding of the meaning, use, and simple computation of the more common fractions will have been introduced to the pupil.

In the fourth stage, namely, Grades 5 through 8, the social experience with numbers is extended rapidly, and increased proficiency in skills and abilities of arithmetic computation develop. During this stage the more abstract number concepts, the more difficult processes in fractions and long division, the more difficult social applications of numbers, and the comprehension of quantitative relationships develop.

In the fifth stage, namely, Grade 9 and beyond, mathematical aptitudes may be discovered and developed in selected students. These stages of development cannot be sharply defined. They merge gradually as parts of a continuous process of growth and development.

### Algebra

Algebra is sometimes called "the science of numbers." In algebra, the quantitative experiences and concepts are translated into formulas that are expressed in abstract letters, numbers, and signs. These formulas represent the so-called "laws of mathematics," which may be applied to the solution of both practical and theoretical problems. In algebra, the numerous computations involving many arithmetic processes are reduced to economical short cuts of computation and, therefore, are relatively complex in derivation. For this reason, algebra is a formal subject including abstract generalizations and provides the foundation of higher mathematics.

The student who enrolls in algebra in the high school should be competent in arithmetic. Unless such competence is present, the student is likely to fail. Studies of achievement in algebra by average high-school students indicate that a majority of them are acquiring so little mastery of the content that algebra should be required of selected students only or that the traditional content should be radically reorganized.

Since algebra is related more closely to the discipline of arithmetic than to the discipline of geometry, which deals with space, the importance of arithmetic mastery is evident. The closest parallel between the two disciplines comes in the use of formulas. In arithmetic the pupil has already had some experience with simple formulas, for example, in percentage, areas of figures, and volumes of some figures. These are simple formulas, and the student can understand the realities represented by the symbols of an abstract nature. These simpler formulas are characteristic of the more difficult and abstract algebraic formulas.

Algebraic ability is highly correlated with intelligence. Thorndike, in his investigations of algebraic computation and problem solving, claims that success in algebra depends emphatically on intellectual ability. Other studies also have shown a high correlation to exist between achievement in algebra and the intellectual ability as measured by abstract intelligence tests. Another related factor, frequently studied by investigators, is the sex differences in ability to achieve in algebra. Although some studies show no significant differences between boys and girls, a majority of the studies indicate that, on the average, boys are slightly superior to girls in achievement in algebra. The reasons for such slight superiority have not been ascertained.

### Geometry

Geometry, as it has been developed functionally, is a science of space and space relationships. The mental processes that are most characteristic of learning in geometry are the ability to master symbols, the ability to apply certain principles of logic, and the ability to think through to the solution geometry problems and hypotheses. In recent years an increasing emphasis has been placed on the development of thinking through geometry teaching. Fawcett's study [25] is characteristic of this trend. Fawcett developed general concepts and abilities related to the nature of proof as applied to solving various theorems in geometry. His emphasis, however, was not only upon the nature of proof in ge-

---

[25] Harold P. Fawcett, "The Nature of Proof," *Thirteenth Yearbook of the National Council of Teachers of Mathematics.* New York: Teachers College, Columbia University, 1938.

ometry, but also upon transfer of such training in thinking to the solution of social, economic, and other problems in daily living. In this approach he emphasized the need for defining terms clearly, for recognizing assumptions or unproved propositions, and for realizing that no demonstration proves anything beyond the limits set by the assumptions.

The new approach in geometry emphasizes: (a) the development of geometric concepts and principles by the individual and by the group in discussion, with special emphasis upon a creative type of logical thinking; and (b) the utilization of non-geometric reasoning situations for introducing, clarifying, and applying logical concepts.

Several studies have shown consistently that not only are students who are taught by this newer method as competent as students in conventional geometry instruction, but also that they have made additional gains in a transfer of powers of thinking to non-geometric situations and problems. The case between the newer and older approach in geometry challenges the ingenuity of both teacher and learner. In the older approach, geometry was often a modified form of drill on relatively abstract and meaningless types of problems. Very often it tended to become a course in memorization of theorems and proofs. The newer approach stresses the importance of meanings, concepts, ability to organize data, ability to see relationships, and ability to think logically.

### Psychology of Music

The growth and development of an individual's ability to appreciate and to perform in music follows a pattern similar to that of the growth of other abilities and aptitudes. General sensitivity to rhythm, melody, and tones develops before finer appreciation and discrimination. The physical or muscular response of young children develops before the ability to make finer co-ordinations. An infant will show some physical response to music on the radio, phonograph, and piano. At the nursery-school age, children spontaneously walk, hop, and clap to the accompaniment of music. At such early stages of development, the child co-ordinates his movements with the rhythmic pattern of music long before he can keep exact time with individual beats. In singing, the young child may hum even before he has ability to enunciate the words of songs or to sing with the correct pitch. Similarly, he is likely to display in his singing many differences in pitch and time even though he may not be able to discriminate these adequately in a song.

The accompanying data from a study by Jersild and Bienstock [26] show the median number of tones or half tones sung by children at various age levels from two to ten years. The tests administered were based on the tones represented in the C major scale.

| Age in years | 2 | 3 | 4 | 5 | 6 | 7 | 8 | 9 | 10 |
|---|---|---|---|---|---|---|---|---|---|
| Median number of tones sung | 4 | 6 | 9 | 9 | 14 | 13.5 | 15 | 16 | 16 |

The findings of this study obviously are limited in interpretation, since they indicate the reproduction of a given tone, and not how consistently a child could reproduce each tone in a series or in a combination with other tones.

Little is known about the age at which the average child is "ready" to learn sight reading or to play one of the usual musical instruments. Important factors that influence musical readiness are the child's intelligence, his aptitude, and his musical background. In musical ability, as in other abilities, large individual differences exist, ranging from genius to little or no ability.

The Kwalwasser-Ruch [27] test of musical accomplishment incorporated many of the standards recommended in a course of study adopted in 1921 by the Music Supervisors National Conference. Kwalwasser's [28] findings on children's mastery of musical concepts and skills at various grade levels are especially important for the psychology of music. In this study, tests were administered to about 4,000 children "representing five different school systems nationally prominent for their superior work in music." The test results indicated that the standards described in the course by the music supervisors' council and designated as easily attainable were, as a matter of fact, to quote Kwalwasser, "so ambitious as to be beyond the reach of the children in the school systems measured." [29]

Among the interpretations emphasized by Kwalwasser [30] in his conclusions are: (1) growth in musical knowledge by children in public schools is unsteady and irregular; (2) skill of reading from notation is not acquired by most grade-school children; (3) girls are more than a grade ahead of boys in musical accomplishment throughout the entire range of elementary and high-school grades; (4) the learning rate in the musical abilities included in

[26] A. T. Jersild and S. F. Bienstock, "A Study of the Development of Children's Ability to Sing," *Journal of Educational Psychology*, Vol. 25, pp. 481-503, 1934.

[27] J. Kwalwasser and G. M. Ruch, *Kwalwasser-Ruch Test of Musical Accomplishment*. Iowa City: Bureau of Educational Research and Service, University of Iowa, 1924.

[28] J. Kwalwasser, *Problems in Public School Music*. New York: M. Witmark & Sons, 1932.

[29] *Ibid.*, p. 145.

[30] *Ibid.*

the tests is twice as rapid in the first four grades as in the later grades.

## Psychology of Reading

### Reading readiness

The importance of providing an adequate background of experience and concepts for young children before they are asked to read more or less formally from textbooks has been emphasized in recent years. The use of trips, visual materials, and experience reading charts are some of the techniques employed to build a background of meaning for concepts and words in reading. The factors that influence reading readiness have been studied carefully, especially by Harrison.[31] The findings indicate that of major importance among all factors are (a) adequate mental age or maturity, (b) adequate visual powers and habits, (c) good hearing, (d) emotional adjustment, (e) adjustment to the school situation, (f) desire to read, and (g) specific skills in the reading process, such as the possession of a range of concepts, ability to follow directions, visual discrimination, auditory discrimination, and comprehension of a short, simple story.

Several notable studies have been made of reading readiness. Fuller[32] found that pupils who had received special language training in the kindergarten were able to achieve better in reading in the primary grades than pupils who did not have such language training. Gates[33] carried on some studies that led him to the conclusion that "the age for learning to read under one program or with the method employed by one teacher may be entirely different from that required under other circumstances." The findings of studies such as these indicate that the relationship of specific factors in reading readiness to the broader process of reading must be studied carefully before definite conclusions can be stated with assurance.

### Value of phonetics

The problem of phonetics in learning to read has been debated extensively. In order to determine some of the values and effects of phonetics as they function in learning to read, Garrison and

---

[31] M. Lucile Harrison, *Reading Readiness*. Boston: Houghton Mifflin Company, 1936.

[32] Lorraine Fuller, "The Effect of Kindergarten Speech Training on Primary Grade Progress and Achievement of Children with Foreign Language Handicaps," *California Journal of Elementary Education*, Vol. 4, pp. 165-173, 1936.

[33] Arthur I. Gates, "The Necessary Mental Age for Beginning Reading," *Elementary School Journal*, Vol. 37, pp. 497-508, 1937.

Heard [34] carried on an extensive experiment. They began with children who entered the first grade and followed these children through the third grade. The children were divided into two groups, namely, the phonetic group, which received training in phonetics during their first-grade and second-grade reading program, and the non-phonetic group, which received no special or systematic phonetic training. The children in the experiment ranged, in terms of mental ability, from dull to bright.

The investigators [35] made detailed studies of the achievement of the pupils in reading and in spelling at the end of each grade. They studied also the amount of loss in achievement during summer vacations. The children who were trained in phonetics were more independent in their pronunciation of words, but the children with no phonetic training were smoother and better oral readers in the primary grades. The bright children profited more than the dull children from the early introduction of phonetics, but for both bright and dull children phonetic training in this experiment proved to be more effective in the latter part of the primary grades. In spelling, the phonetic group made more progress than the non-phonetic group in the primary grades. During the summer vacation, first-grade children who had no phonetic training lost less in reading achievement than pupils who had phonetic training. Although this study does not finally settle the question of phonetic versus non-phonetic training in primary reading, it does point out some of the advantages and disadvantages which follow such types of training.

### Eye movements in reading

Among the most basic skills in reading are those related to eye movements. By means of photographic records some important reading skills can be reliably measured. These include span of recognition, rate of recognition, eye-voice span, and rhythmical progression along the line.

The *recognition span* is measured by determining the number of words that can be observed by the reader in a single attention span. It is obtained from the photographic records of eye movements by finding the average number of eye fixations for the usual line of print. The width of the span provides one measure of fluency of reading. The *rate of recognition* is measured by the duration of eye fixations, which is determined by the speed in terms

[34] S. C. Garrison and Minnie Taylor Heard, "An Experimental Study of the Value of Phonetics," *Peabody Journal of Education,* Vol. 9, pp. 9-14, 1931.
[35] *Ibid.,* p. 14.

of the number of seconds required to read the average line of print. In oral reading, the *eye-voice span* is the number of letter spaces between the words upon which the eye is fixated and the word that the reader is saying. The *rhythmical progression* of eye movements along the line is determined by the number of regressive movements of the eyes for the usual line of print. The immature and inexperienced reader has a number of regressive eye movements as his eyes go back and forth along the line. The mature and experienced reader progresses along the line with few, if any, regressive movements. The regressions of the eyes are symptoms of disabilities or difficulties in reading. Some of the causes of regressive movements are lack of adequate motor control, particularly of muscles of the eyes, lack of word meaning or vocabulary, the difficulty of the reading material, the lack of interest on the part of the reader, and the purposes of reading.

Investigations of eye movements of elementary-school pupils, high-school students, and adults have shown some interesting trends in growth and development. Schmidt[36] found that, when elementary-school pupils read orally, they made from 6.1 to 11.5 fixation pauses in reading the usual line of print. Their average was 8.1 pauses. The high-school students had a range of from 7.2 to 10.2 pauses, with an average of 8.6. In reading orally, adults made from 6.5 to 11.3 fixation pauses in the usual line of print, with an average of 8.2 pauses. From these data it is evident that for the average individual the decrease in fixation pauses for eye movements is largest during the elementary-school period, and that after the age of approximately twelve years the number of fixation pauses does not decrease appreciably.

### Reading interests

Studies of interest in reading among younger children have indicated that they prefer stories about familiar experiences, animals, nature, and fairy stories. As the children grow into adolescence, reading interests are influenced by physical and psychological changes. Boys and girls generally acquire broader and deeper interests in personal, social, and scientific problems. History, biography, and adventure are popular with both boys and girls. Interest in humor is emphasized and usually more subtle than previously, and magazines are read more widely. Boys generally show a preference for articles about their hobbies and such

---

[36] W. A. Schmidt, "An Experimental Study in the Psychology of Reading," *Supplementary Educational Monographs*, Vol. I, No. 2, pp. 39–41. Chicago: University of Chicago Press, 1917.

special interests as science and aviation. The interests of girls in adult fiction of the love-story type and in poetry increase correspondingly. Boys show a preference for newspapers, current events, sports, and materials relating to special occupational or vocational interests. Many boys, also, read sentimental fiction. The reading interests of adolescents, according to a study by LaBrant,[37] under conditions of free choice in reading diet, reveal that youth will respond readily to reading materials related to their own culture pattern and level.

### Developing mature reading habits

The scope and sequence of reading at various grade levels are determined not only by the maturity and interests of pupils, but also by their growth in reading. Children do not reach optimum development in their reading skills and abilities until they have achieved basic skills and habits. The young child in the primary grades must master the basic eye-movement skills and acquire a background of basic concepts and vocabulary before he can read with ease and comprehension. Although children differ widely in the rate at which they reach successive stages of reading, the sequence of growth follows essentially the same pattern. Studies of oral-reading growth, for example, show that pupils make rapid progress in acquiring oculo-motor skills and simple levels of comprehension during the first four grades. The rate of progress decreases somewhat during the fifth and sixth grades, and there is little or no increase in oral-reading growth at the secondary-school level. It is estimated that at the beginning of the fifth grade the average pupil has reached about eighty per cent of his potential development in oral reading.

### Speed of silent reading

In various studies of speed in silent reading, evidence shows that the rate of reading increases rapidly during the first three grades and then continues to improve less rapidly in the fourth through the sixth grades. At the secondary-school level, improvement in speed of silent reading is slight. It may be said, therefore, that the average individual's optimum speed of reading is reached at the end of the elementary-school experience. Such improvement as may occur at the secondary-school level is in the

---

[37] Lou LaBrant, *An Evaluation of Free Reading in Grades Ten, Eleven, and Twelve*. Ohio State University Studies, Contributions to Education, No. 2. Columbus: Ohio State University Press, 1936.

reading of difficult and somewhat specialized material, for example, technical, scientific, and mathematical materials that require reasoning and careful interpretation.

## Comprehension

As in the case of oral reading and speed of silent reading, accuracy in the comprehension of simple materials develops very rapidly in the primary grades and, for the average child, reaches a relatively high rate of development by the end of the third grade. This growth in comprehension of materials continues to increase at a less rapid rate in the fourth through the sixth grades. The depth and quality of comprehension continues to improve gradually throughout the elementary and secondary schools, and in many instances at the adult level, especially in the reading of technical materials.

Related to the general pattern of development in comprehension in reading are the individual's background and experience. If the background and experience are meager, and if concepts are poorly developed, the individual cannot comprehend effectively the materials in the average curriculum. Gray and Holmes [38] have summarized many studies related to growth in word meaning and concepts. The essence of their conclusions is that meanings are generally achieved slowly, and that individuals differ widely in the rate of acquiring meanings. Many individuals have inadequate or incorrect meanings of words and concepts, which tend to persist. Between the ages of nine and fifteen, the number and varieties of meanings acquired are most extensive for the average person. The development of clear and accurate meanings is assumed to be the responsibility of all teachers of the individual in such subjects as the social studies, health, and science, as well as in the language arts. The teachers must be alert not only to develop accurate meanings of new words and terms, but also to correct previous misconceptions.

Because of the importance of developing adequate powers of comprehension, it is encouraging that recent investigators have undertaken studies concerning the nature of comprehension and the factors that influence its development. Dewey,[39] for example, compared the ability of secondary-school pupils to obtain facts and to do inferential thinking about historical materials that they

---

[38] William S. Gray and Eleanor Holmes, *The Development of Meaning Vocabularies in Reading: An Experimental Study*, Publications of the Laboratory Schools of the University of Chicago, No. 6, 1938.

[39] Joseph C. Dewey, "The Acquisition of Facts as a Measure of Reading Comprehension," *Elementary School Journal*, Vol. 35, pp. 346-348, 1935.

had read. His data indicated that pupils cannot be trained to read with understanding merely by being trained to search for the facts as they read. The development of a broader and deeper understanding or interpretation of what is read is of greater educational significance and presents a larger challenge than mere fact-finding ability.

In a brief summary, it is possible to indicate, on the basis of studies that have been made of the reading process, that individuals develop in various stages toward more efficient and mature reading skills and abilities. The rate of growth reached by an individual at various stages is influenced by such factors as mental maturity, emotional maturity, interests, language difficulties, and motor co-ordination as well as the adequacy of instruction in the school. Reading growth may be summarized conveniently in these stages: first, the stage of readiness for reading in preschool and first grade; second, the rapid rate of growth in skills and comprehension in learning to read simple materials in the primary grades; third, the stage of less rapid growth in reading skills accompanying an extension of powers of comprehension and breadth of interests in the intermediate grades; fourth, the stage of broader experience and increased breadth and depth in reading achieved in the junior high school; and fifth, the refining of reading skills, abilities, interests, and attitudes in the high school.

## Psychology of Science

Studies of the growth of children in the various objectives of science have shown that the difference between mental operations of children of the first or primary grades and of children of later grades is mainly one of the complexity of the ideas, attitudes, and generalizations that are grasped by the pupils. Haupt [40] studied the ability of children in the elementary school to generalize with a range of phenomena. From his results he concluded: "The difference between the mental operations of the children of the first and sixth grades was not one of ability to generalize. The difference was one of complexity of the generalizations which were made."

Weller [41] studied the effects of instruction in elementary science on the attitudes of children. Results showed that attitudes and skills may be more definitely developed when they are con-

---

[40] George W. Haupt, "Generalizations in Elementary School Science," *School Science and Mathematics*, Vol. 34, pp. 574-579, 1934.

[41] Florence Weller and others, "A Survey of the Present Status of Elementary Science," *Science Education*, Vol. 17, pp. 193-198, 1933.

sciously kept before pupils. Croxton [42] experimented to discover whether or not children in the various grades were able to formulate and apply a principle after exposure to the essential experience. Demonstrations were performed by the teacher, and pupils were asked a question to test their ability to generalize. The findings indicate that many pupils in the primary, intermediate, and junior high-school grades are capable of generalizing.

At the high-school and college level, studies of growth in information, attitudes, ability to generalize, and ability to apply principles have shown similar results. Studies at this level have shown that students tend to forget specific items of science information but tend to retain and sometimes to increase desirable scientific attitudes, ability to generalize from science data, and ability to apply scientific principles to new situations.

In the field of aids, studies have shown that sound motion pictures and devices such as study guides help to improve the quantity and presumably the quality of learning.

### QUESTIONS AND EXERCISES FOR DISCUSSION AND STUDY

**1.** Is there a best time or mental age at which one should teach certain items, topics, or skills in the various school subjects?

**2.** Is drill in as good repute as a device of instruction as it was several decades ago?

**3.** Should formal arithmetic be introduced in Grade I?

**4.** Is there an optimum mental age for introducing the various processes of arithmetic?

**5.** Explain the tendency in modern instruction in arithmetic to eliminate certain processes that were once emphasized.

**6.** Explain the tendency for the common errors in language to persist throughout the higher grades in spite of the emphasis placed on the instruction in the lower grades.

**7.** Should spelling in the primary grades be emphasized as a special subject?

**8.** Should pupils who are taught manuscript writing in the primary grades be changed to the cursive method in the upper grades?

**9.** Do the same psychological principles of learning hold for learning music as for learning in other fields?

**10.** Discuss the interests in subjects of art for children of various age levels.

**11.** Are there factors other than age that should be considered in determining readiness for reading?

**12.** Show how reading can be integrated with a whole school program and yet provide for consecutive development of skills.

**13.** What are some desirable outcomes of a program of science?

[42] W. C. Croxton, "Pupils' Ability to Generalize," *School Science and Mathematics,* Vol. 36, pp. 627-634, 1936.

14. Are there data to show that children generalize about social studies events?

15. Do the objectives for the social studies apply exclusively to that field of instruction?

### SELECTED REFERENCES FOR FURTHER READING AND STUDY

Buckingham, B. R., "Informational Arithmetic," *The Teaching of Arithmetic.* Tenth Yearbook, National Council of Teachers of Mathematics. New York: Teachers College, Columbia University, 1935. Pp. 51-73.

Croxton, W. C., "Pupils' Ability to Generalize," *School Science and Mathematics,* Vol. 36, pp. 627-34, 1936.

Harrison, M. Lucile, *Reading Readiness.* Boston: Houghton Mifflin Company, 1936. Chapter IV.

Haupt, G. W., *An Experimental Application of a Philosophy of Science Teaching in an Elementary School.* Contributions to Education, No. 633. New York: Bureau of Publications, Teachers College, Columbia University, 1935.

Hildreth, Gertrude, "Number Readiness and Progress in Arithmetic," *Journal of Experimental Education,* Vol. 4, pp. 1-6, 1935.

Horn, Ernest, *Methods of Instruction in the Social Studies.* Report of the Commission on the Social Studies of the American Historical Association, Part XV. New York: Charles Scribner's Sons, 1937.

Mursell, James L., "Application of Psychology to the Arts," *Teachers College Record,* Vol. 37, pp. 290-299, 1936.

————, "Psychological Research Bearing on Music Education," *Music Educators Journal,* Vol. 22, pp. 24-25, 1935.

National Society for the Study of Education, *Child Development and the Curriculum.* Thirty-Eighth Yearbook, Part I. Bloomington, Ill.: Public School Publishing Company, 1939.

————, *Educational Diagnosis.* Thirty-Fourth Yearbook. Bloomington, Ill.: Public School Publishing Company, 1935.

————, "The Teaching of Reading; a second Report," *Thirty-Sixth Yearbook,* Part I. Bloomington, Ill.: Public School Publishing Company, 1937.

"Psychology and Methods in the High School and College," *Review of Educational Research,* Vol. 8, February, 1938. Washington, D. C.: American Educational Research Association.

"Special Methods and Psychology in the Elementary School," *Review of Educational Research,* Vol. 17, December, 1937. Washington, D. C.: American Educational Research Association.

Tharp, James B., "Second Annual Survey of Research in Experimentation in Modern Foreign Language Teaching," *Modern Language Journal,* Vol. 21, pp. 36-41, 1936.

Voorhis, Thelma G., *The Relative Merits of Cursive and Manuscript Writing.* New York: Bureau of Publications, Teachers College, Columbia University, 1931.

# CHAPTER 15

# Appraising the Results of Learning: Educational Measurements and Evaluation

Measurement in education is ~~primarily~~ concerned with gathering evidence of pupil growth so that it may be possible to evaluate the outcomes of instruction and learning. The measurement of pupil growth in concepts, skills, attitudes, academic aptitude, and the like may be done by formal tests and techniques as well as by informal tests and techniques. The teacher who gives a mark, or grade, to the pupil making an oral recitation is using an informal method of measurement. The teacher who marks, or grades, a written report or essay is also using an informal method of measuring growth. Very frequently the accuracy of these informal methods of measuring pupil growth is influenced by factors other than actual accomplishment of the pupil in terms of an aim or objective of the curriculum.

## Evaluation Determined by Aims and Objectives

Evaluation should be made in terms of the aims and objectives of education and of the subject or activity taught. In recent decades, aims and objectives of education for which measures were constructed have become more comprehensive. One of the newer ideas in evaluation is that the scope of any plan for appraisal of pupil growth should include the major objectives of the curriculum or of the subject. Such aims or objectives comprise not only growth in acquisition of information and skills but also the gathering of evidence about attitudes, interests, ways of thinking, work and study skills, and personal-social adaptability. These newer and more comprehensive objectives require the use of appropriate techniques such as tests, rating scales, questionnaires, interviews, diaries, and anecdotal records. As teachers move toward more formal and objective types of measurement, the tests and measures used are reconstructed and revised, so that they become increasingly reliable and valid.

284

### Old and new in evaluation

Twenty years ago, testing and evaluation procedures that were available were of a relatively simple sort. At that time the new-type objective test had just been introduced. The teacher's major instruments of measurement were the essay examination and the oral quiz. The major objective of the curriculum tended, also, to be limited to the simple skills of oral and silent reading, writing, arithmetic, spelling, and the acquisition and reproduction upon demand of certain skills or certain items of information in history, geography, and the other subjects that comprised the curriculum. Many teachers felt that a test of subject-matter mastery was sufficient for evaluating pupil growth.

In recent years, however, a change has occurred, and both elementary- and secondary-school curricula now include an emphasis upon more comprehensive objectives of teaching. The concern for the mastery of information has been supplemented by such newer objectives as pupil growth in attitudes, interests, powers of critical thinking, work and study skills, and personal-social adaptability. Along with this emphasis upon newer objectives has come an increased emphasis upon newer and more objective methods of gathering evidence of pupil growth.

## The Use of Tests

It is important to determine, first, the reasons for administering tests. The proper use of tests requires that one or more important and desirable purposes shall be served. Intelligent planning is basic to the wise use of test results. One way of classifying the use of tests may be according to the functions of various school officers or personnel, namely, the administrator, the supervisor, and the teacher. Many of the purposes may be satisfied by the data from a single test.

### Uses by administrators

The administrator, for instance, may use the test results to provide records of pupil achievement and progress. These may be entered upon the pupil's cumulative record card and may become a basis of the permanent record of the evaluation of the growth and progress of the individual or of the class group. Another use by the administrator is to provide reports to parents. Frequently the principal may find it necessary and desirable to supplement his opinions or the teacher's opinions about a pupil by objective evidence gathered by means of a formal or standardized test. Such evidence may frequently be used in reports to or in conferences with parents. A third use is to make available more systematic and objective records when a pupil is transferred to other schools. Such records permit a better interpretation of a pupil's status and facilitate placement in a congenial classroom in the new school. The administrator may also use test results to provide data for periodic reports of school progress to the patrons in a community. Frequently, also, the data from various tests may be consulted in the classification of pupils for instructional purposes. Although learning is mainly an individual matter, the usual classroom situation demands that each pupil learn as part of a group. When the variation in ability of the pupils in a group is reduced, teaching and learning tend to become more effective.

## Uses by supervisors

The supervisor, likewise, may use the test results for a variety of purposes. His major task is to help the teacher to do a better teaching job. This responsibility can best be realized if both the teacher and the supervisor have evidence about the status of the pupil as well as about his needs and interests. One of the uses that a supervisor may have for tests is to determine the status of a class or a pupil in some of the major objectives of the curriculum. This will permit him to indicate desirable changes in instructional procedures or in learning procedures for various children. Another purpose may be to evaluate teaching methods or instructional materials. Again this may be accomplished by obtaining evidence of the relative contribution which a particular teaching method or particular instructional materials make to the pupils' progress.

## Uses by teachers

The teacher uses the test results for a variety of purposes, many of which are similar to those of the administrator and supervisor. The teacher may discuss the test results with the supervisor in order to arrive at an agreement on various instructional or learning problems. The teacher may use the results of tests and measures: (1) to determine the status of each pupil in various subjects and in various objectives of the curriculum; (2) to evaluate the status and rate of growth of each pupil in terms of his ability and age; (3) to identify the educational needs of each pupil; (4) to identify the gifted pupil, the normal pupil, and the slow-learning pupil; (5) to group pupils for instructional purposes within the class group; (6) to analyze or diagnose an individual pupil's difficulties and rate of growth; (7) to determine the achievement status of the class at the beginning and at the end of the term. These uses of test results can all increase the effectiveness of the learning process and make it possible to provide for the fullest development of the individual pupil.

In summary, then, the major uses of test results may be listed as classification, educational guidance, diagnosis, and vocational guidance—all of which contribute directly or indirectly to the improvement of instruction. Tests have been used to classify pupils in a school into superior, average, and below-average groups so that adaptations of the curriculum might be made more easily, especially in group work.[1] The classification of pupils into these groups, however, should include consideration of special talents and disabilities, social interests, and chronological age if the plan is to be effective.

## Educational guidance

Educational guidance has progressed beyond the concept of a survey of a pupil's abilities. It is now an integral part of the educational program. Skilled guidance has become a part of each teacher's responsibility to her pupils. Individual needs and abilities, rather than uniform grade standards, are the bases of teaching. The teacher uses all pertinent data to counsel or guide her pupil in his educational program. Thus, a pupil in the high school who has the comparatively low I. Q. of 80 would not be counseled or guided to attempt a college-preparatory course.

## Diagnosis

Diagnosis is aided not only by the usual test, but by diagnostic tests which are constructed to provide a pattern or a detailed analysis of individual performance in various skills and abilities. The test items and scoring are arranged so that the specific strength and weaknesses of the individual may be discovered. Special tests have been constructed to diagnose skills and abilities involved in language usage, personality, mechanical ability, reading, arithmetic, critical thinking, and the like. When such a diagnosis is interpreted in relation to the mental capacity and other characteristics of an individual, remedial programs to facilitate the individual's growth may often be established.

[1] See Chapter 7.

## Vocational guidance

Vocational guidance is still in its initial stages. However, some advice can be offered to an individual about whether or not to undertake certain vocations. Data can be obtained in part through intelligence, achievement, and aptitude tests, if necessary, and the individual can be urged to consider other occupational choices adapted to the level of his abilities. A high-school pupil, for example, with an I.Q. of 85 and poor achievement in mathematics and sciences would not be guided to the vocation of engineering or accounting. The attempts at vocational prediction are generally in broad categories such as clerical ability, mechanical ability, musical talent, and the like.

Mechanical aptitude tests in which the student assembles or disassembles doorbells and the like are sometimes used. Other mechanical aptitude tests employ pencil-and-paper techniques. On the other hand, aptitude for music is measured by tests in which exercises are played on a phonograph and the individual responds to discrimination for pitch, intensity, time, consonance, tonal memory, and rhythm. Art ability tests are generally based upon judgment of artistic qualities in pictures. Aptitudes are generally considered as broad patterns of traits inherited or acquired and it is impossible to predict specifically which of the approximately 25,000 occupations an individual should enter. Not only skills, but also interests, temperament, and personality, as well as satisfaction in a given occupation,[2] are important.

## Misuses of results

It is wise, however, to point out that the test results may frequently be misused. If the design of the measurement program is narrow and limited, the testing program may tend to determine the emphasis upon specific objectives of the curriculum to the detriment of others and to the detriment of desirable trends in pupil growth. Frequently test results of a very partial nature are used to estimate or to rate the teacher's teaching ability. While such evidence may be desirable as a part of the data to be considered in rating teachers, few educators would defend a rating made solely upon this basis. Many administrators, however, misuse test results by employing them for purposes such as this.

It should be pointed out also that reliable and valid instruments of measurement are, by their very nature, restricted to an appraisal of limited aspects of pupil behavior or growth. It is im-

---

[2] See Chapter 20.

possible to measure the whole result of an educative experience by any one test or battery of tests. The hope remains, however, that, by measuring many important and vital aspects of experiences, some vital appraisals may be obtained of the relative merits of diverse educational practices.

## Characteristics of a Good Test

### Validity

Any test, regardless of the objectives which it is designed to measure or the item-construction techniques applied, must be *valid*. This means that it must measure the objective or such an aspect of the objective as the authors claim that it is measuring. One method of determining the validity of the test is to study the content of the test from the standpoint of agreement with the particular course of study for which it is designed to be used. If it is a test to measure the knowledge that pupils have developed in a biology course, its items should be a sample of the concepts and the information that have been taught in such a course. This curricular validity may be achieved by analyzing textbooks used in the course, the course of study itself, and the opinions of experts in the field.

Another aspect of validity is called *statistical validity*. A test may be highly valid so far as choice of curricular items is concerned but, because of the form in which they may be stated, the test may have no statistical validity. For example, a biology test may include 100 facts or ideas found frequently in biology textbooks but may present them in exercises almost entirely too difficult for high-school pupils to understand or so easy that practically all high-school pupils can answer them correctly. The test elements, or items, therefore, should be scaled so that they represent a range from very easy to very hard for the students for whom the test is designed.

### Reliability

A test is *reliable* if it measures consistently. Upon a second application, the test should provide an index for ranking of pupils similar to that of the first application of the test. The reliability of a test is not determined by examining the test itself, but the test must actually be tried out to yield desirable information. This may be accomplished either by administering two comparable forms of a test or by a second application of the first test after a given period of time. The scores obtained by the pupils on the first and second tests are correlated, and the coefficient of reliability so obtained permits one to judge how consistent or reliable the test is as a measuring device.

## Norms

Another characteristic of a good test is the fact that certain *norms* are provided for a wise interpretation of the test results. These norms may appear in various forms, such as *grade scores, C-scores, percentile scores,* or *standard scores.* At the high-school level, the percentile scores are becoming more and more widely used, because they permit a good description of a student's status. If a student has obtained on a test a raw score which is translated to a percentile score, let us say, of 35, we can say that on this test the student ranks above 34 per cent of the pupils of his grade or his age, depending upon whether the score is for grade or for age.

## Practicability

The difficulty or ease of scoring a test and of administering it is also an important consideration. The test must prove itself practical, of easy administration, and of easy scoring if it is to be used widely. These characteristics of a test will naturally be kept in mind from the initiation to the conclusion of a test-construction project.

## Varieties of tests

There are many forms and varieties of tests, which range from rather subjective to quite objective methods of measurement and from unreliable to reliable. These can perhaps be discussed under various headings or aspects. Frequently teachers prefer to make their own tests, and it is possible to offer some suggestions that will help teachers to construct items for their own test. Perhaps one of the simplest objectives of the curriculum for which objective tests can be constructed is the acquisition of information and skills.

The kinds of tests vary, according to the types of usage which may be employed. This classification of tests sometimes includes such nomenclature as speed or power tests, survey tests, diagnostic tests, prognostic tests, and achievement tests.

A *speed test* is one in which the individual's ability to react quickly to certain items is tested. The emphasis in this test is upon the rate of answering items, and a definite time limit for completing the test or a portion of the test is established by the author.

A *power test,* on the other hand, is one in which the factor of time or speed is not particularly emphasized. In such a test, the items are usually arranged in the order of difficulty, wherever that is possible, and sufficient time is given for practically all individuals in a grade for whom it is intended to attempt all items of the test.

A *survey test* is one in which the major purpose is to obtain a status, index, or score for a group of pupils rather than for individual pupils. On this account, the test scores for an individual pupil need not be particularly reliable, but the average score for a group of pupils may be highly reliable.

A *diagnostic test* is one designed for use with individual pupils, and it usually contains sufficient exercises of various types so that it is possible for the teacher or supervisor to determine those skills or aspects of an objective of the curriculum in which a pupil may need to have guidance in his growth or development.

A *prognostic test* is one which is useful in predicting the probable growth or future performance of a pupil in a particular subject, activity, or other given line of endeavor.

*Achievement tests* may be described as those which attempt to measure the attainment of pupils in the various important objectives or areas of the curriculum.

## Types of items that are valid for measuring various objectives

The types of items most frequently used in this type of tests may be designated as *true-false* items, *multiple-choice* items, *matching* items, and *completion* items. Various types of item will be needed to measure validly the different objectives of the curriculum. These can be illustrated only in a very incomplete manner at this time and place. The matter of testing for information and concepts, for example, may be discussed first. In order to measure this objective, various types of items have been used. A popular type is the *multiple-choice,* of which the following is an example in a biology test:

Pasteurization of milk is produced by
(*a*) boiling   (*b*) evaporation   (*c*) chemical agents   (*d*) moderate heating
(*e*) freezing

Information and concepts, for example, in biology, may be tested by providing a graphic illustration of a leaf and using an incomplete sentence in which the pupil provides the necessary information. The *completion* item is illustrated in a test where a diagram of a cross section of a leaf is given with statements such as the following accompanying it:

1. The layer marked "a" in the diagram is the _____ layer.

2. The part of the leaf marked "b" is called the _____.

Another method of item-construction used is the *matching technique*, which may be illustrated as follows:

In the left-hand column are listed the following concepts:

1. Pupa
2. Chrysalis
3. Larva
4. Adult
5. Egg

In the right-hand column are the following statements, which are to be matched with three of the concepts in the left-hand column:

1. First stage in complete metamorphosis ..................( )
2. Second stage in complete metamorphosis ..................( )
3. Final stage in development...( )

The *true-false* item is widely used, especially in teacher-made tests. Careful thought must be applied to the construction of such items so that they will not have ambiguous statements or words, such as *always* and *never*, which tend to give away the answer. This type of item may be illustrated as follows:

*Directions:* In the following statements, indicate those which are true by underlining the word *True* and those which are false by underlining the word *False.*

1. The mean, or average, is found by dividing the sum of scores by the number of cases. True False

2. The third quartile is the highest score in the distribution. True False

The types of items discussed are the ones most frequently used in tests of information and concepts. Such items may be carelessly constructed and fail to provide a valid or reliable score. Practice and study will improve their construction.

**Essay examinations**

The essay examination usually is made up of from five to ten questions in which the teacher requires an explanation or description. The student is asked to organize his ideas in paragraphs and sometimes in outline form. One criticism of essay questions is that they do not cover much of the material that may have been studied or discussed. Unless the questions are phrased clearly and unambiguously, the student may misinterpret them. The factors of lack of comprehensiveness, faulty interpretation, and individual judgment sometimes tend to discredit the essay examination. The most serious criticism, however, is that the marking of the essay examination is unreliable.

The ability to organize certain materials is often tested by means of essay questions. This type of question may be illustrated by the following:

Criticize: "Bacteria cause many diseases among men, therefore they should be destroyed."

C. W. Odell [3] gives a scale for rating pupils' answers to this question, from which the following are taken:

Value 0—Bacteria cause many diseases. They cause pneumonia, scarlet fever, appendicitis, tonsillitis and many others.

Value 10—The statement is partially untrue, because it gives no attention to the case "for" the bacteria.

Though some bacteria are responsible for many diseases among men, animals, and plants, others affect our lives in quite different ways. Economically they are very important. Together with the fungi they are the chief cause of decay, thus helping to keep the surface of the earth clean. Bacteria ripen milk and butter and are necessary in cheese making and various fermentations. Those bacteria that fix nitrogen are very valuable in agriculture.

Therefore, the sweeping statement above is not correct, since we should wish to destroy only the harmful bacteria and not the many useful ones.

Essay examinations can be improved and scored quite objectively if certain conditions are met. The first condition is that each question in an essay examination should be planned to measure one definite objective, such as an attitude or an interpretation of facts. A second condition is that the objective should be clearly understood and accepted by all readers of the examination. A third condition is that certain standards of rating, or values to be assigned, should be agreed upon by the readers. The restricted essay questions should be phrased, or stated, so that a clear definition of the intent of the question is available to the student and to the raters of the answer. The teacher or teachers scoring the answer to the essay question must decide first for what objective the question is to be marked. An ideal answer must then be formulated, assigning a certain number of points to each significant part of the answer. Several papers must next be rated independently by separate scorers to determine whether or not the rating scheme is workable. Better than only one ideal answer is an exhibit of several scaled answers assigned to various rating intervals on a

---

[3] C. W. Odell, *The Use of Scales for Rating Pupils' Answers to Thought Questions*. Urbana, Ill.: University of Illinois, Bureau of Educational Research Bulletin, No. 46, 1929.

ten-point scale. Contrary to popular belief, it is more difficult to construct a valid and reliable essay-type test than a new-type objective test. Essay questions are by no means obsolete in instruction, but they usually need radical improvement to make them more than a mirror for a teacher's preconceived estimate of pupil achievement.

### Recent Development in Evaluating Concepts and Information

The most common type of appraisal in schools is to examine the relative amount of concepts and information that pupils may have acquired and remembered. Despite the frequent use and sometimes abuse of subject-matter mastery tests, functional information is an objective with which teachers have been and will be concerned. Many information tests, both formal and informal, however, are so constructed that they encourage rote memorization of words rather than the development of real understanding of meanings and concepts. Tests which use verbatim the terminology of a textbook as the alternative answers to a question, for instance, encourage this undesirable type of rote memory. It is desirable to get and to remember important facts and ideas so that they may be utilized in thinking and acting; but a good test of the acquisition of information will employ language that is not identical with that used in a textbook, and will involve the use of facts and ideas rather than their mere reproduction. On the other hand, the test items should be phrased in as lifelike a setting as possible.

Practically all teachers are familiar with the new-type objective tests which measure the acquisition of information and related skills in reading, arithmetic, spelling, history, geography, science, industrial arts, and fine arts. Any well-known and recent book on "tests and measurements" will provide a wealth of suggestions for tests of this sort. At the elementary-school level, for example, a battery of achievement tests, such as the Stanford,[4] Metropolitan,[4] Modern School,[5] Progressive,[6] and Unit Scales of Attainment,[7] may be cited. At the high-school level, the Sones-Harry or the Cooperative Test[8] series illustrate the available tests for evaluating mastery of various high-school subjects.

---

[4] Published by the World Book Company, Yonkers, N. Y.
[5] Published by the Bureau of Publications, Teachers College, Columbia University, New York City.
[6] Published by the Southern California School Book Depository, Los Angeles, California.
[7] Published by the Educational Test Bureau, Minneapolis, Minn.
[8] Published by the Cooperative Test Service, New York City.

## Evaluating growth in work-study skills

Work-study skills, so far as they have been defined for testing and appraisal purposes, are usually identified with the capacity to read maps, graphs, charts, and tables, to use the table of contents and the index of a book, and to find items of information in reference books. In addition, elementary as well as secondary schools are placing an increasing emphasis upon effective use of the school and local libraries, which involves such skills as knowing the effective use of library privileges, the techniques of withdrawing and returning books, the numbering or filing system of the books, and so on.

At the elementary and junior-high-school levels, the most comprehensive tests of work-study skills now available are the Iowa Every-Pupil Tests of Basic Study Skills.[9] Tests on the use of the library at the elementary-school level have been prepared by Pirtle (Library Test 6B [10]) and by Barker (Informal Testing of the Use of Books and Libraries [11]). Reed has prepared a Test on the Use of the Library for High Schools [12] which is especially adapted for the pupils of the upper grades in senior high schools. A recent test is the Peabody Library Information Test.[13]

## Recent Development in Evaluating Attitudes

Closely related to the evaluation of interests, and using similar appraisal techniques, are scales for the evaluation of attitudes. Although there is some controversy about the nature of attitudes, it is generally assumed that some attitudes that teachers plan to develop through the curriculum may be called specific and others may be called general. There is no universal agreement as to the kinds and significance of either specific or general attitudes that should be developed in schools. These are matters relating to a social and educational philosophy. Certain attitudes, however, which are favorable to social, scientific, and esthetic improvement are generally deemed highly important by most schools. The development of such attitudes is usually not assigned exclusively to any one subject or area of the curriculum.

---

[9] Published by Houghton Mifflin Company, Boston, Mass.

[10] Published by the author, Thomas Jefferson High School, San Antonio, Texas.

[11] Velda Barker, "Informal Testing of the Use of Books and Libraries," *Elementary English Review*, Vol. X (June, September, October, 1933), pp. 143, 274, and 205.

[12] Distributed by the Evaluation Staff of the Progressive Education Association, University of Chicago, Chicago, Ill.

[13] Published by the Educational Test Bureau, Minneapolis, Minn.

Attitudes when defined as expressions of opinions have been measured more or less adequately by such measures as Thurstone's opinion scales on war, the church, God, the Negro, the Japanese, the Chinese, and other phenomena and problems related to topics in the social field.[14] These scales employ an equal-appearing interval technique for weighting the intensity of a statement for or against some object or ideas.

Using the agree-uncertain-disagree technique, other authors have constructed generalized measures of social attitudes toward racial, national, and international ideas and phenomena. The Scale of Civic Beliefs,[15] for example, consists of such statements as "The Japanese are a sly and crafty race" and "Labor unions have accomplished much good." The pupil indicates that he agrees, disagrees, or is undecided in his response to each item. An alternate form of the scale with items of Form A and Form B matched permits a consistency score or index.

### Recent Developments in Evaluating Interests

Interests have long been considered one of the fundamental factors in motivating the acquisition of functional information, skills, appreciations, and discriminations. Interests may perhaps be best defined for purposes of this discussion as those drives that lead the individual to his preferences in personal efforts and conduct.

Various techniques have been employed to evaluate interests. The first recorded study of reading interests, for example, employed an analysis of book withdrawals. It is relatively easy for anyone who has access to the withdrawal records of a school or public library to discover the frequency with which particular books have been withdrawn. Certain limitations inhere in this method: the pupils' choices are limited to books found in the library; moreover, course requirements and other pressures influence the choice, and unless other checks are made, the investigator has no way of knowing whether or not the pupil liked the books he withdrew.

A second technique of evaluating interests may be called the *questionnaire method,* of which there are several variations. The method most frequently reported is to ask the pupil to list the materials he has read or the activities he has performed over a

---

[14] Published by University of Chicago Press, Chicago, Ill.
[15] Published by the World Book Company, Yonkers, N. Y.

given period of time. Then he is asked to indicate those which he liked best. The following example will illustrate one of the interest questionnaires.

Here are some things that some boys and girls like to do. Blacken the spaces as follows:

L—is blackened if you like doing it.

I—is blackened if you are unable to decide whether you like or dislike it.

D—is blackened if you dislike doing it.

|  | L | I | D |
|---|---|---|---|
| 1. Following day-by-day reports of the war.......... 1. | \|\| | \|\| | \|\| |
| 2. Meeting people you have not met before........... 2. | \|\| | \|\| | \|\| |
| 3. Making up problems in arithmetic................. 3. | \|\| | \|\| | \|\| |
| 4. Carving wood, or soap........................... 4. | \|\| | \|\| | \|\| |
| 5. Writing poems or making rhymes................. 5. | \|\| | \|\| | \|\| |

Here again certain limitations are evident. Pupils have difficulty in remembering materials read and activities performed, particularly if some period of time has elapsed between the activities and the recording. Pupils will be influenced, also, in naming their favorite activities by the standards they know to be approved by the teacher.

A third technique uses diaries, logs, or journals which students or teachers keep in a cumulative fashion. This technique may be illustrated by the Reading Records formulated by the Evaluation Staff of the Progressive Education Association.[15a] The Progressive Education Association reading record, after the pupil has made a cumulative log of his reading of books, newspapers, and magazines, is scored so that each entry is assessed in accordance with a predetermined scale of values set up by a jury, and by a special formula to denote the maturity of the reading level of the book, magazine, or newspaper article recorded. Thus it is possible to obtain indexes both of the average maturity and of the range of interests. Adaptations of this technique might be made in other areas of the curriculum of the elementary and secondary schools.

## Recent Development in Evaluating Critical Thinking

An objective to which almost any teacher in any subject area subscribes is the development of pupils' critical thinking powers. This has become a prominent objective of the natural and social sciences. From the work that has been done both in the curriculum and in evaluation, several convenient aspects of thinking may be tested by prepared scales. They are: (1) the interpreta-

---

[15a] This organization is now called The American Education Fellowship.

tion of data; (2) the application of principles and generalizations to new situations; and (3) recognizing the logic of an argument or the nature of proof used in materials presented in the curriculum.

A few tests are available. At the elementary-school level a Test of Critical Thinking in the Social Studies [16] may be recommended. This test is divided into three parts. Part I measures ability to obtain facts from graphs, maps, references, newspapers, and magazines. Part II measures abilities to draw reasonable conclusions from given facts. Part III measures abilities to apply generalizations to new situations.

Some tests developed by the Evaluation Staff of the Progressive Education Association and the Cooperative Test of Social Studies Abilities [17] are valuable at the high-school level. The high-school pupil is presented with a set of facts in narrative, graphic, or tabular form and is asked to check each of a series of inferences which follow as to whether the inference is reasonable in the light of facts given, whether it is contradicted by the facts given, or whether the reasonableness cannot be determined on the basis of facts given.

### Interpreting facts

For the objective of scientific thinking, certain experimental efforts have been made to construct items that measure the ability to generalize experience or to interpret data and to apply principles of a science to a described situation. The test of ability to interpret or to generalize may be illustrated by the following exercise, in which the pupil is asked to indicate whether each statement given is: (1) a true interpretation of the facts given; (2) an interpretation that goes beyond the facts given; or (3) an interpretation contradicted by the facts given.

| Temperature of Surroundings, Centigrade | Calories Lost by Radiation and Conduction | Calories Lost by Evaporation | Total Calories Lost |
| --- | --- | --- | --- |
| 7° | 78.5 | 7.9 | 86.4 |
| 15 | 55.3 | 7.7 | 63.0 |
| 20 | 45.3 | 10.6 | 55.9 |
| 25 | 41.0 | 13.2 | 54.2 |
| 30 | 33.2 | 23.0 | 56.2 |

---

[16] Published by Bureau of Publications, Teachers College, Columbia University, New York, N. Y.

[17] Published by Cooperative Test Service, New York City.

a.  The total heat loss of the human body by evaporation is the same at all temperatures .............................................. (3)a.

b.  At zero temperature no calories are lost from the human body by evaporation ................................................. (3)b.

c.  The number of calories lost by either radiation and conduction or evaporation from the human body increases steadily as the temperature rises ...................................................... (3)c.

d.  If the temperature of the surroundings is higher than that of the human body (about 37° C), no heat can be lost by radiation and conduction from the body ...................................... (2)d.

e.  The human body loses more heat by radiation and conduction than by evaporation at all environmental temperatures from 7° C to 30° C ......................................................... (1)e.

f.  The calories lost from the human body by radiation and conduction decrease as temperature of the surroundings increases, but the calories lost by evaporation increase ................................... (1)f.

In the example above, careful study will indicate why each of the items has been marked either *1, 2,* or *3.* As indicated, the ability called for is that of sifting facts and adding facts together so that a reasonable interpretation can be made.

## Applying principles [17a]

The illustration of the application of principles related to a fact or situation may be comprehended in the following example from an Application of Principles Test:

EXERCISE: Many bare spots in the lawns are not caused by a lack of rain, but by our newest insect pest, the Japanese beetle. It lives in the ground in the winter, and eats the roots of the grass in the spring. After eating the grass roots, the beetle changes its form and comes out of the ground early in July. The beetles come in hundreds, settle on the roses, and eat the petals. Then they eat any other flowers in the garden. When these are eaten, the beetle eats the leaves of trees and shrubs. This beetle, which was accidentally brought into the United States, was first noticed in New Jersey in 1916. Its food was plentiful, the climate right, and best of all, the beetle had no natural enemy here, so it increased in numbers. By 1939 the Japanese beetles were found as far north as Maine, as far south as the Carolinas, and as far west as Michigan and Ohio. Beetle traps and poison sprays have been used to stop the spread of the beetle, but they haven't been successful. The Government has even imported birds which are the beetle's natural enemies in Japan, but the birds died in this country.

---

[17a] Some very helpful articles dealing with the construction of objective tests to measure such abilities as the ability to infer, the ability to generalize, and the ability to apply principles have appeared in the *Educational Research Bulletin* (published at the Ohio State University) since the 1930's. Similar articles have appeared from time to time in other professional journals.

APPLYING A GENERALIZATION TO A FACT

All the statements below are true. Look in the paragraph to see whether or not the statement applies to a particular fact or concept. Then blacken the space under:

    1—if a statement applies clearly to a fact given
    2—if you are not sure a statement applies to a fact given
    3—if the statement is not related to any fact given

|  |  | 1 | 2 | 3 |
|---|---|---|---|---|
| 1. A plentiful food supply is necessary so that insects may live. | 1. | ■ | \|\| | \|\| |
| 2. Some places have cold winters and hot summers. | 2. | \|\| | \|\| | ■ |
| 3. Planting the same crop on land year after year causes good soil material to be used up. | 3. | \|\| | \|\| | ■ |
| 4. Some animals change their form several times till they look just like their parents. | 4. | \|\| | ■ | \|\| |
| 5. Some animals are warm-blooded. | 5. | \|\| | \|\| | ■ |
| 6. Natural enemies check the spread of insects. | 6. | ■ | \|\| | \|\| |
| 7. Some insects live only one season, leaving eggs which hatch in the spring. | 7. | \|\| | ■ | \|\| |
| 8. Insects have very great appetites. | 8. | ■ | \|\| | \|\| |

Careful study of the exercise just given indicates that the student is asked to apply generalizations or principles in order to explain specific facts or concepts. The emphasis here is not on adding elements or facts together to arrive at a generalization, but rather on applying a generalization to a specific fact.

## Recent Developments in Evaluating Personal-Social Adaptability

All areas of the curriculum are assumed to contribute toward personal-social adaptability. At the present time it is difficult to get any clear and precise definition of this objective; hence, many differences of opinion occur in discussions. These differences are often traceable to the fact that different definitions are used for a generalized trait.

Measurement of personal and social adjustment has used a variety of methods and means. These range from the free-association method, self-descriptive adjustment questionnaires, projective techniques, and psychoneurotic inventories to rating scales, anecdotal records, behavior descriptions, case-study methods, and psychoanalysis.

The free-association method, which is not widely used, allows an individual to react to certain words, as in the Kent-Rosanoff Free Association Test,[18] or to certain objects, as in the Rorschach

---

[18] Published by C. H. Stoelting Company, Chicago, Illinois.

Ink Blot Test. Another means of gathering evidence is the disguised test, which may be illustrated by the Maller Self-Marking Test,[19] in which the honesty of pupils in grading their own paper is measured.

Improved rating scales for judging conduct and behavior have appeared. Several of these have been designed for use at the elementary-school level, including the Haggerty-Olson-Wickman Behavior Rating Scale,[20] and the Winnetka Scale for Rating School Behavior and Attitudes.[21]

In self-descriptive scales at the elementary-school level, the oldest and best-known scale is the Woodworth-Mathews Personal Data Sheet.[22] Such scales at the secondary-school level are similar in purpose and pattern of development. They include the Thurstone Personality Schedule,[23] Bernreuter Personality Inventory,[24] and Maller Character Sketches.[25] By means of a pupil's self-descriptive marking, the teacher or school officer attempts to draw inferences about mental health and emotional stability. When supplemented by close and intelligent personal observations, the self-descriptive scales are valuable methods of appraisal.

Sample items from a self-descriptive behavior scale that was devised and used by the author in a large city school system will illustrate this type of scale:

1. Are you troubled at night by dreams about your work?......... Yes No
2. Do you sometimes see spots "swimming" before your eyes?...... Yes No
3. Do you lose your temper and get angry easily?................. Yes No
4. Do you like to see others in pain?............................ Yes No
5. Do you find it more pleasant to live in a "make-believe" world than in the real world?...................................... Yes No

Such items as these may reveal a pattern of fears, nervous habits, escapes from reality, lack of emotional control, and the like, that are often symptoms of present or probable psychoneurotic behavior in an individual. Self-descriptive scales, however, should be supplemented by evidence gathered from interviews, observations, and anecdotal records.

[19] Published by the Bureau of Publications, Teachers College, Columbia University, New York City.

[20] Published by World Book Company, Yonkers, N. Y.

[21] Published by Winnetka Educational Press, Winnetka, Illinois.

[22] Published by C. H. Stoelting Company, Chicago, Illinois.

[23] Published by the University of Chicago Press, Chicago, Illinois.

[24] Published by Stanford University Press, Stanford University, California.

[25] Published by the Bureau of Publications, Teachers College Columbia University, New York City.

## Anecdotal records

*Anecdotal records* and *behavior descriptions* have been used more or less widely to obtain systematic records of children's behavior. The value of anecdotal records has been emphasized by Olson [26] and Randall.[27] Difficulties, however, arise when teachers are not trained observers and when they do not have sufficient time to observe the behavior of individuals or to record it systematically and adequately. Often the record becomes unwieldy, and frequently the anecdotes are not oriented toward any particular point or factors of personality.

*Anecdotal Records by Teacher A about Jane (10 years old) on the Topic of Personal Adjustment*

Sept. 10—Jane cried when she failed to solve an arithmetic problem correctly;

Oct. 3—Shoved without provocation or reason another girl standing near her;

Oct. 9—Refused to take part in playground games with other girls because she was not chosen as leader of one of the groups;

Oct. 15—Used ridicule to belittle Mary, a classmate, who prepared an elaborate report for the social studies class;

Nov. 3—In anger struck Martha, who caught the basketball which Jane missed; sulked when teacher asked reason for striking Martha.

*Interpretation:* In this sample of anecdotal records, Jane reveals a pattern of emotional and social immaturity, and poor adjustment to others of her age. She shows little emotional control and is jealous of others who succeed better than she does. From other data not given here it is known that she is a "spoiled" child at home, is allowed generally to have her own way, and uses crying and tears with her mother when denied something she wants.

The values of the anecdotal record may be summarized briefly as follows: First, the observation and recording of significant conduct and behavior by all teachers should direct attention away from the mere teaching of facts. Systematic observations should be recorded and be available for summarization. Second, teachers should record instances of behavior which indicate both favorable and unfavorable characteristics of the pupil. Practice in recording anecdotes will indicate those which are significant, especially if these anecdotes are discussed in conferences by teachers concerned. Third, the anecdotes should be as concrete and concise as possible, given with a minimum of interpretation: facts are more helpful

---

[26] Willard C. Olson, *The Behavior-Journal Manual of Directions and Forms.* Ann Arbor, Michigan: University Elementary School, University of Michigan, 1935.

[27] John A. Randall, "The Anecdotal Behavior Journal," *Progressive Education,* Vol. 13, pp. 21-26, 1936.

than inferences or interpretations. Fourth, periodic conferences of the teachers should be held to present, review, diagnose, and interpret anecdotal records and related data. All school officers should participate in such summarization and synthesis of data. Anecdotes will fill in gaps in data not gathered by other means.

## Survey of Statistics Frequently Used in Measurement

### Norms

The simplest sort of statistics used in measurement is the so-called *norms*, or *equivalent scores*, which translate *raw scores* on tests into more meaningful language. A *raw score* is the number of items successfully achieved by an individual who is taking a test.

A *norm*, or equivalent score, for a test is a numerical index of the average achievement of pupils of a given grade, age, or other homogeneous group for which the norm is being determined. A norm is a statement of present achievement of a group, and not a universal standard of accomplishment. In most cases the average—mean or median—achievement of a group is taken as the norm, but sometimes other points, such as quartiles or percentiles, are used. Most norms are general norms; that is, they are based upon the scores from a fairly large number of pupils who live in widely scattered parts of the country. In addition to those, however, local norms for particular states, cities, or even buildings are sometimes used. In the elementary school, the grade score is frequently used. Thus, a pupil may have obtained on a reading test a raw score of 35, which score can be translated, let us say, into an equivalent *grade score* of 5.5. This means that his score represents achievement which is at the fifth grade, fifth month, level.

A *grade norm* is a statement of the test accomplishment of pupils in a particular grade. The mean or median score of a large and unselected group of pupils in a single grade is usually employed for this purpose. Grade norms are ordinarily based upon the supposition that a school system contains twelve grades in the elementary and secondary schools. If a school system has a different form of grade organization, adjustments of norms are necessary. Most tests have grade norms for each month of the school year, but others have norms at the end of half-years, such as for February or June.

In a similar manner, equivalent *age scores* are sometimes provided on a test. The equivalent age score for a raw score of 35 might be 10-8, which would mean that this score was the average achieved by pupils who are 10 years, 8 months old.

An *age norm* expresses the mean or median achievement of a group of pupils of designated chronological age. Unless otherwise stated, an age norm is usually an average score made by pupils ranging from the designated age up to the next. For example, a score given as the norm for ten-year-old children is ordinarily understood to be for children who are at least ten years of age but not yet eleven.

*Percentile norms* correspond to the points which divide the total number of cases contained in a frequency distribution of a norm group into 100 equal parts; that is, into 100 parts each of which contains the same number of cases. Although the more common method of reporting norms is in terms of the median, which is the same as the fiftieth percentile, this is frequently supplemented by a statement of other points in the distribution for a given age or grade. Sometimes the scores corresponding to the tenth, twentieth, and every successive tenth percentile are given, and sometimes those at other percentile points are supplied. Such a score may represent, for example, the percentage of pupils of a fifth grade who have achieved a raw score of 35 on the reading test. This score might be translated, let us say, into a percentile score of 53 for fifth-grade pupils. This would mean that a fifth-grade pupil achieving a raw score of 35 ranks at a point above 52 per cent and below 47 per cent of fifth-grade children.

### Educational ages and quotients

Pupils of a given chronological age may vary on a test from the average score of their age group. Some will be far below and some far above it. A ten-year-old pupil, for example, may have a reading ability corresponding to that of the average 7-, 8-, 9-, 10-, 12-, or 14-year-old pupil. If a 10-year-old pupil achieves a score equivalent to that obtained by the average 9-year-old, it is said that he has a *reading age of 9.* If he obtains a score equivalent to that of the average 10-year-old pupil, his reading age would be 10. In a like manner, scores on arithmetic tests, history tests, and tests in geography and other subjects are translated into comparable or equivalent statistics in the interpretation of test data.

The individual's composite or average educational achievement on a battery of achievement tests is called his *educational age,* which means his general ability to achieve in school subjects. The educational age is comparable to the mental age obtained on an intelligence test. When the educational age, or E. A., is divided by the chronological age, or C. A., a quotient called the *educational quotient,* or E. Q., is obtained. Let us suppose that a boy who is chronologically 10 years old has an educational age of 7; his E. Q.

will be 70. On the other hand, if he has an educational age of 10 and a chronological age of 10, his E. Q. will be 100. The E. Q. indicates the achievement status of the pupil in terms of the relation of his C. A. to his E. A.

## Accomplishment quotient

Another quotient sometimes used is called the *accomplishment quotient*. It is computed by dividing the E. A. obtained from a battery of achievement tests by the M. A. obtained on an intelligence test. Since the educational age is divided by the mental age, this means that accomplishment is evaluated in terms of mental age rather than of chronological age. Generally, such complicated statistics seem to have the prestige of scientific treatment. Actually, however, the A. Q. does not work out satisfactorily in practice. The A. Q. has a numerator and a denominator which are derived from other data and are, therefore, liable to have errors, sometimes small and sometimes large. If the errors in the E. A. and the M. A. are large and in opposite directions, the A. Q. will be very much in error. In the second place, the A. Q. favors the dull pupils and penalizes the bright pupil. For example, the A. Q. of a dull 10-year-old with a mental age of 8 will be higher than the corresponding A. Q. of a bright 10-year-old with an M. A. of 12. According to the assumptions underlying the A. Q., the dull 10-year-old has to accomplish at age 10 an M. A. of 10, but the bright pupil has to accomplish an M. A. of 12. The bright pupil has frequently had little opportunity to bring his achievement to the 12-year level because promotions are made in most schools not on the basis of mental age, but on the basis of chronological age. For these reasons it is recommended that the accomplishment quotient should not be used.

## Some Basic Statistical Concepts

Test results are of relatively little value unless they are interpreted wisely and well. To study test data for such interpretation a teacher or school officer may use as tools certain statistical concepts. Only a few of the fundamental concepts are presented here. Those who intend to study the statistical interpretation of tests more comprehensively will need to take special courses in the theory and application of statistical techniques.

The beginning student in psychology and education will doubtless meet many statistical terms and concepts which should have at least superficial meaning for him. A study by Mathews [28] led him

---

[28] C. O. Mathews, "The Introductory Course in Educational Measurements," *Educational Administration and Supervision*, Vol. 21, pp. 431-447, 1935.

to conclude that, based on a consensus of school teachers and officers, the following concepts are most often encountered: construction and interpretation of charts, tables, and distributions; computation of measures of central tendency, quartile points, percentiles, and quartile deviations; interpretation of standard deviation and correlation coefficients.

In an analysis of statistical concepts in professional journals, Dickey [29] found the following most frequently encountered: *measures of central tendency:* mean, median, average; *measures of variability:* standard deviation, range, quartile deviation; *correlation:* Pearson r, rank order correlation.

### Tabulation and Classification

One of the first steps in the handling of test scores is that of tabulation and classification. The teacher may have administered a vocabulary test in reading, for example, to 25 pupils. Various pupils in the class have obtained the following scores: 16, 19, 23, 14, 17, 18, 20, 19, 16, 13, 24, 21, 17, 25, 16, 15, 20, 22, 14, 9, 23, 20, 25, 19, 10. An examination of this group of scores will reveal that the highest score is 25 and the lowest is 9. The teacher will be aided in his understanding of the scores if he will arrange them in descending order, as follows: 25, 25, 24, 23, 23, 22, 21, 20, 20, 20, 19, 19, 19, 18, 17, 17, 16, 16, 16, 15, 14, 14, 13, 10, 9.

This series of scores, however, may be condensed in even more concise form for the 25 pupils. This may be done by setting up the scores into step intervals, let us say, intervals of 5. They might be grouped, for example, as shown in Table X. Such a grouping of scores is called a *frequency distribution,* because the frequency of occurrence of scores for each step interval is indicated in the form of a table.

### TABLE X

GROUPED TABULATION OF SCORES
FOR A VOCABULARY TEST

| Scores | Frequency |
|--------|-----------|
| 21-25 | 7 |
| 16-20 | 12 |
| 11-15 | 4 |
| 6-10 | 2 |
| N = | 25 |

[29] John W. Dickey, "Statistical Ability Necessary to Read Education Journals," *Journal of Educational Psychology,* Vol. 27, pp. 149-154, 1936.

Some suggestions for making the frequency table are: (1) determine the range, which is the difference between the highest and lowest scores; (*a*) select a class interval that will be convenient for tabulation; (3) write the limits of the class intervals in a left-hand column; and (4) tally the scores by making a short line for each score opposite the class interval into which it falls, and count these lines for the frequency of each class.

Table X indicates a frequency of 7 scores in the step interval 21-25, 12 in the step interval 16-20, 4 in the step interval 11-15, and 2 in the step interval 6-10. It is easy to see the advantage of grouping scores into a frequency distribution and using step intervals, particularly if the number of cases which are to be handled is large.

TABLE XI

SCORES ON A READING TEST

| Scores | No. of Pupils (Frequency) | Scores | No. of Pupils (Frequency) |
|--------|--------------------------|--------|--------------------------|
| 35-36 | 1 | 21-22 | 18 |
| 33-34 | 0 | 19-20 | 13 |
| 31-32 | 2 | 17-18 | 13 |
| 29-30 | 4 | 15-16 | 5 |
| 27-28 | 6 | 13-14 | 4 |
| 25-26 | 12 | 11-12 | 2 |
| 23-24 | 17 | 9-10 | 1 |

The handling of a tabulation may be illustrated further by the data that are presented in Table XI, representing the scores achieved by 98 pupils on a reading test. In this instance the scores have been made into a frequency distribution with step intervals of 2, rather than 5 as in Table X.

Sometimes teachers wish to have the distributions of scores represented graphically. For this purpose the frequency histogram is used. It is simple and easily made and shows at a glance the distribution of scores achieved by pupils. Figure 7 is a frequency histogram of the frequency distribution given in Table XI.

The advantages of such concise summarization of test data into the frequency distribution, or its graphic equivalent, the frequency histogram, permit easy visualization and estimation of such statistics as median, mean, quartiles, quartile deviation, and standard deviation.

When data are summarized in a frequency table, it is important to remember that the assumption is made by the reader that all the cases in a step interval are distributed evenly throughout the interval. When the number of cases is sufficiently large, this assumption is well founded. When the number of cases is small, the

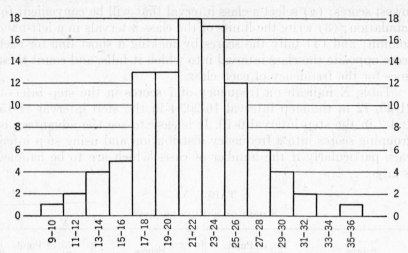

**Fig. 7. Frequency Histogram of Scores on a Reading Test.**

error that may follow basing computations on this assumption is slightly larger than when the number of cases is large.

### Measures of Central Tendency or Average

Measures of central tendency are often called the "average." The term *average* is employed in two different senses by many persons. In statistics it is used as a general term to include the mean, median, mode, and all other measures of central tendency. Its other use is that common in elementary arithmetic and in ordinary conversation. In this sense it is the arithmetic average and refers to the sum of a number of measures or quantities divided by their number. It is recommended by most statisticians, however, that the term *mean* be used in place of arithmetic average.

### Median

Perhaps the most commonly used average in educational literature is the median. Its ease of computation may account for this. The *median* is that point on the scale which divides the total number of measures or cases into two equal groups. For example, if there are 80 cases, the median is a point at which 40 of the cases lie at or below it and 40 at or above it. In other words, it is the fiftieth percentile point of a distribution. Sometimes a distinction is made between a grouped distribution or frequency table and a simple or ungrouped series in that the term *median* is used in connection with the former and *mid-score* or *mid-point* with the latter. The term *median* is generally used to include both series of measures.

Table XII illustrates the method of locating or computing the median in a frequency distribution. The steps of the process are summarized at the side of the table. At the same time, the first quartile, $Q_1$, and third quartile, $Q_3$, are indicated for later reference.

### TABLE XII
#### COMPUTATION OF THE MEDIAN AND QUARTILES

| Score Intervals | Frequency ($f$) | Steps in the Computation |
|---|---|---|
| 95-99 | 1 | *Median* |
| 90-94 | 2 | *Step 1.* Since half (50%) of the frequencies is required, $\frac{1}{2}$ of 98 = 49. |
| 85-89 | 5 | |
| 80-84 | 8 | *Step 2.* To locate the approximate median, count up the frequency column to the interval containing the 49th |
| 75-79 | 10 | frequency, or the top of the 60-64 interval. This provides 37 cases with 12 more required to make 49. |
| 70-74 | 14 | |
| 65-69 | 21 | *Step 3.* The step interval containing the median is 65-69, which contains a frequency of 21; thus, the median |
| 60-64 | 13 | is $\frac{12}{21}$ of the distance up this interval of 5; hence, $\frac{12}{21} \times 5 = \frac{60}{21} = 2.86$, which is the correction to be |
| 55-59 | 9 | added. |
| 50-54 | 8 | |
| 45-49 | 3 | *Step 4.* Add the correction 2.86 to the lower limit, 64.5, of the interval 65-69, and the median is 67.36. |
| 40-44 | 1 | |
| 35-39 | 1 | $Q_1$ *and* $Q_3$ |
| 30-34 | 1 | Follow the same steps as for median, except that $Q_1 = \frac{1}{4}$ and $Q_3 = \frac{3}{4}$ of the frequencies. $Q_1 = \frac{1}{4}$ of 98 = 24.5; $\frac{5}{13} \times 5 = \frac{25}{13} = .19$; |
| 25-29 | 1 | 59.5 + .19 = 59.69. |
| | $N = 98$ | $Q_3 = \frac{3}{4}$ of 98 = 73.5; $\frac{1.5}{10} \times 5 = \frac{7.5}{10} = .75$; 74.5 + .75 = 75.25. |

*Note:* On account of statistical theory, for computational purposes the intervals are considered as beginning .5 of a point below the designation. Thus, 25 = 24.5, 30 = 29.5, and so forth.

In summary, the median, or fiftieth percentile, and any other percentile points are located by dividing the total number of frequencies by the given percentile, counting up the frequency column as far as possible without passing the required point, determining the fractional distance into the next step interval to the required point, multiplying this fraction by the size of the step interval, and adding this result to the lower limit of the step interval in which the median or other percentile is located.

## Mean

A more precise mathematical statistic than the median is the mean. The *mean* is found by adding a series of scores together and

TABLE XIII
COMPUTATION OF THE MEAN AND STANDARD DEVIATION

| Score Intervals | Frequency ($f$) | Deviation ($d$) | $(f) \times (d)$ | $(f) \times (d)^2$ | Steps in the Computation |
|---|---|---|---|---|---|
| 95-99 | 1 | 6 | 6 | 36 | *Mean* |
| 90-94 | 2 | 5 | 10 | 50 | *Step 1.* Guess a mean ($M^1$) near the center of the distribution; here the midpoint of the 65-69 interval, or $M^1 = 67$. |
| 85-89 | 5 | 4 | 20 | 80 | |
| 80-84 | 8 | 3 | 24 | 72 | *Step 2.* Lay off the deviations ($d$) from the guessed mean, as in Column 3 of the table. |
| 75-79 | 10 | 2 | 20 | 40 | *Step 3.* Multiply each ($f$) by its ($d$), as in Column 4 of the table. |
| 70-74 | 14 | 1 | 14 | 14 | *Step 4.* Obtain the algebraic sum of the ($f$) × ($d$) column, $\Sigma fd$, which here are +94 and −93 or +1. |
| 65-69 | 21 | 0 | | | |
| 60-64 | 13 | −1 | −13 | 13 | *Step 5.* Compute the correction $+1 \div 98 = .01 \times 5 = .05$. |
| 55-59 | 9 | −2 | −18 | 36 | *Step 6.* Add the correction to the guessed mean $67.00 + .05 = 67.05$ or the true mean. |
| 50-54 | 8 | −3 | −24 | 72 | |
| 45-49 | 3 | −4 | −12 | 48 | *Standard Deviation* |
| 40-44 | 1 | −5 | −5 | 25 | *Step 7.* Compute the ($f$) × ($d$)², as in Column 5 of the table. |
| 35-39 | 1 | −6 | −6 | 36 | *Step 8.* Obtain the sum of ($f$) × ($d$)², $\Sigma fd^2$, which here is 635. |
| 30-34 | 1 | −7 | −7 | 49 | *Step 9.* Substitute in the formula for standard deviation |
| 25-29 | 1 | −8 | −8 | 64 | $\sigma = i \sqrt{\dfrac{\Sigma fd^2}{N} - c^2},$ |
| $M^1 = 67$    $N = 98$ | | | +94 −93 | 635 | $\sigma = 5 \sqrt{\dfrac{635}{98} - .0001}$ |
| | | | +1 | | $= 5 \times 2.54 = 12.70$ |

$$c = \frac{1}{98} = .01. \qquad c^2 = .0001.$$

$$M = M^1 + \frac{\Sigma fd}{N} i = 67.00 + \frac{1}{98} \times 5 = 67.05.$$

$$\sigma = i \sqrt{\frac{\Sigma fd^2}{N} - c^2} = 5 \sqrt{\frac{635}{98} - .0001} = 5 \times 2.54 = 12.70.$$

dividing the sum by the number of cases involved in order to obtain an arithmetic average, or mean. The mean is different from the median in that it involves a contribution of size from each of the scores in the series, whereas the median is influenced only slightly by any unusual scores at the ends of the frequency distribution. Also, in order to obtain a more precise measure of variability, or spread, which is called the *standard deviation,* it is necessary to compute and to use the mean. In Table XIII a very simple example of how to compute the mean by the so-called "short method" is illustrated. The table also contains the computation of the standard deviation, but this part of the table should be disregarded until it is discussed later. The formula for finding the mean by the "short method" is $M = M^1 + \frac{\Sigma fd}{N}i$. In the formula $M =$ Mean, $M^1 =$ Guessed Mean, $\Sigma fd =$ Sum of frequencies multiplied by their respective deviations, $N =$ Total number of frequencies, and $i =$ interval of grouped scores.

In summary, the steps for computing the mean by the "short method" are to guess a mean near the center of the distribution, to lay off the deviations of intervals from the guessed mean, to multiply the frequency of each interval by its deviation, to obtain the algebraic sum of the frequencies times the deviations, to compute the correction for guessing and to multiply it by the interval, and to add this result to or subtract it from the guessed mean.

The mean obtained by this method will vary slightly from the mean obtained by actually adding all the individual scores and dividing by the total frequencies. As a rule, the difference is so slight as to make no practical difference in the interpretation of this statistic.

## Mode

The *mode* of a distribution is that point on the scale at which more measures are found than at any other point. Thus, in a sense, the mode may be said to be the typical value or case. In a grouped distribution or frequency table, the true mode cannot be determined by inspection but requires rather difficult computations. It is not widely used in educational and psychological research. The mode is also used in a broader and less precise sense to apply to any point on the scale where the frequencies are largest. This point is sometimes called the *major mode.*

When two values appear a large number of times in different parts of the distribution, we have a bi-modal distribution; a trimodal distribution if three modes appear; and so forth.

## Measures of Variability or Deviation

No distribution of scores is adequately described by a measure of central tendency. Two groups of pupils may have the same median or mean score but have different variability, or deviation, of the scores. The spread or scatter of a set of measures about a point, which is almost always a measure of central tendency—that is, an average—is called *deviation*. It is commonly measured by any one of several measures of deviation, or variability, each of which yields a summary statement from a slightly different standpoint. Such measures as the range, the quartile deviation, and the standard deviation are illustrations.

### Range

The *range* of a series of scores or other measures is the distance from the lowest to the highest measure. Thus, the range of a series of test scores of which the lowest is 10 and the highest 53 is from 10 to 53, or 43 points.

### Quartile deviation

The *quartile deviation* is a commonly used measure of deviation, or variability, of a distribution of scores about the median. It is one-half the difference between the points at the twenty-fifth and seventy-fifth percentiles in a frequency distribution of measures. These are denoted as $Q_1$ and $Q_3$, respectively.

For making comparisons between groups which have been administered the same test, one of the most easily computed measures of scatter, or variability, is the quartile deviation Q. It is sometimes called the *semi-interquartile range*. It is one-half the distance from the first to the third quartile. In formula form it may be indicated thus:

$$Q = \frac{Q_3 - Q_1}{2}.$$

Using this formula for the data in Table XII, we find that

$$Q = \frac{75.25 - 59.69}{2} = \frac{15.56}{2} = 7.78.$$

If we assume that the distribution of scores is symmetrical, then the distance from the first quartile to the median would be exactly the same as from the median to the third quartile. In the case of Table XII, this would mean that if the distribution were exactly symmetrical, $Q_1$ would be 7.78 below the median 67.36 and $Q_3$ would be 7.78 above the median. Unless a distribution is decidedly unusual in its shape, the percentage of cases included within the distance of Q on both sides of the median constitutes 50 per cent of the cases.

## Standard deviation

The *standard deviation* is one of the two or three most common measures of deviation, or variability. It is based upon the squares of the actual deviations and is always found about the mean. In a normal distribution or curve, it represents the distance from the mean to the point of inflection, that is, the point at which the shape of the curve changes from an angle of more than 45° with the base line to one of less than that amount. Furthermore, in a normal distribution, a distance of one standard deviation on either side of the mean includes 34.13 per cent of the area of the curve or, in other words, of the number of cases. Therefore, 68.26 per cent of the cases in a normal distribution lie not more than one standard deviation above and below the mean.

In a simple formula form, for a series of ungrouped scores the formula is:

$$\sigma = \sqrt{\frac{\Sigma D^2}{N}}$$

Expressing this in words: the standard deviation is obtained by getting the sum of the deviations squared of all of the scores in the series from the actual mean score and dividing by the number of cases, and then extracting the square root. This computation may sound slightly complicated, but the actual process is fairly easy.

For a series of scores grouped into intervals in a frequency table, the formula is:

$$\sigma = i \sqrt{\frac{\Sigma f d^2}{N} - c^2}$$

The calculation and explanation of this formula are illustrated in steps 7, 8, and 9 of Table XIII. It is essential, of course, to calculate the mean as illustrated for the "short method" of calculation. The additional steps for the calculation of the standard deviation of a grouped series of scores are to multiply each frequency by its deviation squared, to find the sum of these $f d^2$, to divide this sum by the $N$, or total frequencies, to subtract the correction squared, to extract the square root of this result, and to multiply by the interval size, which in this instance is 5. The standard deviation thus obtained may be used for a variety of purposes. One of the most common purposes is to compare the relative homogeneity or heterogeneity of groups of pupils who have been administered the same test.

## Measures of Correlation

When two sets of scores for the same individuals are to be compared, some method of correlation is ordinarily used. If the same pupils have taken a paragraph-meaning test and a word-meaning test, their scores may be correlated to determine how closely similar the achievement of the pupils was on these two tests.

### TABLE XIV

COMPUTATION OF RHO (RANK ORDER) CORRELATION COEFFICIENT

| Students | Test 1 Paragraph Meaning | Test 2 Word Meaning | Rank Test 1 | Rank Test 2 | Difference in Rank | (Difference)² |
|---|---|---|---|---|---|---|
| A | 21 | 14 | 12. | 13.5 | 1.5 | 2.25 |
| B | 26 | 24 | 8. | 7. | 1.0 | 1.00 |
| C | 26 | 26 | 8. | 2.5 | 5.5 | 30.25 |
| D | 20 | 19 | 13. | 11. | 2.0 | 4.00 |
| E | 28 | 26 | 3. | 2.5 | .5 | .25 |
| F | 27 | 26 | 5.5 | 2.5 | 3.0 | 9.00 |
| G | 18 | 14 | 14. | 13.5 | .5 | .25 |
| H | 27 | 21 | 5.5 | 9.5 | 4.0 | 16.00 |
| I | 26 | 21 | 8. | 9.5 | 1.5 | 2.25 |
| J | 24 | 17 | 10.5 | 12. | 1.5 | 2.25 |
| K | 28 | 26 | 3. | 2.5 | .5 | .25 |
| L | 28 | 25 | 3. | 5.5 | 2.5 | 6.25 |
| M | 30 | 25 | 1. | 5.5 | 4.5 | 20.25 |
| N | 24 | 22 | 10.5 | 8. | 2.5 | 6.25 |

Number of Students = 14.        Sum of Differences Squared = 100.50

Step 1. Obtain raw scores on two tests.
Step 2. Assign rank order for each pupil on Test 1, then on Test 2. When two or more scores are of the same size, the ranks are added and the mean assigned; *e.g.*, $1 + 2 + 3 + 4 = 10 \div 4 = 2.5$ in the above table.
Step 3. Compute difference in ranks for each pupil.
Step 4. Compute square of each difference.
Step 5. Add the squares and apply the formula for rho correlation.

$$\text{Rho is } 1 - \left( \frac{6 \times (\text{Sum of Differences})^2}{\text{Number} \times [(\text{Number})^2 - 1]} \right).$$

Applying this formula to the present tests, we have:

$$6 \times 100.5 = 603$$
$$14 \times (196 - 1) \text{ or } (195) = 2730$$
$$603 \div 2730 = .220$$
$$1.000 - .220 = .78$$

The rank-order correlation for the tests is .78.

The two methods most commonly used are called the *rank-order* method and the *product-moment* method. Of these the rank-order method, called *rho,* is the simpler and is especially used when the number of cases does not exceed 30 to 40 individuals. Both correlation methods give approximately the same coefficient of correlation. The rank method, however, does not take into account the exact magnitude of each score, which the product-moment method does. A sample showing of computation of rho is presented in Table XIV.

It will be noted that in Table XIV the rank order for Test 1 was found for each pupil, and in a similar manner the rank order for Test 2. The differences in rank were computed, and then these differences were squared. The formula for rho is given under the table, and the materials are self-explanatory.

## Product-moment correlation

This name is given to the usual method of computing the coefficient of correlation, a method devised by Karl Pearson. For a small number of cases, perhaps less than 25 or 30, the data are usually arranged in two columns, the corresponding entries in which constitute a pair of measures; whereas for larger numbers of cases, a correlation or double-entry table is almost always used. The formula used in product-moment correlation compares the deviations of the corresponding pairs of measures from their means with the standard deviations of the two distributions, and thus yields the coefficient of correlation.

A simple form of this method of calculating the coefficient of correlation is illustrated in Table XV. This form is used when the number of cases is small. The basic formula, however, is exactly the same as for a large number of cases. It is

$$r = \frac{\dfrac{\Sigma xy}{N} - c_x c_y}{\sigma_x \quad \sigma_y}$$

In this formula, the $\sigma_x$ and $\sigma_y$ are computed in exactly the same manner as described in steps 7, 8, and 9 of Table XIII. The entire process of calculation is as follows:

*Steps in Computing the Product-Moment* r

*Step 1.* For each of the two series of scores $X$ and $Y,$ obtain the deviation of each score from its respective mean. Although the true mean may be used, it is seldom a whole number; therefore, it is generally more economical of time and effort to work from an assumed mean. The assumed mean of the $X$ series is selected as 25, and of the $Y$ series as 22. Each deviation of an $X$ score from its assumed mean is indicated by $x,$ and each deviation of a $Y$ score from its assumed mean is indicated by $y$. The plus or minus signs of the deviations must be indicated for use in the next steps. In the $x$ column, for example: $21 - 25 = -4$, $26 - 25 = +1$, and so forth.

*Step 2.* Compute the square of each deviation. Enter these squares in the columns headed $x^2$ and $y^2$. For example, the first three deviations squared in the $x$ column are: $-4^2 = 16$, $+1^2 = 1$, $+1^2 = 1$.

*Step 3.* Compute the product of each pair of deviations. To obtain this, each $x$ is multiplied by its respective $y$. For example, the first three products are as follows: $-4 \times -8 = 32$; $+1 \times +2 = 2$; $+1 \times +4 = 4$; and so forth. It is important to watch plus and minus signs carefully to obtain the algebraic sum.

*Step 4.* Substitute the numbers for corresponding characteristics in the formula, $\Sigma \frac{xy}{N}$. $\Sigma xy = (157)$, which is the algebraic sum of the $xy$ column, is divided by $N$, which is 14. The resulting quotient is 11.21. $c_x$ is the algebraic sum of the $x$ column divided by $N$, and $c_y$ is the algebraic sum of the $y$ column divided by $N$. For the data in Table XV, $c_x$ is $+ .21$ and $c_y$ is $- .14$. Their product, $c_x c_y$, is $- .03$. Since the formula is

$$\frac{xy - c_x\,c_y}{\sigma_x\,\sigma_y}$$

the substitution is $11.21 - (-.03)$ or $11.21 + .03 = 11.24$. The product of $\sigma_x\,\sigma_y$ is $3.32 \times 4.22 = 14.01$. The final calculation is $11.24 \div 14.01 = .80$, which is the $r$.

TABLE XV

COMPUTATION OF THE PRODUCT-MOMENT CORRELATION

| Scores | | Deviations | | Deviations Squared | | Product of Deviations |
|---|---|---|---|---|---|---|
| $X$ | $Y$ | $x$ | $y$ | $x^2$ | $y^2$ | $xy$ |
| 21 | 14 | −4 | −8 | 16 | 64 | 32 |
| 26 | 24 | +1 | +2 | 1 | 4 | 2 |
| 26 | 26 | +1 | +4 | 1 | 16 | 4 |
| 20 | 19 | −5 | −3 | 25 | 9 | 15 |
| 28 | 26 | +3 | +4 | 9 | 16 | 12 |
| 27 | 26 | +2 | +4 | 4 | 16 | 8 |
| 18 | 14 | −7 | −8 | 49 | 64 | 56 |
| 27 | 21 | +2 | −1 | 4 | 1 | −2 |
| 26 | 21 | +1 | −1 | 1 | 1 | −1 |
| 24 | 17 | −1 | −5 | 1 | 25 | −5 |
| 28 | 26 | +3 | +4 | 9 | 16 | 12 |
| 28 | 25 | +3 | +3 | 9 | 9 | 9 |
| 30 | 25 | +5 | +3 | 25 | 9 | 15 |
| 24 | 22 | −1 | 0 | 1 | 0 | 0 |
| $M_x^1 = 25$ | $M_y^1 = 22$ | +21 −18 | +24 −26 | 155 | 250 | +165 − 8 |
| | | + 3 | − 2 | | | +157 |

$c_x = +3 \div 14 = +.21$ $\qquad$ $c_y = -2 \div 14 = -.14$

$c_x^2 = .04$ $\qquad\qquad\qquad$ $c_y^2 = .02$

$\sigma_x^2 = 155 \div 14 = 11.07 - .04 = 11.03$ $\qquad$ $\sigma_x = \sqrt{11.03} = 3.32$

$\sigma_y^2 = 250 \div 14 = 17.86 - .02 = 17.84$ $\qquad$ $\sigma_y = \sqrt{17.84} = 4.22$

$\dfrac{\Sigma xy}{N} = 157 \div 14 = 11.21$

$$r = \frac{\dfrac{\Sigma xy}{N} - c_x c_y}{\sigma_x \sigma_y} = \frac{11.21 - (.21 \times -.14)}{3.32 \times 4.22} = \frac{11.21 + .03}{14.01} = .80$$

The coefficients of correlation range from a maximum of + 1.00 down to zero and to − 1.00. A perfect correlation means that each pupil's score in one series corresponds exactly with his score in the other series on the basis of the relative size of the scores. If the agreement is perfect, a value of + 1.00 is obtained. If the disagreement is as large as possible, a value of − 1.00 is obtained. If there is no relationship at all, neither agreement nor disagreement, it is .00. Intermediate values indicate various degrees of agreement or disagreement.

Correlation has practical uses, which are mainly to discover the relationships between various factors in learning and in testing. Frequently scores on odd items of a test are correlated with scores on the even items for a group of pupils in order to determine the coefficient of reliability of a test. These few indications of the uses of correlation show only elementary application to educational and testing problems.

Knowledge of a few statistical techniques and processes does not qualify a teacher as a statistician. Knowledge of a few processes will assist the teacher in making a better analysis and interpretation of test data. The teacher should be very cautious in making generalizations regarding statistical data until a fuller knowledge of statistical theory and practice has been obtained.

## QUESTIONS AND EXERCISES FOR DISCUSSION AND STUDY

1. In parallel columns list some of the desirable and the undesirable uses of test results.

2. What is meant by the statement that tests may freeze or retard curricular changes?

3. What are some of the advantages of the essay examination and what are some of the advantages of the objective-type examination?

4. What can the teacher do to avoid the usual weaknesses of the essay examination?

5. Prepare an objective test on this or another chapter, using the different types of items which have been illustrated.

6. Why is it undesirable to use an A. Q. for the individual pupil?

7. Define and illustrate the following terms: grade score, educational age, chronological age, arithmetic age, intelligence quotient.

8. Outline a simple measurement problem in which you would use statistical treatment of results.

9. Tell what statistical techniques would be applied to your problem.

10. Suppose you gave a test to 35 pupils and found their range of marks to run from 15 to 70. What size of class interval would you use for grouping?

11. What type of analysis would you use to tell how homogeneous or heterogeneous one class might be compared with another?

12. Which teacher would have the more difficult problem of adaptation to individual differences: one with the class having an S. D. of 15.8, or one with a class having an S. D. of 9.2, on a reading test?

13. What assumption is made in the grouping of measures?

14. Using the data given below, find the (rho) rank-order coefficient of correlation.

15. Compute the mean, median, quartile deviation, and standard deviation from the data below.

| Pupil | A | B | C | D | E | F | G | H | I | J | K | L | M | N | O | P |
|---|---|---|---|---|---|---|---|---|---|---|---|---|---|---|---|---|
| Arithmetic Score.. | 10 | 16 | 13 | 16 | 22 | 17 | 11 | 19 | 13 | 10 | 15 | 10 | 17 | 13 | 4 | 14 |
| Reading Score ... | 14 | 32 | 33 | 22 | 41 | 36 | 22 | 26 | 17 | 25 | 29 | 23 | 37 | 25 | 10 | 27 |

### SELECTED REFERENCES FOR FURTHER READING AND STUDY

Buros, Oscar K., editor, *The Nineteen-Thirty-Eight Mental Measurements Yearbook.* New Brunswick, N. J.: Rutgers University, 1938.

Corey, S. M., "Evaluating Technical Teaching Competence," *The Elementary School Journal,* Vol. XLI, No. 8 (April, 1941), pp. 577-586.

Greene, E. B., *Measurement of Human Behavior.* New York: Odyssey Press, 1941.

Greene, H. A., A. N. Jorgenson, and J. R. Gerberich, *Measurement and Evaluation in the Elementary School.* New York: Longmans, Green and Company, 1942.

————, *Measurement and Evaluation in the Secondary School.* New York: Longmans, Green and Company, 1943.

Hawkes, Herbert E., E. F. Lindquist, and C. R. Mann, editors, *The Construction and Use of Achievement Examinations.* Boston: Houghton Mifflin Company, 1936.

Hildreth, Gertrude H., compiler, *A Bibliography of Mental Tests and Rating Scales.* New York: Psychological Corporation, 1933.

McCall, W. A., *Measurement.* New York: The Macmillan Company, 1939.

Meyer, George, "An Experimental Study of the Old and New Types of Examinations: II. Methods of Study," *Journal of Educational Psychology,* Vol. 26, pp. 30-40, 1935.

————, "The Effect on Recall and Recognition of the Examination Set in Class Room Situations," *Journal of Educational Psychology,* Vol. 27, pp. 81-99, 1936.

Orleans, Jacob, *Measurement in Education.* New York: Thomas Nelson and Sons, 1937.

Purnell, R. T., and R. A. Davis, *Directing Learning by Teacher Made Tests.* Boulder, Colo.: University of Colorado, 1939.

Raths, Louis E., "Appraising Certain Aspects of Student Achievement," *Guidance in Educational Institutions. Thirty-Seventh Yearbook, Part I, National Society for the Study of Education.* Bloomington, Ill.: Public School Publishing Company, 1938. Chap 3, pp. 89-117.

Remmers, H. H., and N. L. Gage, *Educational Measurement and Evaluation.* New York: Harper and Brothers, 1943.

Rinsland, Henry D., *Constructing Tests and Grading in Elementary and High School Subjects.* New York: Prentice-Hall, Inc., 1937.

Ross, C. C., *Measurement in Today's Schools.* New York: Prentice-Hall, Inc., 1941.

Stalnaker, John M., "Essay Examinations Reliably Read," *School and Society*, Vol. 46, pp. 671-672, 1937.

Stroud, J. B., "Evaluating Outcomes of Instruction," Chapter XV in *An Introduction to Modern Education* by C. E. Skinner, R. E. Langfitt, and others. Boston: D. C. Heath and Company, 1937.

Tyler, Ralph W., "Appraising Progressive Schools," *Educational Method*, Vol. 15, pp. 412-415, 1936.

Wahlquist, J. T., *The Philosophy of Education*. New York: Ronald Press Company, 1942. Chap. 10.

Wrightstone, J. Wayne, *Appraisal of Newer Elementary School Practices*. New York: Teachers College, Columbia University, 1938.

————, "Are Essay Examinations Obsolete?" *Social Education*, Vol. 1, pp. 401-405, 1937.

# Part V

# PERSONALITY, ADJUSTMENT, AND GUIDANCE

## CHAPTER 16*

# Emotion and Adjustment

Emotion as a fundamental concern in human living, and therefore in education, has had increasing emphasis in recent years. Without attempting too close a definition, it is worth noting that the Adolescent Study, the report of which was published in 1940, refers to emotion as something not to be considered incidental, but as "intrinsic in every experience, a factor in all conduct."[1] Those who directed this study went on to say that "emotion thus broadly conceived is fused with thinking—for the most part harmoniously —in the healthy, competent individual."

Similarly, the Commission on Teacher Education of the American Council on Education, which has been conducting a co-operative study for the redirection of teacher preparation, in its Bennington Conference of 1939 and in the Division of Human Growth and Development set up at the University of Chicago has stressed a dynamic concept of "learning," in which emotion plays a conspicuous role, and has been encouraging institutions preparing teachers to give careful consideration to this hitherto neglected area of teacher education.

### "Intellect" and "Emotion"

This concept of emotion as inextricably bound up with all other elements in a fused human personality differs from that often held,

---

* For assistance in gathering material for Chapters 16, 17, 18, and 19, the author acknowledges his indebtedness to the Carnegie Foundation for the Advancement of Teaching, New York City.

[1] Caroline Zachry, *Emotion and Conduct in Adolescence* (New York: D. Appleton-Century Company, 1940), p. 5. For a discussion of definitions of *emotion*, see Prescott, *Emotion and the Educative Process* (Washington, D. C.: American Council on Education, 1938), p. 17. Prescott says that emotions are usually defined as "inherited pattern reactions involving extensive visceral behavior and intense feelings, as open to simple conditioning, and as differentiated in quality according to the dominance of the sympathetic or parasympathetic segments of the automatic nervous system," but he calls attention to an oversimplification in the usual treatment of emotions as "definitely misleading to persons seeking an understanding of child development."

if not by psychologists, at least by many teachers and probably most laymen. The fact that much of the early effort in the twentieth-century movement for scientific measurement in education was directed to "intelligence" and "achievement in the school subjects," and that it developed at a period when a restricted view was prevalent as to what education, especially in schools, should be, tended to obscure until recently the importance of the emotions. This was so in spite of the fact that among the psychologists who pioneered in mental measurement there were many (Alfred Binet and Edward L. Thorndike, for example) who never lost sight of the significance of the emotional life and did not make the mistake of isolating "emotion" and "intellect" from each other and from other aspects of the total personality.

That the teaching profession and intelligent laymen have tended to make this separation, however, especially where the schools are concerned, is illustrated by the reply made to the Japanese people of Hawaii by an eminent missionary and authority on Oriental life who had been asked by them whether, in view of the fact that their children attended the American public schools in the Islands under a compulsory education law, the parents should keep up the Japanese language schools of their own. The Japanese were told that they "needed to appreciate the American thought regarding education":

> The educational system of the Islands follows the pattern of that on the mainland. It rests on the postulate that the purpose of school education is to impart intellectual knowledge and mental discipline, and that the moral and religious training of children is the special function of the home. This conviction is based on the fact that moral and religious life is rooted in the emotions. It cannot be orally taught, although, of course, certain intellectual aspects can be. The religious spirit and the moral sense are always "caught" rather than "taught." They are, as a rule, imparted to children by their parents in subtle, indirect ways, chiefly by their example in the home.[2]

The importance of the family and religion for emotional development would be readily conceded. Modern psychologists point out, however, that not only is it impossible and undesirable to make any such separation as is implied in the statement just quoted—since in very fact "the whole child goes to school"—but that actually the process of "learning" rather than "teaching" insisted upon for the home applies with equal force to the variety of learning experiences in the school. It has been the very omission of the emotional elements involved in real living that has tended to make school education sterile rather than lifelike; and one of

---

[2] Sidney L. Gulick, "Sympathetic Insight," *Pan Pacific*, Vol. I, No. 2, April-June, 1937, p. 2.

the chief arguments for the enriched and flexible educational programs of good modern schools, with their provision for wholesome
recreation, practical work experiences, and creative activities in
music, drama, and the fine arts generally, is to give adequate opportunity for healthy play of emotion. Hence the questions raised by
the American Council on Education report of 1937 as to the life
of the child in school in the light of emotional needs:

Is it rich in feeling? Does it have the tang of exciting discovery, the testing
of the stuff that personality is made of, the thrill of feeling that here one is in
the swirls of the stream of real life? Is there an opportunity to enrich life from
beginning to end by guiding children into and through high moments of vivid
exciting experience? [3]

## A Case Study of Emotional Stability

Strictly scientific knowledge of emotional development is
limited. More is known about very young children than about
those of other ages, chiefly because of the work of some half a dozen
centers for research in child development at Iowa, California,
Minnesota, and Toronto Universities, Teachers College, Columbia
University, and the Merrill-Palmer School, Detroit. In the past
few years considerable important work has also been done on the
period of adolescence through the Adolescent Study already mentioned and other investigations. The method of the case study is
used extensively in these researches. One such case study, made
by the Child Research Clinic of the Woods Schools, is reproduced
in shortened form here: [4]

Tom is a bright-eyed, active boy of thirteen, who enjoys the games and
interests of other boys of that age. His story is not a happy one, however. Let
us go back over his brief history to see just what there was, or is, to make him
different from other, happy, thirteen year old boys in schools throughout the
country.

Seven years ago, a worried mother and father brought their young son to
The Woods Schools. Tom was an attractive and well-formed child, but he was
extremely nervous and highly excitable. His hands moved unceasingly, fluttering
aimlessly about, or plucking at his clothing or any nearby object. The boy would
frequently distort his face, shutting his eyes as though in pain, and stretching
his mouth in a grimace. Tom could never be depended upon to react favorably
to even the slightest change in his routine. He would shout and become hysterical
at the slightest deviation from the usual, as was illustrated by his behavior one
day, when he found that his possessions were not as he had left them. He
threw himself on the floor, screaming and kicking. Anything out of the ordinary,

---

[3] Daniel A. Prescott, *Emotion and the Educative Process*. Washington, D. C.:
American Council on Education, 1938, p. 3.

[4] For the full report, see *Toward the Development of Emotional Stability*, Vol. I,
No. 5, of the *Child Research Clinic Series*, The Woods Schools, Langhorne, Pa.,
pp. 5-8.

such as sudden noises, paper blowing about, and the like, frightened him. For several years his parents had been aware of this unusual behavior, and were becoming increasingly disturbed by it. They were constantly comparing him unfavorably with their other son, whose behavior was in every way normal. They were fearful of Tom's influence on this younger brother. Finally, the parents took him to a psychiatrist, who reported some mental retardation and great emotional instability. He recommended that the boy be placed in a carefully regulated environment.

The parents were entirely incapable of handling the situation unaided. Each had been the only and greatly pampered child of wealthy parents, and neither possessed the emotional equipment necessary for handling a nervous, excitable child. The mother was immature in many ways, seeing only the worst side of things, and becoming hysterical whenever a difficult situation arose. At this time, when Tom needed an unemotional, clear-thinking person to guide him, she would throw herself despairingly across a bed, exclaiming: "I can't do a thing with the child!" The boy was devoted to his mother, but her presence invariably proved upsetting to him.

The father's contribution to the case was little better. He was deeply distressed by his son's emotional upsets, but unfortunately seemed totally incapable of doing the right thing at the time it was most needed. Instead of being calm and firm, he would become almost as excited as the child, and demand that something be done at once. It soon became evident that the "carefully regulated environment" of the psychiatrist's recommendation was not to be found in the boy's own home. The solution offered the parents was a school where Tom could live and grow up under the guidance of teachers experienced in handling such cases, a place where routine and discipline would remove, as far as possible, the causes of his emotional outbursts. He should be placed in a comfortable environment where he would have twenty-four-hour-a-day care and supervision, a chance to develop a sense of security, and a real opportunity to succeed. The constant care that he had received at home had resulted only in serious emotional strain to him and to his parents. Persistent nagging and criticism had given him a sense of inferiority.

The report goes on to tell what the teachers did with Tom when he came to its preschool department at the age of six—how they at first quieted his frantic screams (chiefly by ignoring them), then worked with him to get a gradual normal adjustment. At the end of two years, Tom had made progress in his schoolwork, but still remained aloof from other boys. "Emotional outbursts came less often, possibly due to his complete adjustment to the quiet and regulated school environment." When he had reached ten years of age, Tom began to show marked improvement. He was gradually being withdrawn from his solitary interests. There was one emotional upset after what had been a short and satisfactory visit from his father, but it was the last. A psychologist, who had tested him previously, reported one year later:

Tom's greatest problem is not with native intelligence, but with his emotions. A standard intelligence examination gives him a Mental Age below average (Binet, Pintner-Patterson, School Achievement): Chronological Age 11 years 5½ months; Mental Age 9 years; Educational Age 10; Intelligence Quotient 90. This retardation is not one that would prohibit the thought of his carrying on and making a small place for himself. His interests and desires are very much those of a normal boy. He is ambitious, industrious and lovable.

Those who were working with Tom in the school were not discouraged by the report. "We knew that he was not a brilliant boy," says Miss Dorothy M. Odiorne, teacher in the school, "but that he was a good student with excellent power of retention." The school had learned that it could depend upon Tom for handling responsible tasks in the library and in dealing with athletic equipment. As Tom approached his thirteenth birthday, his improvement was in every way marked. "His Intelligence Quotient increased by several points. . . . He took great pleasure in reading. . . . He was taken to concerts and on other one-day trips to the city. . . . He was permitted to make several short train trips unaccompanied, and while showing a normal amount of apprehension at first, soon began to enjoy the sense of responsibility." The final note in the report says:

Excitements, such as picnics or theatre trips, now affect him only as they would a perfectly normal boy. He is boisterous, enthusiastic and happy, but such excitements do not leave him emotionally upset for days afterward, as they formerly did. He recently had a visit from his parents, and this time behaved in a highly satisfactory manner. He was courteous and quiet, showing a normal amount of interest. When asked to choose the afternoon's entertainment, Tom suggested a baseball game. He showed interest and understanding throughout the game. When the time came for his parents to leave, Tom thanked them enthusiastically for having come, and expressed the wish to see them soon again. At no time was there a trace of that old emotional strain and uncontrolled excitement.

Tom is now visiting a boy who was once a student at The Woods Schools, but who is now living at home and doing satisfactory work in a public school. It was a considerable achievement to obtain the permission of Tom's parents for him to make this visit. He is having a very happy time, and, to all appearances, our experiment in letting him pay the visit is proving a success.

Our work now is to continue cautiously to expose Tom to outside influences, and to enrich his curriculum to the fullest extent. Our hope by so doing is some day to impress upon his parents the fact that their boy is able to take his place in the world, however small that place may be. We believe that Tom will continue to progress, but we are still faced with a serious task in parental education, which must be accomplished successfully before we can consider that Tom's problems have been fully met.

The case of Tom is given not only because of its intrinsic interest and its indication of the care and patience necessary in working with individual children, but also because it illustrates the fact that most of what we know about so-called "normal children" derives from experience with youngsters who deviate markedly from the assumed norm and therefore require, more obviously than those who are average or normal, the kind of understanding needed for all children.

## A Complex Process

All the recent investigations into the nature and needs of youth reveal the complexity of the process of growing up and the need for adults, whether teachers, parents, or others, to recognize it as such, at the same time not showing such great concern as to transfer the adult's worry and feeling of insecurity to the boy or girl. Says Zachry:

> The young person's task in growing up is to master, as constructively as he can, his personal fate in his world. He can be helped in any real sense, therefore, only by those, whether in school or elsewhere, who understand his nature and the demands of society. They hold his personality in such respect that they refrain from attempting to instill in him specific personality traits or to impose upon him some plan for growth they have evolved for him.[5]

And Dr. Lois Meek, reporting for a committee of the Commission on Reorganizing Secondary Education, emphasizes social relations as significant for emotional development:

> The members of the Committee have been convinced by their study that for many boys and girls their development in relation to people is thwarted and their resulting emotional tensions are expressed in fears, hatred, and compulsive behavior toward society. We have only to examine the early life histories reported in case studies of school failures, of juvenile delinquents, and of unhappy and antagonistic men and women to realize the important part the development of social relations during puberty and adolescence plays in determining the kind of human beings who make up our society.[6]

The intermingling of the physical with the emotional, and the difficulty of tracing back into the beginnings of emotional disturbance unless all types of motivation are taken into account, is illustrated by the case of Jo, as reported in the Adolescent Study:

> Jo is a boy of twelve who has been feeling very much out of the family picture. He is the youngest child. His sister is soon to be married and his brother has just started to work, but Jo is at an age when he is not particularly interesting to any member of the family. He has been doing only fairly well in his school work and he has definitely neglected his arithmetic.
>
> One morning he went down to breakfast and ate rather heartily: he had oatmeal with cream, eggs, bacon, jam, and milk; and while he was eating he recalled that he was going to have an arithmetic test that morning. He had a queer, twitchy feeling of excitement in his stomach at the thought of the arithmetic test. He started walking slowly to school, thinking more about the

---

[5] Caroline Zachry, *Emotion and Conduct in Adolescence.* New York: D. Appleton-Century Company, 1940. P. 24.

[6] Lois Meek and others, *The Personal-Social Development of Boys and Girls.* New York: Progressive Education Association, 1940. P. 11.

test, and his stomach felt queerer and the oatmeal weighed very heavily on it. He had a vague feeling, which was hardly a thought, that if his breakfast were to come up he wouldn't have to go to school, and the arithmetic test came to mind again. Suddenly he found it hard to keep the breakfast down.

Shortly after his arrival at school, it did come up. He was sent home by the principal with a clear conscience to have a day in bed. The principal telephoned his mother, who immediately became concerned. She put Jo to bed in the guest room and made a fuss over him such as he had not experienced since he was quite a small boy. His sister came in and showed him her wedding presents; his brother stopped and had a talk with him before going out in the evening, an event which had not occurred for months; and his father spent the evening reading to him.

This upset stomach had a high value: no arithmetic test, and solicitude from all the people from whom he had been wishing attention for some time. The next time Jo was faced with a difficult situation and there was a queer feeling in his stomach, it was no longer necessary to go through all the preliminary steps. Now meals just come up without further consideration on his part.[7]

## Dealing with Individuals

One of the most characteristic features of modern studies of emotional development is the emphasis on the uniqueness of each human personality. Gordon Allport's work on the history of personality begins and ends with the notion that every human being is different—uniquely different. The Adolescent Study found that young people have many things in common, but that each is unique in his development. Moreover, as the unpublished studies by Hellersberg show, it is possible for individuals to deviate so far from what is ordinarily considered normal as to be highly conspicuous among their fellows, and yet to be normal in the sense that their adjustments to others in school and in the community are decidedly satisfactory.

It is findings like these with regard to personality that make much of the conventional testing, particularly of the group sort, so dubious for practical purposes. Most of those who worked as pioneers in mental measurement gradually came to give up the device of ability grouping because it became more and more obvious that homogeneity did not exist, even in the restricted academic areas. Similarly with tests for emotional instability: However useful they may become when they are better developed than at present, in the last analysis human society is made up of individuals who mature at varying rates, who interact with their milieu in a complex variety of ways, and whose individualities cannot be dealt with as if they were static for any time, place, or set of circumstances. Hence Wilma Lloyd's warnings as to the use of group

---

[7] Caroline Zachry, *Emotion and Conduct in Adolescence.* New York: D. Appleton-Century Company, 1940. Pp. 69-70.

measures, except for evaluating group trends, and the insistence of Lloyd, Zachry, and others in the Adolescent Study that "however helpful any one systematic procedure may be as a source of supplementary information, none, nor all together, can take the place of the person-to-person responsiveness of the trained educator in the presence of the student." [8]

## Studies of "Emotional Climate"

What has just been said about the individuality of human beings should not be misunderstood as in any way eliminating the effect of the getting together of human beings. It is in this interaction that behavior, emotional and otherwise, develops. A number of studies have been made of what Laura Zirbes and others have called "emotional climate"—the effect of the impact of human beings upon one another and upon their action as a group.

## The Western Electric study [9]

One of the most striking of these studies was made, not in the field of education, but in factory management. The original study, started in 1929, had to do with the intensity of light in a factory and how varying it affected production. As Goodwin Watson tells the story,

The very first experiment was a disappointment. At four different levels of illumination, output bobbed up and down without direct relation to the intensity of light. In another experiment output rose when lights were increased . . . but did not fall back to the original level again! In another, there were substantial gains by groups working at 24, 46, and 70 foot-candles of illumination, but perversely, the control group, with a constant level of illumination, improved output almost exactly as much! The climax of the series, so disturbing to the engineering mind, came with a series of experiments in which illumination was *decreased*, starting at 10 foot-candles and going down gradually to 3. During this time the efficiency of both the control and the test group *increased!* Two girls who volunteered to go on after other operators protested they could hardly see worked down to 0.06 of a foot-candle, an amount equal to an ordinary moonlit night. They still maintained their efficiency, suffered no eye-strain, and insisted that the work tired them less than did the bright lights! The conclusion was inescapable that some variables, far more powerful than differences in illumination, were at large in these "carefully controlled" experiments.[10]

[8] *Ibid.*, p. 23.

[9] F. J. Roethlisberger, W. J. Dickson, and Harold A. Wright, *Management and the Worker.* Cambridge: Harvard University Press, 1939. (Also summarized by Goodwin Watson, "The Surprising Discovery of Morale," *Progressive Education,* Vol. 19, pp. 33-41, January, 1942.)

[10] Goodwin Watson, "The Surprising Discovery of Morale," *Progressive Education,* Vol. 19, pp. 33-34, January, 1942. By permission of the American Education Fellowship.

The "variables" turned out to be human. After exploring all possible hypotheses, the investigators came to the conclusion that the results of these and other experiments they conducted were due to the freer atmosphere, a more democratic kind of supervision, and the improved emotional conditions ("morale") that came from having a share in an experiment. The investigators found that it was a mistake to think of people as mere producers in the mechanical sense: they were members of groups having certain sentiments, codes, routines, and ways of behaving.

Watson summarizes the findings: [11]

Morale improved when the group participated in planning their conditions of work.

Morale rose when the atmosphere was friendly rather than autocratic.

Variety in work helped morale.

Morale was better when the group developed a team-consciousness.

Group incentives did more for morale than did individual rewards.

Morale was built more easily in groups which enjoyed being together socially than in groups too disparate in age.

Problems in morale were found to arise sometimes from personal emotional experiences quite outside the group being observed.

Other problems arose from clashes of group mores. Groups formed themselves and took on distinctive characters which needed to be understood and respected.

Watson's concluding comment is that "when we in education learn to apply some of these simple but fundamental truths, perhaps we, too, shall be amazed at the release of latent energy in pupils once regarded as dull, lazy, weak, and unsocial."

## The Iowa frustration study

To what extent is it helpful to utilize frustration in learning? Are the emotional results good or bad? What is the net accomplishment?

These were some of the questions involved in a recent study at the University of Iowa of frustration among young children.[12] The subjects of the experiment were 30 nursery-school children ranging from 28 to 61 months of chronological age. As Dr. Stoke describes the procedure,

The first stage of the experiment consisted of bringing each child individually into a room equipped with certain toys which were arranged in a standard

[11] *Ibid.*, p. 41.

[12] Roger Barker, Tamara Dembo, and Kurt Lewin, *Frustration and Regression— An Experiment with Young Children.* University of Iowa Studies in Child Welfare, Vol. XVIII, No. I, University of Iowa Press, Iowa City, 1941. (Summarized and discussed also by Stuart M. Stoke in *Progressive Education,* Vol. 19, pp. 42-45, January, 1942.)

pattern within the room. Each child was allowed to play with the toys in any way he chose for 30 minutes. A careful record was made of all he did and said during this time. From this record, his general level of constructiveness at play could be rated. . . . The scale developed had a range of eight points and each child was rated by three judges. . . .

During the period of free play there had been a temporary wall across one end of the room. At the end of the free play part of the experiment, the toys were arranged as before, but now the temporary wall was removed, disclosing a number of unusual and very attractive toys in the new end of the room. The child was taken into the new part of the room, shown the new toys, and permitted to begin playing with them. As soon as his interest seemed thoroughly aroused, he was taken back to the old part of the room with the comment, "You can play on this side now." The experimenter tried to make this transition as impersonal and unemotional as possible, so as to avoid outbursts of crying or other violent behavior. After the child had been taken back to the old part of the room, a barrier of large-meshed wire was padlocked across the room. The result was that the child could see, but could not reach, the more attractive toys in the new end of the room. Here was frustration. The child was compelled to remain in a situation where he was unable to escape the visible reminder of unsatisfied wishes, as well as being unable to satisfy his desire.[13]

The results show an actual loss of functional ability on the part of most of the children, sufficient to cause Dr. Stoke in reviewing the findings to say that "it is evident that frustration can be a most serious impediment to the progress of a group of children." There was also a marked increase of divided attention, and the children were not able to pursue a unit or episode of play as long under frustration as under conditions of free play. Unhappy behavior occurred eight times as frequently during frustration as during free play, and took twelve times as much time. There was an increase in motor restlessness and tenseness. There was also an increase in aggressive behavior, such as knocking, kicking, breaking, and destroying.

In applying the findings of the study to education, Dr. Stoke points out that "perhaps the most frequent cause of frustration in schools is the requirement of a common performance by all pupils, whether they are capable of it or not." Another common cause of frustration, he says, lies in the area of social and play activities:

The child who is rejected by his fellows, or who is unable to compete successfully in the group of which he is a member, or who is of a different level of maturity from his classmates, may feel extremely frustrated in his efforts to establish normal and satisfactory relationships.

The suggestion is made that while it may not always be possible to remove frustrations in this area, they can in many instances be

---

[13] Stuart M. Stoke, "What are the Effects of Frustration on Children?" *Progressive Education*, Vol. 19, pp. 42-43, January, 1942. By permission of Progressive Education Association.

reduced; and that some teacher should offer guidance for the removal or the reduction of the barriers between him and his social goals, or, if they cannot be removed, assist the child to find other outlets as substitutes.

## A study of teacher-pupil relationships

Dr. Bernice Baxter's study of interactions of personalities in the classroom [14] included six teachers, who were described as follows:

Teacher One was dramatic and playful with children, ingenious in utilizing opportunities for teaching, interested in children as persons, optimistic and constructive in comments and manner, original and different in conversation, but was definite and businesslike in exacting pupil accomplishment after she had planned with them as to what they were to do. This teacher was courteous and kindly in her dealing with children. The children were considerate of one another and appreciative of one another's accomplishments. They worked concentratedly and with apparent interest under the careful guidance of the teacher.

Teacher Two was a quietly enthusiastic teacher, who possessed an evident sense of humor and was free from inhibiting restraints. She, too, was conversational, and friendly in tone and manner but was more interested in having pupils direct their own conduct than conform to her plans for them. This teacher was able to guide many simultaneous activities with poise and without evidence of strain. She was particularly interested in the out-of-school life of her pupils and possessed insight into children's emotional and physical needs. There was a naturalness about the pupils in this room. Their standards of conduct and accomplishment were self-imposed, that is, they with the teacher had set up their own goals and assumed joint responsibility for results. They, like the teacher, were free and uninhibited in expressing their own opinions.

Teacher Three showed an eagerness to be kind and helpful to her pupils. She was lacking, however, in her ability to evaluate pupils' efforts and was easily distracted from what she started to do. The pupils in her room took advantage of her confusion and did not conform to her requests. Her bewilderment stirred her pupils to noisy, erratic conduct, and in turn their disorder seemed to distract her to complete loss of control. She resorted to threats and then to cajoling but to no avail. Lesson periods became for the most part veritable riots.

Teacher Four was kind and thoughtful in her relations with her pupils. She lacked spontaneity and enthusiasm and thought that children should learn to work hard. Her pupils were orderly, submissive, and restrained, reflecting the teacher's seriousness of purpose. This teacher recognized abilities and limitations and adjusted her instruction to meet individual needs, but her entire program was teacher-directed. Children in this room responded apathetically and with hesitation.

Teacher Five was dominating and imposing, entirely oblivious of pupil initiative and resourcefulness. Her voice was loud and harsh and her manner aggressive. Pupils in this teacher's room were industrious and hardworking but showed little self-direction. The teacher's expressed aim was to have children learn. She was proud of her pupils' accomplishment as were they. The pupils,

---

[14] From Bernice Baxter, *Teacher-Pupil Relationships*, pp. 25-27. By permission of The Macmillan Company, publishers.

like the teacher, were boisterous and harsh but not unfriendly to each other. Each applied himself with obvious effort to tasks assigned by the teacher.

Teacher Six was habitually quiet, poised, and courteous in her relations with pupils. She possessed a self-restraint in permitting to children freedom of movement and speech and was more interested in thoughtful responses from children than in perfect routine. She was keenly alert to the needs of the children and knew the limitations and capabilities of each. The children in this room were self-directed, knew where to find materials, and evidenced the same thoroughness and quiet persistence in working which characterized the teacher.

Dr. Baxter found a direct relationship between teacher behavior and child behavior. "The six teachers tended to stimulate pupils to the same kind of behavior which they exhibited." Tenseness on the part of one teacher begot tenseness in the children she taught. The relaxed and unhurried manner of another teacher was duplicated in the ease and calmness with which children in her room went to work. The care and painstaking attitude of a third teacher was characteristic of her pupils, even though these pupils were but seven and eight years old. A fourth teacher who worked with driving intensity stirred children to the same blind application as that with which she worked.[15]

## The Locust Point surveys

In some respects the two studies made at Locust Point, a section of Baltimore, Maryland, under the Phipps Psychiatric Clinic of Johns Hopkins University [16] are more illuminating than any others that have been made. In this case the same groups were studied, first, as children in 1914, and later as adults in 1931. The 1914 survey revealed 166 children out of a total of 1502 as seriously substandard in mentality and emotional stability, and destined, in the judgment of the investigators, to be pronounced social liabilities —dependent economically, socially unadapted, and likely to contribute to delinquency, prostitution, and crime. The 1931 study, locating most of the same individuals as adults, found that they had not contributed in anything like the anticipated amount to the prophesied forms of social inadequacy. On the contrary, three-fourths of them were self-supporting, even in a period of financial depression, and nearly all had made satisfactory adjustments in the community.

The investigators who made the follow-up study attributed the

---

[15] Baxter, *op. cit.*, pp. 28-29.

[16] Reported in *Mental Hygiene*, Vol. 1, p. 96, January, 1917, and *Mental Hygiene*, Vol. 17, p. 177, April, 1933. Also summarized by Elise H. Martens in *School Life*, Vol. 16, p. 25, October, 1932, and in W. Carson Ryan, *Mental Health Through Education* (New York: The Commonwealth Fund, 1938), pp. 16-21.

good results from unpromising human material to more directly applicable educational provision resulting from the study, but most of all to the influence of teachers who had been selected specially for their sympathetic and understanding attitudes toward children. "The most striking result of this survey," Dr. Ruth Fairbank said in her final report, "is to be found in the lasting impression made on these people by one of the teachers who came in closest contact with them."

## Studying Children's Emotions

Especially important for better understanding of the emotional life is the recent emphasis on study of individual children. In a recent bulletin in the Teachers College, Columbia University, series on "Practical Suggestions for Teaching," Dr. Gertrude Driscoll lists *clues for determining emotional development*. Pointing out that teachers in the elementary schoool have "unparalleled opportunities to study human behavior," in the classroom, on the playground, and through out-of-school activities, Dr. Driscoll says:

The emotional response of preschool children is characterized by an "all-or-none" reaction. Their joy is extravagant and uncontrolled; their anger is violently expressed. In the primary grades children have begun to experience happiness and contentment as well as joy. They give expression to irritability and annoyance more frequently than to violent anger. They may become sober or silent rather than dejected in their sadness. Changes from one mood to another are less sudden, and the dominant mood is sustained for a longer period of time. Children who come to school happy and contented are able to maintain the mood for a relatively long time even when faced with adverse conditions.

Children in the elementary school seldom express violent anger, though forceful indignation may be shown. The child who loses control in anger and resorts to the more primitive tantrum is usually regarded with distrust by the other children. Unfortunately, exuberance is regarded also with some distrust, as our cultural *mores* frown upon expression of intense emotion. This produces a leveling of emotional expression. Many persons believe that a process of socialization of emotions in which only bland expression of feeling is tolerated is unfortunate. Control of emotions is required in a social world, but it should not be gained at the expense of warm emotional response.[17]

Some of the questions suggested in Dr. Driscoll's analysis are:

1. Are there children in your class who have difficulty in controlling their emotional responses?
2. Do some children resort to tantrums at home but exercise control in school?
3. Are some children regarded askance by their classmates be-

[17] Gertrude Driscoll, *How to Study the Behavior of Children*. New York: Bureau of Publications of Teachers College, Columbia University, 1941. Pp. 44-45.

cause they express emotion vigorously? Have you found a legitimate avenue of expression for these responses?

4. Are there some children whose moods fluctuate during the day?

In all such studies as Dr. Driscoll and others propose there is the basic assumption that exploration into children's needs is highly important. Dr. Lawrence K. Frank says that "probably the most general statement we can make about the child's needs is that he should be protected from distortions, from unnecessary deprivatives and exploitations by adults, parents, teachers and nurses, physicians, psychologists and others dealing with children." He insists, therefore, upon the "primary and inalienable" need of the child to be accepted by adults as a unique individual. He says further:

The little child is frequently disturbed physiologically by emotional reactions, such as anger, rage, and grief, which clamor for expression or release in overt behavior. In a very real sense these physiological disturbances or upheavals seize control of the child and often impel him to act violently and destructively against things and people and even himself. One of the most important of life tasks for the young child is to learn how to manage these emotional reactions and thereby to free himself from this overwhelming experience. It is difficult for adults to conceive or to understand the panic that these emotional reactions may arouse in the child, who finds himself helplessly carried on a tide of feeling so strong that he cannot resist it unaided. If at the same time he meets with a violent response from adults, who strike him or forcibly restrain him, the emotional disturbance may be aggravated cumulatively until terminated by exhaustion. Such an experience teaches the child nothing constructive or helpful, and it may make him so afraid of himself that he begins to be anxious about this behavior and less and less prepared to meet the next provocation. Although the adult may forcibly control the child at the moment, what the child needs is help in controlling the emotional disturbance himself, so that, instead of a persistent conflict within the child between himself and his emotions he can bring these emotional reactions into the pattern of his own living.[18]

Study of the emotions is particularly significant for those students of educational psychology who, while eager to apply whatever they can in the everyday task of teaching, also feel that it is important to look beyond the immediate present and think of understanding human nature as the great requirement of this age. As Henry A. Murray, of the Harvard Psychological Clinic, puts it:

To study human nature patiently, to arrive at understanding, to gain some mastery; there would be little hope in the enterprise if it were not for the history of science, the steady, unassertive, conquering pace of disinterested observation, experiment and reflection. Three centuries ago did the fancy of the most imagi-

18 Lawrence K. Frank, "The Fundamental Needs of the Child," *Mental Hygiene,* Vol. XXII, No. 3, July, 1938, pp. 362-363.

native men foresee the miracles of thought and technics that would mark the way of science? Absorbing this tradition, man may now explore his soul and observe the conduct of his fellows, dispassionate to the limit, yet ever animated by the faith that gaining mastery through knowledge he may eventually surmount himself.[19]

## QUESTIONS AND EXERCISES FOR DISCUSSION AND STUDY

1. If the ideas set forth about "emotions" in this chapter are different from those to which you are accustomed, indicate in what respect they differ.

2. Do you consider yourself "emotional"? Is it bad to be "emotional"? Do you think of some of your associates—members of your family, teachers, school and college friends—as more "emotional" than others, and, if so, are they better or worse off for it?

3. Alfred Binet wrote an article on the importance of the emotions just before his death, but his name is known in American education for something else. What is it?

4. Reread carefully the quotation from Sidney L. Gulick on page 321, and then discuss what he says in the light of your own school, home, and church experience.

5. How would you answer the questions about emotion and school life attributed to Dr. Daniel A. Prescott? (page 322.)

6. Do you think the solution worked out for Tom (page 323) was the right one? What kind of a grown-up do you think Tom will make?

7. Could you cite any cases in your own experience like that of Jo in the Adolescent Study? (page 325.)

8. What do you understand by "emotional climate"? Describe the emotional climate of school and college classrooms you have known.

9. What changes, if any, would take place in schools as you know them if the findings of the following studies were put into effect: Western Electric study (page 327); Iowa frustration study (page 328); Dr. Baxter's study of teacher-pupil relationships (page 330); the Locust Point surveys (page 331).

10. Do Dr. Gertrude Driscoll's suggestions for studying the emotional life of children (page 332) seem to you to have any practical bearing on the everyday work of teaching?

## SELECTED REFERENCES FOR FURTHER READING AND STUDY

Aldrich, Charles A., and Mary M. Aldrich, *Babies Are Human Beings*. New York: The Macmillan Company, 1938.

*American Journal of Orthopsychiatry*. Quarterly. American Orthopsychiatric Association, 25 West 54 St., New York.

Baxter, Bernice, *Teacher-Pupil Relationships*. New York: The Macmillan Company, 1941.

Blos, Peter, *The Adolescent Personality*. New York: D. Appleton-Century Company, 1941.

---

[19] Henry A. Murray, *Explorations in Personality*. New York: Oxford University Press, 1938. P. 35.

Cattell, Raymond B., *General Psychology*. Cambridge, Mass.: Sci-Art Publishers, 1941.

*Child Development*. Quarterly. Society for Research in Child Development, National Research Council, Washington, D. C.

*Child Research Clinic Series*. The Woods School, Langhorne, Pa.

*Child Study*. Quarterly. Child Study Association of America, 221 West 57 St., New York.

Dimock, Hedley S., *Rediscovering the Adolescent*. New York: Association Press, 1937.

Driscoll, Gertrude, *How to Study Children*. New York: Teachers College, Columbia University, 1941.

Dunbar, Helen Flanders, *Emotions and Bodily Changes*, 2nd ed. New York: Columbia University Press, 1938.

*Education for Family Life*. Nineteenth Yearbook of the American Association of School Administrators. Washington, D. C.: National Education Association, 1941.

Folsom, Joseph K., *Youth, Family, and Education*. Washington, D. C.: American Council on Education, 1941.

Goodykuntz, Bess, Beulah I. Coon, and others, *Family Living and Our Schools*. New York: D. Appleton-Century Company, 1941. (Joint yearbook of the Society for Curriculum Study and the Department of Home Economics of the National Education Association.)

Healy, William, *Personality in Formation and Action*. New York: W. W. Norton and Company, 1938.

Husband, Richard W., *General Psychology*. New York: Farrar and Rinehart, 1940.

Kanner, Leo, *Child Psychiatry*. Springfield, Ill.: Charles C. Thomas, 1935.

Keliher, Alice, *Life and Growth*. New York: D. Appleton-Century Company, 1938.

Lund, Frederick L., *Emotions, Their Psychological, Physiological and Educative Implications*. New York: Ronald Press, 1939.

Meek, Lois Hayden, Chairman, *The Personal-Social Development of Boys and Girls*. New York: Progressive Education Association, 1940.

Murray, Henry A., *Explorations in Personality*. New York: Oxford University Press, 1938.

Plant, James S., *Personality and the Culture Pattern*. New York: Commonwealth Fund, 1937.

Prescott, Daniel A., *Emotion and the Educative Process*. Washington, D. C.: American Council on Education, 1938.

*Progressive Education*. Monthly. American Education Fellowship (formerly Progressive Education Association), New York.

Richmond, Winifred V., *Personality, Its Study and Hygiene*. New York: Farrar and Rinehart, 1937.

Rivlin, Harry N., *Educating for Adjustment*. New York: D. Appleton-Century Company, 1936.

Ryan, W. Carson, *Mental Health Through Education*. New York: Commonwealth Fund, 1938.

Shaffer, Lawrence F., *The Psychology of Adjustment*. Boston: Houghton Mifflin Company, 1936.

Tryon, Caroline McCann, *Evaluations of Adolescent Personality by Adolescents*. Washington, D. C.: Society for Research in Child Development, 1939.

*Understanding the Child.* Quarterly. National Committee for Mental Hygiene, New York.

Young, Paul Thomas, *Emotion in Man and Animal.* New York: John Wiley and Sons, 1943.

——————, *The Psychology of Emotion.* New York: John Wiley and Sons, 1942.

Zachry, Caroline B., *Emotion and Conduct in Adolescence.* New York: D. Appleton-Century Company, 1940.

# CHAPTER 17

# Social Adjustment and Conduct Disorders

In the preceding chapter, attention was centered on the emotions as of fundamental concern in a well-ordered, well-adjusted plan of human living. This positive and constructive view of emotional development is of special importance to teachers and other educational workers. It reflects the optimism that many present-day students of personality feel with regard to the possibilities as contrasted with the weaknesses and abnormalities of human beings. "Almost for the first time," says George D. Stoddard, director for many years of the Child Welfare Station at the University of Iowa, "science is reaffirming old principles of social behavior, of friendliness and a regard for others." [1]

It is necessary, however, to examine some of the evidences of maladjustment in cases where, for one cause or another or for a variety of causes, human beings—and specifically children and youth of school age—have failed to make even a reasonably successful emotional and social adjustment. Indeed, much of what is now known and understood with regard to so-called "normal" children and youth has come from scientific study of those who deviate sufficiently from the norm to constitute problems for society.

### Findings of the American Youth Commission

Recent studies of children and youth attribute to emotional difficulties some of the most serious social conflicts of our day. "The tragedies associated with mental ill health are shown most vividly in connection with the increasing number of persons admitted to mental institutions, of whom a considerable proportion are young people," says the report of the American Youth Commission.[2] The same research agency finds delinquency and crime likewise trace-

---

[1] George D. Stoddard, "Pupils Are Persons," *Progressive Education,* Vol. 22, p. 413, December, 1941.

[2] American Youth Commission, *Youth and the Future.* Washington, D. C.: American Council on Education, 1942. P. 111.

able in large part to imperfect adjustments of our complex society in which emotional relationships play a significant role:

> Faulty home life often generates a rebellious attitude toward authority that eventually leads a youth into open infraction of the law. . . . Strained emotional relations between parents may rob the youth of the sense of security he requires and cause him to seek recognition among his contemporaries by conspicuous behavior involving some breach of social customs or codes of law.[3]

There is ample evidence, as the American Youth Commission further asserts, that schools are sometimes a direct and important factor in producing delinquents. This may come about through misunderstanding of the capacities of young persons, or because relations among pupils, teachers, and administrators are such as to "promote the growth of frustrations, grudges, and antagonisms."

### Fears

Back of many of the conflict situations of children and youth, modern students of personality find, is the element of *fear*—fear that is often the result of experiences in early childhood. Cases of the most aggravated aggressiveness are sometimes revealed as desperate efforts to compensate for deep-seated timidity and fear. In reporting one particularly interesting case of this type to the 1940 meeting of the American Psychoanalytic Association—that of a 20-year-old college student who suffered an acute breakdown during his first semester—Dr. Robert P. Knight made the following comment:

> Psychoanalysts have long been aware that an individual who feels driven to intimidate and frighten others is defending himself against intense anxiety and insecurity. They have found that such a person has a powerful need for affection which he cannot let himself admit. However, his aggressive attitude constantly frustrates in reality his needs for love, he becomes progressively more insecure and anxious as he provokes hostile responses from his fellows, and he finds himself in a vicious circle gradually growing more intense. The task in the analysis of such a patient is to uncover the fears which drive him to intimidation techniques and then analyze these fears and insecurities. When this is done the strong needs for love become conscious and can gradually be accepted by the patient as he finds satisfaction of these needs in his interpersonal relationships.[4]

One of the most important questions that students of personality have to answer, as Lawrence K. Frank has shown, is whether hostility and aggression are inborn characteristics or whether they are the reactions of individuals who, as infants and preschool chil-

---

[3] *Op. cit.*, p. 196.

[4] Robert P. Knight, "Intimidation of Others as a Defense Against Anxiety," *Bulletin of the Menninger Clinic* (Topeka, Kansas), Vol. 6, pp. 4-14, January, 1942.

dren, were deprived of needed affection and security and so were driven by the "unrelieved pressure of socialization" to hostile, aggressive, destructive conduct. This question is clearly of the utmost importance educationally—"the answer involves the future of our society and of the civilized world":

If man is innately hostile and aggressive, prone to destructive antagonisms and rivalries, then the prospects for a better, more humanly desirable society are not very bright. If human nature, as theological tradition and many of our contemporary students of personality tell us, is born wicked, sinful, and hostile, and must be forced to be social, cooperative, and altruistic, the task of education is essentially a coercive one, that of curbing the hostility, of teaching individuals to "handle their aggressiveness." If, on the other hand, human nature is essentially plastic, subject to educational direction toward friendliness, cooperativeness, gentleness, and genuine group or social activity, then the task of education is to prevent the early distortions and unnecessary deprivations that arouse resentment and aggressiveness, by providing as much affectionate reassurance and toleration of individual, temperamental differences as possible for the children who have been ill treated or neglected by their parents.[5]

Fear, and the resentment or hostility that it often generates, constitute, in the judgment of Frank and other writers of our day, major emotional drives that lead to much unsocial and antisocial behavior:

The traditional manner of teaching, by calling the child bad or wicked when it is the behavior that should be defined as undesirable, makes the child fearful, guilty, and unhappy, and, if continued, may establish a persistent feeling of guilt and inadequacy and of being rejected. To assuage that feeling of guilt and to overcome the sense of inadequacy and rejection, the child may commit more antisocial or forbidden acts to get the punishment he needs for his guilty feelings or to prove that he is not worthless.[6]

And Dr. Frank calls attention to the fact that Healy and Bronner have shown [7] that the delinquent generally has had an unhappy childhood, characterized by feelings of rejection, inadequacy, and guilt, and by lack of affection.

Recognition of social or environmental factors as of special significance in the study of children's behavior is comparatively recent. In a review of the literature, Dr. Ruth Pearson Koshuk [8] notes three stages—social influences were at first ignored or discounted, then they were recognized but deplored, and lately they

---

[5] Lawrence K. Frank, "The Fundamental Needs of the Child," *Mental Hygiene,* Vol. 22, p. 372, July, 1938.

[6] *Op. cit.,* pp. 375-376.

[7] William Healy and Augusta Bronner, *New Light on Delinquency.* New Haven, Conn.: Yale University Press, 1936.

[8] Ruth Pearson Koshuk, "Social Influences Affecting the Behavior of Young Children," *Monographs of the Society for Research in Child Development* (Washington, D. C.), Vol. VI, Serial No. 28, No. 2, 1941.

have been looked upon as highly important. Sociologists have been partly responsible for drawing the attention of psychologists and educators to the need for research on the social side. Returns from a canvass of representative sociologists in 1935 brought out the following as subjects for needed research in child development: conditioning factors in home life; the extent to which the expectancy of others affects the interests and actions of children; development of in-group consciousness, leadership tendencies, and psychopathic trends; differences of development in various racial and economic groups.[9]

### Types of Studies

Reference has been made in the preceding chapter to the prominent part played by case studies in modern research dealing with children and youth. With the increase in the number of child guidance clinics since 1909, Dr. Koshuk points out, "A growing body of data has been amassed concerning the adjustment of particular children and particular environments." Still more recently, and especially within the past four or five years, reports of "longitudinal" studies have appeared covering the same individual or group of individuals over a period of years.[10] Illustrative of this method are the studies by Jean Macfarlane at the University of California on family influences on children's personality development, child guidance, and the relation of environmental pressure to the development of the child's habit patternings. These studies are considered important for the light they throw on parent relationships and marital adjustment in their effects on children. William E. Blatz and associates have made continuing studies of the Dionne Quintuplets in which personality differences are increasingly apparent, "in spite of presumably identical heredity and an environment as standardized as is humanly possible."

Indirect or "projective" methods of personality study, intended to explore more extensively than has hitherto been possible the child's inner life, have come into wide use recently. They range from "Rorschach ink blots to artistic production and creative and

---

[9] M. Smith, "Suggestions of Sociological Research in Child Development," *Journal of Educational Sociology*, Vol. 9, pp. 105-110, 1935. (Cited in Koshuk, *op. cit.*, pp. 8 and 68.)

[10] The "Harvard Growth Study," begun in the fall of 1922, had as its predecessors a study by H. P. Bowditch of the Harvard Medical School, 1872 (the measurement of 12 males and 12 females over a period of 25 years), and a "longitudinal" study by W. T. Porter, also of the Harvard Medical School, 1910 to 1920— "as against the cross-section method in vogue." See Koshuk, *op. cit.*, pp. 46-48, for a summary of the later "longitudinal" studies.

cathartic play." [11] Dr. Lois Barclay Murphy characterizes this type of study as indicative of a new trend in psychology that has significant possibilities for the future. She says:

> The work of Freud, Jung, Lewin, Stern, Piaget, Rorschach, and others will, one hundred years from now, be recognized as basic in the growth of a tradition concerned essentially with dynamic functioning of personality in relation to its environment.[12]

Some authorities consider it necessary to caution against too great reliance upon what they refer to as the "psychologic or psychoanalytic interpretation of behavior disorders in children." Thus, Louis A. Lurie, director of the Child Guidance Home, Cincinnati, Ohio, while admitting that "suppressions, frustrations, rejections, identifications, feelings of hostility, feelings of inferiority and inadequacy and the like" are potent and frequent factors in the causation of abnormal behavior, and that great profit has accrued from this psychologic approach to the study of human behavior, nevertheless insists that attention needs to be paid to other reactions as well—such as somatic, endocrine, and neurologic conditions.[13] In Lurie's view the "environmentalist," with his social approach to the problem child, was the first to supplant the "organicist," and now he in turn is being supplanted by the psychologist and the psychoanalyst. What Dr. Lurie argues for is a comprehensive viewpoint and technique on the part of all concerned with child guidance:

> The successful child guider is he who understands that the total integrated personality is a composite of the totality of the individual . . . plus the totality of the environmental situation. In other words, the molding of the personality is the resultant of the interactions of two dynamic systems, namely, a psychologic organism and a socio-economic physiochemical environment, working conjointly to produce in the child a type of reaction that gives him his distinctive personality. These two dynamic systems are composed of numerous separate component parts, each of which is capable of changing or modifying the personality. It is hardly necessary to point out the effect of climate, geographic location, economic status, and many other environmental factors on the personality. Likewise, every physician is acquainted with the devastating effects of such diseases as encephalitis on the personality make-up. Furthermore, the work of Stockard, Kretschmer, and others has demonstrated that certain patterns of abnormal behavior may conform with certain types of physical structure or constitution. Similarly, the

---

[11] Koshuk, *op. cit.*, p. 17.

[12] Lois Barclay Murphy, "Shall the Rorschach Method Be Standardized?" *American Journal of Orthopsychiatry*, Vol. 9, pp. 526-527, 1939. (Cited in Koshuk, *op. cit.*, p. 17.)

[13] Louis A. Lurie, "Endocrinology and the Understanding and Treatment of the Exceptional Child," *Journal of the American Medical Association*, Vol. 110, pp. 1531-1536, May 7, 1938. (Reprinted in *Proceedings of the Fourth Institute on the Exceptional Child* [Langhorne, Pa.: Child Research Clinic of the Woods Schools, October, 1937], pp. 6-19.)

endocrine glands have their part in the determination of the pattern types of behavior.[14]

Of the cases of behavior disorder studied in the Child Guidance Home of Cincinnati, 49 per cent were found to be endogenous, or psychophysical in origin. In only 23 per cent of the cases were the causes exogenous, or environmental. In the remaining 28 per cent both endogenous and exogenous factors were responsible for the behavior difficulties. "Furthermore, in approximately 75 per cent of the cases in the endogenous group the causes were organic." Lurie found endocrine disturbances present in approximately 20 per cent of his cases, and in 10 per cent the glandular disturbances were the principal causes of the difficult behavior.

## The Family and Maladjustment

Those who seek for the causes of maladjustment in environmental conditions put the family ahead of everything else in importance. "It has become clear to me," says Dr. William Healy, "that the two most serious threats to satisfactory personality development, at least in early years, lie in parentage and sexual problems." And he adds:

I could fill volumes with case histories bearing on this central theme of the personality changes which derive from the emotional traumata that some children suffer when they are brought face to face with problems of their parentage. There would be many variations of the problems and the settings, and the child's reactions thereto. These latter would be conditioned, of course, by many other things, but they would all point to the same conclusion, namely, that striking changes in personality may result from upsetting emotional experiences.[15]

Exploring into the outcomes of treatment of problem children in the child guidance clinics, Dr. Helen Witmer and her students at the Smith College School for Social Work found no constant factors in therapy except those involved in family relationship:

When the "emotional tone" of the home was harmonious, failure occurred in only a few cases. Degree of marital adjustment showed an even closer relation to treatment outcome, while in the behavior of the parents toward the patients was found a surprisingly clear index to the probable therapeutic results of treatment. Cases in which the parents, particularly the mother, overtly rejected or, in an unharmonious home atmosphere, greatly over-protected the child, made up the bulk of the unsuccessfully adjusted cases.[16]

[14] Louis A. Lurie, in the *Journal of the American Medical Association, op. cit.*

[15] William Healy, *Personality in Formation and Action.* New York: W. W. Norton and Company, 1938, p. 119.

[16] Helen Witmer, "The Outcome of Treatment in a Child Guidance Clinic: A Comparison and an Evaluation," *Smith College Studies in Social Work,* June, 1933, p. 371.

And summing up the various attempts on the part of psychologists to analyze the course of personality development and chart its path, Winifred Richmond says: "However they may differ in regard to theories or explanations, they are all in agreement concerning the importance for future development of the interplay of psychological forces within the family during the child's earliest years." [17]

Neurotic personality in the case of a man of 42 described by Dr. Franz Alexander was cleared up when the early family situation was revealed. Analysis showed a common emotional situation:

In his youth as a middle child between an elder brother and a younger sister, the patient had developed a strong envy toward both the younger sister and the elder brother. The younger sister had all the advantages of the smallest in the family. When she was born, she took away from him all the privileges of the little child, the parents' attention and special care, and all the satisfactions of the receptive claims of a child. His elder brother, on the other hand, had all the privileges of the eldest. Thus the patient had neither the advantages of the baby nor the privileges of the eldest. The result was a strong, competitive, hostile attitude toward his brother, which became the basis for his severe sense of guilt toward him.[18]

What sometimes happens when maternal care is interrupted at too early an age and there is no real or substitute family relation to nourish the child's personality is indicated in a case reported by Dr. Lauretta Bender at the Second Institute on the Exceptional Child:

There is in the Children's Ward of the Bellevue Psychopathic Hospital at the present time a girl of eleven named Molly who presents this type of behavior problem. She was the youngest of six children. When she was six months old her mother suffered from a temporary psychotic episode for which she was committed to a state hospital for several months. Molly spent some time in several baby hospitals as a feeding problem, and on account of mild infantile illnesses. She was placed in various boarding homes, each for a short period. When the mother returned home it was felt best for her not to attempt to care for Molly, although the rest of the children returned and have not presented any special social problems at any time. Molly's history has been a long sequence of maladjustments to boarding homes. She not only did not develop any attachment to any of the boarding mothers, but left each with a growing sense of bitterness because no one loved her or cared for her. She has gradually become guilty of every form of unfavorable and antisocial behavior, and has failed to adjust in model council homes, schools, and even in disciplinary institutions that usually take girls older than Molly. At the present time she has been returned to our ward for the second time because of her noisy, over-active, abusive, aggressive behavior, and her inability to adapt to any social

---

[17] Winifred Richmond, "The Exceptional Child and the Family Constellation," *Child Research Clinic Series*. Langhorne, Pa.: Woods Schools. Vol. II, No. 5, pp. 5-6.
[18] Franz Alexander, "Meeting Emotional Depression," *Hygeia*, March, 1933, p. 218.

situation. She openly expresses her hatred for everyone, and makes herself disliked, at the same time that she demands love and complains bitterly of the lack of it. She is physically and verbally abusive to everyone, yet constantly grumbles at the lack of sympathy toward her. She is unable to accomplish anything in her school work, because she cannot apply herself in spite of good intelligence, and accuses her teachers of not teaching her. She destroys her clothes with incomprehensible success and laments that no one gives her clothes. She is not only aggressive in her relationship to others, but is constantly destroying whatever of her own she herself values.[19]

Even when there is no such extreme situation as that of the case just described, adults frequently complicate the social adjustment of children and young people, especially, as Dr. James S. Plant points out, by failure to realize that symbols used by adults have no real meaning to the child.[20] Dr. Plant cites as a simple example in every home the word *hurry*. "The parent says 'hurry,' and is exasperated over the child's continued dawdling, and amazed when the child says 'I *am* hurrying.' " Even more tragic is the situation in education, where, Dr. Plant says, "each year we are learning more clearly what a large fraction of our reading and arithmetic troubles arise out of our giving these things to children before they are 'ready' for them."

In the difficulties of adjustment that come through premature use of generalizations and symbols, Dr. Plant and other authorities have thought they saw one of the most serious tendencies in modern life—the tendency to substitute symbol for reality:

Is my experience unique if I see most adults mistaking money for what it symbolizes? Or street address or make of automobile for happiness or success? Or grades or marks for education? A word-centered culture has certain advantages—certainly it clothes life with a gaudy array of intellectual achievements. But where these run ahead of an emotional development, where these go beyond being expressions of and generalizations of our emotional needs and experiences . . . they eat away at life rather than enrich it.

Is there an answer? I don't know, but I should like to suggest the following. I will use the example of literature, although the same could be done in any other subject. The great masterworks are read and (in my clinic experience) something like one in fifty children recognizes that these are expositions of his own life. Done with beauty and solemnity—yes, but still generalizations of life in his family or on his street. Note the difficulty that we have had in getting any appreciable number of people to recognize that the stories of the Old Testament are master pictures of the problems of our own everyday personal relationships. Or take the teaching of civics. The schools in my area are busy with "preparing children for democracy." I observe classes busy as bees

[19] Lauretta Bender, "Emotional Problems in Children," *Proceedings of the Second Institute of the Exceptional Child.* Langhorne, Pa.: Child Research Clinic of the Woods Schools, October, 1935, pp. 52-53.

[20] James S. Plant, "A Psychiatrist Looks at Teacher Education," *Educational Record*, Vol. 22, p. 141, April, 1941.

learning the structure of our government and the responsibilities placed upon the voters, where even so personal a matter as the child's going to the basement (if a person can't decide this for himself, what *can* we expect of him?) is subject to authoritarian rules.[21]

## Work and Maladjustment

How essential it is to have worth-while work to do, and how serious it is when there is no employment, has come out dramatically in many of the studies. Howard Bell in his investigations for the American Youth Commission found the *need for a job* the chief preoccupation of young people.[22] One investigator who studied the disintegrating effect of unemployment found that "some unemployed become as downcast as mental patients and develop a negative or catastrophic outlook on life." [23] Girls as well as boys are affected. "The danger in a group of unemployed youth like this," says R. Fedder in her study of unemployed girls, "is not so much that they will start a revolution, as that they will eventually become community charges":

At first they *do* rebel. Then gradually they adjust to whatever circumstances befall. They disintegrate—stagnate intellectually, emotionally, and morally. A few eventually become adjusted in a job or in marriage; the others go insane, commit suicide, embark on criminal careers, become prostitutes, or drift aimlessly.[24]

One of the special problems revealed in studies of the transition from school to work is that of the stigma that attaches to many types of employment, especially of a manual sort. The "white-collar bias" still has to be reckoned with among youth, parents, and teachers. In Canton, Ohio, for example, according to a recent survey, 53 per cent of the high-school seniors looked forward to entering the professions, whereas the city of Canton had at the time of the survey professional positions for only 5 per cent of its population.[25] Similar findings came out of the North Carolina Youth Study of 1940. Yet, as Dr. Vernon Jones has pointed out, "If youth find an easy, normal transition from school to work, and

---

[21] Plant, *op. cit.,* p. 142.

[22] Howard Bell, *Youth Tell Their Story.* Washington, D. C.: American Council on Education, 1939.

[23] N. Israeli, cited in C. Darl Long, *School-Leaving Youth and Unemployment.* New York: Teachers College, Columbia University, 1941. P. 14. (Contributions to Education, No. 845.)

[24] R. Fedder, "The World Is Laying For You," *Progressive Education,* Vol. 12, 1935, p. 521. See also: "Occupational Adjustment and the School," *Bulletin of the National Association of Secondary School Principals,* November, 1940.

[25] "From School to Work," *Proceedings of the Joint Conference of Educators and Employers of Youth.* Worcester, Mass.: Clark University, 1941.

if they can satisfy through legitimate means their wants for money and what it can buy, then there is less motivation for the development of antisocial attitudes and conduct." [26]

Race discrimination in employment has been recognized as a serious cause of maladjustment. In times of economic depression, particularly, members of minority races and groups find themselves in a peculiarly difficult position, with highly dangerous emotional tensions as a result.

### Schools and Behavior Difficulties

That schools are themselves responsible for maladjustments of a serious nature has been indicated in numerous studies. A classic study is that of E. K. Wickman, who found that teachers (at the period the investigation was made, at least) were disposed to regard as important types of misbehavior those acts of children that were annoying to the peace and quiet of the classroom, and to overlook almost entirely less noticeable aspects of behavior that were far more significant for possible future mental and emotional difficulty.[27]

The whole system of "failures" in schoolwork has been attacked in recent years, not only as interfering with adequate learning, but as having bad effects on personality development. The fact that constant failure is a deterrent, and that children need to be successful, as well as to learn to be realistic with respect to their limitations, has been accepted as a basis for important educational changes recently in many schools. Dr. Wilford M. Aikin, Director of the Commission on the Relation of School and College, which has made one of the most significant investigations of recent years, tells of a boy in one of the high schools he visited who had reached the age of 20 before he became a senior. This boy had failed again and again and repeated course after course. On each repetition the results would be little better than the first, but teachers finally passed him along and he was enrolled as a senior. He had a hang-dog look:

Then one day his English teacher thought he saw possibilities in the boy. The class was reading *Macbeth* preparatory to its presentation before the school. The boy had been given minor parts to read, but he had not read well. The teacher, taking some students into his confidence, suggested that the boy be offered the part of Macbeth. They agreed. The result was an astonishingly

---

[26] *Ibid.*, p. 44.

[27] E. K. Wickman, *Children's Behavior and Teachers' Attitudes.* New York: The Commonwealth Fund, 1928. A pamphlet summary of the main findings of the original report is also available from a later printing (1938).

good performance. The boy's head thereafter was up; the hang-dog expression disappeared; all of his school work improved; and he graduated respected by all and confident of the life of usefulness and honor he has since lived.[28]

That modern schools can and do recognize even the more subtle cases of difficulty is indicated in the case of Janet, as reported by a dean of girls:

I did not hear of Janet until she had been in school a whole semester. She never caused any disturbance that might send her from her class to my office. In fact, she was so very quiet that few people, except her teachers, knew of her presence in school. Fortunately, I received a telephone message one day from her mother, who requested that Janet be told about a change in plans for an appointment after school. As no one in the office seemed able to take care of the message at the time, I went to the classroom to deliver it myself. The class was one in General Education. The teacher of such a class is the counselor for the entire high school period of three years. Before I opened the door, I noticed that a lively discussion was going on at one side of the room. (Miss R. does a splendid job of teaching.) The last two rows of seats were unoccupied except for one girl who sat in the rear with her eyes down close to a book and her head leaning on her hands as if to shut out the noises of the classroom. When I asked the teacher for Janet, this isolated person jumped, dropped her book, and flushed noticeably. I called her outside into the hall and delivered her mother's message. "Oh, is that all? I was scared to death. I've never seen you before," said Janet. Intrigued by the girl's manner, I went back to ask Miss R., the counselor, about her.

"She simply will not mingle with the class and they ignore her. She refuses to contribute to a discussion, so we don't bother her any more. We just let her read. She failed in everything but English the first semester. Her other teachers say that her conduct in class is good but that she contributes nothing. I've been going to speak to you about her but haven't found the time yet. You might like to see the test data in her folder. She is a queer person."

I did indeed desire to see the test data and found to my amazement that she rated *excellent* and *superior* in all factors measured for English Usage, Literature, Music, History, Reading, Comprehension, and Reading Vocabulary. In Science, Spelling, and Contemporary Affairs, she rated *below average*. From her Cumulative Record, I found that her hobby was reading, and that her teachers in Junior High School had marked her *low* in Initiative, Sense of Humor, Ability to Get Along With or to Influence Others, and *high* in Trustworthiness.

This information made me determine to find out from her other teachers what they thought about Janet, so I went the rounds and found them all of Miss R.'s opinion: that the girl needed help but because she had been so quiet in class and had never caused any trouble at all, they could postpone dealing with her problem until time presented itself; nevertheless, they were willing to meet together in a case conference to talk over the possibilities of helping her now. The result of this conference was that, after consideration of the possible implications of her withdrawnness, her counselor, Miss R., was asked to write up all the available facts in the form of a case study. Our school is not provided with a psychiatrist, but we do have available the facilities of the Child Guidance

[28] Wilford M. Aikin, *New York Times Magazine,* September 7, 1941.

Clinic, attached to the State General Hospital. To refer a case we need only present to the head of the clinic the written case study and he will arrange for a conference with the student and her family. In the course of time this was accomplished for Janet, but none too soon, as the first report to the school from the clinic referred to her as a "borderline case of adolescent dementia praecox."

"Do you suppose we discovered the need of help in time?" is the query of all the teachers concerned.

Both Miss R. and I have been called to the clinic in consultation and we have learned from the doctors the amazing and significant facts in the case of Janet. Janet has conferred with the psychiatrist every week, and her mother less frequently, during the past year. We are beginning to note a slight interest on her part in her classmates and teachers and some willingness to enter into class activities, but we are told that the process of helping a sick mind is a very slow one and we must be patient.

After the last more encouraging report from the clinic, Miss R., Janet's counselor, remarked in the case conference, "And to think that we were all willing to set Janet's need aside because she did not annoy us. I'm sure that we have all been impressed with the importance of paying attention to every child's problem and of using the data provided for us through tests and records."

"Amen," said I to myself.[29]

## Resources for Studying Adjustment

Studies of emotional maladjustments and the more serious conduct disorders associated with them may be said to have a double usefulness. They are usually designed in the first place to find out what treatment can be provided to help the individual who is in difficulty. At the same time, however, they are an essential means for learning to understand human conduct in its more usual manifestations and for establishing positive and preventive mental health measures for all—not merely for those who deviate so markedly as to be a problem for society. Just as early efforts to do something for the blind, deaf, and other types of handicapped children in the nineteenth century led to some of our most significant changes in educational philosophy and practice with respect to normal children, so the child guidance clinics and other services of the twentieth century have not only helped those who were sorely in need of aid to better adjustment, but have marked the beginnings of a more thorough understanding of children and youth who more nearly approach the "normal."

### Child guidance clinics

The child guidance clinic began in an attempt to make available in one central place in a given community the resources of modern

---

[29] Ruth H. Anderson, "Leaves From A Counselor's Notebook," *Progressive Education*, Vol. 17, pp. 211-212, March, 1940.

science with respect to the behavior problems of children—particularly of the psychiatrist, the psychologist, and the psychiatric social worker. The functions of the original demonstration clinics established in the 1920's were thus described in one of the early reports of the Commonwealth Fund, the foundation which sponsored the pioneer work in this field:

1. To develop the psychiatric study of difficult, predelinquent, and delinquent children in the schools and the juvenile courts; and to develop sound methods of treatment based on such a study.

2. To develop the work of the visiting teacher whereby the invaluable early contacts which our school systems make possible with every child may be utilized for the understanding and development of the child.

3. To provide courses of training along sound lines for those qualified and desiring to work in the field.

4. To extend by various educational efforts the knowledge and use of these methods.

There are now several hundred child guidance clinics scattered throughout the United States and Canada, though these are as yet by no means sufficiently numerous to reach all children and youth who need help.[30]

Especially useful for schools in early determination and care of behavior difficulties has been the work of the visiting teacher, or school social worker—a qualified social case worker who operates between the home and the school—with or without the complete services of a child guidance clinic.

### The Adolescent Study and the Institute on Personality Development [30a]

One of the research activities of recent years that has been most influential in transferring some of the knowledge and insights with regard to human behavior gained through experience with serious maladjustments over to the practical situations of normal boys and girls is the Study of Adolescents carried out by Dr. Caroline B. Zachry and her associates for the Commission on Secondary School Curriculum of the Progressive Education Association.[31] To the

---

[30] A directory of child guidance clinics and other similar services in the various states can be obtained from the National Committee for Mental Hygiene, New York City. For a summary description of child guidance clinics, visiting teachers, and school psychiatric service, see W. Carson Ryan, *Mental Health Through Education* (New York: Commonwealth Fund, 1938), pp. 190-221.

[30a] This Institute is now called the Institute of Human Development.

[31] Two reports of the Study of Adolescents are: *Emotion and Conduct in Adolescence,* by Caroline B. Zachry, and *The Adolescent Personality,* by Peter Blos, both published by D. Appleton-Century Company, New York, 1940, 1941.

Study of Adolescents was assigned the special task of gathering material for a fuller understanding of adolescent personality and development. Extensive use was made of the case-history approach, and the staff that was drawn upon included educators, psychologists, psychiatrists, physicians, social workers, anthropologists, and specialists in other disciplines. The purpose was to find out as much as possible about ordinary youth in their typical school, community, and family setting.

An important outgrowth of the Study of Adolescents has been the Institute on Personality Development, which began its work in 1939. Seminars are held in New York City during the winter months, and a workshop is maintained as part of the Institute of Euthenics at Vassar College, Poughkeepsie, New York. The following aims are emphasized in the Institute's program:

(a) To gain an understanding of the theoretical assumptions underlying the interpretation of personality.

(b) To develop discrimination between the important and unimportant data and procedures in both reading and recording case histories.

(c) To show the relationship between concepts from various disciplines represented by the professional background of staff and participants; to relate findings of physical examinations to personality development; to coordinate findings and results of psychological and physical examinations with insight into other areas of experience such as speech, reading, social anthropology, social work, home and family relationships, et cetera.

(d) To assist participants in developing skill in interview techniques; to develop the ability to deal directly with guidance problems.

(e) To help participants distinguish between normal phases of development and neurotic problems, and to consider how each of these may be dealt with within the school or agency. To assist guidance workers and teachers in determining when and how a case may be referred to outside experts and how to cooperate with these experts after referral.

(f) To discuss implications of the above for educational procedures, vocational guidance, records, the curriculum, et cetera.[32]

## Division of Child Development and Teacher Personnel

Direct application to the preparation of teachers and other educational workers of research material from all sources has been the task of the Division of Child Development and Teacher Personnel of the Commission on Teacher Education of the American Council on Education. Made possible largely through grants of funds from the General Education Board of the Rockefeller Foundation, the Division has sponsored since 1939 at the University of

---

[32] Bulletin of the Institute on Personality Development of the Progressive Education Association, 1942, pp. 4-5.

Chicago a center of "documentation and collaboration in the study of human growth and development." More than fifty psychologists, college teachers of education, and public school officers and teachers have spent from three to ten months as members of the group of collaborators studying recent research findings and discussing the educational implications of these findings. The group had the benefit of short visits by many of the psychologists and child development specialists who had carried on the research being studied. They also had the opportunity of examining many unpublished research findings, case studies, and the like. It is planned to make these materials available to all institutions and individuals concerned with teacher education. Dr. Daniel A. Prescott has been in charge of this work.

## Group work

In the preparation of social workers, materials gathered in the study of social maladjustment and conduct disorders have long occupied an important place. In recent years one branch of social work has come to be recognized as having a special function in informal education carried on "in relatively small groups possessing a high degree of self-propulsion and direction." This is what is known as "group work," or group education. Originating in the Young Men's Christian Association work of the mid-nineteenth century and carried forward in the settlement movement a generation later, the work now includes a large number of agencies working in behalf of youth—Boys' Clubs, Y. W. C. A.'s, Boy Scouts, Girl Scouts, 4-H clubs, church programs for youth, summer camps, and many others. The Section of Social Group Work of the National Conference of Social Work, which represents these various agencies, went into action for the first time in 1935.

Some of the outcomes claimed for group work that have a direct bearing on the problems of conduct considered in this chapter are:

Personalities otherwise thwarted may find the satisfactions of comradeship, of the sense of belonging and at-homeness in a social group, and of a sense of worth that is yielded by participating in worthy enterprises.

Individuals may be rescued from wretched routine and stimulated to find creative and satisfying expression in a wealth of cultural and creative pursuits.

The threat of a leisure for which we were almost totally unprepared may be turned into a constructive influence in the enrichment of personality and the community.

The individualistic ideals and motives that were the inevitable result of an individualistic culture may be rechanneled into social motives, ideals, and patterns of conduct, as persons participate in enterprises that seek to achieve a larger measure of the good life for themselves and others.[33]

## QUESTIONS AND EXERCISES FOR DISCUSSION AND STUDY

1. Describe any individual—child, youth, or adult—whom you consider to have been definitely "maladjusted." What do you think were the causes of the maladjustment, what happened to him, and what was the outcome? After reading this chapter, would you have any different view of the case than you had before?

2. Find out all you can about the American Youth Commission and its work. What other publications of the Commission (besides the general report referred to on page 337) deal with adjustment problems of young people?

3. Family relationships are mentioned at various points in this chapter as especially important for social adjustment. Does your own experience bear this out or refute it?

4. Do you agree with Lawrence K. Frank (page 338) that a very important question for psychologists is whether or not "hostility and aggression are inborn characteristics"? What is your own view? How would schools differ from what they now are if one or the other of the two viewpoints Dr. Frank describes were accepted?

5. What was the worst *fear* you ever experienced? Has it had any after-effects that you know of on your own personality?

6. What do you understand by "longitudinal" studies of human growth and development? (Page 340.) By "projective" methods of personality study? (Page 340.)

7. What is the significance of a "Rorschach ink blot"? (Page 340.) How many of the other names in Dr. Lois Murphy's statement can you identify?

8. What did Dr. Helen Witmer and her students at the Smith College School of Social Work find out about the effects of family relationships in the treatment of child-guidance clinic cases?

9. Discuss the case of Molly (page 343). Do you think some other procedure might have had better results?

10. The word *semantics* is sometimes used in discussing the problem of symbols and reality posed by Dr. James S. Plant (page 344). What is meant by "semantics"?

11. Discuss failures in schoolwork as an emotional problem. Are failures useful in learning?

12. Did the English teacher mentioned by Aikin act wisely or not in the case of the 20-year-old senior and the production of *Macbeth?*

13. Is there a child guidance clinic in your community or near by? If so, find out to what extent the local schools use its services.

14. Why was it considered necessary to have a long-continued research such as the Study of Adolescence? What bearing would the results of such a study have on the work of the schools?

---

[33] Hedley S. Dimock, Charles E. Hendry, and Karl P. Zerfoss, *A Professional Outlook on Group Education.* New York: Association Press, 1938.

15. Find out from the leaders of your local Y. M. C. A., Y. W. C. A., or other similar agency what they understand by "group work" and its significance for help with social maladjustment and conduct disorders.

## SELECTED REFERENCES FOR FURTHER READING AND STUDY

Aichhorn, August, *Wayward Youth*. New York: The Viking Press, 1935.

Appel, Kenneth E., and Edward A. Strecker, *Practical Examination of Personality and Behavior Disorders, Adults and Children*. New York: The Macmillan Company, 1936.

*Dealing with Delinquency*, 1940 Yearbook of the National Probation Association.

French, Lois Meredith, *Psychiatric Social Work*. New York: Commonwealth Fund, 1940.

Glueck, Sheldon, and Eleanor T. Glueck, *Juvenile Delinquents Grown Up*. New York: Commonwealth Fund, 1940.

Groves, Ernest R., *Personality and Social Adjustment*. New York: Longmans, Green and Company, 1936.

Gruenberg, Sidonie Matsner, *We, The Parents*. New York: Harper and Brothers, 1939.

Healy, William, and Augusta F. Bronner, *New Light on Delinquency and Its Treatment*. New Haven, Conn.: Yale University Press, 1936.

Heath, Esther, *Approach to the Parent*. New York: Commonwealth Fund, 1933.

*Journal of Educational Sociology*, Vol. 12, No. 2. (October, 1938.) Articles on social adjustment and the teacher and delinquency.

Koshuk, Ruth Pearson, *Social Influences Affecting the Behavior of Young Children*. Washington, D. C.: Society for Research in Child Development, 1941. (*Monographs*, Vol. 6, No. 2.)

Myerson, Abraham, *Social Psychology*. New York: Prentice-Hall, Inc., 1934.

Preston, George H., *Psychiatry for the Curious*. New York: Farrar and Rinehart, 1940.

Richards, Esther Loring, *The Origin of Conduct Problems in School Children*. Iowa City, Iowa: University of Iowa, 1934. (Child Welfare Pamphlets, No. 34.)

Stevenson, George S., and Geddes Smith, *Child Guidance Clinics—A Quarter Century of Development*. New York: Commonwealth Fund, 1934.

Taylor, Katherine Whiteside, *Do Adolescents Need Parents?* New York: D. Appleton-Century Company, 1938.

Witmer, Helen Leland, *Psychiatric Clinics for Children*. New York: Commonwealth Fund, 1940.

*Youth and the Future*. General Report of the American Youth Commission. Washington, D. C.: American Council on Education, 1942.

# CHAPTER 18

# Adjustment and Guidance of the Exceptional Child

With the increased attention given by psychologists to emotional development, there has come a change in the attitude toward those individuals who are physically handicapped—the blind, the deaf, the crippled—and toward all other "exceptional children" who are in need of what is generally called "special education."

It is now recognized that personality problems assume particular significance in any program for the physically handicapped. "The most important element in the approach to the solution of the problems presented to schools and communities by these groups," says the California State Department of Education, "is the recognition of the personality of the child, and his various relationships with his family, the community, and general society, and of the relative part to be played by clinics, schools, and other agencies of care, correction, and education." [1]

This view precludes, as the California authorities are careful to point out, the treatment of any person as primarily a cripple, or blind, or deaf, or even as gifted, "for such a course misses the main point in specialization of treatment or education." The tendency is clearly in the direction of having the so-called handicapped individual make the best possible normal adjustment to social living, with a minimum of isolation from his fellows, and with special treatment justifiable only to the extent that this will contribute to a rich and complete personality.

## Who Constitute Exceptional Children?

Various terms have been used to designate those groups that include different types of physical or mental handicaps or any other deviation from an assumed norm. "Atypical," "special," "excep-

---

[1] *The Education of Physically Handicapped Children*, prepared by the Commission for Special Education of the California State Department of Education, Sacramento, Vol. X, No. 12, December, 1941, p. 3.

tional," have all been current, with "exceptional" the term now most frequently employed as a collective designation. A committee of the White House Conference of 1930 included under "the handicapped and the gifted" the following groups: (1) the deaf and hard of hearing; (2) the blind and partially seeing; (3) the crippled; (4) the speech defective; (5) children of lowered vitality; (6) the gifted; (7) the mentally retarded; (8) the emotionally or socially maladjusted. The California Commission classifies the school children who should receive the services of special education as follows:

1. Blind and partially sighted
2. Sight-saving cases
3. Deaf
4. Hard of hearing
5. Crippled (that is, "orthopedic cases")
6. Those with lowered vitality
7. Those with speech defects and disorders
8. Mental defectives
9. The nervously and emotionally unstable
10. The socially maladjusted, that is, those presenting various types of behavior problems traceable primarily to environmental conditions
11. The gifted

A typical conference of the International Council for Exceptional Children has sections devoted to crippled children, behavior problems and delinquents, the hard of hearing, the deaf, the epileptic, the blind, sight-saving, the mentally handicapped, the gifted, speech correction, lowered-vitality children, and the clinical psychology of exceptional children.

Only a cursory glance at these several lists is needed to show how difficult it is to group individuals on the basis of any one disability, defect, or condition. The more classification is attempted, the more evident it becomes that, though there are unquestionably common problems, each individual is different, and that physical, emotional, and social elements are inextricably commingled. "How many blind children are also deaf, or also defective in speech?" asks Edgar A. Doll. "Likewise, how many feeble-minded children are deaf and blind and speech defective? It is not simply a question of double handicap—there are triple and quadruple handicaps as well. How many defects are present in the same person and what are the frequencies of these multiple abnormalities?"[2] The danger

---

[2] Edgar A. Doll, "Coordination of Effort for the Education of Exceptional Children," U. S. Office of Education *Bulletin*, 1935, No. 7, p. 65.

of setting individuals apart for any one handicap is more and more recognized. As a participant in the Third Conference on Education and the Exceptional Child put it:

> Not the classes and schools for exceptional children, but the child, is what counts. Is not every child an individual and exceptional child? There is no true "normal." That we must accept as axiom. The boy or girl who has a handicap in speech or mind or body has only in intensified form an obstacle to overcome, which each of us, to some degree after all, meets also. Is one among us quite perfectly the counterpart of the "norm"? Do we not all belong in the group of the "different"? [3]

The director of special education for the city of Minneapolis said at a conference on exceptional children called by the United States Commissioner of Education: "In all our efforts I am convinced that the emphasis should be placed upon the positive points of contact between the regular and special groups instead of upon their differences." [4] And Dr. Charlotte Grave, commenting on the statement by the head of a well-known school for exceptional children that the school "represents the progress in methods of dealing with exceptional children," makes the point that actually progress in a school of this type indicates progress in methods of dealing with *all* children, since, in Meta Anderson's words, "special education at its best is simply *good* education." [5] Indeed, says Dr. Doll:

> The field of special education is exerting a tremendously good influence on education in general. If we now have 40 per cent of children labeled as "exceptional," shall we not soon reach the point where the education of every child is individualized according to his special abilities or special disabilities? A particular ability or disability is relatively merely an exaggeration of a single characteristic of the individual. Those who are defective in vision, for instance, may be of normal mentality, or, conversely, those who are mentally subnormal may be visually normal. . . . Several sections of the White House Conference, especially that section dealing with the handicapped child, urged capitalizing the normal aspects of handicapped children rather than merely providing for their deficiencies. [6]

### Special Problems of the Physically Handicapped

Not a great deal is known about the emotional difficulties of the physically handicapped, though there is much popular opinion

[3] Elizabeth Gertrude Stern, "Society and the Exceptional Child," *Proceedings of the Third Conference on Education and the Exceptional Child,* The Woods Schools, Langhorne, Pa., May, 1937.

[4] May E. Bryne, in "Coordination of Effort for the Education of Exceptional Children," U. S. Office of Education *Bulletin,* 1935, No. 7, Washington, Government Printing Office, 1935, p. 8.

[5] Meta Anderson, "Twenty-Five Years of Progress in Education at the Woods Schools," *Journal of Exceptional Children,* Vol. 6, No. 2, December, 1939, pp. 83-90.

[6] Edgar A. Doll, U. S. Office of Education *Bulletin,* 1935, No. 7, p. 65.

and some scientific data. That special problems of adjustment do exist for the blind, the deaf, and the seriously crippled is, of course, generally assumed. "If a program for the emotional adjustment of children with a full complement of senses is considered important," says Gabriel Farrell, head of the Perkins Institution, "certainly such a program is even more essential for those in whom one of the five senses is missing." [7] And Thomas D. Cutsworth, who is himself sightless and who wrote his doctor's thesis at the University of Kansas on the emotional problems of the blind, speaks of the blind, after a century of special education in this country, as "still laboring, hopelessly, with their problems of personality, and wrestling ineffectually with their social adjustment." [8] Elbert A. Gruver, superintendent of the Pennsylvania School for the Deaf, said at the Office of Education conference of 1935:

> The deaf are disturbed in heart and mind. They are confronted by unusual and puzzling problems which are causing them deep concern. Hard times have made a lasting impression upon them. Their emotions have been stirred, their thoughts quickened, and their ideas stimulated. They are not easily aroused, but new conditions confront them, new experiences confuse them, and new inventions intrigue them, until it has become very difficult for them thoroughly to analyze their feelings, properly diagnose their troubles, and logically apply a remedy. This is not surprising. We, too, are confounded and confused. Add a physical handicap and the burden becomes heavier and the game of life harder to play.[9]

As for other types of physical disability, "the personality is often profoundly altered by physical deformities," writes Louis A. Lurie. "The tendency toward self-pity that so rapidly develops may lead to introversion, to withdrawal from the realities of life and to neurotic manifestations." Or, "the personality may be modified along definitely anti-social lines. Incorrigibility, delinquency, and even criminality may be the end-results of interference with the normal development of the ego instinct of the personality." [10]

Calling attention to the fact that the estimates of the White House Conference indicate 300,000 crippled children in the United States with less than 12,000 receiving the advantages of special education, 200,000 youth coming into the juvenile courts every

[7] Gabriel Farrell, "Mental Hygiene for the Blind," *Mental Hygiene*, Vol. XXIII, No. 2, April, 1939, p. 215.

[8] Thomas D. Cutsworth, *The Blind in School and Society*. New York: D. Appleton-Century Company, 1933. (Cited in Farrell, *op. cit.*)

[9] Elbert A. Gruver in U. S. Office of Education *Bulletin*, 1935, No. 7, p. 19.

[10] Louis A. Lurie, "Endocrinology and the Understanding and Treatment of the Exceptional Child," *Journal of the American Medical Association*, Vol. 110, May 7, 1938, pp. 1531-1536. (Reprinted in *Proceedings of the Fourth Institute on the Exceptional Child* (Langhorne, Pa.: Child Research Clinic of the Woods Schools), Oct., 1937, p. 10.

year, and half a million so defective in hearing that they should be taught lip-reading, Esther Lloyd-Jones finds no cause for complacency.[11] Nor can complacency be based, she asserts, on any hope that youngsters with these and similar problems will "outgrow them" or that satisfactory adjustments will take place by themselves:

> Think of the load of misery that is represented in the following figures: 500,000 persons in prisons, hospitals for mental diseases, almshouses and institutions for the feeble-minded; 70,000 new individuals being admitted each year for the first time to hospitals for the mentally diseased; 300,000 men and women committed every year to prison. . . .
>
> Why, in the face of this situation, are we content to go on, relatively placid about the provisions we are able to make for the education of exceptional children? The only possible explanation is that the tools are not prepared to our hand, and without the necessary tools our social inertia is so great that we are content to let the matter rest.

Over against such vivid statements as this of the plight, emotional and otherwise, of the vast group we call "exceptional" must necessarily be placed the evidence that numerous individuals ordinarily so classified have made markedly successful adjustments, not only surmounting their handicaps but often adapting themselves far more effectively than many persons regarded as normal. Blind violinists and deaf musicians are part of the tradition of the arts, and modern examples of supremely adequate adjustments would include leaders of our generation from Helen Keller to Franklin D. Roosevelt. The California Commission cites some interesting examples:

> One of California's most famous ministers of religion and pulpit orators was a man of insignificant stature, a hunchback who stood less than four feet six inches in height. In the pulpit he surmounted his handicap by his convincing eloquence and radiant personality until every thought of deformity was banished from the thoughts of his congregation. There is, too, the story of a well-known Scotch divine who was a noticeable cripple but a very eloquent preacher. On one occasion, a thoughtless stranger, in complimenting him on his sermon, said that she had often wished to hear the famous *lame* preacher. His quick retort was, "Lame man, I admit, but lame preacher, never!" Clarence Hawkes, the distinguished naturalist, might equally exclaim, "Blind man, yes, I admit it, but blind author and blind naturalist, never! For what I describe I once saw and still see, and what I describe I see perhaps more vividly and penetratingly than most of those who possess a good pair of functioning eyes."
>
> "Handicap," and other like terms, are, after all, relative, and it is the actuating mind that makes the senses and muscles do effective work. . . . A

---

[11] Esther Lloyd-Jones, "Training Opportunities for Workers with Exceptional Children," *Proceedings of the Fourth Institute on the Exceptional Child*, The Woods Schools, Langhorne, Pa., October, 1937, p. 29.

deaf Douglas Tilden can still see unrevealed beauty of form, and from his creative brain call forth imperishable works of the sculptor's art.[12]

## The Blind and Emotional Adjustment

In a recent discussion of mental hygiene for the blind,[13] Dr. Gabriel Farrell finds that there is a difference of opinion among the blind themselves as to the direct responsibility of blindness for personality difficulties. "Maladjustments frequently attributed to blindness in reality may be the result of institutional environment, or an unsatisfactory adjustment to other children," says Ralph V. Merry in his doctoral dissertation at the Harvard School of Education, while Thomas D. Cutsworth, whose book has already been cited, is certain that "blindness changes and utterly reorganizes the entire mental life of the individual," and that the earlier this frustration occurs, the greater the reorganization demanded and the greater the effect of the frustration upon other individuals whose attitudes determine the hygiene of the blind. Dr. Farrell's own conclusion is that, despite the conflicting evidence given by blind persons, "living in perpetual darkness must levy its toll on the emotional life." He points out that the emotional problem is complicated by the fact that the number of completely blind persons is very small, and the outlook on life of a person with some sight differs from that of one who is totally blind. Even the existence of some sight, instead of easing the individual's situation, often adds additional burdens—"the constant fear that remaining vision may depart and the confusion that arises from not seeing things clearly."

Especially difficult is the problem of the younger person who loses sight unexpectedly. With older people, Dr. Farrell says in his account, the loss of sight does not always create serious mental difficulties, but with a young person there is likely to be an emotional maladjustment which changes the whole of life. He gives the following case of a young girl who had lost her sight in an automobile accident and "simply would not accept blindness as her permanent fate":

She lived in another state, but would not go to the state school because she was afraid that her friends would think her queer if she had to go to a school for the blind. She kept her eyes completely bandaged so that no one could see them, even though there was no necessity for this. After some persuasion she

[12] "The Education of Physically Handicapped Children," *Bulletin of the California State Department of Education*, Vol. X, No. 12, December, 1941, pp. 5-6.

[13] Gabriel Farrell, "Mental Hygiene for the Blind," *Mental Hygiene*, Vol. 23, pp. 215-227, April, 1939.

was prevailed upon to come to Perkins.[14] Our first step was to make her remove the bandages, though we compromised by allowing her to wear dark glasses. Next we showed her that she could work within the school and carry on a definite program, which would occupy her mind. Our third step was to make her associate with pupils in the school and, gradually, to go down town, where she would be seen by other people. Finally, we got her to go out independently so that she became completely adjusted to her station in life as a blind person. She has now returned to her own state school, where she is doing excellent work and showing a fine attitude. We feel that that was a successful case of emotional adjustment.[15]

One of the teachers at Perkins Institution cites four ways in which blindness affects personality: (1) it inhibits normal physical activity and limits the sources of stimulation; (2) it thwarts wish-fulfillment; (3) it increases nervous and physical strain; and (4) it make the individual an exceptional member of his group. A member of the staff of the California School for the Blind [16] lists as primary characteristics of blind children: (1) lack of initiative due to emotional blocking rather than to physical causes; (2) feelings of inferiority often compensated for by bravado; (3) worry about the present and the future; (4) a varied phantasy life of a wish-fulfilling or a sadistic nature. Dr. Cutsworth puts as the two most acute problems in dealing with the blind, apart from emotional difficulties common to all youth, *verbalism*—the problem of words versus reality—and the phantasy life of the blind. Of the special emotional problem involved in the phantasy escape from reality he says:

> The phantasy life of the blind does not arise from a primary physical disability, but it does arise from the social relations that such a disability involves. . . . The most unfortunate aspect of phantasy building lies in the fact that it is not the signal of social maladjustment in a small part of each personality. On the contrary, it signifies a defective organization of the whole self. Escape into unreality derives its nature from the total situation and for any individual the greater part of the environment is the self. The blind are chronic phantasy builders.[17]

A program for guidance and adjustment of the blind as worked out at an institution such as the one Dr. Farrell describes would include a psychiatric social worker, "who builds up a relationship between the family and the school"; psychometric and psychological

---

[14] The Perkins Institution and Massachusetts School for the Blind, Watertown, Massachusetts, founded by Samuel Gridley Howe, pioneer worker for the handicapped.

[15] Gabriel Farrell, "Mental Hygiene for the Blind," *Mental Hygiene,* Vol. 23, April, 1939, pp. 215-227.

[16] Cited by Farrell, *op. cit.,* pp. 221-222.

[17] From the summary by Farrell, *op. cit.,* p. 223, of Thomas D. Cutsworth's *The Blind in School and Society.*

work to bring understanding of the cases that come and meet "the maladjustments that blindness brings to each individual in varying scope and intensity"; clinical work in speech correction; a program of physiotherapy to overcome "blindisms"; an extensive program of outside activities "to keep the children normal and in contact with the seeing world for which they must fit themselves." Dr. Farrell says:

> Month by month we meet together, those of us who are engaged in the personnel work of Perkins, at a large table in the board room, to discuss from the respective angles of our specialties the various aspects of pupils' difficulties, so that, working together, we may bring a full-rounded program of rehabilitation, guidance, and adjustment to bear upon the needs of our boys and girls. . . .
>
> [Our aim is] to prepare our young people to lead poised and purposeful lives. Poised, in that they are to be kept free from the mannerisms which are often a greater handicap than defective vision; they are to be taught to stand firmly upon their feet, confident of their ability to face life squarely. Purposeful, in that they will have the conviction of a real and worth-while purpose in life. It is our responsibility to help them find that purpose. This means that we must study the traits and characteristics of each pupil, until we find out what is the best contribution that each can make to society and how we can guide each one into the most useful and satisfying life. To my mind that is our great challenge, and in meeting it we must muster all the forces that combine to form an adequate mental-hygiene program.[18]

Special emphasis has been given in recent years to sight-saving cases, on the ground that, as the California Commission says, vision is so essential to the general conduct of life that "any nonremediable defect, impairment, or loss of vision has the effect of slowing down or seriously weakening or even eliminating certain functions or processes often of vital importance in the normal conduct of an individual's affairs." Most authorities stress the necessity for keeping children with limited vision in close touch with other children, but giving them the special individual training and equipment that may be necessary. The partially seeing are that group consisting of those who, in the words of Mrs. Winifred Hathaway, "after everything possible has been done for them, have too little vision to make use of the ordinary school equipment but too much to benefit by the education for blind children." [19] Mrs. Hathaway points out that, for this group and others with seriously progressive eye defects, considerable research is needed to clarify standards and clear up differences of opinion among opthalmologists, educationists, and others. Research is also needed to determine what vocations partially seeing children may enter with the best possibilities of successful adjustment.

---

[18] Gabriel Farrell, *op. cit.*, p. 227.
[19] Mrs. Winifred Hathaway, "Coordination of Effort for the Education of Exceptional Children," U. S. Office of Education *Bulletin*, 1935, No. 7, pp. 17-18.

## Problems of the Deaf

Few specific data are available on the emotional aspects of deafness, although the problem has been recognized as an important one. The American Instructors of the Deaf, in their discussions of research needs, recently put on record their determination to "utilize information resulting from the endeavors of those interested in research in fields far removed from education." They spoke of the physics of sound, but they also emphasized the physiology and psychology of hearing, the psychological effects of deafness, the psychology of the different types of deafness, prevention and treatment, and "social and emotional adjustment, mental hygiene, and studies of the normal child." [20]

Speaking of the "semi-deaf," the Vermont report on atypical children (which finds aproximately twice the percentage of hard of hearing for that state ordinarily quoted for the nation) asserts that these are handicapped in many ways. They are precluded from full enjoyment of the theater, motion pictures, and lectures, it is pointed out. Many occupations are closed to them. And, "unless especially favorable conditions exist, the psychological and social effects of impaired hearing are also grave." The Vermont investigators believe that the semi-deaf person is under a strain and tension that make him subject to unusual fatigue and "perhaps to morbidity." For this reason, it is asserted, the semi-deaf should be helped to enter vocations that will keep them busy and happy, and the schools should be particularly careful to discover hearing deficiencies early enough to plan the right kind of care and education.[21]

In a careful study based on clinical records, Antonio Ciocco and Carroll E. Palmer have pointed out that one of the difficulties with deafness is that, while hearing impairment can be classed among those physical handicaps which reflect on the behavioristic personality and create special problems of economic and social adjustment, nevertheless impaired hearing is not an ailment that admits of much dramatization. "It is not fatal, it is not contagious, nor does it evoke the popular sentimental reactions of some less prevalent if more widely discussed diseases." The Ciocco-Palmer investigation did not go into emotional factors to any extent, but its conclusions on prevention of deafness among school children are significant not only for their practical applications but for the re-

---

[20] American Instructors of the Deaf, *Proceedings*, 1935. Washington, D. C.: Government Printing Office, 1936. The words quoted are from President A. E. Pope's presidential address.

[21] Verner E. Parker, "Atypical Children in the Public Schools of Vermont." Burlington, Vermont: University of Vermont. (Mimeographed.)

lationship they suggest between the physiology and psychology of hearing. Future research work among school children, these investigators maintain, would contribute most to prevention of deafness if directed toward: (1) the development of a more efficient means of detecting auditory defects of slight degree; (2) increased knowledge of the etiology of middle ear infection; (3) a more complete study of the pathological changes of structures of the ear and its adjacent organs. The investigators closed their report with the significant statement that "the need for further study is self-evident when it is considered that every year, on the average, 4.6 per cent of children develop some impairment of hearing and .6 per cent of children with good hearing acquire a defect so marked as to impair the understanding of speech in one or both ears." [22]

### Other Physically Handicapped Children

Among the group of "exceptional children" it has been customary to designate one section of those who are seriously crippled in some way. Here again, however, it is important to free ourselves from too definite labelings, especially those that imply stigma, inferiority, and undesirable difference. Every child, with or without what are usually thought of as handicaps, is first of all a person, especially a person in a family. In the words of Winifred Richmond:

He is first of all a physical being; upon the kind of body that he has, upon its health and strength and the proper functioning of its organs, will depend the reactions he is able to make to his environment, and thus the habits that he will build up. The child who has been birth-injured, for instance, may be unable to use his body to get the experiences normal to childhood. He cannot run and play games, he cannot manipulate objects with his hands, or he cannot talk so as to be understood. Willy-nilly, he is forced into the role of an exceptional child. The family that can accept such a child and absorb it, so to speak, give it its proper place in the family group and its utmost chance for development, is a rare one. Grief and disappointment, unwillingness to accept the verdict of physicians, a frantic search for someone or something that may ameliorate the condition, is the usual parental reaction. In this atmosphere the child is ill at ease and unhappy, and as he grows older—if of normal intelligence, as many such children are—he develops a bitterness and pessimism that add a most unpleasant disposition to the burden of a crippled body.[23]

[22] Antonio Ciocco and Carroll E. Palmer, "The Hearing of School Children, A Statistical Study of Audiometric and Clinical Records." Washington, D. C.: National Research Council, 1941. (*Monographs of the Society for Research in Child Development*, Vol. VI, Serial No. 29, No. 3.)

[23] Winifred Richmond, "The Exceptional Child and the Family Constellation." Langhorne, Pa.: The Woods Schools, 1937. (*Child Research Clinic Series*, Vol. II, No. 5, p. 7.)

The concern for the individual in family and community here expressed is, as has already been noted in these chapters, one of the most characteristic elements in the modern case-work approach to all children and human beings generally, but it is particularly evident in the work with so-called crippled children. If we really think in terms of the individual and his needs in the case of the physically handicapped child, as Esther Dimchevsky has pointed out, "can we still offhandedly label and pigeonhole him as a deformed limb, a sightless eye, or a curved spine, paying small heed to the fact that attached to that limb, that eye, and that spine is a total personality in reaction to and within a total environment, and that there is a steady interplay of factors—physical, intellectual, emotional, as well as social, economic, and cultural?" [24]

Take the case of Tony, for example. Instead of merely accepting the fact that Tony's difficulty has been diagnosed as a cardiac involvement, says Dimchevsky, and therefore prescribing a boarding-home placement, must we not, viewing the situation from the standpoint of a total personality behaving with meaning within a given environment, pause and ask ourselves:

> What type of person is this boy who, though convalescing, still has a heart that is incapacitating him? What is the meaning of this disability to Tony himself? Why can he not accept its limitations? Is it the restriction of the physical handicap that is the irritating factor, or is some deeper inner need expressed as resentment of enforced inactivity? What will be the emotional effect on him of removing him from his home? What is his place in the family unit? How does he feel toward the other members of the family, and how do they feel toward him and his illness? Does he dislike school now because he cannot climb those stairs, or because he cannot compete physically with his schoolmates; because his intellectual capacities cannot comfortably meet the demands of his grade, or because he is emotionally unable to take his place in group life at the eleven-year-old level? What are *his* interests, and how can *he* most satisfactorily express them in *his* way? Is reading *his* interest or *our* idea of his interest? [25]

Another case cited in this same report is that of Marjorie, who at the age of eight was brought to the hospital with a fractured femur. Between periods of hospitalization, the account shows, Marjorie busied herself at home cheerfully with doll-centered girl playmates, "concerned only with the day's affairs, not looking into the future, content to submit to a mother's solicitude, and in that setting not overly conscious of crutches or brace." But seven years later, at age fifteen, Marjorie's needs have changed. Now an ado-

---

[24] Esther Dimchevsky, "The Social Content of Work with Crippled Children," *Mental Hygiene*, Vol. XXIII, No. 3, July, 1939, p. 422.

[25] *Ibid.*, pp. 422-423.

lescent, her small group of girl friends do not satisfy her; "the brace makes me self-conscious"; she sees herself frustrated in the nursing career she had chosen; and her mother's solicitude has become irksome. Then:

A short time ago, the brace discarded behind the door, Marjorie took to the highway, limping along toward a nearby town where relatives "let me do things and treat me like the other kids." A puzzled mother blames the leg for what seems to her a change in personality. The behavior might easily be labeled simply a "reaction to bodily deformity." But can we really consider it as mainly an outcome of the hampering condition imposed by the *osteitis fibrosa cystica,* or is it the result of a basic adolescent need—the attainment of emancipation from home—with the leg intensifying the problem and the brace helping to determine the nature of Marjorie's solution? [26]

Whatever the type of physical handicap, questions like these are being asked more and more by teachers and workers in both day and residential schools, and special attention is being given to social and emotional adjustment in programs of education and training. Pointing out that the physically handicapped child must sooner or later make the adjustment to a more or less competitive world, "learning to overcome difficulties by his own efforts is especially important," says the California Commission. Best of all compensating factors, in the judgment of the Commission, "is the discovery of some accomplishment in which he may excel." [27]

A useful summary of the literature on the influence of chronic illness upon the behavior of children has recently been provided by Lyon, Rauh, and Carroll. As a result of their own study of social adjustment arising in the treatment of heart disease, these workers find the following special problems arising: worry of the child over his illness; resentment of the fact that he has heart disease; concealment of his illness in order to participate in the full activities of his companions; use of the presence of heart disease as a protective measure; subjection to ridicule by his siblings because of "laziness"; lack of co-operation with the outlined program of rest because of the indifference or the oversolicitude of parents.[28] Many of these difficulties were removed, the investigators say, by conferences with school-teachers and school principals by advice to parents and other children in the family, and by the provision of special activities and vocational training for the patients.

---

[26] *Ibid.,* p. 426.
[27] "Education of Physically Handicapped Children," pp. 58-59.
[28] R. A. Lyon, Louise W. Rauh, and Mary G. Carroll, "The Social Adjustment of Children With Heart Disease," *Mental Hygiene,* Vol. 25, pp. 443-449, July, 1941.

## Speech Difficulties

The White House Conference estimated that approximately a million children in the United States have handicapping speech defects.[29] Dr. Smiley Blanton, President of the American Speech Correction Association, lists three types of the speech disorders included in this group as having a large emotional element: (1) indistinct speech, (2) lisping speech, and (3) stuttering and stammering. Stutterers, of whom there are at least 200,000 in our schools, "suffer from a definite and specific emotional difficulty," Dr. Blanton says, which prevents them from adjusting in a satisfactory manner to playmates, schoolwork, and the world in general:

> The stuttering child, because of his feeling of anxiety and timidity, develops marked feelings of inferiority in his relation to other people. . . . It may be asked: Why do some children stutter because of fear and others do not? Probably in those cases in which anxiety causes stuttering there is some inadequacy in the speech mechanism, so that fear and anxiety interfere with the proper functioning of the complicated and delicate speech mechanism.[30]

Blanton and others working in this field believe that preventive work must be accomplished by bringing to the parents the knowledge of mental hygiene and child guidance that will help prevent the development of stuttering.

The California Commission, likewise insisting that the causes of functional nervous speech disorders are psychological, and the speech disorder itself an external manifestation of some difficulty that may have a psychoneurotic origin, emphasizes the importance of early home and school environment:

> If the child with the nervous speech disorder is living in a home where there is a lack of understanding, inconsistency, or laxity in discipline, tyranny, quarreling, sarcasm, or unfavorable comparison of that child with another, the speech disturbance is likely a result of the environment. The school environment must also be considered. If the teacher is too severe or impatient, or if the child is subjected to ridicule by his classmates, his confidence in his power to control himself may be seriously shaken.[31]

## "Retarded" Children

Less interest has been expressed in recent years than formerly in what has been known as "retardation" of school children. On the theory that a certain amount of accomplishment was normal for a school year or grade, those children who could not achieve

---

[29] U. S. Office of Education *Bulletin,* 1935, No. 7, p. 33.
[30] *Ibid.,* p. 34.
[31] California State Department of Education *Bulletin,* December, 1941, p. 77.

this were regarded as "retarded." To some extent in theory, and to a considerable extent in practice, this notion still prevails. With the expanding concept of education, however, and the recognition of many more aspects of human living than the narrowly "intellectual," a less rigid theory has come into considerable acceptance. Even in the earlier days of intelligence and achievement testing, Elizabeth Farrell, supervisor in charge of "ungraded classes" in New York City, could write: "The teacher of the future, not too far distant, will want to know, not that the child is backward, but in what particular area of his mental functioning he is strong, and where weakness dominates." More recent statements would be even more inclusive. They would be likely to say, with Dr. Elise H. Martens and others, that "the basic philosophy underlying the education of retarded children is no different from that recognized for all children; the fundamental aim of all education is to teach children to live wisely and well in the environment in which they find themselves." [32]

Even when such statements are made specific with respect to so-called retarded, backward, or "slow-learning" pupils, it is quite evident that they apply with equal force to all children, as when Dr. Martens and her group supplement the general objectives given above with the following: "Happy social relationships, physical efficiency, wise use of leisure time, earning capacity, and acceptance of home responsibilities are of major importance." Certainly these apply to all children, not just to those of limited mental ability, but it is to a considerable extent true that in practice those who for one reason or another deviate sufficiently from the assumed norm as to be troublesome are likely to get a better, more individualized education than those who are merely "normal."

One reason why the attitude toward retardation has changed is the evidence that gradually accrued as to the lack of any really homogeneous groups even in so-called mental abilities and academic subjects, to say nothing of the other things in life. As Ruth Hankins says:

No two individuals are alike. Children cannot be lumped together in groups according to I.Q. In a group of a hundred children with I.Q.'s from 55 to 60, for example, there will be just as wide a range of physical, social, and emotional differences as in a group of a hundred with I.Q.'s from 120 to 130. Each child must be treated as an individual. By way of illustration, in one group with which I worked there were Sally and Ann. Both were eleven years old, and both had

[32] Elise H. Martens and others, "Twenty-Five Years of Progress in Education at the Woods Schools," *Journal of Exceptional Children*, Vol. 6, No. 3, December, 1939, pp. 83-90.

I.Q.'s between 55 and 60. Sally was a quiet child, willing to sit and watch the activities of the other girls, or just as willing to attempt any work which was placed before her. She talked very little, and nothing apparently bothered her. Ann, on the other hand, was nervous and restless. She talked constantly in a high-pitched voice, even when working alone. Any criticism, however slight, upset her completely, and she continually demanded encouragement and affection. Naturally, the two girls could not be approached in the same way, or treated in like manner.[33]

Moreover, the direct relationship between school success in "academic" subjects and the child's emotional life—working both ways—has been made clear in many studies. Reading disabilities are frequently due to causes deep in the emotional life of the child.[34] Enrollment in special classes for the mentally handicapped is still dependent for the most part on the approximate I.Q. range or degree of mental retardation, but "it is also generally understood that all pertinent factors are to be considered in recommending a child for such placement," the United States Office of Education reports.[35] In Massachusetts and other states, the services of the "visiting teacher" or school social worker are often utilized in connection with these placements, which indicates an interest in social and emotional factors as well as in the more usual tests and measurements. The change that has taken place is clearly indicated in a recent report by Dr. Neil A. Dayton, of the Massachusetts Division of Mental Deficiency:

The variety of problems now being presented to the clinic shows the rapidly changing trend in the demands made upon our traveling school clinic. Formerly it was expected that all of our children would be referred to the clinic because of retardation. In fact, that was the primary reason for the creation of the clinics. Now we see that other problems are arising within the public schools and giving the educators serious concern. These, of course, are problems quite apart from retardation, although in some instances there is a combination of retardation and another type of problem. We see now that the clinics are offering a broader and more useful service to the public schools in that they are examining various school and behavior problems which are often the cause of such serious difficulties within the various school systems.[36]

---

[33] Ruth Hankins, "Principles of Teaching Exceptional Children in the Elementary Schools." Langhorne, Pa.: The Woods Schools, 1939. (*Child Research Clinic Series*, Vol. III, No. 1, p. 6.)

[34] See Phyllis Blanchard, "Reading Disabilities in Relation to Difficulties of Personality and Emotional Development," *Mental Hygiene*, Vol. 20, pp. 384-413, for a number of cases.

[35] Elise H. Martens, "State Supervisory Programs for the Education of Exceptional Children." Washington, D. C.: U. S. Government Printing Office, 1941. U. S. Office of Education *Bulletin*, 1940, No. 6, p. 36.

[36] Neil A. Dayton, Report of the Division of Mental Deficiency. Boston: The Commonwealth of Massachusetts [1939], p. 4. (Reprint from the Annual Report of the Commissioner of Mental Diseases, P.D. 117, 1937.)

The tendency on the part of many school systems that once stressed "ability grouping" or "homogeneous grouping" is to move forward to other plans that take into account the needs and possibilities of each child as an individual. Thus, a bulletin of the National Association of Secondary School Principals devoted to pupils who are frequently referred to as "nonacademic" or "unscholarly" says flatly: "Since no two individuals are ever identical in characteristics, needs, and capacities, the education of each pupil should be adapted to him accordingly. . . . Within any framework of general instruction there should exist a flexibility that will insure the adaptability of the program to the individual's need to a maximal extent." [37]

Studies have shown, however, that those who test low by the ordinary instruments of measurement—whether we refer to them as "mentally retarded" or not—do seemingly contribute more than their share of emotional and behavior disorders. No matter how good the organization, says A. Leila Martin, how well prepared the teachers, how worthwhile the projects and pupil endeavors, how sensitive the whole school plan to the mental hygiene possibilities of school life, "there will still be problem cases among the exceptional group, whatever its make-up, that do not respond to the educational program." [38] And she suggests that there will in such cases be need for analysis and re-education through the efforts of a personnel staff that will include:

The psychologist, who through interviews gets the child's point of view—his interpretation of his problem, and through tests, his strengths and weaknesses.

The visiting teacher, who brings the picture of the home and its environment—the relationship with the family.

The physician and school nurse, and in special cases the psychiatrist, to advise, and in some cases to supervise the corrective program.

Still another factor that psychologists have begun to take into account in "retardation" is the effect of economic and social conditions, as analyzed by sociologists. One recent study of the educational, social, and economic backgrounds of thirty-six children in a sixth-grade classroom revealed three to be of superior intelligence and twenty-seven to be normal or average in ability, with only six classified as dull, according to the Kuhlmann-Anderson Intelligence Test. Nor did physical defects account for the retardation. The explanation for the fact that these children were in a

---

[37] *Bulletin of the National Association of Secondary School Principals,* Vol. 23, Number 85, November, 1939, p. 21.

[38] A. Leila Martin, "Solving Emotional Problems of Exceptional Children Through an Educational Program," *Proceedings of the Third Conference on Education and the Exceptional Child.* Langhorne, Pa.: The Woods Schools, May, 1937.

lower grade than called for by their chronological age lay almost entirely in the social environment.[39]

## Gifted Children

It has been customary to include in the group of exceptional children those who are of very superior intelligence, not only because of the fact that they deviate so markedly from the norm, but also because they present problems of one sort and another that society has by no means solved. "I am much concerned about the superior children and what is happening to them," Dr. Lawson G. Lowrey, formerly director of the Institute for Child Guidance, told the U. S. Office of Education Conference of 1934:

> For example, there recently turned up in one small clinic to which I go, a youngster of 6 years 8 months of age, doing very good work in the second grade, with a mental age of 12 years 11 months and an I.Q. of almost 200. What do you do with a chap like that? He says that the reason he doesn't like the second grade is because they won't give him mathematics. He is given word tests and he uses words like "luminosity" and "economics" and "encyclopedia," which at 7 or a little under 7 I think is doing well.[40]

On the whole, the work of Terman seems to indicate that a normal proportion of highly gifted children make satisfactory adjustments to life. But there are those who are concerned at what they regard as the failure of society to discover and conserve its highest talent. Thus, Harvey Zorbaugh, Director of the Clinic for the Social Adjustment of the Gifted, New York University, writes:

> It is because of the loss to society that results from the relative ineffectiveness and lack of productivity, and the inadequate social interest, of its gifted members, that the community must concern itself with its gifted children. It is in the interest of making them more productive members of the community that research on the nature and growth of gifted children, and experiments in their education and guidance, are being conducted here and there throughout the nation. The problem that confronts the community is not so much that of the maladjustment of these children; it is the problem of helping them to realize their potentialities for growth and function and of integrating their interests with the community's interests.[41]

That gifted children do have definite problems of adjustment is clear from the experience of many child guidance clinics. Moreover, the staff of the New York clinic are increasingly impressed

---

[39] Alice Bell Finlayson, "Social and Economic Background of Retarded Children," *Journal of Educational Sociology*, Vol. 15, pp. 38-45, September, 1941.

[40] Lawson G. Lowrey, U. S. Office of Education *Bulletin*, 1935, No. 7, pp. 46-47.

[41] Harvey W. Zorbaugh, "How May the Community Utilize Its Gifted Children?" *Mental Hygiene*, Vol. 24, January, 1940, p. 2.

with the fact that, important as is the too often sterile educational environment in creating problems for gifted children, "the roots of these problems usually are found to extend down into the child's earlier developmental experiences within the family."

## Instability and Genius

At one of the conferences on the education of exceptional children, Professor Zorbaugh began a discussion of giftedness and emotional instability by quoting Deems Taylor's description of an individual case:

He was a man who had a gift for getting himself talked about. He was an undersized little man, with a head too big for his body; a sickly little man. His nerves were bad. He had skin trouble. It was agony for him to wear anything next to his skin coarser than silk. And he had delusions of grandeur. He was a monster of conceit. Never for one minute did he look at the world, or at people, except in relation to himself. He believed himself to be one of the greatest dramatists in the world, one of the greatest thinkers, and one of the greatest composers. To hear him talk, he was Shakespeare, and Beethoven, and Plato, rolled into one.

He had a mania for being in the right. The slightest hint of disagreement, from anyone, on the most trivial point, was enough to set him off on a harangue that might last for hours, in which he proved himself right in so many ways, and with such exhausting volubility, that in the end his hearer, stunned and deafened, would agree with him for the sake of peace. He had theories about almost any subject under the sun, including vegetarianism, the drama, politics, and music; and in support of these theories he wrote pamphlets, letters, books—thousands upon thousands of words, hundreds and hundreds of pages. He not only wrote these things, and published them—usually at somebody else's expense—but he would sit and read them aloud, for hours, to his friends and his family.

He had the emotional stability of a six-year-old child. When he felt out of sorts, he would rave and stamp, or sink into suicidal gloom and talk darkly of going to the East to end his days as a Buddhist monk. Ten minutes later, when something pleased him, he would rush out of doors and run around the garden, or jump up and down on the sofa, or stand on his head. He could be grief-stricken over the death of a pet dog, and he could be callous and heartless to a degree that would make a Roman emperor shudder.

He was almost innocent of any sense of responsibility. Not only did he seem incapable of supporting himself, but it never occurred to him that he was under any obligation to do so. He was convinced that the world owed him a living. In support of this belief, he borrowed money from everybody who was good for a loan—men, women, friends, or strangers. He wrote begging letters by the score, sometimes loftily offering his intended benefactor the privilege of contributing to his support, and being mortally offended if the recipient declined the honor.

An endless procession of women marched through his life. His first wife spent twenty years enduring and forgiving his infidelities. His second wife had been the wife of his most devoted friend and admirer, from whom he stole her.

And even while he was trying to persuade her to leave her first husband he was writing to a friend to inquire whether the friend could suggest some wealthy woman—any wealthy woman—whom he could marry for her money.

He was completely selfish in his other personal relationships. His liking for his friends was measured solely by the completeness of their devotion to him, or by their usefulness to him, whether financial or artistic. The minute they failed him—even by so much as refusing a dinner invitation—or began to lessen in usefulness, he cast them off without a second thought.

He had a genius for making enemies. He would insult a man who disagreed with him about the weather. He would pull endless wires in order to meet some man who admired his work, and was able and anxious to be of use to him—and would proceed to make a mortal enemy of him with some idiotic and wholly uncalled-for exhibition of arrogance and bad manners.[42]

The name of this monster, Professor Zorbaugh reminds us, was Richard Wagner. "Not a madman, but from the point of view of modern psychiatry surely a highly unstable personality. Was his instability inherent in his genius?" [43]

From the Wagner illustration Dr. Zorbaugh goes on to summarize the data given in Wilhelm Lange-Eichbaum's study of the biographical data on three hundred geniuses,[44] which indicated that 21 per cent had "clearly psychotic episodes at one point or another in their careers":

Among them he mentions Baudelaire, Hugo, Nietzsche, Manet, and Maupassant—all paretic; Newton, Lenz, Halderein, and perhaps Van Gogh—schizophrenic; Martin Luther—manic-depressive; Rousseau—paranoid; Blake—paraphrenic; and Dostoievsky—epileptic; as well as Kant, Copernicus, Stendhal, and Faraday who developed senile dementia. He holds further, that a large percentage of the rest were highly unstable personalities, characterized by inward cleavage, nervous tension, neurosis, drug addiction, depravity, exaltation and depression, crises of conversion, a craze for creation and preposterous convictions of inspiration—among them Michelangelo, Byron, Schopenhauer, Heine, Wagner, Bismarck, DeQuincy, Coleridge, Poe, Wilde, Napoleon, Molière, Raphael, Richelieu, and Hegel.

Of the seventy-eight greatest of these geniuses, Lange-Eichbaum found 37 per cent to show evidence of at least one psychotic episode; an additional 46 per cent to have displayed markedly "psychopathic" personalities; and another 10 per cent to have displayed mildly "psychopathic" personalities. Of the seventy-eight greatest geniuses, then, Lange-Eichbaum found 83 per cent to have been highly unstable or psychotic, and only 7 per cent to have been "normal." [45]

---

[42] Deems Taylor, "The Monster," in *Of Men and Music.* New York: Simon and Schuster, 1937. Used by permission of the author and publisher.

[43] Harvey W. Zorbaugh, "Is Instability Inherent in Giftedness and Talent?" *Proceedings of the Third Conference on Education and the Exceptional Child,* The Woods Schools, Langhorne, Pa., May, 1937, p. 17.

[44] Wilhelm Lange-Eichbaum, *The Problem of Genius.* New York: The Macmillan Company, 1932.

[45] Zorbaugh, *op. cit.,* pp. 19-20.

Professor Zorbaugh's own experiences with the Clinic for the Social Adjustment of the Gifted, of which he is the head, lead him to question any such inherent association between instability and the potentiality of genius as Lange-Eichbaum and popular opinion assume. Dr. Zorbaugh points out, however, that it is possible to debate the desirability of children of genius "growing into adult life too well adjusted in the ordinary meaning of the word," although there have certainly been stable and adjusted men of genius—Titian, Rubens, Verdi, and Dürer, for example. Furthermore, Dr. Zorbaugh argues, even though the gifted children he has studied should come through into adult life as reasonably stable and adjusted personalities, their adjustment is likely to be on a different level, of a different quality, than that of persons we commonly think of as adjusted:

These children are vastly more sensitive to and reactive to the experiences of living than are children in general. Their minds are more active in organizing their experiences into an inner reconstruction of reality. Their reconstructions of reality are more personal, less cultural. Their adjustments are more largely to the demands of this personal reality. From this fact springs much of their creativeness. From this fact springs much of the impression of being socially unique which they make upon others. From this fact must spring, as well, a certain sense of conflict with their environing culture. There is little danger of these children feeling so at peace with their social world that their creative fires are dampened.[46]

## Present Trends

In 1875 the United States Office of Education was reported as dealing with 40 institutions for the instruction of deaf mutes, 28 for the blind, 9 for the feeble-minded, 400 for orphans, and 45 for "the reformation of misguided youth." We have gone some distance since then in recognition of the problem, at least, if not in actually filling the requirements of children in need of special assistance.

Possibly the most noteworthy change has been with respect to institutional care. Recent Office of Education figures stress day-school attendance of handicapped children; they show that special schools or classes in public day schools for one or more of the different types of exceptional children have been established in 46 states, "encompassing approximately 750 cities, and enrolling at least 300,000 children in special classes, including home and hospital groups." [47] Residential schools still exist for the blind,

---

[46] Zorbaugh, *op. cit.*, p. 24.
[47] Katherine M. Cook, in *Proceedings of the Fourth Conference on Education and the Exceptional Child*, Langhorne, Pa., 1938, p. 8.

deaf, socially maladjusted, or mentally deficient to the number of between four and five hundred, and many of them are doing valuable work, but it has been found that much more can be done than was formerly assumed possible with handicapped or difficult children without removing them from the natural home and community setting. Some of the residential schools are particularly useful, not only for working with those cases where institutional care is found to be desirable or necessary, but for the pioneering they do in better methods of working with exceptional children to the end that "their happy adjustment becomes a challenging responsibility." [48]

The same philosophy that encourages American society to keep as many as possible of those with special difficulties in a living relationship with their family and friends in the home and community rather than isolated in an institution applies also, many believe, to the so-called gifted children, or children with a high I. Q., discussed in a preceding section. Some, however, maintain that there are values as well as disadvantages in organizing superior children into a class or school, where this is administratively possible. It is interesting to find emotional as well as intellectual factors insisted upon for the special educational program of a genius:

> Above all, the teacher must be a warm, human sort of a person. . . . The genius retires to his books because he gets little satisfaction from the usual opportunities for human relationships. But surround him with schoolmates of equal potentialities, place him in the charge of a friendly, mature, and able teacher, and he soon will blossom forth to be at least as sociable as a normal child.[49]

Whether gifted or defective, the exceptional child will derive benefit from a program that has a place for the arts. "The arts are invaluable," said Elizabeth Moos at the Third Conference on Education and the Exceptional Child, "not only as a means for the creative expression of the child, but as diagnostic and therapeutic agents":

> Through the arts, conflicts that could not otherwise appear may be expressed. Antagonisms, fantasies, the child's inner life, may come into external being, to his own great satisfaction, and to the benefit of the teacher.[50]

---

[48] See "Residential Schools for the Handicapped." Washington, D. C.: U. S. Government Printing Office. (U. S. Office of Education *Bulletin*, 1939, No. 9.)

[49] Irving Lorge and Raphael D. Blau, "The Education of a Genius," *School and Society*, Vol. 54, p. 574, December 20, 1941.

[50] Third Conference on Education and the Exceptional Child, *Proceedings*, p. 29.

It is the teacher's business, says Ruth Hankins, to cultivate an appreciation of what is worthwhile in artistic fields.[51] "To the mentally retarded, who are seldom creative to any great extent, it is important that they learn to gain pleasure and profit from the enjoyment of beauty in all its forms—in music, in literature, in color and form." Miss Hankins emphasizes the value of playing some musical instrument as an outlet for emotions otherwise blocked. "Drawing and painting, pencil, pen and ink, pastel, crayon, show card paints, finger paints, water color, oil—here again, although the mode of expression may be mediocre, yet the time spent on these activities is happily and productively occupied."

That these and other desirable educational opportunities are needed for all children, and not only for those who are markedly deviant, is emphasized in much of the recent literature. The report of the National Association of Secondary School Principals on non-academic children finds "nothing that would lead to the assumption that these young people are in any way peculiar":

> The same personal urges for affection, security, and self-realization are paramount in all groups. Certainly the social demands for vocational efficiency, intelligent citizenship, good character, and all the values that constitute a stable society are equally desirable for every type of individual, whatever his gifts and limitations. . . .
>
> Only in the degree to which a school can adjust its instruction to satisfy the present real and personal needs of all pupils can it hope to provide the conditions that lead to the larger objectives of preparation for an adjusted and satisfying adult life.[52]

This emphasis upon the possibilities of every individual for making his own contribution, large or small, to human life is brought out admirably in Goodwin Watson's discussion of "The Exceptional Child as a Neglected Resource."[53] In Watson's view, human beings can be considered uniquely valuable in themselves:

> But can everyone contribute? My answer is an unqualified "yes." We can conceive no society so perfect, run by people so talented, that you or I could not do some humble service to help make it better. . . .
>
> I want to apply this same concept whenever a child is added to the two billion inhabitants of the earth. Potentially, he is a valuable resource. . . . Something he can learn to do will make life interesting for him and more satisfying to the rest of us. In this complex culture of ours there could be uncounted

[51] "Principles of Teaching Exceptional Children in the Elementary Schools." Langhorne, Pa.: Woods Schools, 1939. (*Child Research Clinic Series*, Vol. III, No. 1, p. 13.)

[52] "The Needs of the Educationally Neglected," in *That All May Learn. Bulletin of the National Association of Secondary School Principals*, November, 1939, p. 60.

[53] Goodwin Watson, "The Exceptional Child as a Neglected Source," *Child Research Clinic Series*, Vol. II, No. 6, Part II. Langhorne, Pa., 1937, p. 6.

opportunities for personal happiness and for social usefulness, for exceptional as well as typical persons.

## QUESTIONS AND EXERCISES FOR DISCUSSION AND STUDY

1. If you can do so without embarrassment, try to find out whether people you know who have so-called physical handicaps—blindness, deafness, weak heart, and so forth—are subject to any special emotional difficulties.

2. Why are "gifted" children discussed in this chapter as one group of "exceptional" children?

3. Do you accept or reject the notion advanced by several authorities cited in this chapter that "there is danger in setting 'handicapped' individuals apart from others"? Why?

4. What did Dr. Edgar A. Doll mean by referring (page 356) to 40 per cent of all children as "exceptional"?

5. Do you know personally any cases, like those cited in the chapter, of individuals who have made very acceptable adjustments in spite of physical or other handicaps? To what do you attribute their success?

6. Would the guidance and counseling procedure described by Dr. Gabriel Farrell (page 360) be desirable for all children and youth, or only for the blind?

7. From the facts given about Tony, the boy with the heart ailment, would you think it best for him to live at home or go to a boarding home? What additional data would you need to have before making a recommendation?

8. What do you understand by "retardation"? Did you go to a school where there was "homogeneous" or "ability" grouping? What are the emotional implications of it, good or bad?

9. "Reading disabilities are frequently due to causes deep in the emotional life of the child." Discuss this statement in the light of your own experience and your reading in psychology.

10. The work of the visiting teacher is mentioned in connection with the Massachusetts program (page 368). Find out whether visiting teacher service is available in your community and near by, and, if it is, what has been accomplished through it.

11. Do the examples cited in this chapter incline you to the belief that "gifted" individuals have more than their share of emotional difficulties, or not? Should the education of "gifted" children differ from that of "normal" children?

12. What is a "normal" child?

## SELECTED REFERENCES FOR FURTHER READING AND STUDY

Baker, Harry J., *Introduction to Exceptional Children*. New York: The Macmillan Company, 1944.

Best, Harry, *Blindness and the Blind in the United States*. New York: The Macmillan Company, 1934.

————, *Deaf and Deafness in the United States*. New York: The Macmillan Company, 1943.

Brunschwig, Lily, *Personality Study of Deaf Children*. New York: Teachers College, Columbia University, 1936. (*Contributions to Education*, No. 687.)

California State Department of Education, *The Education of Physically Handicapped Children*. Sacramento: State Printing Office, 1941. (*Bulletin*, Vol. X, No. 12, December, 1941.)

Child Research Clinic of the Woods Schools, Langhorne, Pa., *New Contributions of Science to the Exceptional Child*. (1935 to date.)

————, *Psychotherapy for the Exceptional Child*. (Proceedings of the Tenth Institute, 1943.)

Ciocco, Antonio, and Carroll E. Palmer, *The Hearing of School Children*. Washington, D. C.: National Research Council, Society for Research in Child Development, 1941.

Cutsforth, Thomas D., *The Blind in School and Society*. New York: D. Appleton-Century Company, 1933.

Davies, Stanley P., *Social Control of the Mentally Deficient*. New York: Thomas Y. Crowell Company, 1930.

Dodds, B. L., *That All May Learn. Bulletin of the National Association of Secondary School Principals*, Vol. 23, November, 1939.

French, Richard S., *From Homer to Helen Keller*. New York: American Foundation for the Blind, 1932.

Habbe, Stephen, *Personality Adjustments of Adolescent Boys with Impaired Hearing*. New York: Teachers College, Columbia University, 1936. (*Contributions to Education*, No. 667.)

Hilleboe, Guy L., *Finding and Teaching Atypical Children*. New York: Teachers College, Columbia University, 1930. (*Contributions to Education*, No. 423.)

Martens, Elise H., *The Deaf and the Hard-of-Hearing in the Occupational World*. Washington, D. C.: U. S. Government Printing Office, 1936. (U. S. Office of Education *Bulletin*, 1936, No. 13.)

————, *Teachers' Problems With Exceptional Children*, II. *Gifted Children*. Washington, D. C.: U. S. Government Printing Office, 1933. (Pamphlet No. 41.)

———— and Florence E. Reynolds. *An Annotated Bibliography on the Education and Psychology of Exceptional Children*. U. S. Department of the Interior, Office of Education, Washington, D. C.; U. S. Government Printing Office, 1937. (Pamphlet No. 71.)

Merry, Ralph V., *Problems in the Education of Visually Handicapped Children*. Cambridge, Mass.: Harvard University Press, 1933.

Meyer, Max F., *Fitting into a Silent World; the First Six Years of Life*. Columbia, Mo.: University of Missouri, 1934. (*Studies*, Vol. 9, No. 2, April 1, 1934.)

Skinner, Charles E., Philip L. Harriman, and others, *Child Psychology*. New York: The Macmillan Company, 1941. Chap. 16.

Walker, Helen M., and Mary C. Shauffler, *The Social Adjustment of the Feebleminded*. Cleveland, Ohio: Western Reserve University Press, 1930.

White House Conference, Committee on Physically and Mentally Handicapped, *The Handicapped Child*. New York: D. Appleton-Century Company, 1933.

# CHAPTER 19

# Mental Hygiene

Mental hygiene has to do primarily with the development of more wholesome human relationships. It means applying to everyday living what has been learned with regard to the behavior of human beings. On the negative side, it has been concerned with more humane and intelligent care and treatment of the mentally ill. Positively, it has meant the early discovery of mental and emotional difficulties, the prevention of as much threatened serious illness and disorder as possible, and the provision of healthful living for the greatest conceivable number of individuals as members of a modern society. For teachers, social workers, and others whose daily activities have to do with children, youth, and other human beings, mental hygiene involves not only a better understanding of human growth and development with respect to those with whom they work, but also an understanding of the worker's own personality and his own relationship to his family, associates, school, and community.

## The Nature of Mental Health

Human behavior, according to Daniel Prescott and L. L. Jarvie of the Commission on Teacher Education of the American Council on Education,[1] is the outcome of the interaction of certain fundamental aspirations and motives from within the individual and the demands, pressures, and influences exerted upon him by other persons and by the world about him. "If surrounding conditions and pressures make it impossible for the individual to meet his needs and satisfy his aspirations, unpleasant emotions and inacceptable or ineffective behavior inevitably result. If circumstances permit the satisfaction of needs and the realization of aspirations, effective behavior . . . and personal happiness ensue."

---

[1] As reported in "A Conference on Personnel Relations in Public Education," *Report of the Study Conference of Representatives of the Schools of Los Angeles City, Los Angeles County, Pasadena, Santa Monica, and Burbank, California.* Los Angeles: Office of the County Superintendent of Schools, 1941, p. 27.

Certain ends or objectives that are more or less continuously sought by all human beings are listed by Prescott and Jarvie as follows:

a. The maintenance of the health of the body by proper nourishment, elimination, avoidance of infection, etc.

b. The spending of energy (activity) at a rate that is natural for the physique concerned.

c. The functioning of the body in the various ways its design implies function.

d. The alternation of activity and rest in accord with the natural rhythm of the body.

e. The growth and maintenance of a body that attracts the admiration of others and gives a sense of personal effectiveness and beauty to the individual.

f. The winning of evidences of love and affection from others and of the right to show love and affection to others.

g. The experience of evidence that most of the persons with whom one works and one's associates are glad that one is present.

h. The experience of having one's associates turn to one for advice, companionship, approbation, sympathy, and active help.

i. The experience of evidence that those less privileged or developed (subordinates) look up to and respect one.

j. The experience of evidence that those more privileged or developed (superiors) have confidence in and respect for one's judgment, skill, and personal integrity.

k. The experience of evidence that one is making progress toward increased professional and personal effectiveness.

l. The experience of evidence that increased professional effectiveness is being recognized and will be acknowledged and rewarded (promotion, salary increase, time adjustments, greater freedom to make decisions, being consulted about problems, praised before others, etc.).

m. The feeling that one is competent to meet any situation likely to arise in one's professional and personal life.

n. The sense of having a rich background of general and professional experience and of being in the process of moving toward many more interesting and satisfying experiences in the future.

o. The feeling that one understands life and one's place in it and that one is seeking and doing "significant" (important) things.

p. The sense of having significant roles among groups of persons that are working toward the improvement of contemporary and future life—the nation, the church, the community, the profession, the family, the clubs, etc.

q. The sense of a steadily improving quality in one's own living—"better" car, "better" music, "better" people in one's circle of friends, "better" home, "better" position.

r. The experience of evidence that one has "risen above" or "conquered" personal handicaps, traits or background that limited one's personal development (physical disabilities, personal eccentricities, inferior family social status, a "foreign" background, poverty, lack of education, lack of "savoir faire," etc.).

s. The experience of evidence that one is "free" to do that which he believes is best and most satisfying in his professional and personal life.

t. The feeling that one's values and behavior are consonant with the ultimate forces and authorities of the universe—that one "does the will of God," "promotes the brotherhood of man," "improves the lot of the unfortunate," promotes the power and stability of the nation, etc.

u. The experience of evidence that the area of knowledge, the type of service, or the type of institution with which one identifies oneself is becoming increasingly useful in the community, and is receiving increased recognition and support by superiors, subordinates, and the public.[2]

## The Extent of Mental Ill-Health

That relatively few persons achieve these objectives, and that "effective behavior and personal happiness" do not ensue for vast numbers of human beings is only too evident. Man has by no means mastered the elements of a satisfying existence for himself and his fellows. He has not even used to any appreciable extent the folk wisdom, the spiritual insight, or the scientific knowledge already available to him for this purpose.

How serious and widespread mental illness and emotional disorder really are is not generally understood. One indication of the magnitude of the problem is the amount of institutional provision necessary. It takes approximately half a million hospital beds to care for the mentally ill and "insane," or more than are necessary for all other types of illness. This does not take into account the vast number of those who, while not in institutions, are nevertheless the despair of their families and friends because of their inability to cope with modern conditions of living. The late William A. White, for many years head of St. Elizabeth's Hospital in Washington, once remarked that mental hygiene would not mean much until it affected not only the more obvious difficulties of the maladjusted, but the way of life for all people. Indeed, the scope of mental ill-health may be said to embrace every form of human conflict, from war on the international scene to gloom at the breakfast table.

When the president of the Rockefeller Foundation in a recent report was describing the activities of his organization in this field, he spoke of mental hygiene as a branch of medical science, but it is clear from his statement that he had in mind also psychology and other areas of human knowledge:

Why mental hygiene? Because it is the most backward, the most needed, and potentially the most fruitful field in medicine today. The number of hospital beds devoted to the care of mental cases exceeds in many countries the number of hospital beds for all other diseases put together. If there were any way of knowing the number of hospital patients whose apparent bodily illnesses are the result or concomitant of mental disorders, the picture would expose even more vividly the discrepancy in our effectiveness against "diseases of the

[2] *Ibid.*, pp. 27-29.

mind" as contrasted with "diseases of the body." Our tragic lack of knowledge in this backward field may be deduced from the economic, moral, social, and spiritual losses occasioned by the feeble-minded, the delinquents, the criminal insane, the emotionally unstable, the psychopathic personalities, and—less dramatic but far more widespread—the preventable anxieties, phobias, tantrums, complexes, and anomalous or unbalanced behavior of otherwise normal human beings.[3]

That body and mind cannot be separated for purposes of treatment is further emphasized in this Rockefeller Foundation report. "Whether he will or no, the doctor's office is a confessional of spiritual as well as physical disability. 'Mankind's eternal cry is for release, and the physician must answer it with something more than a test tube.'"

Dr. Louis Hamman, of Johns Hopkins University Medical School, told the symposium on mental health at the Richmond meeting in 1938 that of some five hundred patients brought under his care as a specialist in internal medicine, not one had consulted him for an overt psychiatric condition, yet 116, or 23 per cent, had no discoverable organic cause for the symptoms of which they complained; 56, or 11 per cent, presented minor organic lesions, but not such as to account for the symptoms. In other words, Dr. Hamman concluded, "one third suffered solely or predominantly from functional disorders," and at least a fourth were essentially psychiatric problems.[4]

Mental ill-health is not confined to any one section of the population. Although some statistics seem to indicate a disproportionate amount in professional and higher-income groups, this is undoubtedly due in part at least to the fact that those in this group are more likely to be conscious of the problem and in a better economic position to provide the costly care and treatment that are required. Studies of college students show a fairly high percentage in need of psychiatric service. Among 1619 University of Pennsylvania freshmen entering in 1937-1938, the incidence of "real mental disease" was low, but 16.4 per cent were adjudged, after being interviewed by a psychiatrist who had previously collected certain life-history data, to have problems "severe enough to warrant a continuation of therapeutic interviews."[5] Kenneth Heaton and other investigators have found evidence that the freshman year in

[3] "The World of the Mind," *Annual Report of the Rockefeller Foundation,* New York, 1936.

[4] "Mental Health," *A Report of the Symposium of the Section on Medical Sciences,* American Association for the Advancement of Science, Richmond, Virginia, December 28-30, 1938. (Lancaster, Pa.: Science Press.)

[5] Harold D. Palmer, "Common Emotional Problems Encountered in a College Mental Hygiene Service," *Mental Hygiene,* Vol. 23, pp. 544-553, October, 1939.

college is particularly difficult for youth. Many of the maladjustments seem to be due, they report, to the fact that "many students are not prepared for the personal and social adjustments required when they leave the old familiar environment of home, parents, and friends, and enter into the new environment of college campus and new associates." [6] The transition is considered less onerous for those who have in pre-college years been given responsibility for the completion of their own work, for the selection of their own friends, for making their own decisions, for managing their own money, for association with a variety of social groups, and for adjustment to rules and routines similar to those imposed in college. That the problems are definitely in the mental health field is asserted by most authorities. "No college student ever suffered a nervous breakdown as a result of over-work," says Dr. Palmer in discussing the Pennsylvania study mentioned above. "At least I have never encountered a case. Mental conflict is the thief that steals the mental efficiency of the student." [7]

## Remedial and Preventive Measures

What can be done about this problem of mental health, both from the remedial and the preventive point of view? The fight against mental disease, Dr. C. Macfie Campbell says, is a war in which all elements in the population must take part. As a physician, he urges not only the necessity to increase the body of medical knowledge as rapidly as possible, but also "to bring the facts within this field of medicine into their natural relationship with other branches of science." [8] Dr. Harry Stack Sullivan, another medical man, points out that "both the social sciences and psychiatry have been relatively sterile in the practical direction of human affairs":

The mental hygiene movement has corrected many abuses in the case of those who fail; child guidance and the psychiatric repercussions in education have saved many from more serious warp. The debit side of the ledger is not as red a picture as it was fifty years ago. On the credit side, however, the sum total of positive constructive changes in the fabric of society is woefully small. The instrumentalities of psychiatry and the social disciplines have been unsuited to ready use by legislator, jurist and statesman, not so much because of technical abstruseness as because of inherent narrowness and overspecialization of purview. Hope for the general conservation of mental health would seem chiefly

[6] Kenneth L. Heaton, "The Contributions of Research to the Redefinition of College Entrance Requirements," *Educational Record*, April, 1941, pp. 167-168.

[7] Palmer, *op. cit.*, p. 549.

[8] "The Gist of It," *Summary and Conclusions of the Symposium on Mental Health, Section on Medical Sciences*, American Association for the Advancement of Science, Richmond, Virginia, December 28-30, 1938.

to reside in a pooling of the techniques available in the social and the psychiatric disciplines, a redefinition of the fields to be explored, and a vigorous support of research into the currents of social change and personal experience, so that we can rapidly discover relationships that make for the healthy expansion of personality and the effective collaboration of people.[9]

It would be tragic if we did not attempt to solve this enormous problem of mental health, to build on what has already been achieved. "If a majority of those committed to institutions were not cured and able to resume everyday life, the toll taken by mental ill-health and crime would cripple our civilization," say Cutts and Moseley. "If a large number can be cured, it stands to reason that in many cases their breakdown could have been prevented. This is our hope and our challenge."[10]

Any program for work in mental health necessarily cuts across many sciences and fields of knowledge—for example, physiology, psychiatry, psychology, sociology, anthropology, social case work, and education. Illustrative of the diverse approaches that have been made is the list of activities and agencies cited in the Rockefeller report previously mentioned:

Appropriations now operative under this Foundation program include such diverse approaches as the University of Illinois, for teaching and investigative work in *psychiatry;* Johns Hopkins University, for the development of *neurology;* the Institute of *Child Welfare* of the University of California; the Institute for *Psychoanalysis* in Chicago; the Institute of Human *Genetics* at the University of Copenhagen; the National Committee for *Mental Hygiene;* Galton Laboratory, University of London, for research in *genetics;* Maudsley Hospital, London, for research in *psychiatry;* College of Physicians and Surgeons of Columbia University, for *psychiatric* research; Worcester State Hospital, Massachusetts, and the University of Amsterdam, Netherlands, for work in *dementia praecox;* University of Leiden, Netherlands, for research in *child psychology;* and other institutions and agencies.[11]

### Attitude of Adults

In recent years mental hygienists have turned to education and the schools for help in preventing mental ill-health and for building up wholesome personalities. It has been pointed out, however, that before much can be done through the schools, the attitudes of adults will have to receive consideration. Dr. James S. Plant, speaking as a psychiatrist with many years' experience as director of the Essex County Juvenile Clinic at Newark, New Jersey, has

[9] *Ibid.,* p. 9.
[10] Norma E. Cutts and Nicholas Moseley, *Practical School Discipline and Mental Health,* p. 3. Used by permission of, and arrangement with, the publishers, Houghton Mifflin Company.
[11] *Rockefeller Foundation Report for 1936.*

described his impressions from contacts with thousands of adults who have had long-time relationships with teachers and the schools. "The most startling and pervasive thing about these adults," says Dr. Plant, "is their fear of and resistance to change." Only about one in six of the parents with whom he has dealt sees the close relationship between change and growth:

> Adults seem somehow to resent the growth and development of family life and parenthood as though it had been enough to undergo the process in childhood and that it now wasn't "cricket" that they had to begin all over again, in a much more realistic way, to grow up. Something over four-fifths of our population has as its answer to pressing social problems that we get back to something we used to have—the family we used to have, the political integrity we used to have.[12]

Plant says that this resistance to change becomes fairly crystallized before the child goes to school. Schoolroom personal relationships undoubtedly play their part, he thinks; but, whether they do or not, "the psychiatrist is thoroughly accustomed to a conditioning of the child to be afraid of all venture for three or four years before he goes to school." Dr. Plant also finds as significant among adults a "feeling of personal futility" with respect to human affairs—failure to realize that social institutions are, after all, only what "we as individuals acting in groups" make them. "People are society."[13]

In an effort to help a girl student at college whose difficulty went back into her family life, Dr. Harold D. Palmer found the following—a father who was difficult, explosive, selfish, hateful, egotistical, revengeful, who hated his son and ignored his only daughter; a mother who was also unstable, stormy, and quick-tempered. There was constant family strife, the case history showed, with threats of divorce, violence, and desertion, and the children were caught between these two fierce antagonists. "The patient clung to the mother, who lavished affection and admiration upon her."[14] She apparently represented to her mother a vicarious escape, she *must* achieve in order to compensate for and fulfill the mother's unhappy life. She was scourged through grade school and high school, not allowed play and recreation. She must have perfect grades. "Her mother met her at the door after she had hurried home from school in order to study and read; there was cross-examination about tests, recitations, what grades others got, then

---

[12] James S. Plant, "A Psychiatrist Looks at Teacher Education," *Educational Record,* April, 1941, pp. 137-138.

[13] *Ibid.,* p. 140.

[14] Harold D. Palmer, "Common Emotional Problems Encountered in a College Mental-Hygiene Service," *Mental Hygiene,* October, 1939, Vol. 23, p. 552.

lavish praise for perfection in grades. Social contacts were forbidden; recreation consisted of sewing and practicing the piano." [15]

She was graduated from high school at sixteen and entered the university; then contracted pneumonia and lost a year as a result of mastoid complications followed by a long, slow convalescence. On her return to college, she soon discovered her complete lack of social adaptation or of any capacity in that direction. The result was that intellectual compensatory strivings became more acute, failure in social adjustment became a more and more fixed pattern. The foundations of the "social neurosis" were obvious throughout. The need was great for some replacement of maternal solicitude, for a constant giving on the part of others of praise, admiration, and recognition. Failing to find these, the pattern of life that had been to the child sufficient for years now began to fall apart. The need for security was obvious. A new integration of personality on a sounder, more mature basis was imperative.[16]

Most college youth in the process of growing up face situations that may cause them special difficulty, Dr. Clements C. Fry, of the Student Mental Hygiene Department at Yale, told the freshman counselors. He explained how a psychiatrist goes behind the scenes to try to learn why one student fails, why another is a drifter, why a third antagonizes people and rebels against authority; and how, in doing this, he takes a whole history of the individual. For example:

A student was referred to us by his physician because he had been excitable and fearful during a recent illness. When seen, the boy was agitated and complained of having "jitters." This student had always appeared calm, easy-going, and steady. His fellow students regarded him as a good athlete, dependable in a game, and a leader in the group. Their only complaint was that he was lazy because he refused to go out for a major team.

This student's laziness was in reality a strong desire not to go out for the team. He disliked the strain of play, for he feared that the tension would bring out his excitability. When he was excitable, he was "jittery," fearful, and—he thought—foolish as well.

A study of the boy's history revealed many unsuspected elements in his background. First, in personality he was fundamentally an anxious, fearful individual. These temperamental qualities were aggravated by difficulties in his impulsive life and by the uncertainty of his status in relation to his family. He had been a protected child, and he missed his parents and their customary attention. At the same time, however, he did not want to be too closely involved with the family—he was beginning to desire some freedom. In addition to all this, he had not done so well scholastically as he had anticipated, and this disappointment was deflating. Altogether, this student's problems embraced nearly the whole of his life. Staying away from sports was a necessary protection—for he didn't want to risk revealing all these problems when in a tight spot.[17]

---

[15] *Ibid.*, p. 553.

[16] *Ibid.*, pp. 552-553.

[17] Clements C. Fry, "Mental Hygiene and Freshman Counseling," *Mental Hygiene*, April, 1939, Vol. 23, p. 271.

A further suggestion of adult responsibility is found in the attitudes of college teachers. Some authorities look upon the faculty as the chief stumblingblock in a college mental-hygiene program. The problem arises, Dr. Palmer believes, not so much from active hostility toward college mental hygiene efforts as from the fact that the college faculty member "seems to lack any criteria for judging the severity or the depth of emotional problems in college students." Others point to the fact that college and university teachers are themselves likely to be difficult personalities. Thus, Lawrence K. Frank says:

> Those schools and colleges that have made an attempt to help individual personalities to reach a saner, more mature level of functioning are regarded with suspicion and disdain by the others who cling to the purely intellectual program, in which alone they feel professionally secure. The irony of this situation is that the emotionally distorted, unhappy individual often makes the best scholar or scientist, because he finds a socially sanctioned way of living with his maladjustments in an academic career, wherein he sacrifices all else to his professional work as defense against mental ill-health. Thus we are forced by the shining example of a few brilliant, but neurotic, professors to sacrifice all other students upon the altar of intellectual achievement.[18]

## Mental Health and Education

Although other forces count for much in mental health or the lack of it, the responsibilities and opportunities of education in this field have been widely acknowledged in recent years. It is generally conceded that "teachers are in a strategic position to discover maladjustment," and their long-continuing association with a child gives them an opportunity to help him straighten out his difficulties. "Next to the parent and the family, the teacher and the school can do most for mental health," was the statement made over and over again by psychiatrists consulted in the course of a study for the Commonwealth Fund in 1936-1937.[19] "If we cannot, as a very fundamental part of the educational process," Dr. Plant says, "teach children the relationship between change and growth—a willingness to ask at least how much of change is growth —we face further generations of anxiety and timidity as the human race works out its problems." [20]

By some authorities the principles of mental hygiene and of modern education are held to be identical. Thus Dr. C. E. A. Wins-

---

[18] Lawrence K. Frank, "The Reorientation of Education to the Promotion of Mental Hygiene," *Mental Hygiene,* October, 1939, Vol. 23, p. 533.

[19] W. Carson Ryan, *Mental Health Through Education.* New York: The Commonwealth Fund, 1938.

[20] James S. Plant, in *Educational Record,* April, 1941, p. 139.

low, in the health volume of the report of the New York State Regents' Inquiry, says:

> The principles of modern education are identical with the principles of mental hygiene. Both are directed toward cultivating self-confidence, self-respect, self-management, courage, the ability to take responsibility, the ability to overcome difficulties and to carry things through to completion, friendliness, sympathy and cooperation with others, the development and expression of affection, tolerance of differences, the sharing of experience, the freer expression of initiative and creative abilities and interests, freedom from the stigma of guilt and shame, the ability to acknowledge an occasional defect frankly, the honest facing of unpleasant realities, and a capacity for assuming and submitting to authority in a spirit of good will.[21]

And a writer on sociology draws a similar picture of the joint aims of education and mental hygiene:

> The aims of education and mental hygiene should be the same, the development and training of the individual for effective living in a social environment. Both are concerned in leading the child toward habits and attitudes that make the individual better able to attack his life problems. The child comes to the school as a whole, and it is impossible to separate his intellectual functions from his motives, emotions, and social adjustments. Teachers and schools cannot ignore these facts and shirk their responsibilities. They must accept the mental-hygiene viewpoint and free their methods of practices that might cause pupil maldevelopment and maladjustment.[22]

"Acculturation," the process of initiating the child through education into the "culture" of our world, and what this means for the personality of the individual, are receiving increased attention as important aspects of mental health. Mental hygiene is helping us, says Lawrence Frank, to see that this early cultural training is necessary and inevitable, since the young child must be socialized, not only for the protection of society, but for his own guidance and self-management as well. But:

> Mental hygiene also makes clear that the mental health of the individual may be seriously jeopardized by the way in which these interferences and deprivations, these compulsions and prohibitions, are taught to him, and by the way authority in general is administered. That is to say, the personality of the child and his adjustment to society depend upon the way he *feels* about people and situations and especially about himself.[23]

[21] C. E. A. Winslow, in *The School Health Program.* New York: The Regents' Inquiry, 1938. Pp. 22-23.

[22] Darrel Boyd Harmon, "The Teacher and Delinquency from the Mental-Hygiene Point of View," *Journal of Educational Sociology,* Vol. 12, pp. 78-86, October, 1938.

[23] Lawrence K. Frank, "The Orientation of Education to the Promotion of Mental Hygiene," *Mental Hygiene,* October, 1939, Vol. 23, p. 530.

Here again the charge is likely to be made, with some justification, that the school may be responsible for much of the difficulty and, indeed, may itself constitute a menace to mental health:

As we see the young child emerging from this family training, bearing the impact of these cultural lessons, we can begin to evaluate formal schooling in terms of its contribution to mental health or its accentuation of the already established personality difficulties in the young child. Here we see the child entering school at five or six, to face the demands for standardized academic achievement, for rigid conformity and for adjustment to his contemporaries, bringing to these encounters all the perplexities and anxieties of his family background and training. It is evident that much of what is now done in the schools is inimical to mental health, since the child is confronted with more anxieties and exposed to frequent and devastating humiliations. Thus many of the attitudes and feelings he brings from his family training are crystallized and intensified by the school program and discipline.[24]

Likewise, Plant refers disparagingly to the sort of thing one still sees in many schools—"100 per cent present today," or "0 tardy today." This "mass-blackballing," he says, of the child whose absence or tardiness is perhaps already evidence that he is in some difficulty in his home or neighborhood only serves to increase isolation.[25]

Both remedial and preventive measures are involved in a recent discussion of mental hygiene from the point of view of "discipline" problems in the schools. After pointing out that the principles of mental hygiene should be applied not only in dealing with children who are "causing trouble," but even more in the day-by-day work of the school, Cutts and Moseley say:

In negative form, these principles may be summed up as demanding that we do nothing to hinder the physical development of the child, that we do not use shame, sarcasm, or ridicule, and that we do not humiliate him in any way, that we do not ask him to work beyond his physical or mental ability, that we do not place him where he will fail constantly, and that we avoid anger and scolding in our dealings with him. In positive form, these principles tell us to promote the child's health and happiness, to like him, to make him certain of his place in our affections and his membership in the group, to adjust his work to his physical and mental ability to the point where effort will bring success, to express our approval of the good things he does and to praise his effort and improvement, and to be sure that he has a task for which he is responsible which he can do with interest and satisfaction.[26]

---

24 *Ibid.,* p. 532.
25 James S. Plant, in *Educational Record,* April, 1941.
26 Norma E. Cutts and Nicholas Moseley, *Practical School Discipline and Mental Hygiene,* p. 5. Used by permission of, and arrangement with the publishers, Houghton Mifflin Company.

Like other investigators,[27] Cutts and Moseley stress the importance of "emotional climate," and in particular, the desirability of making a good start under favorable living and working conditions:

For the first day of school, the teacher should not only put on a pretty, colorful dress and have her hair attractively done, but also try to see that the room itself is as attractive as possible. Calendulas, asters, cosmos, zinnias are all in a profusion of bloom when school opens; [28] if they can be begged, borrowed, or bought, make the room gay with them. Fill the bulletin board with pictures of summer travels and clippings of current interest. Have new books and illustrated magazines on the library table. Do everything to make the room bright and cheerful and to provide a place the children will take pride in coming to and keeping clean. Start them quickly on adding new items to the bulletin board, drawing pictures for the walls, and stocking the aquarium with fish. It is hard to associate misbehavior with a room of this kind, and one rarely finds it there.[29]

In her *Practical Procedures in Mental Hygiene for Public Schools*,[30] Nora Alice Way quotes approvingly a set of questions for teachers propounded some years ago by a well-known worker in a progressive school. Miss Way thinks teachers would do well to ask themselves from time to time:

1. Do I practice good self-control?

2. Do I maintain an attitude of cheerfulness and optimism toward all my pupils and their problems?

3. Do I attempt to avoid worry?

4. Do I get along well with fellow workers?

5. Do I in every way avoid giving the impression of hurrying?

6. Am I willing to face squarely my own personality handicaps and try to correct them?

7. Am I able to create an atmosphere of happiness? [31]

### Effect of the Teacher's Personality

That teachers through the impact of their own personalities play an important part for good or ill in mental health is emphasized by investigators. Analyzing the factors that conduce to truancy and juvenile misbehavior, Wallin puts the first responsibility upon the teacher:

[27] Bernice Baxter, for example. Also see Chapter 16.
[28] The writers are speaking chiefly in terms of the northeastern United States.
[29] Norma E. Cutts and Nicholas Moseley, *Practical School Discipline and Mental Health*, p. 17. Used by permission of, and arrangement with, the publishers, Houghton Mifflin Company.
[30] Summit, New Jersey, 1939. (Published by the author.)
[31] Bess B. Lane, "The Teacher Looks at Herself," *Progressive Education*, March, 1931, Vol. 8, p. 212.

The first factor is the maladapted, tactless, uninspiring, sarcastic, dyspeptic, emotionally maladjusted or immature teacher, or the taskmaster type of teacher who possesses little insight into personality problems, the mechanisms of the child mind, the dynamics of emotional conditioning or malconditioning in children, the effects of teacher behavior patterns upon the learning and affective attitudes of the learner, or the teacher who is solely or mainly concerned with the development of certain kinds of subject matter skills, oblivious of or unconcerned about the influences that the learning procedures used may exert upon the personality integration of the pupil.[32]

Wallin concludes that the role of the teacher is strategic and dynamic in all phases of pupil adjustment, in the development of effective or ineffective teaching or learning methods, in the development of desirable or undesirable pupil attitudes and pupil liking or disliking for school, in the stimulation of enthusiasm for learning, and in the acceptance of a life ideology that makes for mental and social health.

But when we undertake any exploration into the personality of the teacher, Rivlin warns us, "We are faced with the fact that we really don't know what the teacher's personality is like, or what it should be like in the ideal situation." [33] There is always the danger, Rivlin says, of accepting the cartoonist's caricature of a teacher as realistic; similarly with respect to the studies that have been made of the teacher's personality by psychologists and psychiatrists, "it is often the extremely maladjusted teacher who is investigated and not the kind of teacher who is to be found in most of the classrooms of the country." [34]

Rivlin analyzes the factors in teacher personality and then illustrates how one would go about effecting a change:

For example, what can be done for the teacher who is over-sensitive to criticism, who is easily offended by any suggestion that is made by his supervisor, even though the criticism is merited and the suggestion is sound? Is it enough merely to tell him that he must learn to accept criticism graciously? Hardly. Before we can offer any specific suggestions to the over-sensitive teacher, we must agree on the fundamental procedures to be used in the modification of personality traits.[35]

Basically, Rivlin points out, the procedures in modifying the teacher's personality are the same as would be used when the teacher seeks to modify behavior in a youngster.

---

[32] J. E. W. Wallin, "The Nature and Implications of Truancy from the Standpoint of the Schools," *Proceedings of the Fourth Conference on Education and the Exceptional Child.* Langhorne, Pa.: The Woods Schools, May, 1938.

[33] Harry N. Rivlin, "The Personality Problems of Teachers," *Mental Hygiene,* Vol. 23, p. 12, January, 1939.

[34] *Ibid.,* p. 13.

[35] *Ibid.,* p. 15.

All teachers realize how futile it is merely to tell the disobedient child that he must be good, to tell the truant that he ought to come to school, or to tell the child who has been stealing that theft is dishonest. The only method by which the teacher can actually cure the child is to find out why he is truant, or why he steals. It is only by removing the underlying cause that the teacher can hope to change the student's behavior pattern.[36]

Just so with the teacher's own personality—the surest way of effecting a lasting change is to discover the cause. But Rivlin warns, of course, that "inasmuch as it is often difficult to discover the cause, it is no easy matter to change personality," whether with children or with teachers.

Rivlin puts it in the last analysis up to selection by the training institutions:

Can new entrants to our profession be so selected and educated that future teachers will have the kind of personality that is needed in the classroom? Here, too, the possibilities of a preventive program are far greater than are those of a program of correction. The key to the improvement of teacher personality is to be found in schools of education, where future teachers are now enrolled as undergraduate students. The school of education must select its students carefully and give them the kind of experiences that will make certain that the new teacher brings to the classroom not only a keen mind, a rich background, and skill in teaching techniques, but also a stable personality, one that will exert a wholesome influence on the personalities of his students.[37]

Any assumption, however, that even approximately valid instruments are available for determining the personality of a teacher —or any other human being—is unwarranted. One of our best-known contemporary educational psychologists [38] has expressed the hope that teacher-education institutions and school systems engaged in redirecting the education of teachers will go at the task from a point of view that will include: (1) willingness to look at the individual as an organism; (2) an interest in the experimental courses that will give adequate attention to "intellect" (a good deal depends upon what one means by "intellect": one should mean by it that the individual has to *learn* effective behavior, which, in turn, depends upon the capacity of the organism to learn by experience); (3) willingness to study the future effects of experience in leading to *ideals* or value *concepts* (which are dynamic with respect to human behavior); (4) an understanding of the evolution of social behavior—relationship of the youngster with parents, siblings, play group, school, occupation group, political

---

[36] *Ibid.*, p. 16.
[37] *Ibid.*, p. 24.
[38] Daniel A. Prescott, of the University of Chicago and the Commission on Teacher Education of the American Council on Education. For the views of Dr. Prescott and his staff, the reader is referred to the reports of the Commission.

group, and world citizenship; (5) acknowledgment of the role of emotion in human life.

Emphasizing the fact that modern industry has begun to develop new personnel procedures in which the human needs of the workers are recognized, Dr. Prescott urges similar attention to the professional personnel in education. "The teacher of the future will be of more help to children in the process of growing up," he says, "because he will understand children better and because he will be more grown-up himself." [39] Moreover, he adds, changes in the education of teachers and in organizing and operating schools that will be necessary to secure such a teacher are all "within the range made possible by present knowledge of human development and behavior."

It is generally agreed that nursery schools and nursery-school teachers have been especially helpful in mental hygiene. The first objective of many such schools has been to aid in the emotional adjustment of children. Free from conventional preconceptions as to what schools should be and do, the nursery schools were able to focus on "a better physical, mental, and emotional development of the child." Summarizing the literature of nursery-school education, Dr. Douglas A. Thom of Boston said with respect to the preschool contribution to mental hygiene:

If a generation of children were permitted to enjoy during the pre-school years an environment which fulfilled their physical, intellectual, and emotional needs as outlined and as expressed in the proposed plan for pre-school education, there is reason to believe that they well might attain a greater sense of security in all personal relationships resulting in a harmonious adjustment with parents, contemporaries, and those in authority. They would acquire confidence in self as a result of personal achievement, and adequate recognition, and something very much worth while and far-reaching would be accomplished. Such a group would find a happier and more efficient adjustment to the demands of life and relatively less conflict with society in general.[40]

What can schools and colleges do directly to improve mental health? Several ways of helping have already been suggested or implied in this chapter—seeking to understand the development of children and youth, searching out causes of behavior, recognizing the significance of the emotions, and maintaining the right kind of "emotional climate." In the case of the girl of college age cited by Dr. Palmer,[41] the college had no hesitation in saying that, regard-

---

[39] Daniel A. Prescott, "The Teacher of the Future," *Understanding the Child,* June, 1941, p. 11.

[40] Douglas A. Thom, "The Psychiatric Implication of Education," *American Journal of Psychiatry,* January, 1936, p. 834.

[41] Harold D. Palmer, *op. cit.,* p. 552.

less of the fact that the college did not produce the problem, it should be responsible for trying to solve it. Moreover, Dr. Palmer insisted that there was real hope of success. The "simple therapeutic program" put into action in such a case as this was as follows:

1. "Therapeutic interviews are held once or twice a week to give opportunities for the unloading of tension.

2. "Contact is made at once with the dean of the college for women and she is told of the student's need for success in social relations and for achievement in extracurricular activities.

3. "A schedule is drawn up which has a certain fixed pattern; as much emphasis is laid on hobbies, cultural interests, physical recreation, participation in social groups as on scholastic application.

4. "Endocrine studies are made to see whether further physical growth is possible and the question of growth stimulation by endocrine substances is considered.

5. "Remedial exercises are prescribed for postural correction.

6. "The dermatologist is asked to see the patient in order to begin therapy for her acne at the earliest possible moment.

7. "Endocrine and gynecological studies are also undertaken in an effort to determine the cause of dysmenorrhea, irregularity, and scantiness of menses." [42]

In a statement referring especially to the co-ordination of all mental health forces in college, but applicable also to work with children and youth in the schools, Dr. Palmer pictures the psychiatrist at an educational institution as visualizing (in a sort of wish-fulfillment fantasy) "the mobilization of mental-hygiene forces in a campaign for penetrating the whole of college life, the organization into an integrated system of all the agencies capable of fostering the growth of stable, mature personalities in the students."

An example of organized mental hygiene facilities at the public school level is that of Essex County, New Jersey, where the Bureau of Child Guidance in the city schools of Newark and the Essex County Juvenile Clinic have taken the lead in mental hygiene work both within and without the schools.[43] The work started in 1923 with the setting up of a tax-supported child guidance clinic to serve the county courts. Out of this have developed "a number of

---

[42] Harold D. Palmer, "Common Emotional Problems Encountered in a College Mental Hygiene Service," *Mental Hygiene*, October, 1939, Vol. 23, p. 554.

[43] "The Essex County Program," *Understanding the Child*, Vol. VIII, No. 3, October, 1939.

autonomous psychiatric, psychological and psychiatric social worker services."

From the start, we are told, the philosophy of this Essex County movement has differed somewhat from that of other similar developments in that the parent, the teacher, the nurse, the policeman, the foreman, and the minister have been viewed as the "chief purveyors of mental hygiene," with the technical workers (psychiatrist, psychologist, and social worker) considered as having their place only in assisting those who naturally are the child's environment:

We believe that it is only as these latter persons are trained to think in terms of what experiences *mean* to the child and in terms of *why* a child acts in a certain way, that a program truly preventive in the areas of crime, mental breakdown, and maladjustment can be set up. Again, in the field of treatment we turn the patient back to his familiar milieu (and depend upon it ourselves) much more than is the case with other guidance programs. This has involved an intensive educational program and a wide use of clinic material to illustrate to parents, teachers, nurses, and others concerned, the fundamental point of view involved.[44]

A comprehensive change in curriculum, whereby activities and experiences are provided to meet the needs of individual children, with creative opportunities in the arts, music, health, and work, is one of the essentials in a school program designed to conserve and strengthen the mental health of children and youth. This may even include, as in Dr. Alice Keliher's discussions based on films, or in the Delaware Human Relations Classes with children of the seventh and eighth grades, participation by the children themselves in attempts to understand the difficulties and possibilities of human behavior. Among the subjects discussed in the Delaware seventh- and eighth-grade classes were the following:

The importance of friends.
Personality traits of a "regular fellow."
Our inner human drives—self-preservation (security); recognition (desire for approval); interest in the opposite sex; adventure.
The value of facing up frankly to personal and social problems—overcoming personal handicaps.
Relationships with younger brothers and sisters.
The necessity for self-discipline—learning to lose gracefully.
Wholesome school relationships—problems of a new pupil in school.
Problems of having older relatives or outsiders living in the family.
First impressions—how we look, talk and act.
The advantages and disadvantages of being timid and shy.
How various types of punishments affect us.
Personality qualifications for various types of vocations.

---

[44] *Op. cit.*, p. 3.

Emotional problems of children in wartime.
Use and abuse of comic books.
Emotions and their effect on behavior.
The result of continued failure on personality development.
Sharing our emotional problems with others.[45]

For those working in the field of education, one way to find out whether what is done tends toward better mental hygiene is to try to answer the following questions:

1. What is the concept of education that prevails? Is it that of narrow schooling, or all-round development? Are we really concerning ourselves with individual human beings and their needs?

2. Does "health" (both mental and physical) actually come first? Do we think of health, work experiences, music and the fine arts, learning to live with other people, as fundamentals in education, or just "extras"?

3. What kind of "emotional climate" do we have—in the classroom, in the administrative office, in the shops, on the playground, everywhere in the enterprise? Are teachers and other school workers friendly, understanding, human?

4. What is the attitude toward "individual differences"? Are we concerned chiefly with the "I.Q.'s" and "subjects," or do we think of individual possibilities in all areas—emotional, aesthetic, social?

5. Do we understand and act on the principle that "behavior is caused"? Do we tend to explore into the conditions that explain what an individual is doing, and help him on the basis of that to make a better adjustment?

6. Has the community learned to provide a child guidance clinic, visiting teachers, and similar service to help youngsters with special problems, and to assist educational workers in understanding the needs of individual human beings?

7. Is the educational situation "authoritarian," or is it genuinely democratic, with children, teachers, parents, and others sharing in planning and carrying out the program?

8. Do the community and the educational administration understand that "administration" is not something that exists for itself, but is justified only as an agency to facilitate the essentially *human* task involved in education?

9. Is our underlying philosophy such that we have faith in the possibilities of human beings—building on what they can do rather than on what they cannot do?

---

[45] "The Human Relations Class," *Understanding the Child*, October, 1941, and October, 1944.

## Mental Health a World Concern

It is important to remember, however, that mental health is much more than a schoolroom problem—that it involves the welfare of communities, states, nations, in fact, our whole world order. The progress of mental hygiene has been impeded by many and serious obstacles, as a philanthropic survey recently showed: "Charlatans masquerading in the livery of its servitors, misconceptions of what it is and does, controversy among its followers, public apathy and unawareness." [46] Support is needed, according to this authority, for extending the gains in control of mental illness, and especially for hastening the possibilities of mental hygiene that now lie largely in the future:

We face a troubled world, its unhappy difficulties due in great, perhaps greatest part to the mental, physical and moral maladjustments of its peoples. These maladjustments are intimately related. No one of them can be corrected in any large way without correction of the others.

The problems of mental disorder involve the most fundamental issues of human life and happiness. For the first time in his history man is making an intelligent effort for their solution. Already he has been richly rewarded. The future that stretches before him is fascinating in its possibilities. Nowhere is support more needed than here—nowhere does it give more generous promise of return.

It needs to be made clear, particularly when mental hygiene is considered in relation to schools, that it is not "merely an added embellishment or auxiliary service to be added to education." It is, as Frank points out, "a far-reaching and all-embracing concept for the reorganization of our culture in terms of human needs and values." If and when we become convinced, as this writer points out, that mental health must be conserved in education, we will call for teachers who are genuinely concerned with the personalities of children and not interested merely in their mental processes, who will continuously recognize the emotional needs and problems of the little boys and girls in their pupils of all ages.

And finally, in Lawrence Frank's words:

Mental health and democracy are goals to be achieved anew by each generation who must give to their children a faith in human nature and a courage to live with love and understanding that can be transmitteu only by warm, intimate human relationships. If each generation will strive to free its children from its emotional handicaps and personality distortions, and bid them go forth to live fully and sanely, mental health and democracy will be secure. A program of mental health education must enlist families and schools, and all other agencies

---

[46] *The Mental Hygiene Movement from the Philanthropic Standpoint.* New York: Central Hanover Bank and Trust Company, 1939.

for human guidance in a united effort to protect and cherish the personalities of all children, if we are to realize our human potentialities.[47]

## QUESTIONS AND EXERCISES FOR DISCUSSION AND STUDY

1. Make a list of the experiences in your own life that seem to you to have (a) helped, or (b) hindered, your mental health.

2. Of the people you know best, how many are examples of "good mental health"?

3. Visit one of the following types of institutions and try to find out what its function in a mental hygiene program is: (a) a hospital for mental diseases; (b) a juvenile reformatory or "reform school"; (c) a nursery school.

4. Check yourself on the list of "ends or objectives" described by Prescott and Jarvie, of the Commission on Teacher Education as "more or less continuously sought by all human beings." (Pages 378 to 380.)

5. What influence, for good or ill, in mental hygiene wielded in your community by the family, the church, the school, the movies?

6. Find out whether any statistics have been compiled for your school or college comparable to those given for University of Pennsylvania freshmen (Page 381.)

7. "How much of change is growth?" Try to answer this question suggested by James S. Plant. (Pages 384 and 386.)

8. Make an investigation to find out how many of the teachers you know accept Winslow's statement (page 386) that "the principles of modern education are identical with the principles of mental hygiene." Then try to decide whether you yourself accept the statement or not.

9. Discuss the procedure for the first day of school recommended by Cutts and Moseley (page 389). Does this seem to you important as mental hygiene?

10. Give your opinion of the importance for mental health of the following plans described in the chapter: (a) the Essex County program; (b) the Human Relations Class; (c) the college program outlined by Harold D. Palmer.

11. Can you justify the statement on page 396 that "mental health is much more than a schoolroom problem—it involves the welfare of communities, states, nations, in fact, our whole world order"?

12. What is the effect of war on mental health?

## SELECTED REFERENCES FOR FURTHER READING AND STUDY

Averill, Lawrence A., *Mental Hygiene for the Classroom Teacher*. New York: Pitman Publishing Corporation, 1939.

Bassett, Clara, *Mental Hygiene in the Community*. New York: The Macmillan Company, 1934.

Beers, Clifford W., *A Mind That Found Itself*. New York: Doubleday, Doran and Company, 25th printing, 1940.

Burnham, William H., *Wholesome Personality: A Contribution to Mental Hygiene*. New York: D. Appleton-Century Company, 1932.

Crow, Lester D., and Alice Crow, *Mental Hygiene in School and Home Life*. New York: McGraw-Hill Book Company, 1942.

[47] Lawrence K. Frank, "The Reorientation of Education to the Promotion of Mental Hygiene," *Mental Hygiene*, October, 1939, Vol. 23, p. 543.

Cutts, Norma E., and Nicholas Moseley, *Practical School Discipline and Mental Health*. Boston: Houghton Mifflin Company, 1941.

Deutsch, Albert, *The Mentally Ill in America*. New York: Doubleday, Doran and Company, 1937.

Fenton, Norman, *Mental Hygiene in School Practice*. Stanford University Press, 1943.

Groves, Ernest R., *Readings in Mental Hygiene*. New York: Henry Holt and Company, 1936.

Howard, F. E., and F. L. Patry, *Mental Health*. New York: Harper and Brothers, 1935.

Keliher, Alice V., *Life and Growth*. New York: D. Appleton-Century Company, 1938.

*Mental Health in the Classroom. Thirteenth Yearbook of the Department of Directors and Supervisors of Instruction,* Washington, D. C.; National Education Association, 1940.

*Mental Health. Symposium of the American Association for the Advancement of Science*. Lancaster, Pa.: Science Press, 1939.

*Personality Adjustment of the Elementary School Child. Fifteenth Yearbook of the Department of Elementary Principals.* Washington, D. C.: National Education Association, 1936.

Ruggles, Arthur H., *Mental Health—Past, Present, and Future*. Baltimore, Maryland: Williams and Wilkins, 1934.

Ryan, W. Carson, *Mental Health Through Education*. New York: The Commonwealth Fund, 1938.

Shaffer, L. F., *The Psychology of Adjustment*. Boston: Houghton Mifflin Company, 1936.

Sherman, Mandel, *Mental Hygiene and Education*. New York: Longmans, Green and Company, 1934.

Skinner, Charles E., and associates, *Readings in Educational Psychology*, Part V. New York: Farrar and Rinehart, 1937.

Thorpe, L. P., *Psychological Foundations of Personality*. New York: McGraw-Hill Book Company, 1938.

Tiegs, E. W., and B. Katz, *Mental Hygiene in Education*. New York: Ronald Press Company, 1941.

Wallin, J. E. W., *Minor Mental Maladjustment in Normal People*. Durham, N. C.: Duke University Press, 1939.

Way, Nora Alice, *Practical Procedures in Mental Hygiene for Public Schools*. Summit, N. J.: published by the author, 1939.

Weill, Blanche C., *Through Children's Eyes*. New York: Island Workshop Press, 1940.

Witty, Paul A., and Charles E. Skinner, editors, *Mental Hygiene in Modern Education*. New York: Farrar and Rinehart, 1939.

Zachry, Caroline B., *Emotion and Conduct in Adolescence*. New York: D. Appleton-Century Company, 1940.

### PERIODICALS

*Child Study*. Quarterly. Child Study Association of America, New York.

*Mental Hygiene*. Quarterly. National Committee for Mental Hygiene, New York.

*Progressive Education*. Monthly. American Education Fellowship (formerly Progressive Education Association), New York.

*Understanding the Child*. Quarterly. National Committee for Mental Hygiene, New York.

# CHAPTER 20

# The Nature and Techniques of Guidance

## Introduction

The purpose of this chapter is to explain the psychological nature of guidance and to make clear the relationship of guidance procedures and techniques to the whole process of learning and adjustment. Since past discussions of guidance have tended to neglect searching inquiry into the psychological essence of guidance, such inquiry will be the main burden of emphasis. Because it is the purpose of this book, primarily, to describe the psychology of learning and teaching, it will not be possible to enter into a detailed description of certain aspects of guidance commonly included in a treatment of guidance proper.

It may be said at the outset that there is nothing new about guidance as a feature of the education of the young. As a matter of fact, it is a venerable educative procedure. It is interesting to note that in primitive educational systems considerable care was taken to induct the young into a proper understanding of the customs and habits of the tribe. Tribal rituals are a case in point. A study of anthropology furnishes us examples of the stereotyped and formalized tribal functions into which the young were initiated. In fact, primitive guidance devices were so effective that, with few exceptions, it was virtually impossible for primitive man to escape the closed orbit of their restricting influence. Personal habits thus built up constituted a lifelong determinant of conduct, often to the disadvantage of the individual himself.

Rome had an interesting plan of child direction. The first phase of the Roman plan was identically the one that we have today in a well organized guidance program—namely, selection. This selection was somewhat brutal, it is true, consisting of the exposure of newborn infants to the elements with the purpose of weeding out weak stock. The training of the Roman youth (incidentally, largely for the boys) consisted in having the young boy follow his father around in the course of the daily routine of activity. This form of guidance is in accord with the most approved modern methods, which in many cases involve excursions to witness the actual operation of various industries, trades, and so forth. Finally, the young Roman was put through the traditional ritual of adolescence, after which he was allowed to assume the toga and was regarded as a full-grown man.

The apprenticeship system of the Middle Ages, to which, curiously enough, we are now showing some tendency to return, illustrates another historical example of this most vital element of the educative process. Psychologically speaking, the apprenticeship system is excellent. It is in considerable accord with the theories of activity-education and specific learning. Apprentice training produced excellent craftsmen. This training was a particularly advantageous type of guidance in a society in which many things, including industrial progress, moved slowly. Modern economic development, with its extremely rapid growth of new industries, presents a different and more complicated problem, the solution of which may result in a modified system of apprenticeship.

All of these early efforts at guidance, and many others, illustrate the fact that there is something deep-seated in the whole process—a fundamental fact recognized for a long time. The problem of today is complicated, and the variables not only change rapidly but affect each other in a partially predictable but far from simple manner.

Shortly after the turn of the present century, there developed conscious and increasingly emphatic attention to guidance. This interest preceded the full flowering of experimental psychology and the development of statistical procedures just enough to result in the emergence of some unfortunate developments, such as the attempt to direct every pupil into the specific trade for which he was supposed to have a peculiar aptitude. We are just beginning to counteract the deleterious effects of these unscientific practices. Taken generally, this guidance of two or three decades ago made an effort to determine more or less absolutely the exact trade, profession, or occupation which an individual should follow, the entire process being based upon a faulty conception of special aptitude, a shaky neurology, and a sort of psychological predestination. Few follow-up studies kept account of the errors of prediction that were made. Under this system, the guidance expert was a sort of educational yogi. What few statisticians there were ranted in vain —and, for that matter, had little better procedures to substitute.

### The nature of guidance

Our brief examination of a few historical episodes from the background of the present concept of guidance as an educative procedure makes it clear that there is nothing novel about attempting systematically to direct the young or to develop behavior patterns calculated to produce easier adjustment to existing social conditions. We shall shortly examine in some detail the general and specific purposes of guidance.

The principal difference between the guidance of today and that of yesterday probably is not in the general philosophy underlying the effort or its social purpose. The superiority of modern guidance techniques, if such superiority they do indeed possess, depends more upon advances in psychological technique in general than upon any radical alterations in thinking concerning what the purpose of guidance may be. Psychology itself, in passing from soul-study to mind-study and thence to behavior-study, carried along with it a number of concomitants, including guidance. And, as psychological technique passed from intuition to introspection, and from introspection to experimentation, the technique of the school procedures dependent upon psychology became correspondingly, although perhaps not proportionately, objective and scientific. For example, as medical and mental measurements of the maturity level of the child became more precise and reliable, guidance officers found their work materially easier in those areas.

In discussing the nature of guidance, we shall consider three major phases. The first of these phases is *counseling*. Counseling is in all probability the oldest of surviving guidance practices. It has always been the function and habit of the elders of the race to transmit to the young information on the *mores*. The function of counseling in former times, however, was narrow and fatalistic in nature and implied a far more exact knowledge of the individual's potentialities than was really at hand. The tendency in bygone days for cobblers' sons to become cobblers was the result of more than mere slowness of transportation and communication: it was a consequence likewise of a narrow, over-paternalistic guidance system. Numerous conspicuous social misfits were the victims of this system. Some of the world's outstanding leaders have had to wrench themselves out of the grasp of an overly rigid parental or teacher domination. The counseling of today makes only moderate effort to convince the child that he must go this way or that. By far the greater effort is given over to pointing out the possibilities in various fields and the problems that will confront the individual in terms of his own analyzed strengths and weaknesses. One example of this method of job analysis is explained by Trabue: [1]

---

[1] Marion R. Trabue, "Functional Classification of Occupations," *Occupations*, Vol. XV, No. 2, November, 1936, p. 129.

Among the broad characteristics commonly recognized as being important in determining one's success in different occupations are the following:

*Int.*   Intellectual power to reason, infer, and learn.

*Mec.*   Mechanical ability and insight.

*Soc.*   Social understanding and effectiveness.

For convenience with reference to any one of these three characteristics, the total adult population might be divided roughly into four quarters.

| * | ** | *** | **** |
|---|---|---|---|
| Lowest Quarter | Low Average Quarter | High Average Quarter | Highest Quarter |

By using these ratings, it is possible to group families of jobs requiring similar characteristics. One family, for example, might permit "lowest quarter" in social understanding. In this family might be such jobs as auto assembler, cook in restaurant, dairy hand, paper-hanger, roofer and slater, and stagehand.

For the vocational guidance of youth, the value of the families or "constellations" of similar jobs . . . is quite obvious. A youth should be guided toward a whole group of occupations, any one of which would be quite appropriate to a person of his make-up, rather than toward a particular job.[2]

A second phase of modern guidance is the *mathematical* side. No one any longer believes that efficiency in guidance is anywhere near perfect. That is, guidance is primarily an effort to estimate probabilities. To estimate probabilities with any degree of accuracy, large amounts of data are necessary. Such numerous data simply decrease the error of prediction. There is nothing at all unique about this approach; the method is a fixture in the field of industry. The man who is making a large investment in a new business is almost certain to require an ample demonstration of its operation. A race-horse breeder keeps extensive data on the performance of the strains that he is breeding in order better to predict the future performance of the individual horses.

Third is the *demonstrative* phase. One of the most conspicuous errors of early guidance in the American system of education was that it consisted almost entirely of expository and hortatory advice. Particularly in the field of vocational guidance, although less so in educational and social guidance, is it possible to demonstrate to the person being guided the exact nature of the several choices with which he is confronted. Hence we see developing a planned program of excursional education. The purpose of vocational trips to various industrial plants is not merely to provide a pleasant outing for the pupils, but to furnish them with first-hand data upon which to base their own choices. This demonstrative phase of modern

---

[2] *Ibid.,* p. 130.

guidance is really the key to the whole effort. There is no better way to conclude this discussion of the nature of guidance than to summarize the opinions of over a thousand teachers on some of the things that guidance should and should not be. Such a summary [3] has been compiled and is herewith quoted:

> Question: Do you accept the thesis that the schools, with the cooperation of parents, should attempt to guide pupils toward what seem to be the best educational and vocational careers for them? If not, why not; if so, with what reservations, if any?

Eleven hundred and twenty teachers answered this question. Only 16 teachers answered "No!" The other 1104, who represent 98½ per cent of those who replied, answered "Yes," thus giving an endorsement for guidance in secondary schools that is almost unanimous.

Their reservations, if such they must be called, constitute some of the best common-sense rules for administering guidance that have yet appeared. The following statements are a consensus of these reservations:

1. Guidance should be rational advice based on factual information.

2. Guidance should not be compulsion, force, domination, cut and dried planning, regimentation, prescription, neither should it be dictatorial or arbitrary.

3. Neither teachers nor parents should force children to follow an unwanted career.

4. The financial and economic status of the family is an important element in guidance.

5. A pupil's desire to enter a field, if great enough, often overcomes seemingly insuperable odds.

6. An efficient and comprehensive guidance organization should be provided for testing and interviewing each child and for evaluating all data about each child.

7. Regular follow-up of all guidance given should be a part of the program.

8. Much guidance must be marked "tentative," to provide for changed circumstances or conditions in the child, the family, and society.

9. Extreme care should be exercised by teachers to avoid "selling" their subjects to pupils when some other subjects might be more useful to them.

10. School guidance should avoid, in so far as it is possible, conflict with home guidance.

11. While parents naturally have their children's interests at heart and try to give them sincere advice, they are prone to error because of the following factors:

---

[3] *Guidance Service Standards for Secondary Schools,* New Jersey Secondary School Teachers Association, 1937, pp. 8-11.

(*a*) The awareness of the child's aptitudes and capacities, and the implications of these facts, are apt to be dulled by sentiment.

(*b*) Their lack of knowledge of a very complex occupational world makes it difficult for them to give the child an adequate picture of career possibilities.

(*c*) Their eagerness to obtain information about both the child and careers in general leads them to accept statements that are based on mere hearsay and that therefore tend to be scant, unreliable or biased.

12. Parent guidance is as necessary as pupil guidance.

13. Guidance should be done by trained guidance counsellors. Guidance by well-intentioned, but untrained, people may do more harm than good.

14. Since guidance is an individual matter, no grade norms for accomplishment of course choices and careers can be expected.

15. Guidance requires much more information about the individual pupils than most schools now possess.

16. Guidance should not take the sole responsibility for making people successful or happy or good. It is but one of the agencies helping people to help themselves to achieve these ends.

17. Guidance should be broadly conceived. Ideally, a child's vocational interests and choices should arise out of attitudes and experiences developed through adequate educational guidance during the whole of his school career.

18. The composite picture of the pupil as constructed by parents and teachers is probably the most accurate obtainable. Hence, close cooperation between teacher and parent is necessary in any guidance program.

19. The social implication of guidance is that each individual should be engaged in that type of occupation which he can successfully pursue and in which he can render his maximum contribution to society and to his fellow men.

20. Guidance should overcome the standard advice given by some people about college, *viz.:* "You don't need a college education. Look where I got without it!"

21. The home room teacher should share, under specific direction, many general guidance responsibilities.

22. Schools must make it their business to know the facts about industrial and occupational conditions.

23. Overloaded teachers cannot be expected to function in the capacity of guidance counsellors, since counselling is basically an individual matter requiring the entire time and energies of the worker.

24. Guidance workers should remember that since it is the child who must live with his choice, it should be the child who makes the choice of a career whether educational or vocational. The guidance worker's job is to help the child make that choice as intelligently and as wisely as possible.

25. Guidance should not mean coddling the student. However, for some students, it should provide more suitable programs. Some of these will be harder, some easier, than the average. The goal should be an individually tailored program for every child.

26. Guidance, properly functioning, should eliminate to a very great extent maladjustments of individuals to school life.

27. Guidance should eliminate pupil choices of snap courses if the school authorities have not been wise enough to eliminate the courses themselves.

28. The theory that every teacher should be a guidance teacher is based on the false belief that every teacher can be a guidance teacher. Many teachers do not have the type of personality, the training, or the interest required for this work.

29. Guidance workers must never forget that maturity frequently brings vast changes in pupils.

30. The time is past when ordinary business people, craftsmen, and many workers in service occupations do not need a good general education. It should be considered a prerequisite for every career.

31. Guidance workers should be practical people of the widest culture and interests.

32. Most occupational guidance should be toward types of work rather than toward specific jobs.

33. Guidance workers should keep a careful record of the help given pupils. Hence, a complete system of personnel records is a necessity for every counsellor.

34. Vocational tendencies are latent in many cases until adolescence is well over. Hence, it is necessary that much guidance be given late in the high school period.

35. Placement in college or work is the natural fruit of the well-nurtured guidance plant.

36. It is idle to talk of guiding pupils toward the courses for which they are best fitted unless the schools provide such courses.[4]

## Types of guidance

In the preceding paragraphs, we have examined certain psychological phases of guidance. These phases may be regarded as attributes of all kinds of guidance interacting in various ways. We shall now consider the several types.

One type of guidance is the *educational* or *academic*. This is closely related to the other two types—the vocational and social. For many years, educational guidance was viewed as primarily an effort to assist the pupil in selecting subjects. Modern philosophy of education, however, has abandoned the idea that education can be regarded primarily as taking subjects. With this change in philosophy, educational guidance was forced to change its techniques. Educational guidance today tries to assist the pupil to take an inventory of himself and to plan his educational program so as to develop his strength and improve his weaknesses. Sometimes

---

[4] *Ibid.*

this self-inventory can be accomplished by self-rating; at other times it is necessary for the guidance officer to gather the data.

A second type of guidance is *vocational*. There are two distinct phases of this type of guidance—namely, the problem of supply and demand in various professions, trades, industries, and so forth, and the problem of training the individual for a vocation for which he is mentally, physically, and temperamentally fitted. In this area of guidance, aptitude testing, the purpose of which is to survey the natural attributes of the individual, is a prime requisite. At present, for example, national defense is a keynote of American industry and economic organization. During wartime, the Army and the Navy receive into the service many thousands of men. The military services themselves are vast and complex societies with unique specialization. Every effort is made to fit a man into his proper place, an aim which requires aptitude testing of a high order.

In the vocational field as well as in the military services, the picture is increasingly complex and ever changing in the most rapid fashion imaginable. Several research institutes are given over to the primary business of keeping account of new developments in supply of and demand for labor. No teacher must be more alert to the constantly changing social panorama than the teacher who is attempting to give vocational guidance.

A third type of guidance is *social*. Here we encounter many perplexing variables, all of them comparatively intangible in nature and difficult of measurement. In the field of social guidance, character education and personality development are the primary effort. Moreover, in this field, prejudice is rife and individuality of point of view a factor with which definite reckoning must be had. The millions of school children who are the beneficiaries of free public education in the United States of America come to the schools from extremely heterogeneous home backgrounds. Furthermore, five or six years of early home environment have already laid down a groundwork of habits, some of them undesirable, which must be broken and reconstructed. In the field of social guidance also comes the significant problem of developing attitudes. Strictly speaking, we have in the United States forty-nine separate systems of education, and yet our national morale, even our national existence, depends upon our having a unity and integration of viewpoint that can cope with those of much more highly centralized systems, such as dictatorships. At the present time, to develop such unity of viewpoint is requiring one of the major efforts of the entire educational system of this country, and it will probably continue to do so for some time to come.

Social guidance is effected partly by precepts, partly by example, and partly by the long, tedious, and delicate process of building up generic attitudes. The calculated fusing of a wide variety of individual experiences is also a basic factor. Patriotism, a highly meritorious primary objective of social guidance, cannot be taught in the way that the number combinations can. It must be the result of growth and experience sharply graduated in difficulty. Particularly is social guidance the work of every teacher, for it is impossible to delegate to one unit of the school system the development of behavior patterns that are so generalized and that are connected with every phase of the educative process.

## The purposes of guidance

Up to this point we have considered the psychological nature and essence of guidance and have briefly examined its principal types. It is fitting, therefore, to analyze the basic purposes of the process itself.

The purposes of guidance may be considered under four main headings:

1. Social and mental adjustment of the individual.
2. Economic balance of society.
3. Discovery of new talents and values.
4. The correlation of the school with society.

The social and mental adjustment of the individual is a primary aim, not only of the specialized guidance services themselves, but, indeed, of the entire process of education. Modern psychological theory lends considerable credence to the point of view strongly held by some guidance experts, that fundamentally education is guidance. If the educational development of the child is viewed as a process of passive reception of ideas transferred from the teacher or parent, the theory that education is guidance has slight validity. However, if it be held that education is a process of reaction and response to stimulation rather than a transfer of ideas, directional and guidance efforts become vital. Since most modern psychologists do not believe in the doctrine of innate ideas or the transfer of the same, the directional concept of education has become a very important one and holds special significance for guidance.

Let us for a moment consider the problem from its negative aspect. The converse of adjustment is maladjustment. There are two principal ways in which we may look at gross maladjustment with society. We may hold the theory that social maladjustment and mental unbalance are the result of faulty inheritance. In its extreme form, this notion constitutes a sort of biological predestination. The second, and to most modern thinkers the more plausible, explanation is that maladjustment is caused largely by improper conditioning. The fact that cork will float and lead will not does not mean that cork is good material and lead is poor material, except with floating as the criterion. Since there are many kinds of human material exhibiting the same tremendous diversity of potential usage as exists between cork and lead, it is thoroughly reasonable to hold that the discovery of the proper usage is a basic function of education and guidance. To state that social or mental maladjustment can often be explained on the theory that human beings are equally gifted, even in the case of those who have similar aptitudes, it must be recognized that there are both quantitative and qualitative differentiations, and that differentiation itself may be the result of natural or acquired influences.

Social conflict and maladjustment are sometimes the result of encountering a situation in which personal inadequacy becomes distressingly apparent. Society itself makes many efforts to prevent this occurrence. Prize fighters not scaling a certain weight are not allowed to fight for the world's heavyweight championship. Golf and tennis tournaments are carefully arranged on a handicap basis in order to equalize competition. Income tax percentages are higher in the higher-income brackets than the lower, not only to provide more revenue, since the additional revenue is relatively inconsequential, but also in the interest of social equality and the reduction of social conflict. A tax of ninety per cent on a million-dollar-a-year income results in far less conflict and instability than would be the case were a yearly income of a thousand dollars taxed the same percentage. If the example seems far-fetched to the reader, let him consult the history of taxation.

Even the eugenist has slight cause for alarm or for disagreement with the description of guidance as directed behavior. There is in it no essential barrier to improving the racial stock or the quality of the human biological product. But being given material of varying quality, modern guidance procedures try to find for such material a place where it may most adequately function.

The problem becomes more acute when one considers the following statement, taken from a publication of the Educational Policies Commission: [5]

The groups in the United States which are at present reproducing at rates far above actual replacement needs are located in certain rural areas, and pre-

---

[5] *The Effect of Population Changes on American Education.* Washington, D. C.: Educational Policies Commission, 1938. P. 28.

dominately in communities that are at the lowest economic levels and most remote from those educational and cultural influences which are held typical of social progress. For the United States as a whole, fertility in the poorest areas is 77 per cent in excess of that necessary to replace the population in those areas. This stands in contrast to a deficit of 17 per cent in the areas with the highest level of living. . . . Each new generation of Americans is tending to be disproportionately recruited from areas with low standards of living and inferior educational resources.

The second purpose of guidance is to assist in maintaining the economic balance of society. Obviously, the preparation of large numbers of workers for industries that are not able to absorb them is contributory to economic unbalance, with its serious accompanying factors of unemployment, social unrest, and so forth. There are two general theories of the way in which guidance as given in schools can contribute to economic and social equilibrium. The first theory holds that modern industry is so specialized in nature that it is virtually impossible to give adequate specialized training of any material value at the high-school level. This theory advocates a more general education through the secondary level. The second theory holds that, because of this very specialization of modern industry and business, a long period of training is necessary; and that, this being the case, it is imperative that the high-school student determine as early as possible the vocation he intends to follow and begin training for it.

Both the theories of general unspecialized secondary education and the theory of early choice of vocation have advocates. To attempt to demonstrate the unquestioned superiority of either one would be impossible with the evidence now at hand. Where early specialization is deemed desirable, there is no doubt that statistics on supply and demand in various vocations are a prime requisite for showing the pupil the probability of securing employment after he has completed his training.

That progress is being made in the direction of charting occupational patterns is evidenced by the recent work of Anderson and Davidson.[6] This research furnishes a basis for studying the composition and changing conditions of the American working population.

A third purpose of guidance is the discovery of new talent and values. Schools are not always successful in discovering the aptitudes of pupils. Probably, in a system of mass education which necessitates each teacher seeing dozens, or even hundreds, of pupils every day, the situation will never be completely remedied. The

---

[6] H. Dewey Anderson and Percy E. Davidson, *Occupational Trends in the United States*. Palo Alto: Stanford University Press, 1940.

concept of education as guidance, however, taken in conjunction with the notion that every teacher in the school is a guidance officer, can go far toward solving the problem. Modern psychology does not believe in compartmentalized mental functions or the idea of compensatory mental endowments. A person mentally superior in one field is likely to be superior in any other field to which he turns. Therefore, the search for new talents does not mean that we shall expect to find a child brilliant in history if he is naturally very slow in mathematics. There are, however, physical attributes in which people differ markedly and which serve as the fundamental basis of success. In addition to physical endowments is the fact that shortly after birth and in succeeding years, interests have developed upon which later training must be based.

A fourth purpose of guidance is the correlation of the school with society. Many pedagogical theorists feel that the school is unduly remote from and unconcerned with social problems. The cause of this is often gratuitously assumed to be the reactionary nature of administrators and teachers. Such an explanation would appear to be a naïve one. Undoubtedly, a huge institution like the school is bound to suffer somewhat from social inertia. In a system of democratic education, it is dangerous for the school to represent many extreme opinions, a fact which has negative as well as positive values. But, apart from normal social inertia, there is always the danger that the schools may have dropped out of touch with society through sheer inattention, indifference, and laziness. One purpose of the school, therefore, which has been stressed on numerous occasions by educational philosophers and sociologists is the presentation to the pupil of a picture of society as it exists. A guidance procedure which puts emphasis upon the pupil's own choice of recognized alternatives instead of upon arbitrary assignment in a regimented society must not fail to take cognizance of this major purpose of guidance.

### General psychological techniques of guidance

It has not been the purpose of this chapter, as was stated at the outset, to give a complete discussion of all phases of guidance. Many routine duties, such as keeping records, which have an entirely proper place in a complete treatment of guidance, have no place herein. The attempt has been rather to deal with all those elements of guidance that are definitely psychological in nature.

Guidance comes about in many ways. It requires a careful administrative setup and the co-operation of the entire teaching staff. It requires an excellent system of cumulative record keeping.

Certain of the mechanisms of guidance which are definitely psycho-logical in nature are:

1. Interview and conference.
2. Measurement and rating.
3. Excursional devices.
4. Special methods of teaching.

A revered locale for the guidance conference used to be, and in some places still is, the family woodshed. When father took his erring young son out to the woodshed, he was, in his own thinking, attempting to offer some inducement for the redirection of be-havior. A consultation with a psychoanalyst is an attempt to secure social guidance by the conference method. Personnel work at the secondary and college levels comes under the same heading. These various types of guidance all represent an effort at redirection of behavior trend and the substitution of other activities. Very few experienced principals use the conference which they have with their problem cases solely for punitive purposes.

The psychological strength of the case method of guidance lies in the demonstrable susceptibility of human beings to suggestion. When a pupil has confidence and trust in his preceptor, satisfactory results may often be expected. The writer cannot bring himself to accord with those who say that all interviews and conferences are words written in the wind and come to naught. The power of words as determiners of conduct is altogether too obvious and well estab-lished to allow such an assumption.

Another psychological device which has become a guidance technique is measurement and rating. In the First World War, intelligence tests were used as one of the criteria for selection of officer material. Intelligence tests are today used in some schools as an aid in giving advice to pupils on curriculum and vocational choices. Of the various kinds of measurements which are available, physical measurements are probably the most objective and best standardized. Intelligence measurements, in spite of all the criti-cisms which have been directed at them, would probably come next. A type of measurement that we need badly, and in which substantial progress has been made in the last few years, is aptitude testing. This field is bound to become standard in the future, and the tests themselves will doubtless be greatly refined and given higher reliability.

In the field of rating, efforts to determine pupil interest are worthy of note, as is self-rating. That one works harder at some-thing in which he is interested is axiomatic, and when it is possible to base guidance upon interest, much is gained. It is probably not demonstrable that interest and ability are very highly correlated, in spite of the recognized fact that we tend to like that which we do well. There are at present too many students at the collegiate level pursuing curricula far beyond their capacities, talents and abilities to master.

Self-ratings are valuable in guidance because they give the pupil training in self-evaluation and self-analysis. Without the specialized training which the self-rating technique gives, many persons are not able to make an objective and systematic canvass of their own abilities. Merely the taking of a self-rating test contains certain values for guidance.

Excursions are among the most interesting techniques of guidance. We have mentioned previously that modern education, which is based upon experience, reaction, and a stimulus-response psychology, stresses the value of sensory data as the basis of education. It has been shown that there is a definite tendency for young people, even in a mobile modern society, to secure employment in industries and vocations in the midst of which they have been reared. Therefore, in terms of the probable locale and type of occupation, excursions to such fields are valuable. Many pupils, however, will be interested in trades and vocations which cannot be demonstrated at first hand in their communities. In recent years devices have been developed which materially help this situation. Reference is had to the growth of audio-visual enrichment of the curriculum. It is now possible, far in excess of what it would have been a very few years ago, to give pupils a first-hand idea of what the nature and possibilities of various occupations are. Not only has the technique been perfected mechanically, but a wide array of both transcriptions and pictures is available.

The fourth technique of guidance of psychological significance is the use of special methods of teaching and curricular organization. It is in this area especially that every teacher in the staff is a guidance officer. A curriculum which is integrated within itself and correlated to society is a very potent tool of guidance. A curricular organization which is internally inconsistent and taught by teachers of different points of view and methodology not only results in uncertainty in the pupil but destroys his power of self-determination as well.

Technique of teaching should offer possibilities for self-exploration on the part of the pupil. In spite of all the criticisms that can be leveled at some of the modern methods of teaching in terms of waste motion, high laboratory expense, and so forth, it nevertheless must be admitted, from the standpoint of learning the valuable art of self-direction, that the cost is in many instances justified. The socialized recitation, allowing as it does a maximum of pupil self-direction, contributes much to the pupil's progress in self-direction.

Hence, we may say that guidance according to the modern educational and psychological theory is less specific than according to the former theory of exact job placement. With respect to the specious notion that placing every pupil in a definite type of work early is scientific because of its objectivity, the modern trend is an unfortunate one, but it is in better accord with democratic ideals and education. Furthermore, it is in more complete harmony with modern psychological theory, which holds that the normal individual who has a reasonably wide latitude of interest may turn in any one of a number of directions with equal chance of success in each.

## Psychological factors in group guidance

Guidance, like all other phases of a system of mass education, must cope with the problem of making its procedure effective for the individual with a teaching staff that is inadequate to permit each pupil being given much time. Even the norms of class size set up as satisfactory by the various accrediting associations permit far more pupils to come under the direction of one teacher than can be given adequate attention. Of necessity, therefore, there have developed various plans of group guidance which attempt to conserve time, energy, and staff by disposing of many guidance problems collectively instead of individually.

The fact that necessity compels us to do a certain amount of group guidance does not mean that group guidance is ineffective or, for that matter, not the best type for meeting some problems. Modern psychology teaches us that learning is often, if not usually, a specific phenomenon that takes place best under natural circumstances in which the learning will later need to be used. From this point of view, a considerable amount of guidance is directed learning, and, to follow the general principle, it should take place near the environment in which it is expected to function. Therefore, social groups are a natural guidance environment for the obvious reason that no small part of guidance is directed at trying to teach the pupil how to adjust to his social surroundings. It is an axiom of psychologically based education that activity participation is the best teacher. This being the case, it is far better to give the pupil many forms of social direction in a group than individually.

Another psychological factor which contributes to the effectiveness of group guidance is group pressure. Even the Pollyanna school of theorists is for the most part willing to grant that some coercion is necessary occasionally in the redirection of pupil conduct, particularly where antisocial behavior has gained considerable intrenchment through time and force of habit. Group pressure is the strongest and most natural of all such inducements. Used in a kindly but calm and intelligent manner by the master teacher, group pressure has on more than one occasion been a potent force in guiding the life of some child.

Another situation that makes group guidance frequently a logical choice is the commonality of interests among young people. So much is heard at present about the psychology of individual differences and what we should do to take cognizance of such differences that it is easy to fall into the error of assuming that human beings are more unlike than alike. One has only to stop and think a minute to realize that the likenesses of people are much larger in number than their differences. More than that, all adjustments and deviations themselves fall into categories which permit of another type of group guidance, namely, the handling together of groups that have similar problems.

One of the pressing needs of most educational and social guidance when an attempt is made to handle it through groups is for quick and accurate methods of diagnosis. This is a problem of first magnitude, since even in group guidance, as it is ordinarily conducted, there is considerable effort to individualize within the group. Therefore, the better data the guidance director has, the better ramified will be the guidance procedure. Some extremely ingenious devices have been worked out to give these types of data. An example of such devices are the class personnel charts in use in Providence, Rhode Island, which are described by Dr. Allen in his Manual for the Use of the Providence Class Personnel Chart. [7] These Personnel Charts provide in a very small space a complete array of data for use in educational and vocational adjustment work. The material is in such form that a continuous record is available, and the record indicates the cases which need remedial instruction and assistance. This chart also makes use of statistical procedure in simple and functional form—a thing which in itself is definitely advantageous because so many teachers have not had an advanced course in statistics, and because, as has been pointed out elsewhere in this chapter, mathematical procedures are un-

---

[7] Richard D. Allen, *A Manual for the Use of the Providence Class Personnel Chart.* New York: Inor Publishing Company, 1935.

avoidable in a scientific attempt at guidance and aptitude diagnosis.

## Individual guidance technique

Jones [8] states that data on the individual pupil constitute the most important single material in the guidance field. This is probably not an overstatement. When we undertake to deal with a definite problem of a specific pupil, we find ourselves in much the same position as does the physician whose diagnostic efforts are concentrated heavily on the segregation of data unique to the case. The guidance laboratory and clinic, like the large hospital, have certain routine procedures in charge of routine assistants, called in the one case "nurses" and in the other "guidance assistants." In addition, however, the counselor needs data unique to the individual child when that child is an acute guidance problem. We shall now consider some of the phases of the information which the guidance officer needs.[9] Guidance officers must have a definite understanding of the growth and maturity phases of childhood. Modern psychology views many phases of conduct as purely phenomena of mechanics and chemistry. Therefore, to understand child behavior, it is necessary to be familiar with certain purely mechanical data. Behavior problems, as well as probable vocational adjustments, have frequently been solved almost entirely by proper understanding of physical factors.

Another side of the child's nature that teachers should understand, in order to do effective guidance work, is "mental" ability. Some psychologists today regard the mind as simply a name given to one specialized phase of physical behavior. Fortunately for our purpose here, it is not necessary to settle this question. However the mind may be defined, objective evidence in the greatest quantity is available to prove that children differ widely in the performance of the specialized sort of test commonly called "mental." Since it has been shown that the incidence of failure in certain specialized professions is related to mental ability, obviously the information such tests give cannot be ignored by the counselor.

Another sort of evidence which the guidance officer should

[8] Arthur J. Jones, *Principles of Guidance,* 2nd ed. New York: McGraw-Hill Book Company, 1934. P. 83.

[9] Ruth M. Strang, "Characteristics of Pupil Population," *Review of Educational Research,* Vol. IX, No. 2, April, 1939, Chap. 1, pp. 147-160.

Giles M. Ruch and David Segel, "Minimum Essentials of the Individual Inventory in Guidance," *U. S. Department of the Interior, Vocational Division Bulletin* 202, Washington, 1940.

have is the achievement record of the pupil. Investigation has shown that there is far from a perfect correlation between mental ability and achievement. Probably there is no more common guidance problem than that of attempting to get an individual who is superior mentally to work up to his potential capacity.

Attitudes and interest are determining factors in effectiveness of learning. Since modern psychology holds that many attitudes and interests are learned at an early age, it is necessary to explore for these in each child to discover their exact pattern. It is almost entirely beside the point to say that, since we know the entire range of attitudes and interests which a person may have, there is no point in determining them for each individual. The important thing is not cataloging the list, but discovering the exact pattern and potency.

Another and still more subtle attribute upon which we need information is personality. Personality itself in some of its phases is a learned, changeable, and changing thing, but it can be defined socially and measured, since one of its phases is the interaction between the individual and his social environment.[10]

Finally, it is of definite value, particularly in social guidance, to have an understanding of the special behavior problems in each child. Again mere knowledge of the range of difficulties to be encountered is of secondary importance and the prime object of search is the individual's combination of traits and the particular way in which these traits are functioning to cause the individual difficulty.

### Guidance clinics and laboratories

A word is in order at this point concerning a highly specialized type of service to be found only in larger cities and universities, but one that contributes materially to the progressive advancement of scientific practices in the field of guidance. This is the guidance laboratory or clinic. The modern guidance laboratory is equipped with facilities to undertake tasks that would be far beyond the range of a counselor in a small school working with no budget and no trained personnel. Such a guidance laboratory as has been maintained at Teachers College in Columbia University, for instance, not only provides a wide range of personal appraisal services but continually does research work to improve practices throughout the country. Below, for example, is a brief summary of the miscellaneous services for one year of the Teachers College guidance laboratory:

---

[10] Francis F. Powers, T. R. McConnell, and others, *Psychology in Everyday Living.* Boston: D. C. Heath and Company, 1938. Chapter IV, "Personality."

1. Administered about one hundred audiometer tests to outside children.

2. Prepared lists of schools in the environs to increase guidance placement service.

3. Co-operated with speech department by making speech-recording apparatus.

4. Co-operated with the music department by making recording apparatus.

5. Co-operated with the French department by making recording apparatus available.

6. Co-operated with individual professors in making recording apparatus available for research projects.

7. Arranged many special demonstrations for students in education and other classes.

8. Interviewed a number of students referred by the admissions office.

It is obvious that the sorts of service referred to above can be performed only in a large, well-equipped, well-financed laboratory. One excellent objective for the future development of the guidance movement would be to get a similar laboratory within easy traveling distance of every school in the United States. The number at present is completely inadequate. Furthermore, there are many areas which are amply able to support and finance such a clinic or laboratory but which are not doing so. The tendency of the larger cities has been to restrict their services, for obvious reasons, to the children coming from within the city limits. In the opinion of the writer, it would be extremely wasteful both economically and professionally for every school to attempt to set up a guidance clinic. There are schools at present with something corresponding to "guidance clinic" written on the door of some nearly empty room. One who has seen a real clinic in operation knows that this is subterfuge. A clinic properly equipped and staffed can handle a very large number of cases by reference, and in those situations where this has been the practice, little difficulty has been encountered. It is recommended that every state department of education take this matter under advisement with the idea of serving all states in the future as well as some localities are served at the present time.

One further statement needs to be made about guidance laboratories or clinics. There are those, shrewd in their insight but far from altruistic in their intent, who have discerned this need and have attempted to commercialize it. In other words, there are numerous so-called guidance services and clinics run on a purely commercial basis to supply a demand which should be supplied in a systematic manner by the educational setup of every state. These establishments range all the way from personality-building factories to institutions which will train you for any kind of job that you want to undertake. Although the failures are less gruesome than in the case of medical quackery, the amount of money wasted is far more than one who has not looked into the problem would imagine. This statement does not mean that a privately run type of laboratory is perforce unscientific and composed of charlatans. Such is far from being the case. There are excellent private laboratories, in some cases far better financed than even the large school system could hope for. But it is well, in the course of the ordinary guidance procedures in the schools, particularly in the field of vocational guidance, to warn the pupil against the deceptive allure of some of the less meritorious establishments which still exist in some communities.

Finally, attention should be called to the fact that there are some schools that do not avail themselves of clinic and laboratory service when it is to be had for the asking. The writer is aware, for example, of a large university clinic which has an excellent staff and is capable of handling a considerable number of cases, although some school people within the area have been very much surprised to learn that such a service existed. School administrators and guidance officers should be thoroughly posted on the nature of this service available within their own areas, including the important factor of medical clinics, some of which, in the hands of an imaginative and educationally interested director, can very easily add a guidance adjunct.

### Representative guidance programs

There are hundreds of effective guidance systems in the United States. Naturally, it would be impossible within the scope of one chapter to sample anything like a representative number of them. It is worthwhile, however, to describe a few of the outstanding programs illustrative of trends in the field.

One of the urgent needs in the field of guidance is for research, especially in the form of follow-up studies to measure the results of the guidance. Unfortunately, very little of this type of research has been done. Another type of research that is needed is research on how well we are doing what we are doing. Fortunately, some of this research has been done. One of the most interesting investigations of this sort was carried on by the research committee of the Southern California Counselors' Association.[11] All counselors in Southern California were given a list of 97 items and asked to indicate the extent to which they practiced the activities described in their guidance setups. Ratings were as follows: never, 0 times per semester; seldom, 1 to 10 times per semester; often, 11 to 20 times per semester; frequently, 21 or more times per semester. The data thus derived were treated as described in the following quotation: [12]

The markings "Never," "Seldom," "Often," and "Frequently" were given a position on a quantitative scale as follows:

| Marking | Position on Scale |
|---|---|
| Never | 0 |
| Seldom | 1 |
| Often | 3 |
| Frequently | 4 |

In terms of this scale the average deviation from the standard was worked out for each of the 97 items for the 102 replies. For example, on Item 1 the distribution of replies was as follows: Never 12, Seldom 43, Often 15, Frequently 32. Since the key for this item was "often," the average deviation was:

| Never | $12 \times 3 = 36$ |
|---|---|
| Seldom | $43 \times 2 = 86$ |
| Often | $15 \times 0 = 0$ |
| Frequently | $32 \times 1 = 32$ |

$$102 \qquad 154 \div 102 = 1.51$$

A distribution was made of the average deviations of the 102 replies. The range from highest deviation to lowest was divided into four equal spaces, and labeled "Very Unsatisfactory," "Unsatisfactory," "Satisfactory," and "Very Satisfactory." The classification of the distribution follows:

2.83-2.19......................Very Unsatisfactory
2.18-1.57......................Unsatisfactory
1.56-0.94......................Satisfactory
0.93-0.30......................Very Satisfactory

Below are listed some of the items with their ratings. On the assumption that all of these items represent valid and worthy guidance activities, it is very evident from the study that there is a tremendous differential in the effectiveness of various guidance procedures.

---

[11] *Report of the Committee on Guidance of the Association of California Secondary School Principals* (Monograph No. 1), California Society of Secondary Education, Berkeley, California, December, 1938, pp. 5-11.

[12] *Ibid.*, p. 6.

## TABLE XVI

### Item by Item Evaluation[13]

| | Key | Deviation | Rating |
|---|---|---|---|
| **(a) Group activities with students.** | | | |
| 1. Explaining courses, offerings, and opportunities to students in contributing schools.............................. | Often | 1.51 | Satisfactory |
| 2. Giving tests and compiling data for students in contributing schools........ | Seldom | 1.37 | Satisfactory |
| 3. Acquainting new students with plans and schedule........................... | Seldom | 2.06 | Unsatisfactory |
| 4. Acquainting late entrants with plant and schedule........................... | Seldom | 2.11 | Unsatisfactory |
| 5. Preparing plans and instructions for group guidance...................... | Often | 1.08 | Satisfactory |
| 6. Supervising group adjustment to school life................................. | Frequently | 2.02 | Unsatisfactory |
| 7. Promoting activities and courses in preparation for life choices............... | Often | 1.42 | Satisfactory |
| 8. Preparing for further educational choices. | Often | 1.27 | Satisfactory |
| 9. Preparing for and making vocational choices............................ | Often | 1.17 | Satisfactory |
| 10. Directing visitation to future schools and to industrial establishments........... | Often | 2.14 | Unsatisfactory |
| **(b) Counseling activities.** | | | |
| 1. Contacting parents of prospective students when possible.................. | Frequently | 2.83 | Very unsatisfactory |
| 2. Holding individual conferences for programming new students.............. | Frequently | 1.59 | Unsatisfactory |
| 3. Providing significant data for teachers about new students................... | Seldom | 1.56 | Satisfactory |
| 4. Considering previous work taken in programming new students.............. | Frequently | 0.87 | Very satisfactory |
| 5. Interviewing for placement in curriculum. | Frequently | 0.84 | Very satisfactory |
| 6. Helping select subjects for program..... | Frequently | 0.80 | Very satisfactory |
| 7. Providing significant data for teachers about old students................... | Often | 1.18 | Satisfactory |
| 8. Checking up on situation for late entrants (credits, etc.)........................ | Often | 1.39 | Satisfactory |
| 9. Making program adjustments for late entrants............................. | Frequently | 0.80 | Very satisfactory |
| 10. Providing significant data for teachers about late entrants.................... | Often | 1.19 | Satisfactory |
| 11. Holding individual conferences as needed. | Frequently | 0.30 | Very satisfactory |
| 12. Conducting a periodic check-up on all students........................... | Frequently | 1.23 | Satisfactory |
| 13. Considering failures and their adjustment................................ | Frequently | 0.67 | Very satisfactory |
| 14. Checking up on unsatisfactories........ | Frequently | 0.77 | Very satisfactory |
| 15. Advising on changes of curriculum..... | Often | 1.18 | Satisfactory |
| 16. Making adjustments through changes of program............................ | Often | 1.02 | Satisfactory |
| 17. Considering the progress of students.... | Frequently | 0.93 | Very satisfactory |

[13] *Ibid.*, pp. 8–11.

TABLE XVI—(*Continued*)

ITEM BY ITEM EVALUATION

| | Key | Deviation | Rating |
|---|---|---|---|
| (b) *Counseling activities.*—(*Continued*) | | | |
| 18. Checking on plans and causes showing need for guidance.................... | Often | 1.71 | Unsatisfactory |
| 19. Counseling students regarding changes of school............................ | Seldom | 1.63 | Unsatisfactory |
| 20. Holding individual conferences with teachers on pupil cases................ | Often | 0.87 | Very satisfactory |
| 21. Coöperating with teachers on the adjustment of failures..................... | Often | 0.91 | Very satisfactory |
| 22. Contacting parents at school for mutual understanding and guidance of pupils... | Often | 0.93 | Very satisfactory |
| 23. Handling recommendations for trade schools............................. | Seldom | 1.04 | Satisfactory |
| 24. Checking credits for certificates and diplomas............................. | Frequently | 1.29 | Satisfactory |
| 25. Distributing information and forwarding applications for summer school........ | Seldom | 1.40 | Satisfactory |
| 26. Answering inquiries about the offerings and opportunities of the school.......... | Often | 1.21 | Satisfactory |
| (c) *Activities common to both group and individual guidance.* | | | |
| 1. Preparing entering students for changes of situation......................... | Often | 1.55 | Satisfactory |
| 2. Testing for abilities (re-checks)......... | Often | 1.32 | Satisfactory |
| 3. Testing of late entrants............... | Often | 1.40 | Satisfactory |
| 4. Discovering unmet needs and making recommendations.................... | Often | 0.81 | Very satisfactory |
| 5. Directing the use of standardized tests and interpreting the results............ | Often | 1.26 | Satisfactory |
| 6. Promoting discussions and interviews on problems heretofore recognized........ | Frequently | 0.92 | Very satisfactory |
| 7. Interpreting life problems.............. | Often | 1.41 | Satisfactory |
| (d) *Administrative and supervisory activities.* | | | |
| 1. With teachers, department chairmen, and principals. | | | |
| (a) Directing group guidance by teachers. | Frequently | 1.47 | Satisfactory |
| (b) Interpreting principles of guidance... | Often | 1.42 | Satisfactory |
| (c) Holding group meetings for plans and discussions...................... | Often | 1.33 | Satisfactory |
| (d) Preparing aids for homeroom guidance........................... | Often | 1.55 | Satisfactory |
| (e) Explaining forms and reports........ | Seldom | 2.01 | Unsatisfactory |
| (f) Interpreting curriculum and graduation requirements................. | Seldom | 2.32 | Very unsatisfactory |
| (g) Interpreting rulings and changes..... | Seldom | 1.83 | Unsatisfactory |
| (h) Assisting and furnishing guidance in the use of standardized tests......... | Often | 1.27 | Satisfactory |
| (i) Making recommendations for grouping of pupils..................... | Seldom | 1.68 | Unsatisfactory |
| (j) Taking part in department heads' meetings....................... | Often | 1.71 | Unsatisfactory |

TABLE XVI—*(Continued)*

Iᴛᴇᴍ ʙʏ Iᴛᴇᴍ Eᴠᴀʟᴜᴀᴛɪᴏɴ

| | *Key* | *Deviation* | *Rating* |
|---|---|---|---|
| *(d) Administrative and supervisory activities.*<br>—*(Continued)* | | | |
| (k) Taking part in principals' staff meetings............................ | Often | 1.41 | Satisfactory |
| (l) Encouraging teachers in guidance activities........................ | Often | 0.95 | Satisfactory |
| 2. Patrons and community contacts. | | | |
| (a) Securing visits from representatives of other schools..................... | Often | 2.03 | Unsatisfactory |
| (b) Securing speakers on vocations...... | Often | 1.92 | Unsatisfactory |
| (c) Arranging for advisers from other schools and from industry to interview students.................... | Often | 1.93 | Unsatisfactory |
| (d) Developing necessary form and bulletins for students in contributing schools......................... | Often | 1.37 | Satisfactory |
| (e) Maintaining helpful relations with P.-T. A., service clubs, coördinating councils, etc...................... | Often | 1.47 | Satisfactory |
| (f) Contacting parents in the home..... | Seldom | 1.00 | Satisfactory |
| (g) Making surveys and studies of employment conditions............... | Seldom | 0.93 | Very satisfactory |
| (h) Assisting with employment service... | Often | 2.31 | Very unsatisfactory |
| 3. Pupil groupings, records, and testing. | | | |
| (a) Grouping students as needed........ | Often | 1.60 | Unsatisfactory |
| (b) Guiding arrangements for receiving new students..................... | Seldom | 1.25 | Satisfactory |
| (c) Making suggestions and plans for further programming.............. | Often | 1.20 | Satisfactory |
| (d) Organizing records for interviews and guidance........................ | Frequently | 0.58 | Very satisfactory |
| (e) Organizing records for interpretation to teachers....................... | Often | 1.04 | Satisfactory |
| (f) Organizing records for consideration in problem and discipline cases...... | Frequently | 0.76 | Very satisfactory |
| (g) Organizing records for interviews and guidance with parents............. | Often | 0.96 | Satisfactory |
| (h) Making master program or assisting with master program.............. | Frequently | 1.39 | Satisfactory |
| 4. Articulation with lower and higher schools. | | | |
| (a) Maintaining helpful relations and understandings with contributing schools............................ | Often | 1.36 | Satisfactory |
| (b) Keeping in touch with requirements and conditions in higher schools..... | Often | 1.12 | Satisfactory |
| (c) Attending conferences and making visits to other institutions.......... | Often | 1.11 | Satisfactory |
| 5. General school service. | | | |
| (a) Encouraging offerings of vocational instruction as electives............ | Often | 1.59 | Unsatisfactory |
| (b) Serving on committees within the school........................... | Often | 1.05 | Satisfactory |

TABLE XVI—(*Continued*)

ITEM BY ITEM EVALUATION

| | Key | Deviation | Rating |
|---|---|---|---|
| (d) *Administrative and supervisory activities.* | | | |
| —(*Continued*) | | | |
| (c) Representing school on outside committees........................ | Often | 1.74 | Unsatisfactory |
| (d) Representing school and reporting conferences...................... | Often | 1.66 | Unsatisfactory |
| (e) Calling attention to new books and articles on guidance.............. | Often | 1.48 | Satisfactory |
| (f) Writing articles, or interpreting schools to the community.......... | Often | 2.01 | Unsatisfactory |
| (g) Making and interpreting questionnaires for necessary data........... | Seldom | 1.22 | Satisfactory |
| (h) Conducting research studies and making reports...................... | Often | 1.41 | Satisfactory |
| (e) *Activities of a clerical nature.* | | | |
| 1. Evaluating transcripts when received... | Never | 2.65 | Very unsatisfactory |
| 2. Revising lists and removing cards from files............................... | Never | 2.58 | Very unsatisfactory |
| 3. Telephoning data or copying and forwarding............................ | Never | 2.28 | Very unsatisfactory |
| 4. Compiling data for all entering students. | Never | 2.68 | Very unsatisfactory |
| 5. Compiling significant test data subsequently obtained.................... | Never | 2.68 | Very unsatisfactory |
| 6. Compiling significant information from all other sources.................... | Never | 2.74 | Very unsatisfactory |
| 7. Preparing information for forwarding to other schools....................... | Never | 2.79 | Very unsatisfactory |
| 8. Securing and maintaining a file of catalogs of future schools............... | Never | 2.15 | Unsatisfactory |
| 9. Maintaining files of information on vocational opportunities.................. | Never | 1.93 | Unsatisfactory |
| 10. Posting records on permanent record cards and cumulative records........... | Never | 2.16 | Unsatisfactory |
| 11. Making and forwarding transcripts...... | Never | 1.61 | Unsatisfactory |
| 12. Making class adjustments to equalize class size........................... | Never | 2.30 | Very unsatisfactory |

It has been stated repeatedly in this chapter that, to be effective, guidance must be worked into the regular curriculum. Every subject must be made to contribute to its maximum potential extent to building up the ideals and attitudes deemed desirable by the counselor. One city with a highly organized and functioning guidance program is Providence, R. I. On the next page is reproduced a typical unit of work from this program.

## SIXTH UNIT OF WORK—GRADE 9A

CASE CONFERENCE

(A Question of Study)

Time: Two Periods

NOTE TO TEACHERS:—This particular unit is submitted not so much with the idea of suggesting the topic but rather to offer a pattern by which any subject of case conference may be presented. Optional topics are listed near the end of this unit. Teachers should select that which seems to offer the more pertinent interest at the time.

Bill and Jack are pals who share many interests. Each boy is an enthusiastic and skillful swimmer. Both enjoy track and football very much. They agree that success is the result of effort and work on the athletic field and in the classroom. But there is one subject about which they have exactly opposite ideas. Bill believes that home study each evening is a waste of time and that whole-hearted application the evening before the examination is more economical.

Jack says, "I cannot learn for keeps your way, Bill. In order to remember I have to learn small portions at a time. So my way is more economical for me."

1. What do you think of Bill's and Jack's efforts to find an economical method of study?

2. What advantages are there for the students who do not waste time at their home study?

3. In trying to discover a successful way to save time, what points should the student consider?

4. What is your opinion of Bill's idea of time saving?

5. What about Jack's idea?

6. What helpful study hints can you suggest?

*Objectives:*

1. To awaken an appreciation of efficiency in study as well as in other pursuits.

2. To expose the weaknesses of cramming.

3. To observe class reaction.

4. To summarize good study habits.

The testing program is a vital part of every guidance setup. There is far more to a testing program than the mere administration of a large number of tests. Los Angeles, California, has a splendidly integrated testing program, probably because it is built on certain definite, proved theories of measurement. Herewith are given basic considerations underlying this program.[14]

---

[14] *Outline of Procedure for Educational Guidance in Elementary Schools,* Los Angeles City School District, Division of Instruction and Curriculum: Educational Research and Guidance, revised February, 1939, p. 21.

In working out his program, the principal should be guided by certain basic considerations.

1. Effective educational procedure requires a continuous appraisal of children's achievement.

2. An important reason for achievement testing is to determine the extent to which each child has mastered the so-called tools of learning. It is, therefore, desirable to have such tests given at the beginning of the term, so that the results may help the teacher to know each child's needs.

3. An important result of achievement testing is the careful diagnosis of the data which will help in developing individual programs for the children.

4. All entering children should be thoroughly studied as to health, mental development, physical condition, social maturity, and emotional stability.

5. Each child should be given a group intelligence test at least every two years.

6. Schools should record, at least once a year, data on each child which will include chronological age, mental age, intelligence quotient, and tool subject achievement. The results are sent in to the central office for summarization. Schools using Expectancy Ages should supply such data annually.

7. Our present educational procedure demands that "failure" be reduced to an absolute minimum. Before a child is required to repeat a grade, it should be clearly established that he is unable to work in the next level with happiness and profit.

8. Since desirable attitudes and appreciations are among the most important goals of the school, attempts should be made to observe pupil growth in the field of personality.

9. The testing program should be based on the needs of each individual school.

10. The principal should plan the scope of the testing program with the Supervising Counselor.

11. The principal should indicate his plans for the semester on the blank provided by the Educational Research and Guidance Office, entitled "Principal's Testing Program in Elementary Schools."

Stephens College of Columbia, Missouri, is justly noted for the excellence of its personnel work. Undoubtedly part of the success of this program depends upon the care with which psychological principles are attended to in guidance work. The following five principles [15] described by Dr. C. N. Rexroad, Professor of Psychology at Stephens College, are illuminating.

The following principles bear upon these and similar problems.

1. Merely lending a sympathetic ear to the story is of some help, often all that is needed, for (a) in telling it the student thinks through her problem more clearly, and probably more unbiasedly, than when she is alone with her

[15] W. P. Shofstall, *Stephens College Handbook for Advisers.* Columbia, Mo.: Stephens College, 1939. Chap. VII, "Using Psychological Principles in Advising," pp. 24-25.

own confused thoughts, and (*b*) she leaves the conference with the feeling that someone whose opinion is worth while understands her.

2. It is often more advantageous to attempt to build up already strong traits than to try to strengthen weak ones. We cannot say that a student's personality is no stronger than the weakest trait; rather it is the sum of all her strong and weak traits. The whole personality is strengthened as much by increasing assets as by decreasing liabilities.

3. No person is described by reference to a few of his traits. Each student probably has some very strong traits, a large number in which she is average, and a few weak traits. The presence of a few extreme traits (good or bad) should not blind the adviser to the fact that his advisee possesses many other traits which must be considered in completing the picture of her personality.

4. Anything one can do to give a student justified confidence is desirable. To discourage is unquestionably bad, and to encourage when the encouragement will be immediately shattered by experience is to destroy the possibility of being of further help; however, some traits can always be found in every student that are worthy of praise, and every student has some ability, the development of which will meet with the success which is so necessary to insure confidence. Praise, if there is the least excuse for it. Wholesale censure is likely to breed antipathy as well as discouragement.

5. To label a student as stupid, shy, over-sensitive, uncoöperative, unattractive is bad manners as well as bad psychology—bad because it is misleading and inaccurate, and because it solves no problems.

One of the essential elements in successful vocational guidance is the necessity of having pupils occupation-minded as early as possible. "Occupation-minded" does not mean having chosen a life work at an early age. It does mean being mindful of the wide variety of possible choices and thoughtful about them. Minneapolis, Minnesota, where all pupils are required to study occupations in the ninth grade, has an excellent statement in its bulletin [16] on the *Care of the Individual Child* on this point.

With the constantly increasing opportunities and growing complexities of modern life have come added responsibilities in orienting young people in a highly specialized and rapidly changing world of occupations. A person should be taught not only to appreciate and to respect the work and the problems of all kinds of workers but also the importance of and means of fitting himself into a kind of work suited to his interests and abilities. We have recognized both the economic and social implications of such responsibilities and have accepted them as worth-while aims in the ninth grade social studies.

Many students even at the college level are vague concerning the objectives and purposes of courses which they are taking. This vagueness is not conducive to a good attitude toward work or toward success in it. Many schools are now realizing the paramount

---

[16] Carroll R. Reed, *Care of the Individual Child in the Minneapolis Public Schools,* Minneapolis, Minnesota, May, 1937, p. 14.

importance of orienting the student toward his work and of informing him of the exact contribution which each course will make toward his final training. West Seattle High School of Seattle, Washington, does an excellent job of this type of orientation. The following description [17] of their junior business training course is typical.

## JUNIOR BUSINESS TRAINING

Junior Business Training has two major objectives:

I. Exploratory—to aid in discovering aptitudes, abilities, and interests which will help pupils in planning a school program and finally in selecting a vocation.

II. Teaching of fundamental business activities from the standpoint of the consumer so that the course is valuable to all pupils regardless of their future occupation.

Junior Business Training I and II are prerequisites to Bookkeeping and required of all pupils taking the commercial course. Credit may be made in Junior Business I without taking the second semester's work and is particularly recommended as it covers those business activities needed by every person, such as Insurance, Investments, Budgets, both personal and family, Money and Banking, Mail, and Travel.

The second semester gives an introduction to business correspondence, filing, bookkeeping, salesmanship, commercial law, economics, personality. Pupils have an opportunity to test their abilities and interest in these subjects as well as to provide a background for the study of other commercial subjects.

Getting a job is a task of paramount importance to the young man and young woman of today. It is one that unfortunately even many well-trained people bungle. The Department of Educational and Vocational Guidance of Rochester, New York, has concerned itself vitally with bridging the gap between high school and employment. In the Rochester plan, the student is given specific, practical instruction in how to find a job. The following quotation from the Rochester manual [18] on the subject should be interesting to guidance officers everywhere.

## HOW TO PROCEED TO FIND A JOB

Analyze yourself to determine what type of work you are best qualified to perform. Consider:

*Your Preference.* What kind of work would you like? In what business establishments will you find the type of work you are seeking?

*Your Ability.* What is your scholastic standing? What desirable attributes do you think you possess? What service do you feel you can render to an employer?

*Your Special Training.* What shops or special courses have you taken to fit yourself for employment?

---

[17] *Learning to Live: Educational Guidance Manual for West Seattle High School.* Seattle, Washington: Seattle Public Schools. P. 8.

[18] *High School—Then What?*, Department of Educational and Vocational Guidance, Board of Education, Rochester, New York, pp. 1-3.

Analyze the avenues of approach to the job you want. Jobs are usually found through one of the following:

New York State Employment Service, 65 Broad Street, the official public placement bureau. (The procedure to be followed in registering here should be familiar to all graduates.)

Private employment agencies. These agencies have a fee connected with their services, ordinarily a charge equal to a certain percentage of the salary to be earned.

Employment offices in large business and industrial establishments.

Newspaper advertisements.

Friends and acquaintances.

The teachers, department heads, and principal of your school.

Information about industries and data about firms can be obtained from the following sources: *

"Books About Jobs," published by the American Library Association.

Trade papers and magazines serving specific industries.

Government publications describing particular trades and occupations. Reports of the U. S. Census Bureau.

Various types of directories—city, telephone, manufacturers'.

Publications of local chamber of commerce which contain valuable job information and data about local firms.

Local newspapers.

Trade directories. Names of such books are given in a "directory of directories," such as Morley's "Mailing List Directory," or Dartnell's "Mailing List Handbook."

Employees of the firm with which there is hope of connection.

*Map out a plan for yourself.*

Prepare a list of prospects, firms you think would find your services useful, and become as well-informed as possible about them.

Try to secure information about the executives of these firms, and study the various methods of approach to them.

Study the application blank and the technique of the interview.

Find your employer and try to sell him your services.

*Before starting out to search for a job look in the mirror and answer the following questions:*

Are my face and hands clean? My ears and neck? Are my teeth and fingernails in good condition?

Is my hair neatly combed? Am I shaved?

Is my clothing clean and neatly pressed? Suitable? (Dress plainly.) Collar tidy? Shoes clean and polished?

Am I wearing gaudy trinkets? (Avoid any buttons or pins of an advertising or political nature.)

Have I used too much rouge, lipstick, or colored nail polish? (Employers object to over-use of cosmetics.)

*Points to consider when you go for an interview with an employer:*

Arrive at your destination on time, *and alone.*

Be prepared to submit to a written or oral examination.

Be provided with a pencil or pen; and with sufficient money for carfare, lunch, or any other emergency which might arise.

---

*Sources are from *What About Jobs?* by Theodore Barrett.

Allow sufficient time for the interview.

Wait outside a private office until you have been invited to enter.

State as briefly and pleasantly as possible your reason for calling. ("Good morning, Mr. Blank, I am John Jones from Blank High School.")

Secure a person's permission when using his name as reference. Your high school principal and teachers are always willing to make a statement regarding your school achievement.

Remain standing until you are asked to be seated.

Sit erect, in a comfortable position. Appear calm and self-possessed. Avoid playing with ties, rings, or bracelets. Chewing gum, smoking, or the use of perfume are out of place in an employment office. (Some employers have decided likes and dislikes.)

Let the employer take the initiative in carrying on the conversation.

Answer all questions in a straightforward, truthful manner.

Show no interest in conversation not directed to you, or in private material which may be lying on the interviewer's desk. (This is very important!)

Do not press your case. Remember the employer has the right to interview other applicants before selecting you.

If a point of difference or misunderstanding comes into the interview, do not argue.

Do not joke or be flippant with the employer, nor employees, even if they be old friends.

Be pleasant at all times.

After the employer has offered you a position, you have a right to know the kind of work you are to do; the hours of service; the salary or rate of pay; and any other facts which might influence your decision.

Be courteous at all times, and especially if you do not receive the position.

Throughout the interview be careful to use good, concise English. Face the interviewer and speak clearly; avoid slang and such expressions as "Gee," "Yeah," "Sure," "O. K."

## QUESTIONS AND EXERCISES FOR DISCUSSION AND STUDY

1. *Project:* From a standard encyclopedia or other reference books, expand the material in the introduction on the historical systems of guidance.

2. What are some differences between the guidance programs of today and those of yesterday?

3. *Project:* Draw a diagram to represent the guidance setup in the school in which you are a pupil.

4. Explain briefly the counseling, the mathematical, and the demonstrative phases of guidance.

5. What are the types of guidance, and why is each important?

6. Name and discuss the purposes of guidance as treated in the chapter.

7. What is a eugenist, and what is the interest of the eugenist in a guidance program?

8. Give some examples of measurement and rating in the field of guidance. How are these used, for instance, in the Army training programs?

9. What are some of the things that you personally feel cannot be well done by a group guidance technique?

10. What are some of the things that it would be possible for guidance laboratories, even small ones, to have in the clinic?

11. Describe one of the guidance setups to which reference is made in the chapter.

12. If you were organizing a guidance program, what factors would you emphasize most strongly?

### SELECTED REFERENCES FOR FURTHER READING AND STUDY

Allen, Richard D., *A Manual for the Use of the Providence Class Personnel Chart*. New York: Inor Publishing Company, 1935.

————, *Organization and Supervision of Guidance in Public Education*. New York: Inor Publishing Company, 1934.

Anderson, H. Dewey, and Percy E. Davidson, *Occupational Trends in the United States*. Palo Alto, Cal.: Stanford University Press, 1940.

Baker, Harry J., and Virginia Traphagen, *The Diagnosis and Treatment of Behavior-Problem Children*. New York: The Macmillan Company, 1936.

Brewer, John M., *Education as Guidance*. New York: The Macmillan Company, 1933.

Cox, Philip W. L., and John Carr Duff, *Guidance by the Classroom Teacher*. New York: Prentice-Hall, Inc., 1938.

Cyr, Frank W., consulting editor, *The Continuity of Guidance*. Scranton: International Textbook Company, 1939.

*Effect of Population Changes on American Education*. Washington, D. C.: Educational Policies Commission, 1938. P. 28.

*Guidance Service Standards for Secondary Schools*, New Jersey Secondary School Teachers' Association, 1937, pp. 8-11.

Hamrin, Shirley A., and Clifford E. Erickson, *Guidance in the Secondary School*. New York: D. Appleton-Century Company, 1939.

*High School—Then What?* Department of Educational and Vocational Guidance, Board of Education, Rochester, New York, pp. 1-3.

Jones, Arthur J., *Principles of Guidance*, 2nd ed. New York: McGraw-Hill Book Company, 1934. P. 83.

*Learning to Live: Educational Guidance Manual for West Seattle High School*, Seattle Public Schools, Seattle, Washington, p. 8.

*Outline of Procedure for Educational Guidance in Elementary Schools*, Los Angeles City School District, Division of Instruction and Curriculum: Educational Research and Guidance, revised February, 1939. P. 21.

Paterson, Donald G., Gwendolen G. Schneidler, and Edmund G. Williamson, *Student Guidance Techniques*. New York: McGraw-Hill Book Company, 1938.

Powers, Francis F., T. R. McConnell, and others, *Psychology in Everyday Living*. Boston: D. C. Heath and Company, 1938. Chapter IV, "Personality."

Reed, Carroll R., *Care of the Individual Child in the Minneapolis Public Schools*, Minneapolis, Minnesota, May, 1937, p. 14.

*Report of the Committee on Guidance of the Association of California Secondary School Principals* (Monograph No. 1), California Society of Secondary Education, Berkeley, California, December, 1938, pp. 5-11.

Ruch, Giles M., and David Segel, "Minimum Essentials of the Individual Inventory in Guidance," *U. S. Department of the Interior, Vocational Division Bulletin* 202, Washington, 1940.

Shofstall, W. P., *Stephens College Handbook for Advisers*. Columbia, Missouri: Stephens College, 1939. Chapter VII, "Using Psychological Principles in Advising," pp. 24-25.

Smith, Charles M., and Mary M. Roos, *A Guide to Guidance*. New York: Prentice-Hall, Inc., 1940.

Strang, Ruth M., "Characteristics of Pupil Population" (Chapter 1), *Review of Educational Research*, Vol. IX, No. 2, April, 1939, pp. 147-160.

————, *Pupil Personnel and Guidance*. New York: The Macmillan Company, 1940.

Trabue, Marion R., "Functional Classification of Occupations," *Occupations*, Vol. XV, No. 2, November, 1936, pp. 127-131.

Traxler, Arthur E., editor, *Guidance in Public Secondary Schools*. New York: Educational Records Bureau, 1939.

Williamson, E. G., *How to Counsel Students*. New York: McGraw-Hill Book Company, 1939.

————, and J. G. Dailey, *Student Personnel Work*. New York: McGraw-Hill Book Company, 1937.

————, and M. E. Hahn, *Introduction to High School Counseling*. New York: McGraw-Hill Book Company, 1940.

# Index of Subjects

433

# Index of Names